MW01625511

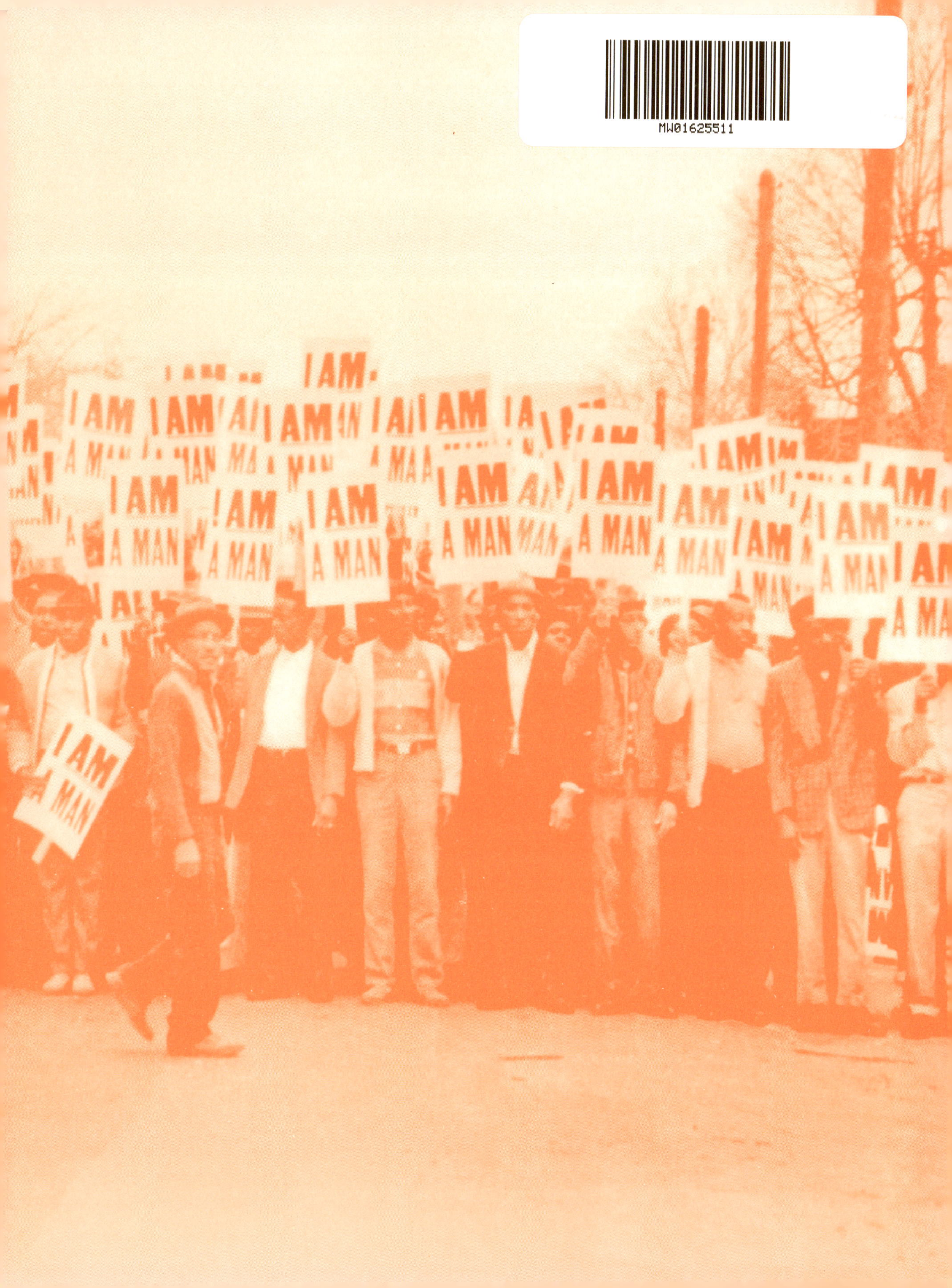

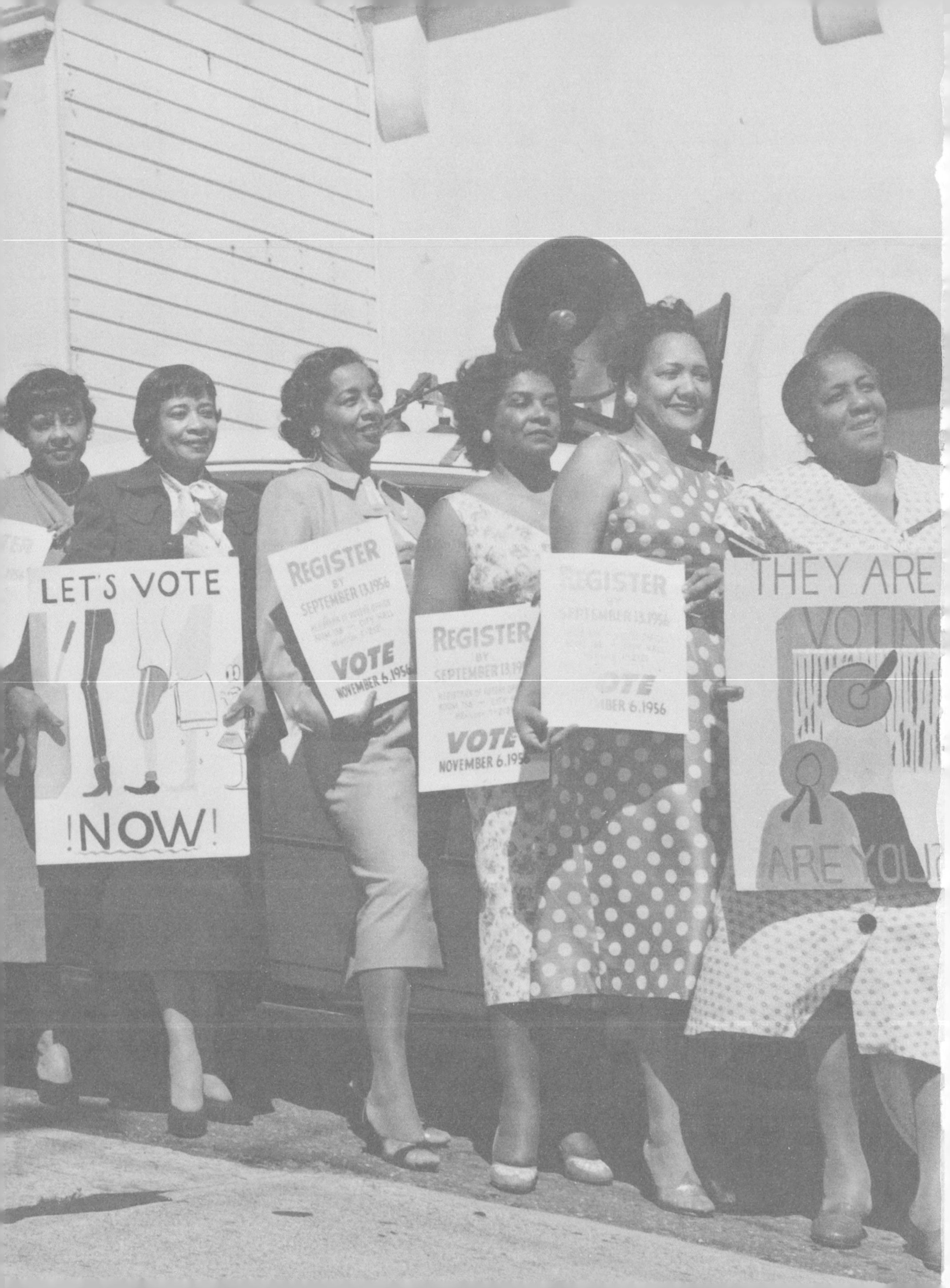
LET'S VOTE
!NOW!
REGISTER
BY
SEPTEMBER 13, 1956
VOTE
NOVEMBER 6, 1956
REGISTER
BY
VOTE
NOVEMBER 6, 1956
THEY ARE
ARE YOU

STRIKETHROUGH!

Typographic Messages of Protest

STRIKET

IROUGH!

Typographic Messages of Protest

Silas Munro
Cocurated by Stephen Coles

Introduction by Colette Gaiter

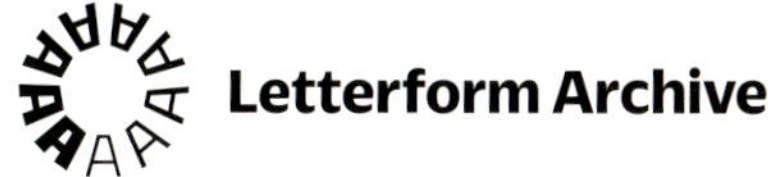

The official catalog for the
2022–2023 exhibition

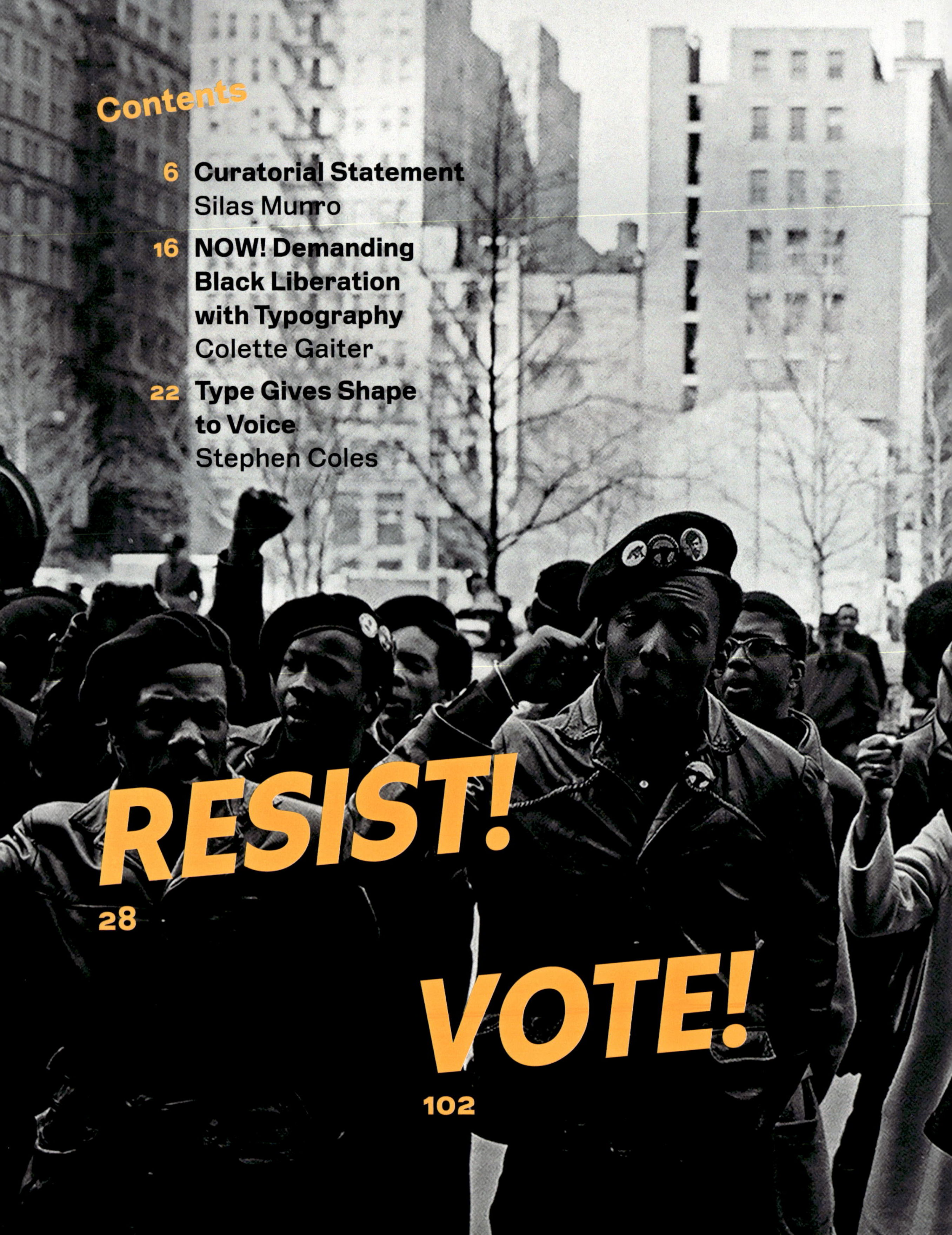

Contents

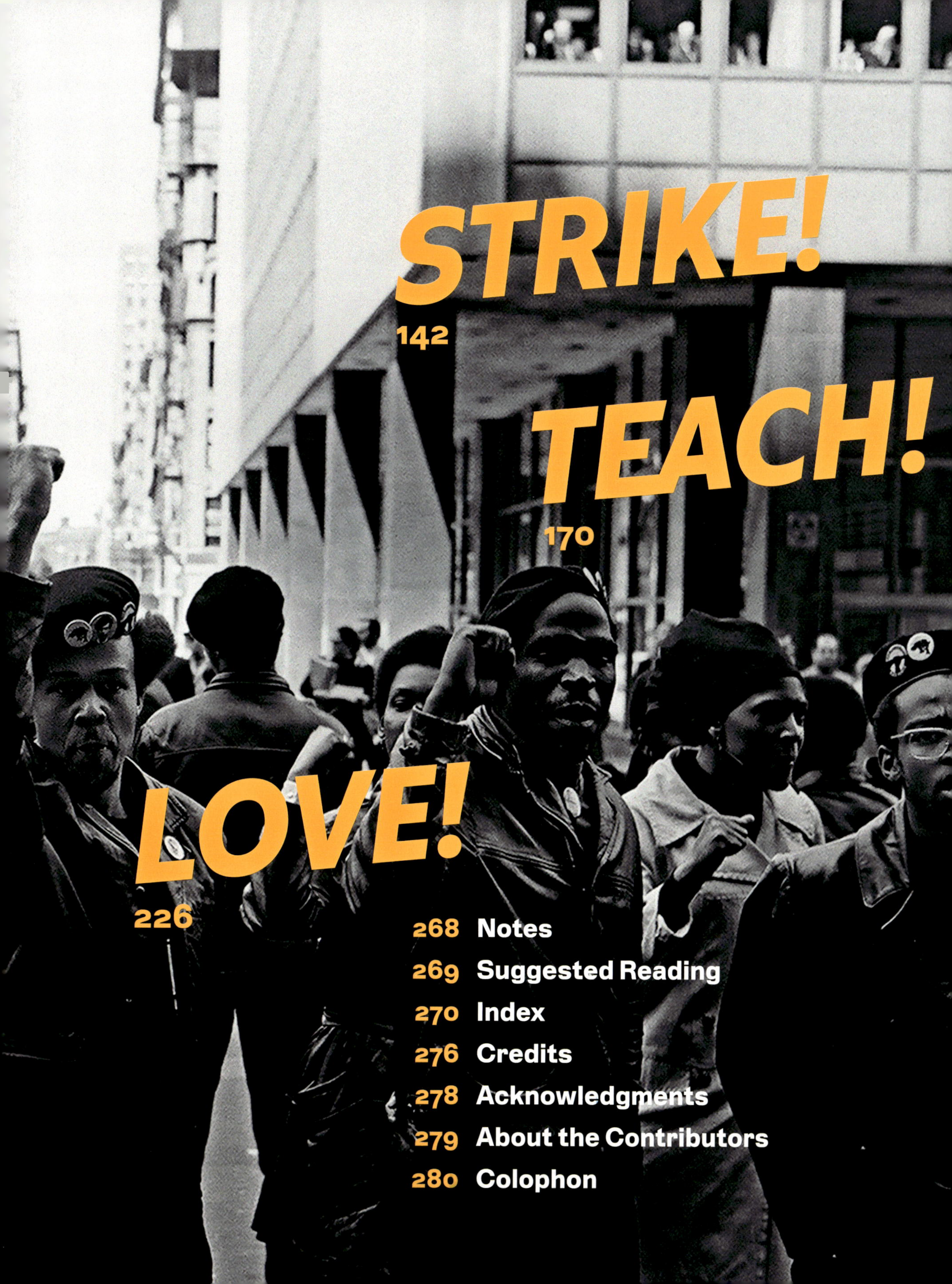

Curatorial Statement

strikethrough: (n) the penetration of ink through paper in the printing process; (v) to draw a line through text to call for the deletion of an error

Silas Munro

Protesters have long used typography to strike through myriad forms of oppression. Their urgent, often handmade signs, placards, and posters put bigots on notice that their hate has been marked for correction. Curated in the wake of the 2020 police murders of Black Americans, including George Floyd and Breonna Taylor, and on the upswell of ensuing Black Lives Matter protests, this exhibition and book showcase examples of typographic anger and agency from across moments, places, and movements—as it is seen in the streets, on the printed page, and even on the bodies of demonstrators.

We begin this overview in the nineteenth century, with abolitionist printers rendering their rage in support of the antislavery cause with bold Victorian wood type. We see this typeset fury recur in the 1963 *I Am a Man* placards carried by Memphis garbage men striking to prevent more of their coworkers from dying on the job. We encounter it again in the ragged handlettering on posters made by students expressing shock at the U.S. war crimes in Southeast Asia and the 1970 shooting deaths of student protesters at Kent State. And we witness it re-emerge near the end of the century in AIDS-awareness public service announcements, skillfully crafted through the wrath and sorrow of designers who were losing friends, and sometimes even their own lives, to the stigmatized disease.

We see anger in these graphics, but we can also discern cause for hope: in the 1914 convention badge worn by a Black suffragist, determined to claim her right to vote; in the brave eloquence of the gay Harlem Renaissance poet who declares space for himself in *Fire!!*, one of America's early queer publications; and in Sister Corita Kent's prints, which reverberate in spiritual solidarity with the civil rights movement.

From across the United States and beyond, the designs shared in *Strikethrough* stage a march through time and space to declare that, while the specific chants of protest may vary by movement and medium, one refrain remains the same: the demand to speak, to be heard, and to be seen and respected as a human being.

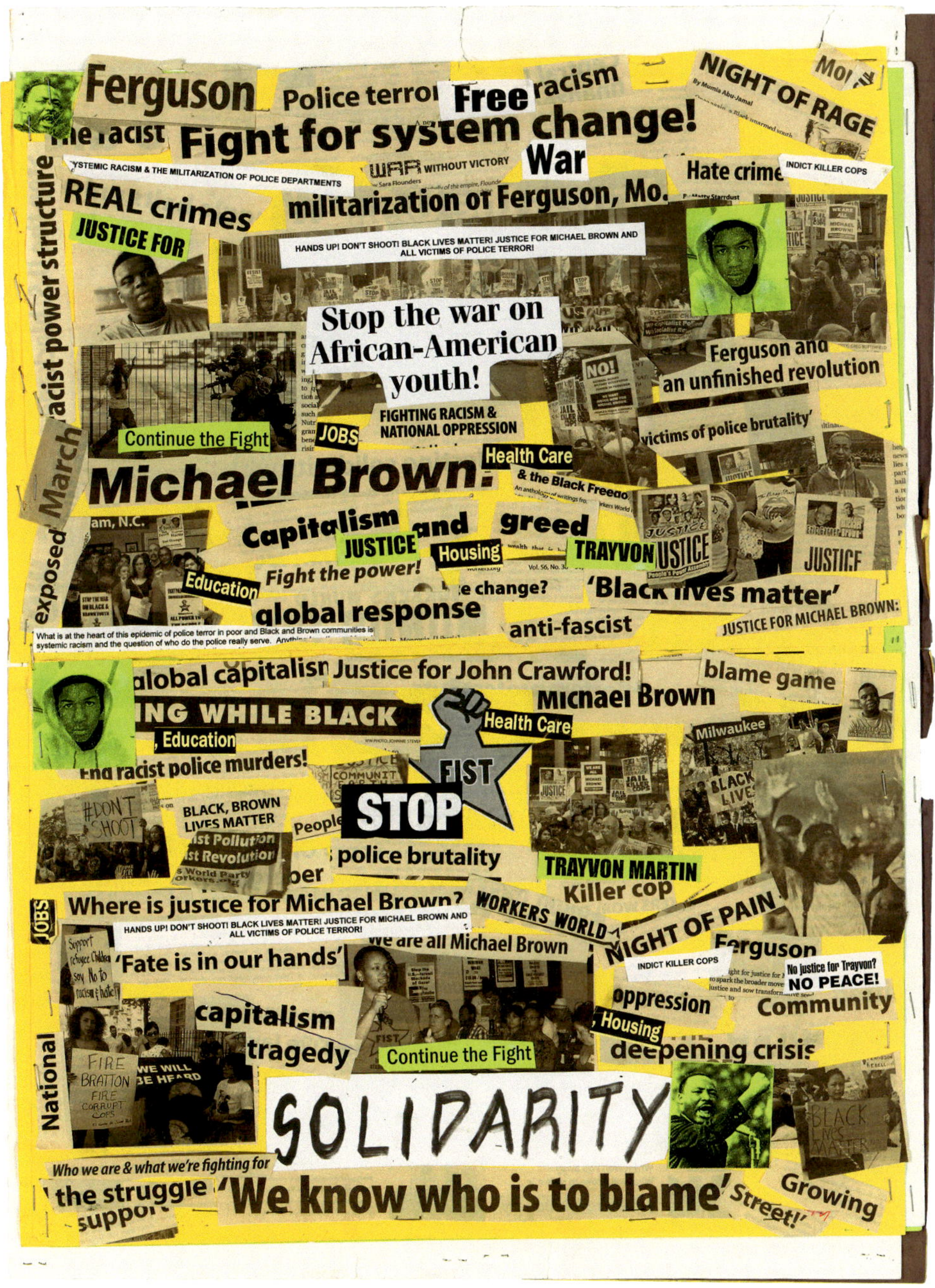

Sara E. Benjamin, untitled poster for a Black Lives Matter protest, 2014, newsprint and digital print collage on paperboard with metal staples, 24 × 18 inches (61 × 46 cm), Baltimore. Collection of the Smithsonian National Museum of African American History and Culture.

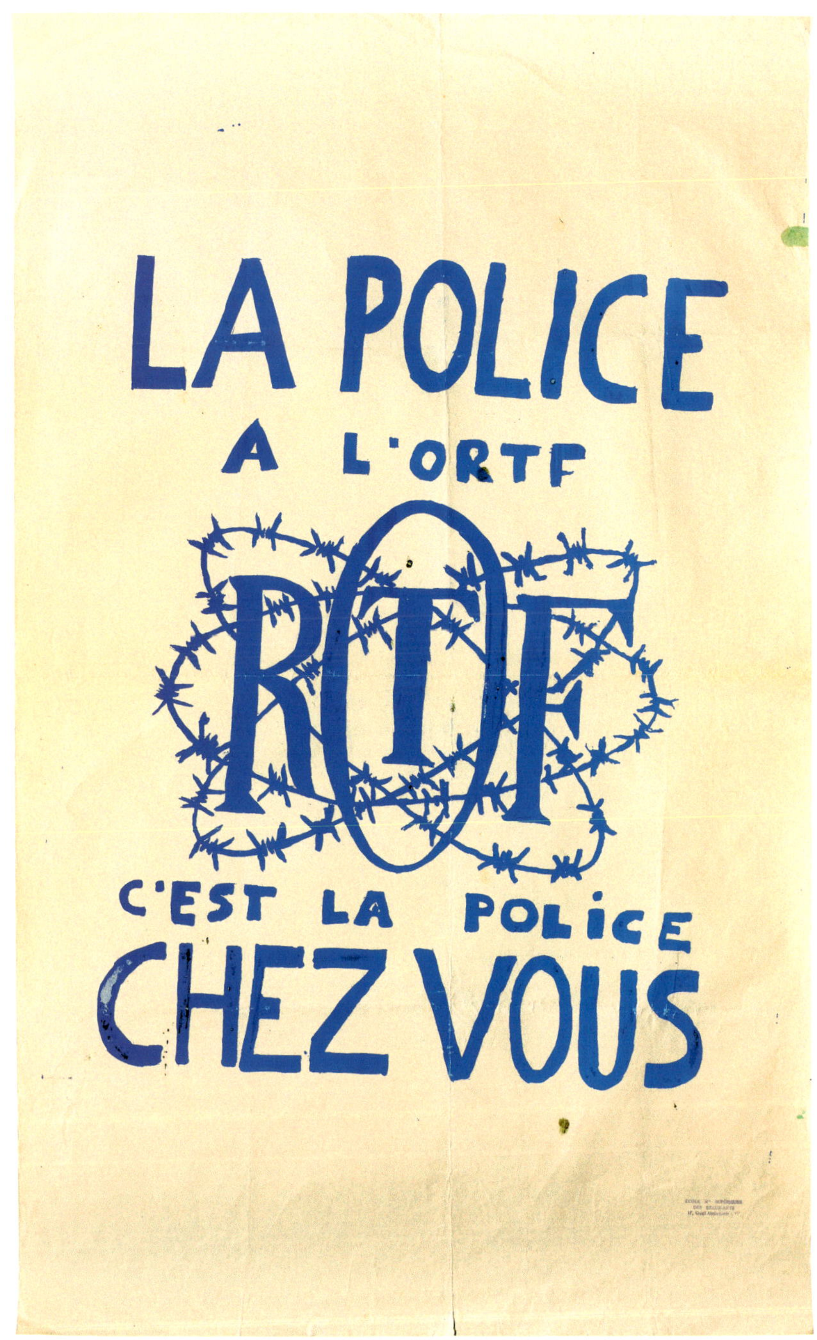

Atelier Populaire, *Police at the ORTF Means Police at Your House* (*La police à l'ORTF c'est la police chez vous*), 1968, screen print on newsprint, 35⅜ × 22 inches (89.5 × 56 cm), Paris.

The Typographic Origins of Strikethrough

In letterpress printing, a strikethrough occurs when the blunt mechanical force of printing pushes ink through the page. But the mark more commonly associated with the term—a line crossing through a written word to call for that word's omission—actually predates movable type. In Europe, medieval scribes used the horizontal bar to call out gaffes in illuminated manuscripts, as mistakes were too painstaking and expensive to redo.[1] Some scholars identify Laurence Sterne's typographically ambitious work of fiction, *The Life and Opinions of Tristram Shandy, Gentleman* (1759), as the mark's first appearance in printed book form.[2] Over time, the strikethrough took its place in copyediting markup and was implemented across many different cultures. In Japan, for instance, it is formed with a double line so as not to be confused with strokes in *kanji* or *kana*.[3] In the late 1970s and early 1980s, the strikethrough became an indelible part of digital life when it appeared in the first word processors' revision tools. And in the early twenty-first-century Tumblr days, bloggers used the strikethrough to coyly take back internal dialogue or controversial text while actually emphasizing their retention.[4]

The term *strikethrough* does not appear in Robert Bringhurst's book *The Elements of Typographic Style*, the definitive usage guide for many English-speaking type nerds. Perhaps its perpetual use in proofreading and infrequent appearance in finished printed works disqualified it from mention.[5] Nonetheless, the strikethrough has earned a place in our typographic idiom.

In the context of this exhibition, striking through means marking oppression for deletion while making it visible to all. It means wielding letterforms—be they letterpress, woodcut, stencil, Letraset, Xerox, or laser-cut—to call out societal ills so that they can be fixed. It means engaging with the issues at the level of the typeset line, interrogating the role that print plays in changing minds.

In list-making, the strikethrough is also used to mark a task as completed. It is our hope that the institutional wrongs called out in this book will, over time, be struck through, one by one, so they no longer pose a harm to future generations.

Making Design Under Duress

Protest graphics vibrate with urgency, as their makers tend to rush to the streets without the time—or often the financial means—to fastidiously produce their signs. *Strikethrough* is concerned with the formal and material codes of people making design under this duress. It also charts the parallels between waves of social transformation and the printing technologies that helped spread their messages.

The French art collective Atelier Populaire ("popular workshop") demonstrated this urgency when its members overtook the

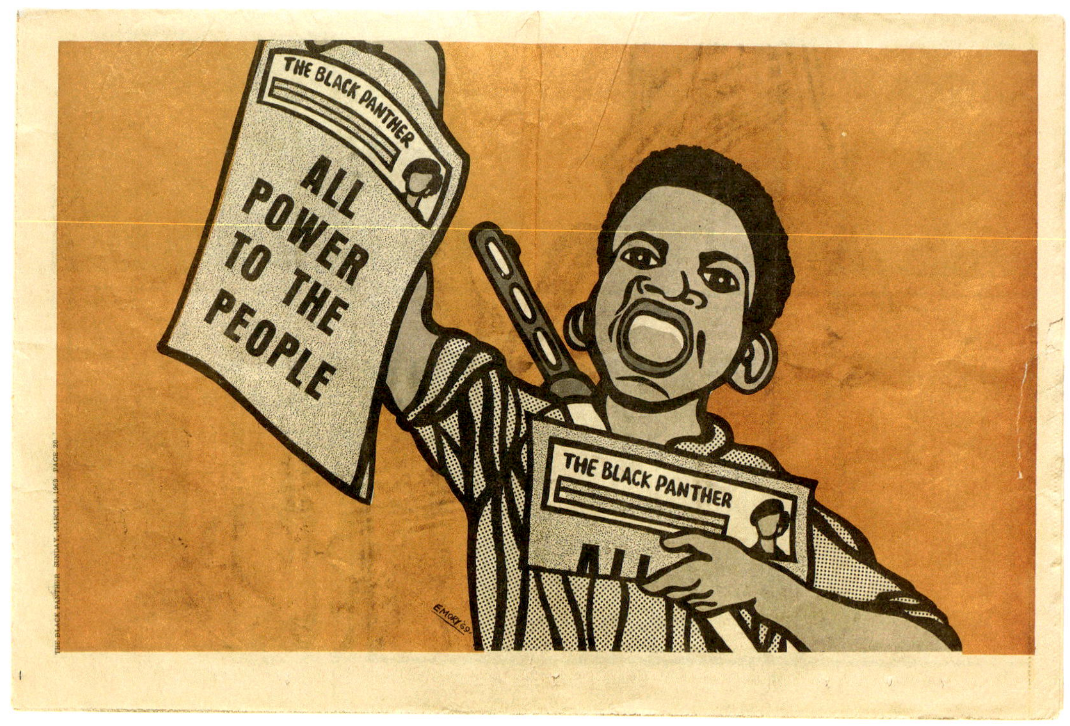

lithography studio at the École des Beaux-Arts in critique of a broken education system and the authoritarianism of French president Charles de Gaulle. Printing thousands of posters, the students soon realized that using silkscreens was faster and cheaper than stone lithography. You can see evidence of their frenetic pace in the work itself: in the letterforms' uneven strokes, the use of limited colors, and rudimentary but effective illustrations (see pages 8 and 150–51).

Simultaneously, U.S. protesters in the civil rights, women's liberation, countercultural, and LGBTQIA+ movements were also embracing an economy of means, thanks to inexpensive newspaper printing. One of the most iconic and prolific publications of this time was produced by the Black Panther Party, based in Oakland, California. While the organization was a collective, it was the vision of Emory Douglas, the Party's official minister of culture, that helped define the visual aesthetic of Black liberation. Mastering the art of working lean, he used a cost-effective typographic palette consisting of fonts for the IBM Selectric typewriter and from dry-transfer Formatt letters (a cheaper version of Letraset). Emblazoned with his handlettering and illustration, and printed in a rotating set of eye-popping spot colors, *The Black Panther* newspaper was a weekly tour de force that, at its height, circulated to 300,000 households, schools, and businesses.

In the following decades, designing lean became even easier, with increased access to publishing via copy shops and cheap offset printing, which gave rise to underground publications such as *IGTimes*. Art-directed by graffiti writer and

Emory Douglas, back cover of *The Black Panther*, vol. 2, no. 25, 1969, offset, 11½ × 17 inches (29.5 × 45.5 cm), Oakland, California.

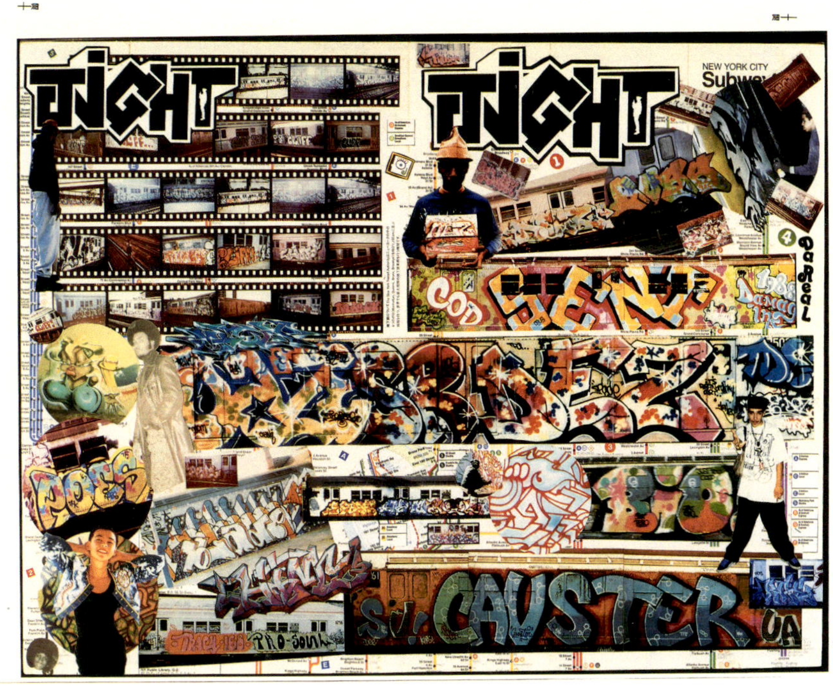

block-party-flyer designer Phase 2, this DIY zine came to define the 1990s Wild Style aesthetic, with its hip-hop collage look merging urban photography and drippy spray-paint textures with an eclectic typographic language borrowed from transfer type and the handstyles of various graffiti artists. Developed during one of the bleakest economic times in New York City, this cutting-edge visual language served as a precursor to the postmodern typography that would soon be co-opted by white design agencies and television shows like *Yo! MTV Raps*.

IGTimes and its scenemakers were plagued by racial tensions, accusations of gang warfare, and police violence. These struggles not only echo those of the Black Panthers, who were relentlessly pursued by the FBI, but also foreshadow those of the protesters in the Black Lives Matter movement, which has been a target of both police and vigilante violence, as well as disparagement in the press.

The Revolution Will Be Digitized

As technology advances, so does the creation of additional spaces for the production and display of protest graphics. Today, smartphones allow more people to virtually attend a protest than could ever turn out in person. Crafted to catch the attention of the digital masses, tweets and typographic Instagram posts function as the digital broadsides of our day, acting as a bullhorn for the cause and helping protesters connect and organize.

We saw the first wave of such digital protest in the spring of 2011, when a series of popular uprisings in primarily Muslim countries, including Bahrain, Egypt, Libya, Morocco, Syria, and

Phase 2 (designer/editor), *IGTimes*, vol. 14, 1993, offset, 19 × 25 inches (48 × 63.5 cm), New York.

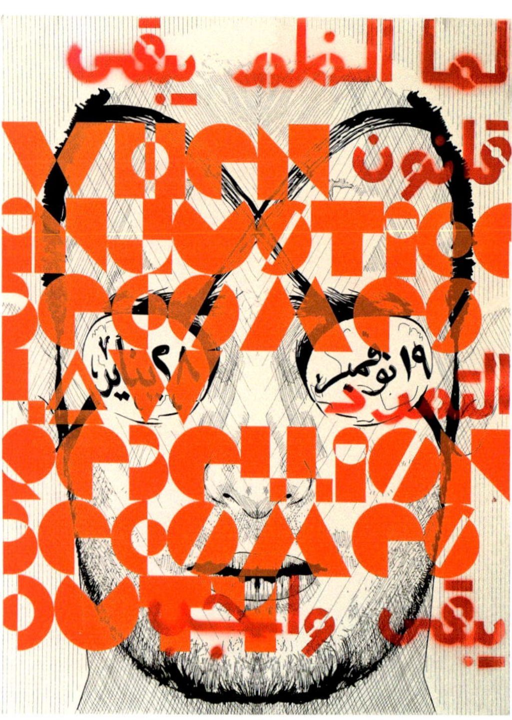

Tunisia, were heavily documented on Facebook and Twitter. Images of young Arab protesters wielding handmade banners, posters, and flags ricocheted across social feeds. After the Egyptian military abused protesters demonstrating against President Hosni Mubarak, artist Ganzeer created a series under the sarcastic title *Of Course the Army Protected the Revolution*. In the four designs in the series, he layered a formal silkscreen and an ad hoc stencil over a portrait of an injured or murdered demonstrator, each of whose experience of state violence went viral online.

Egypt-born book artist Islam Aly similarly borrowed from the streets in *The Square*, a chunky tome assembled using traditional Egyptian coptic binding (see pages 84–87). Aly laser-cut the phrase "The people want to bring down the regime" ("al-sha'b yurid isqat al-nizam") in the Arabic script Kufic. He mimics the escalating calls of the crowd at Cairo's Tahrir Square by repeating the phrase in denser and denser layouts as the book progresses. Triumphantly, this typographic chant crescendoes into "The people have brought down the regime" at the book's end.

Digital production has also revolutionized the typographic language of protest graphics. For the series *A Queer Year of Love Letters*, Nat Pyper created five digital typefaces based on the lives of important but overlooked gay liberation activists.[6] In their research, Pyper looked to early queer media and translated the letterforms into expressive digital offerings. With references as varied as American Sign Language (used by gay Chinese American painter Martin Wong) and

Ganzeer, *Justice for Harara*, from the *Of Course the Army Protected the Revolution* series, 2020, spray paint on screen print, 25 × 19 inches (63.5 × 48.5 cm), Houston. Courtesy of Ganzeer.

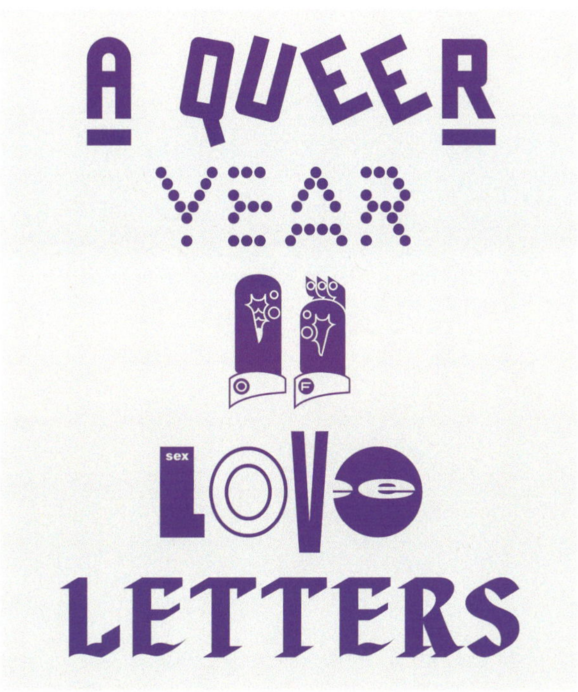

the children's toy Lite-Brite (which inspired the title sequence of one of G. B. Jones's low-budget queer films), Pyper's typefaces refuse to flatten heroes into stereotypes. Available for free, the fonts serve as both an archive of queer liberation and new tools to use in the ongoing fight.[7]

Typographic Call and Response

Brought from Africa to the colonies in America via the transatlantic slave trade, call and response is a pattern in music in which two distinct phrases are connected in dialogue, meaning the first phrase (the call) elicits the second (the response).[8] This rhythmic exchange also shaped early ideas of civic participation in which community leaders and members call and respond to each other to facilitate conversation. Today, you can witness it at work between speaker and audience throughout Black culture, particularly in religion, music, and community organizing (the last of which can be seen in the speeches of Dr. Martin Luther King, Jr., and President Barack Obama).

Strikethrough traces a typographic version of call and response across time and also across print and digital material. The substrates of protest are as diverse as the movements themselves, taking shape as placards, signs, pamphlets, typefaces, phone apps, and more. Despite this variety, these methods of communication are often united by graphic lineage in the form of recurring typefaces and illustrative motifs, which are all too often underscored by the sense that history is repeating. One of the goals of this exhibition is to highlight these forms

Nat Pyper, samples from the typeface series *A Queer Year of Love Letters*, 2018, digital fonts, Chicago and New Haven, Connecticut. From top to bottom: Ernestine Eckstein, G. B. Jones, Martin Wong, Robert Ford, and Women's Car Repair Collective.

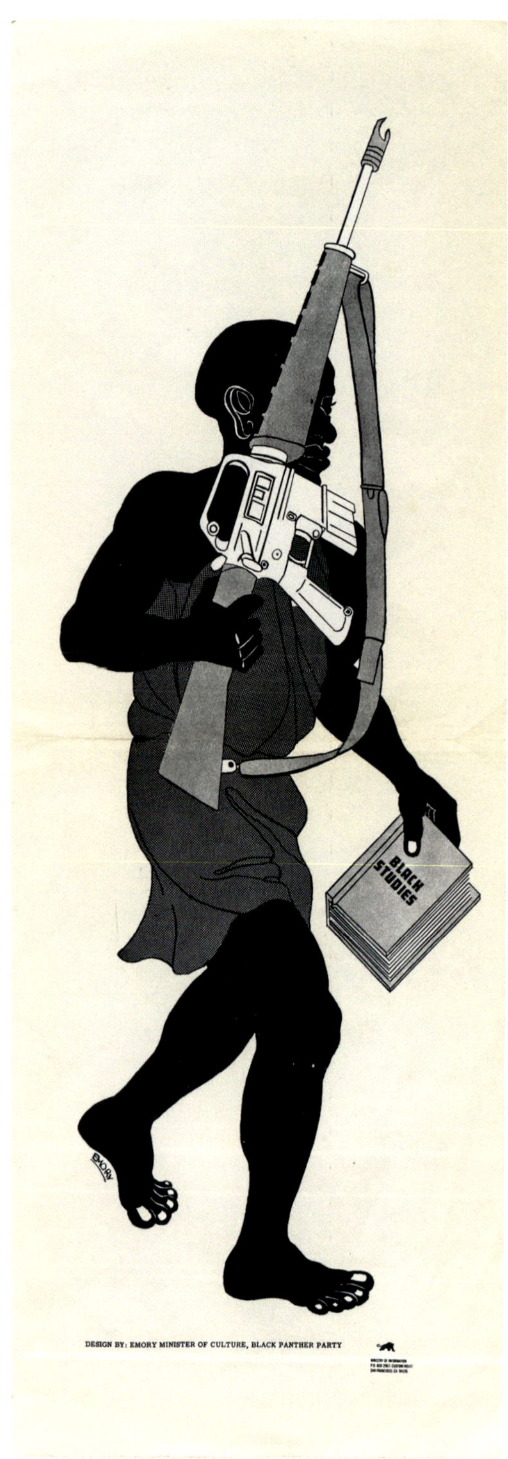

Emory Douglas, *Black Studies*, circa 1970, offset, 22¾ × 8⅛ inches (58 × 20.5 cm), Oakland, California.

of visual call and response via letterform and iconography. Another goal is to share the stories of the designers themselves, many of whom have also worked as activists and used their craft to facilitate change.

In seeing so many chants made visible among these materials, five core proclamations stood out, transcending the issues of the individual demonstrators-as-designers: Resist, Vote, Strike, Teach, and Love. Using these calls to action as organizing principles, we are able to witness waves of protesters iterating on each theme across generations, geography, media, and sociopolitical values.

A True Collective Action

Like the movements of protest in *Strikethrough*, the creation of this show and book was a collective effort of call and response. In the period of the exhibition's curation, design, and production, we were all processing the one-two punch of a global pandemic and a national reckoning catalyzed by the 2020 Black Lives Matter protests. As designers, historians, and archivists, our every choice echoed with the struggles of many histories and lineages. Together with Letterform Archive (the host of the exhibition and publisher of this catalog) and members of collective design studio Polymode, we worked side by side to look at the history of protest graphics from a uniquely typographic perspective.

A key ask was to expand the Archive's existing collection of graphic design with acquisitions from outside the white, Euro-American, and often cis male constructs of type and design history. Through friends of the Archive and Polymode, we endeavored to include the work of BIPOC, women, LGBTQIA+ artists, international designers, activists untrained in graphic design, and other voices that are often excluded from canonical discourses.

Despite our best efforts, however, we are still left with the curatorial lament that *Strikethrough*—while expansive—does have its limits. Long histories of colonialism, white supremacy, misogyny, homophobia, and ableism have worked against the legacies of many of the makers, artists, and designers of protest art, and much of their work was not saved for preservation in libraries, museums, and archives. Further, because the graphic materials of protest are often by their very nature ephemeral, we were also challenged by pieces of unknown provenance or authorship. The global COVID-19 pandemic additionally limited and slowed our access to many archives and collections.

That said, the posters, prints, apparel, buttons, signs, books, periodicals, and software in *Strikethrough* serve as ample typographic receipts of wrongs in need of righting. They demonstrate a constant revision of our society in real time. Each letterform is a push back against the denial of freedoms. Every design makes the error of injustice visible while also effectively calling for its erasure. Every protester featured here generated text as evidence of a moral mistake that they felt must be struck through.

Our hope is that *Strikethrough* will call out for typographic responses that echo for years to come. What might future conversations around human life look like typeset in a refrain for dignity, safety, and equality for all?

NOW! Demanding Black Liberation with Typography

Colette Gaiter

One of the most surprising things about 1960s and early 1970s African American protest graphics is that they ever existed at all. Jim Crow laws across the United States restricted every aspect of life for Black people. Even after the Civil Rights Act of 1964 technically banned segregation and discrimination, racist restrictions continued to block access to print media production. But determined activists, artists, and designers made a way out of no way—as the African American saying goes—to deploy printed words in the fight for liberation. They put out a call and expected a response.

According to Lincoln Cushing, the McCarthy era and its anti-communist scare tactics shut down many post–World War II progressive presses. "It's a remarkable fact that the civil rights movement and the free speech movement of 1964 relied on almost every medium *but* posters," he writes.[1] Instead, activist organizations usually distributed smaller flyers and pamphlets that could be reproduced on office machines. Posters from the early civil rights movement are also rare because Black designers for the most part worked on Black publications, and segregation denied those publications access to the small presses that printed posters.

One exceptional series of iconic posters that did make it into production came from the Student Nonviolent Coordinating Committee (SNCC), which formed in 1960 and organized sit-ins, voting rights campaigns, and other critical actions. A caption in Hal Elliott Wert's book on campaign and political posters explains why the SNCC graphics were so effective: "The unerring SNCC design team often cropped [civil rights photographer Danny] Lyon's photos and added pertinacious captions . . . . *NOW* is one of the top photos and posters from the entire sixties civil rights struggle."[2] Lyon shot the image on the poster—one of five made by the SNCC that feature his photography—at the March on Washington on August 28, 1963.

Other photographs of that historic day show marchers carrying placards that typographically shouted out specific demands. Black photographer Ernest Withers's famous image of sanitation workers striking in Memphis in March of 1968 (see pages 144–45) poignantly echoes the sea of protesters at the 1963 March on Washington. As liberation movements progressed, posters repeated this rhetorical approach and added color, images, and graphics, as the means of production allowed. Oversized text became a universal element in protest signs, representing loud calls to action.

The Memphis protests for better working conditions occurred after two sanitation

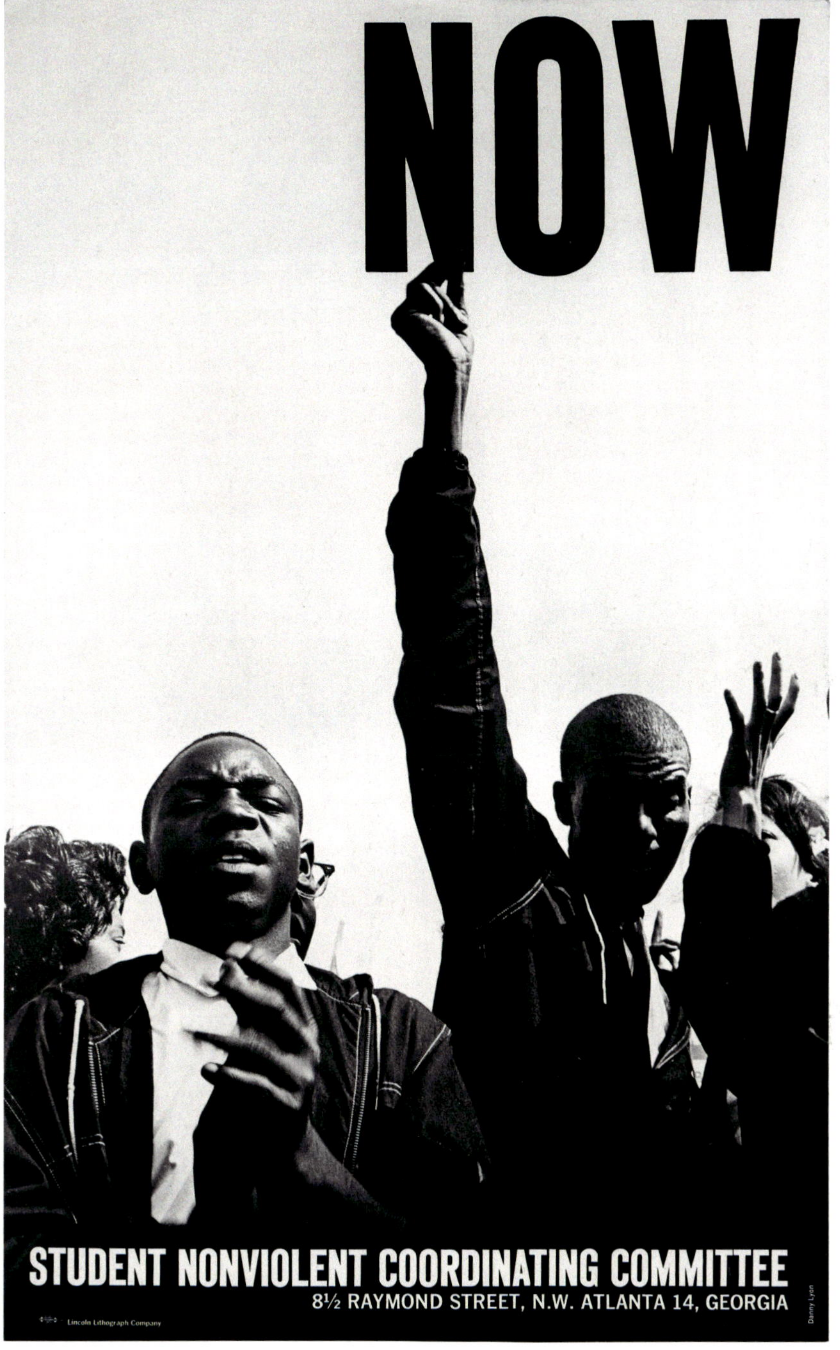

Unknown designer for the Student Nonviolent Coordinating Committee (SNCC), Danny Lyon (photographer), *NOW*, 1963, offset, 22 × 14 inches (56 × 35.5 cm), Atlanta. Courtesy of Magnum Photos.

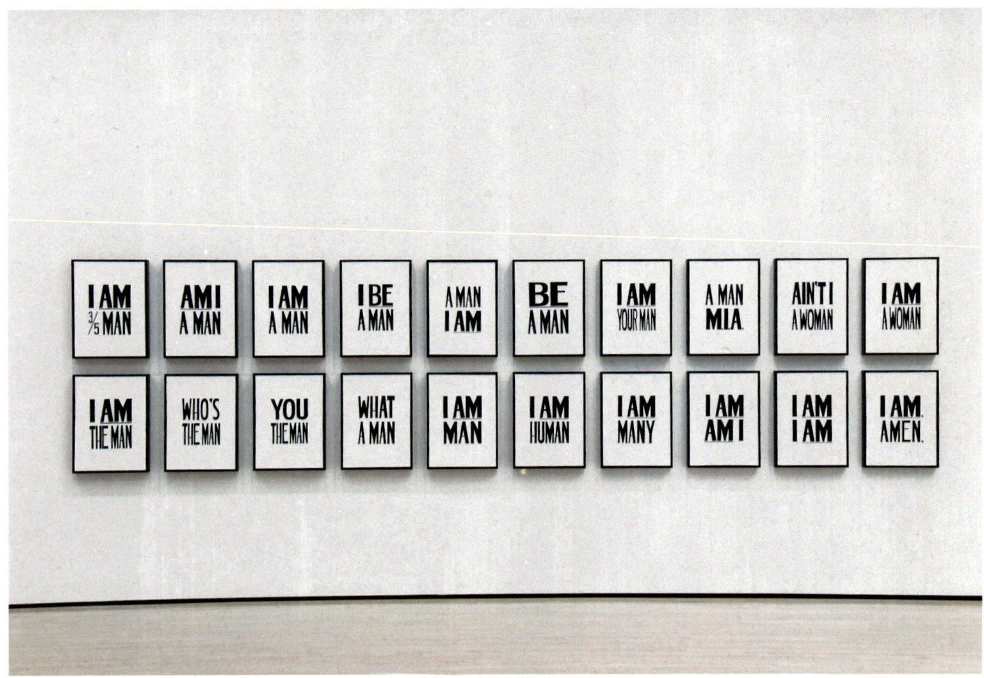

employees were killed on the job. The events might have remained local news, except that Dr. Martin Luther King, Jr., was assassinated the day before he was scheduled to march in solidarity with the cause. Over time, the placards carried in Memphis became typographic symbols of the frustration and anger expressed by the protesters but felt by nearly all African Americans. Most of the placards were discarded after the march, but the sign remains a powerful metonym for Dr. King's last act of leadership before his death. Like the word "NOW" on the SNCC poster, accompanied by a snap of a protester's fingers, the four words "I AM A MAN" visually scream a declaration and, with it, a demand. Contemporary artists Hank Willis Thomas and Glenn Ligon later incorporated the latter image/text in separate works that conceptually expand the words' meaning and legacy.

The cover of the June 7, 1969, issue of *The Black Panther* newspaper, designed by Emory Douglas, continues the placard sensibility of calling out a demand. Black Power activism, which evolved from the civil rights movement, included self-defense as a liberation strategy. Because the Black Panthers legally armed themselves against the extreme actions of law enforcement, many were arrested and jailed for crimes they did not commit.[3] The late 1960s and early 1970s saw a steady stream of textual demands in support of these prisoners, including "Free Angela [Davis]," "Free Bobby [Seale]," and the long-running "Free Huey [Newton]." Posters, banners, buttons, and flyers proliferated at organized marches that advocated for their freedom. Most Black Panther political prisoners were acquitted, although some not until decades later. As of 2021, thirteen former Panthers were still serving sentences handed down in the late 1960s.[4]

Hank Willis Thomas, *I Am a Man* series, 2009, liquitex on canvas, 25¼ × 19¼ inches (64 × 49 cm) per panel. Courtesy of the artist and the Jack Shainman Gallery, New York.

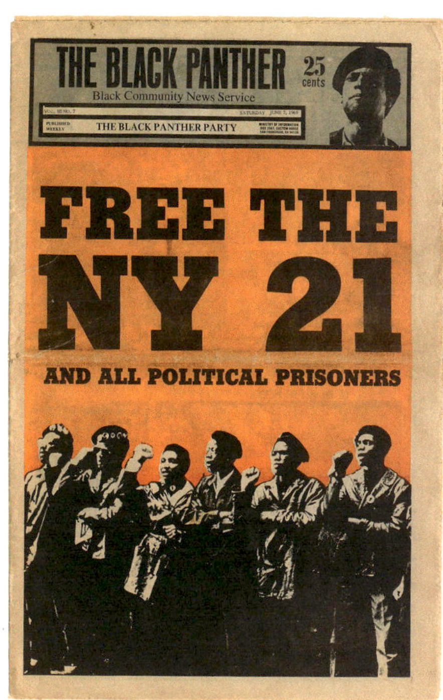

THE BLACK PANTHER
25 cents
Black Community News Service
THE BLACK PANTHER PARTY
FREE THE NY 21
AND ALL POLITICAL PRISONERS

The Black Panther Party also advocated for direct political action through their newspaper, and the wider community of visual artists took up the same protest themes in their work. Starting in 1965, the Black Arts Movement provided a cultural complement to Black Power's political organizing. Larry Neal, a Black Arts leader, described this new movement as the "aesthetic and spiritual sister of the Black Power concept. As such, it envisions an art that speaks directly to the needs and aspirations of Black America." He went on: "One is concerned with the relationship between art and politics; the other with the art of politics."[5]

This nationally dispersed but associated group of musicians, poets, prose writers, playwrights, and visual artists promoted Black expression as a vehicle for solidarity and the improvement of Black life. One prominent group in the Black Arts Movement was the African Commune of Bad Relevant Artists (AfriCOBRA). Based in Chicago, AfriCOBRA included Barbara Jones-Hogu, whose 1971 screen print *Unite* re-creates the protest experience (see page 20). Instead of carrying placards, people raise their fists, and the word "UNITE" fills the air around them in a visual and almost out loud call to action.

In a similarly dynamic typographic treatment, Faith Ringgold's 1971 *Women Free Angela* poster (see page 21) explores various word relationships in a tessellating op art pattern in the Black liberation colors of red, black, and green.[6] In a 2010 blog post, Ringgold's daughter, the writer Michele Wallace, explains that the poster, which is one of a pair of designs, was "meant to be distributed at public meetings [and] displayed at spontaneous protests" and was "conceived as art for the people in the egalitarian spirit of

Emory Douglas, front cover of *The Black Panther*, offset, vol. 3, no. 7, 1969, 17 × 11½ inches (45.5 × 29.5 cm), Oakland, California.

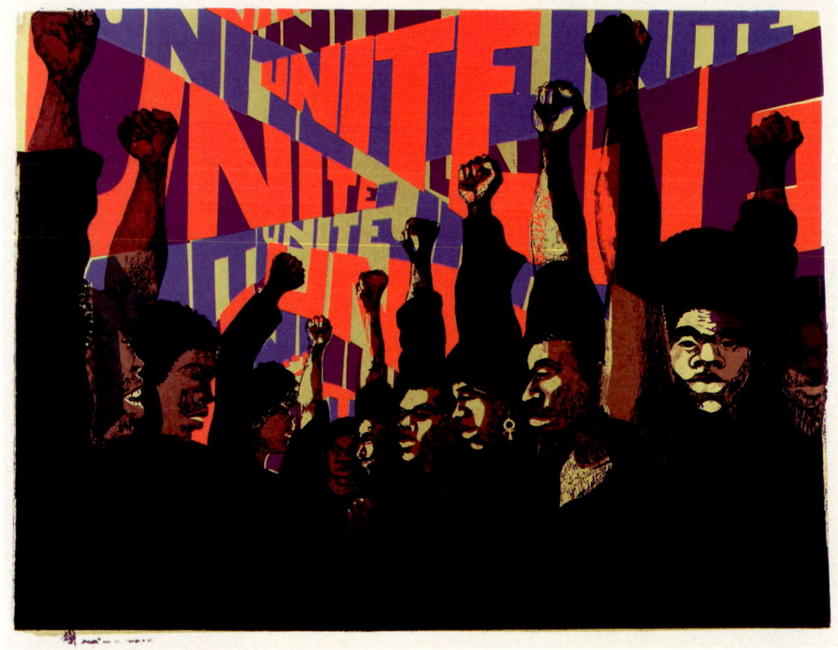

the times.”[7] The late 1960s prints draw from textile designs known as Kuba cloth, created by the Kuba people from the Democratic Republic of the Congo (formerly Zaire). With the words arranged to be readable in many directions, the textual configurations also visually represent the literary spoken-word structures of Black Arts Movement poets.

After 1964, Black artists and designers expanded their options in protest media as they moved out of the long shadow of legally institutionalized segregation and racism. Before the 1964 Civil Rights Act, political posters that demanded change could be hung only in sympathetic spaces such as the offices of the SNCC and other African American activist organizations. The call and response tradition of early civil rights speeches proved equally effective in Black Power typographic images of the 1960s and 1970s, and previously silenced messages of Black liberation became visible and practically audible when posted on walls. Typography became an oratory device that called for liberation with a resonance that, while it could not be literally felt in the body like the voices of preachers and leaders, had the advantage of reaching more people.

Speaking in 2022 at Howard University, art historian Huey Copeland described the 1968 *I Am a Man* sign as a “multi-vocal demand for the recognition of Black manhood, nationally and locally . . . in the face of a vehemently racist political culture.”[8] Citing the concept of “collective intelligence,” developed by Cedric Robinson, a late scholar of the Black Radical Tradition,[9] Copeland posits that the sign echoes a range of voices from different times and places—including those of African and enslaved ancestors—all of them calling for universal respect of Black bodies. Today, the typographic legacy of Black protests carries on, with the protest placards of the civil rights movement evolving to declare that “BLACK LIVES MATTER.” The African American and ancestral African aesthetics of oration and design continue to call Black people together in pursuit of the only correct response: Black liberation—NOW.

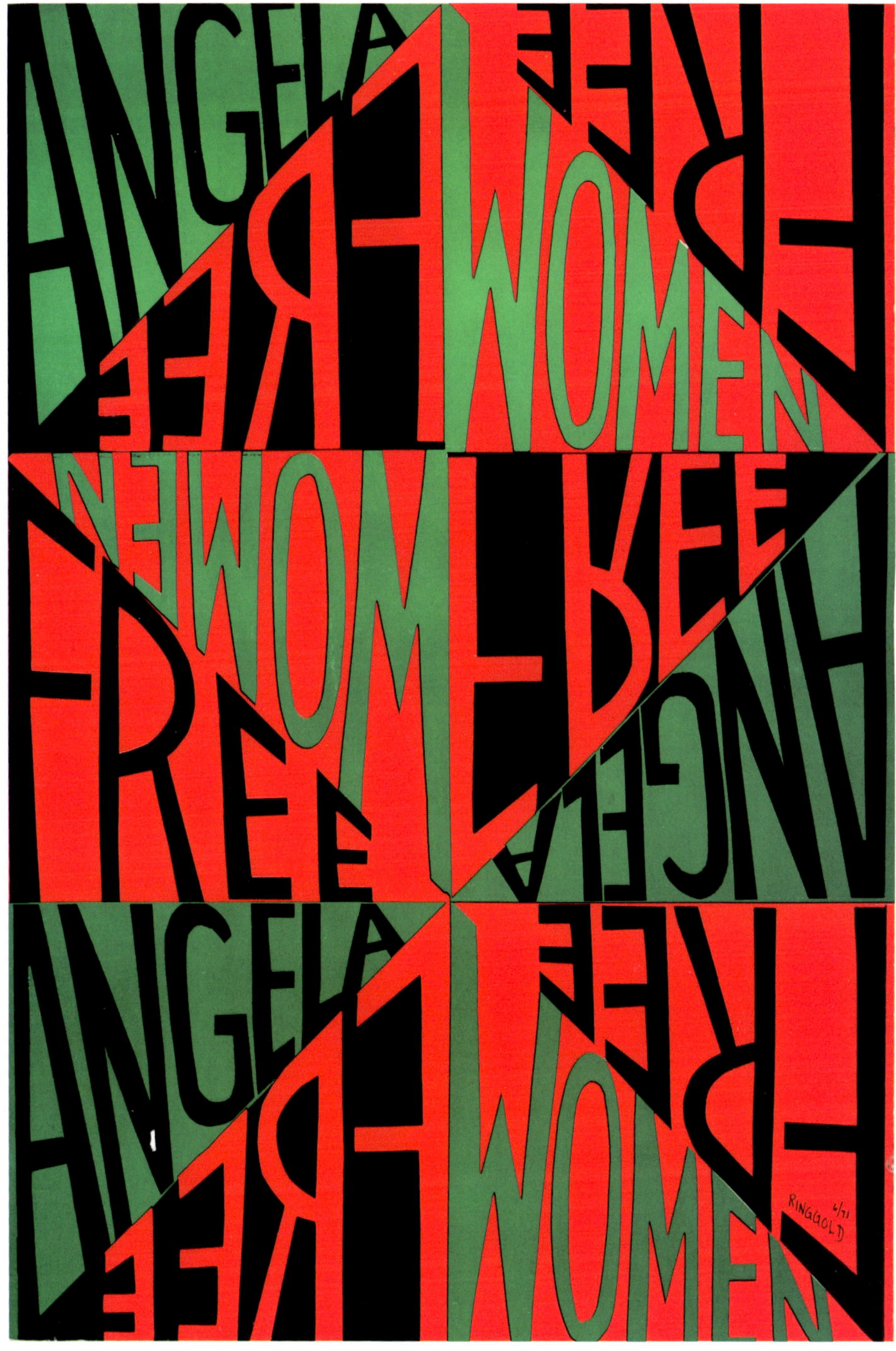

Barbara Jones-Hogu, *Unite*, 1971, screen print, 22½ × 30 inches (57 × 76 cm), Chicago. Courtesy of Lusenhop Fine Art.

Faith Ringgold, *Women Free Angela*, 1971, screen print, 28¼ × 19½ inches (72 × 49.5 cm), New York. Courtesy of ACA Galleries, New York.

Type Gives Shape to Voice

Stephen Coles

Typography is often discussed in terms of fashion. Printing historian and type marketer Beatrice Warde famously described typefaces as "the clothes that words wear." Fonts are also sometimes compared to building tools or materials: The process of typeface selection is all about picking the right one for the job. As we selected the objects for this exhibition and accompanying book, however, the theme that repeatedly rang in our ears is how type gives shape to voice.

The text of these posters and patches, books and buttons transforms the spoken into the seen. Through the power of printing, demands that may otherwise go unheard are documented, reproduced, and distributed. Audible calls for action are translated into a visible, repeatable form. They transcend the moment when they are uttered and travel into other times and places to impact new audiences and take on new meanings.

In this work, we see how activists talk with type. Anger, fear, conviction, and strength are frequently conveyed through extrabold typefaces like Compacta, Franklin Gothic, Futura Condensed, and Impact. These implements of commerce, commonly found on billboards and magazine ads, are repurposed for deeper causes, yet with the same effect: grabbing attention. Designed to fit large text in any space, their heavy weight and narrow proportions pack a punch and fill a page.

These type styles also do it without frills or pretension. Compare a bold sans to a delicate serif, a decorative novelty face, or an ornate script. The first of these speaks, without wavering, the common language of the proletariat. It is the typographic equivalent of shouting the truth out loud.

Ever since their invention in the middle of the nineteenth century, workhorse sans serifs (grotesques) have flourished in commercial messaging. Initially, they delivered brief texts at small sizes in books and newspapers. Then, as cities grew and literacy increased, mass communication expanded to the walls of the city. Following the lead of urban advertising, proclamations of protest came in the form of *broadsides*: oversized flyers or posters, usually printed on letterpress. The need for larger letters that could be seen from the street also required a type material that was lighter and cheaper than metal: enter wood. Blocks could be several inches or even feet high—much bigger than any metal type. Bold, condensed gothics

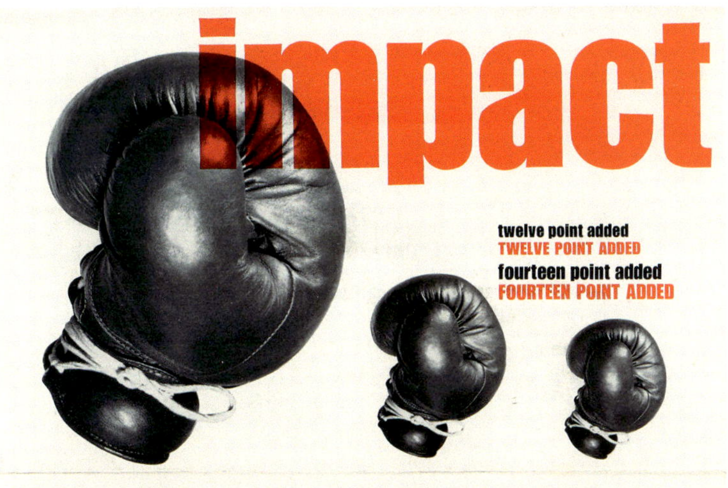

see the proportion of x height to CAP height
see the design detail, ALTERNATIVE J J terminal r r

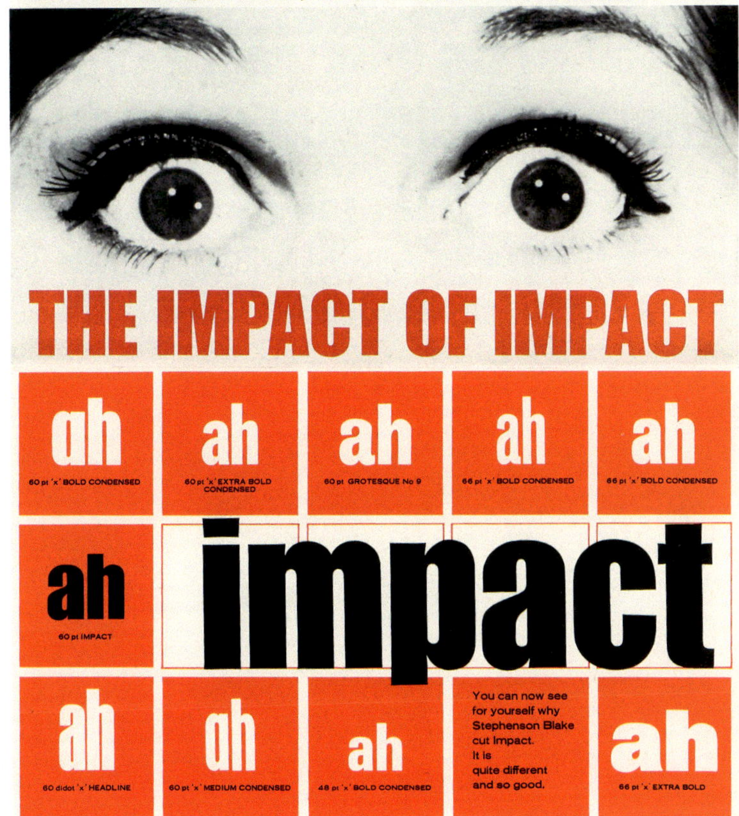

Geoffrey Lee (type designer) for the type foundry Stephenson Blake, detail of a type specimen for Impact, circa 1965, letterpress, 20 × 5 inches (51 × 12.5 cm) unfolded, Sheffield, England.

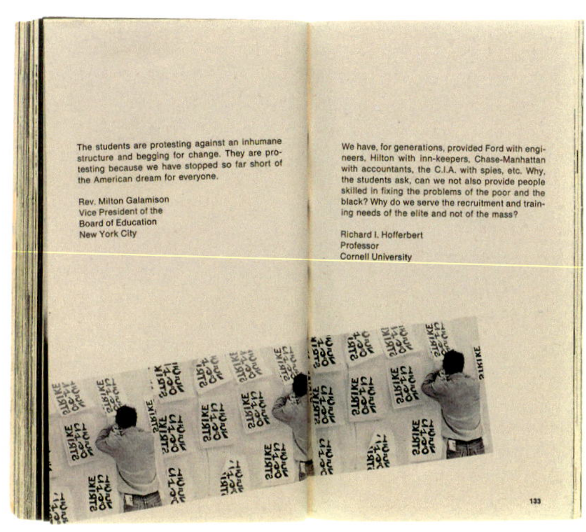

The students are protesting against an inhumane structure and begging for change. They are protesting because we have stopped so far short of the American dream for everyone.

Rev. Milton Galamison
Vice President of the
Board of Education
New York City

We have, for generations, provided Ford with engineers, Hilton with inn-keepers, Chase-Manhattan with accountants, the C.I.A. with spies, etc. Why, the students ask, can we not also provide people skilled in fixing the problems of the poor and the black? Why do we serve the recruitment and training needs of the elite and not of the mass?

Richard I. Hofferbert
Professor
Cornell University

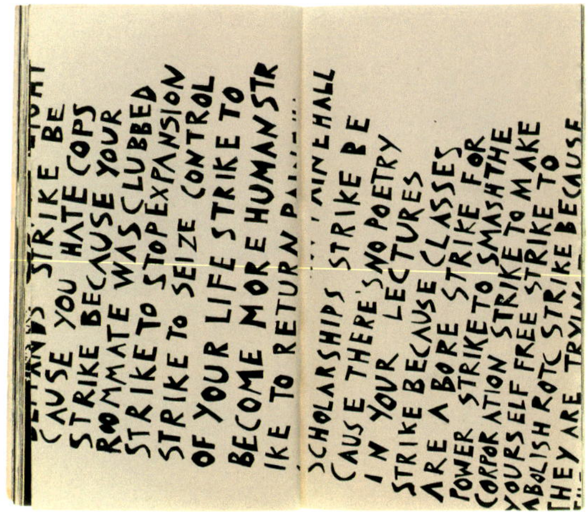

and slab serifs were common wood type styles, which the printer would use to fit as many big words as they could on each line. Examples of wood type at work in *Strikethrough* include abolitionist broadsides (see pages 34–37), the *I Am a Man* sign (page 148), Ben Shahn's *McCarthy Peace* poster (page 91), and the prints of Amos Paul Kennedy, Jr. (pages 124–27).

Later, the vintage typefaces that originated in wood type found their way into protest materials via updated font technologies. Some were simply reproduced photographically, such as Playbill, a typeface derived from nineteenth-century styles sometimes called French Antique and that Corita Kent often put to use in her posters (see pages 52–53). As the century went on, other artists incorporated digital revivals of wood type, including Favianna Rodriguez and Anthony Burrill, whose respective uses of Knockout (see page 138) and Champion Gothic (page 217) modernize but retain the edge of the hefty wood type traditionally used for the iconic "tale of the tape" posters promoting boxing events.

By the middle of the twentieth century, activists were regularly co-opting the principles of commercial typography for noncommercial purposes. Designers like Herb Lubalin, of the magazines *Fact*, *Avant-Garde*, and *Eros* (see pages 116–17 and 242–45); Archie Boston (page 38); and Tibor Kalman, of the quarterly *Colors* (pages 210–13), understood the persuasive power of bold typefaces, straightforward typography, and plainspoken copywriting, and they put all of this to work in the service of advocacy.

In other pieces we see how lettering, particularly handmade lettering, reflects the voice of its maker. There is no better way to say that something comes from the heart—and especially the heart of someone personally affected—than to write it (see the Guerrilla Girls' *Dearest Art Collector* on page 209), to draw it (Ganzeer's *Of Course the Army Protected the Revolution* series, on pages 12 and 82), or to cut it by hand.

Hand-cut letters frequently appear in screen-printed work, a result of both the production process and the desire to retain a human element. See the lettering of See Red Women's Workshop (pages 74–77), Jane Norling (page 51), Melanie Cervantes (page 137), and Thea Gahr (page 101), as well as the many striking posters reproduced inside and on the cover of *Right On!* (pages 188–91). Digital type may have enabled Ward Schumaker to churn out hundreds of *Trump Papers* (pages 130–31), but it was the

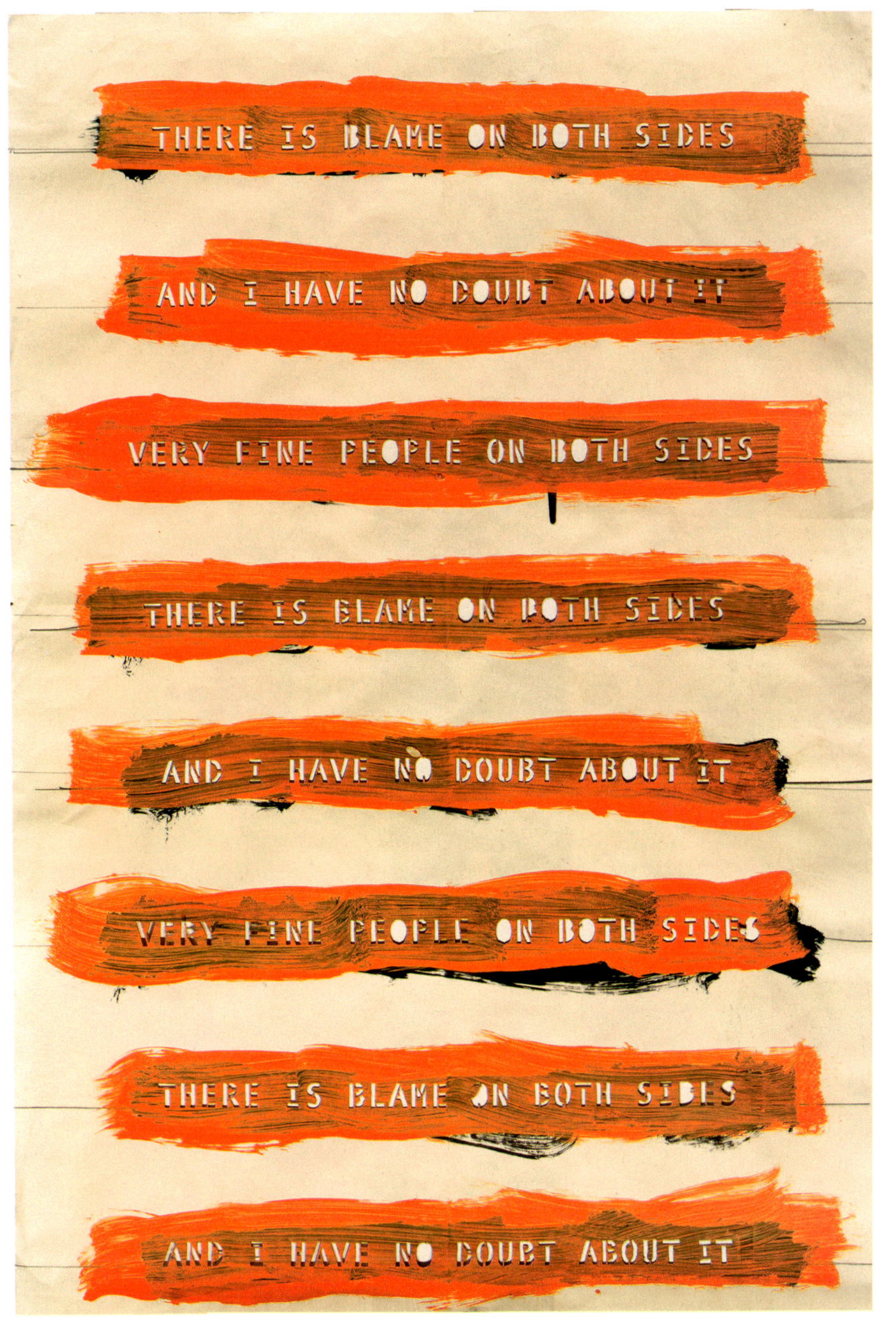

David L. Burke (designer), Maryl Levine and John Naisbitt (authors), interior pages from *Right On!: A Documentary of Student Protest*, 1970, offset, 7⅛ × 4¼ inches (18 × 11 cm), New York.

Ward Schumaker, stencil for *Jews Will Not Replace Us*, from the series *Trump Papers* (*Hoisted by His Own Petard*), 2018, acrylic on cut paper, 37 × 25⅜ inches (94 × 64.5 cm), San Francisco. For the title of this poster, Schumaker appropriates a hate slogan that was chanted at a 2017 white supremacist rally in Charlottesville, Virginia.

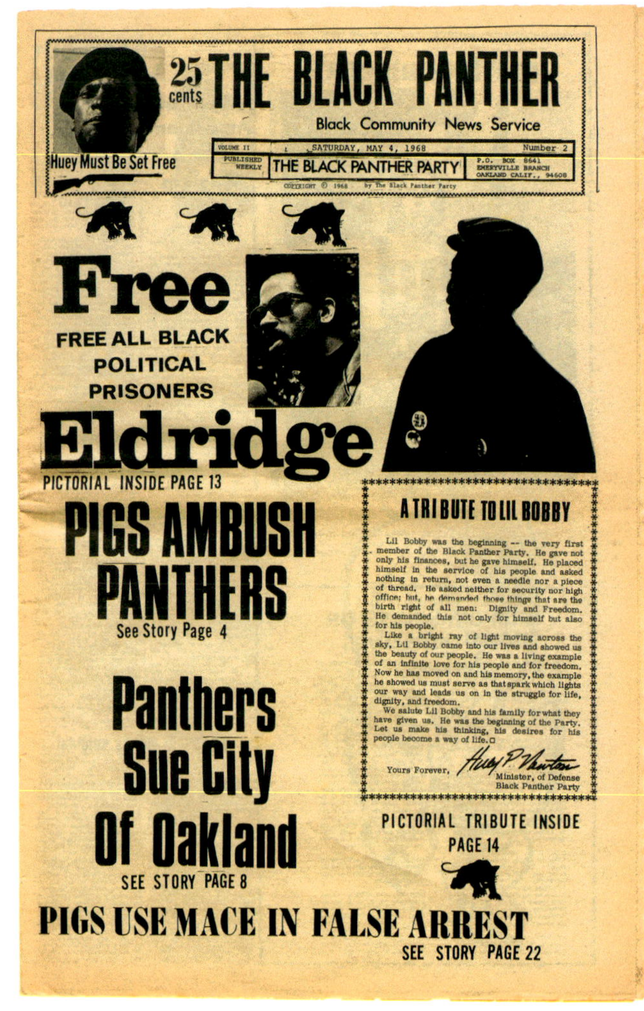

25 cents THE BLACK PANTHER

Black Community News Service

VOLUME II — SATURDAY, MAY 4, 1968 — Number 2

PUBLISHED WEEKLY — THE BLACK PANTHER PARTY — P.O. BOX 8641 EMERYVILLE BRANCH OAKLAND CALIF., 94608

COPYRIGHT © 1968 by The Black Panther Party

Huey Must Be Set Free

Free

FREE ALL BLACK POLITICAL PRISONERS

Eldridge

PICTORIAL INSIDE PAGE 13

PIGS AMBUSH PANTHERS

See Story Page 4

Panthers Sue City Of Oakland

SEE STORY PAGE 8

A TRIBUTE TO LIL BOBBY

Lil Bobby was the beginning -- the very first member of the Black Panther Party. He gave not only his finances, but he gave himself. He placed himself in the service of his people and asked nothing in return, not even a needle nor a piece of thread. He asked neither for security nor high office; but, he demanded those things that are the birth right of all men: Dignity and Freedom. He demanded this not only for himself but also for his people.

Like a bright ray of light moving across the sky, Lil Bobby came into our lives and showed us the beauty of our people. He was a living example of an infinite love for his people and for freedom. Now he has moved on and his memory, the example he showed us must serve as that spark which lights our way and leads us on in the struggle for life, dignity, and freedom.

We salute Lil Bobby and his family for what they have given us. He was the beginning of the Party. Let us make his thinking, his desires for his people become a way of life.□

Yours Forever, Huey P. Newton
Minister, of Defense
Black Panther Party

PICTORIAL TRIBUTE INSIDE PAGE 14

PIGS USE MACE IN FALSE ARREST

SEE STORY PAGE 22

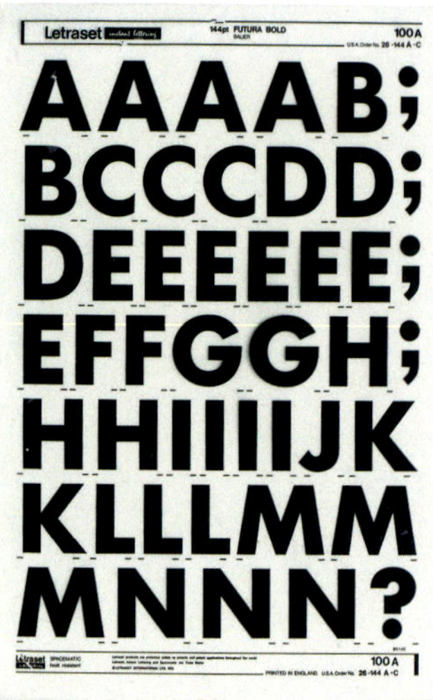

Emory Douglas, front cover of *The Black Panther*, vol. 2, no. 2, 1968, offset, 17 × 11½ inches (45.5 × 29.5 cm), Oakland, California.

Paul Renner (type designer) for original foundry Bauer, Letraset (transfer type manufacturer), Futura Bold transfer type, 1972, 15¼ × 10⅛ inches (38.5 × 26 cm), London.

Morris Fuller Benton (type designer) for original foundry ATF, Geotype (transfer type manufacturer), detail of Franklin Gothic Extra Condensed transfer type, circa 1970s, 12¼ × 16 inches (31 × 40.5 cm), Blaine, Washington.

manual act of cutting and painting each stencil that achieved the fiercely personal result.

We also see how other typographic choices are simply defined by what is possible. In many cases, the "look" of protest material is a product of the techniques and technologies available to the protester. For those whose lives or livelihoods are on the line, the best way to get the word out is to do it quickly and cheaply—and sometimes without the privilege of professional training.

This was never more true than in the late 1960s, which saw a confluence of newly accessible typographic and reproduction technologies. Rub-down lettering allowed for quick headlines in a variety of eye-catching styles, while increasingly sophisticated yet affordable typewriters produced galleys of text in a variety of typefaces. Flyers and publications could be reproduced on mimeograph machines and, later, photocopiers. All of this meant that activists on a budget could publish and disseminate many things on their own without relying on professional typesetters and printers. It freed them economically and also politically. They could finally print anything they wanted to say.

You can see this newfound freedom in countless independent publications and print pieces, from *The Black Panther* (see pages 10 and 56–61) to *IGTimes* (pages 11 and 79–81). Here, the front cover of an early *Black Panther* issue reveals the edges and guidelines of cut-and-paste transfer lettering. While designer Emory Douglas typically kept font styles to a minimum, he stacked this cover with lines of Futura, Alternate Gothic, Ultra Bodoni, Clarendon, and Compacta. With text calling for justice for Black people, it reads as a typographic descendant of nineteenth-century abolitionist broadsides, on which line after line of wood type in various typefaces urged the end of enslavement (see pages 34–37).

The curation of the *Strikethrough* exhibition and the selection of materials for this accompanying catalog is a political act. The choices we made reflect our choices not just as curators but as people. Because visual culture never lives in a vacuum, we understand that it is impossible to separate art and design from politics. So, with this show, we take a stand. Like Elvin Willie and the Alcatraz occupiers, we acknowledge that San Francisco (home to Letterform Archive, where this exhibition was first mounted) is part of the unceded ancestral homeland of the Ramaytush Ohlone people. We join the Feminist Majority Foundation and See Red Women's Workshop in demanding equal rights and equal pay. We concur with Mark Fox and the creators of *Occupy George* that unfettered capitalism only increases the imbalance of power. And we declare, without hesitation or equivocation, that Black Lives Matter. *Strikethrough* is a reminder to our community, and to ourselves, to consider typography not simply as an aesthetic or utilitarian enterprise but as a megaphone for justice.

RES
Freedom
MAB
MAB
People Power

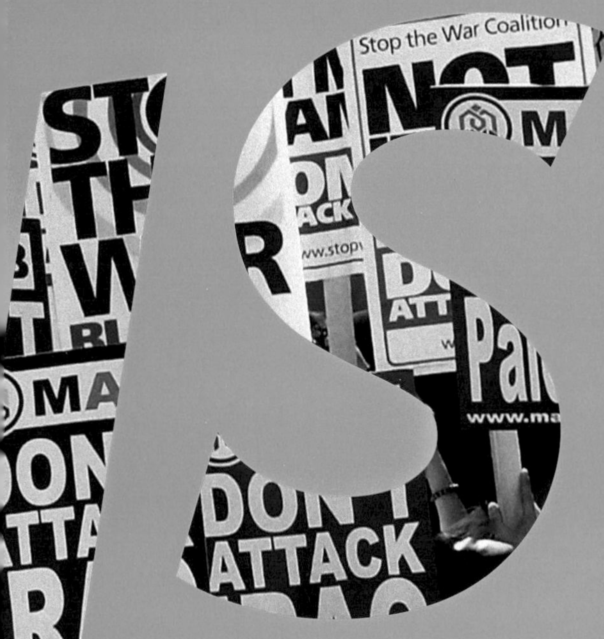
Stop the War Coalition
NOT
ATTACK

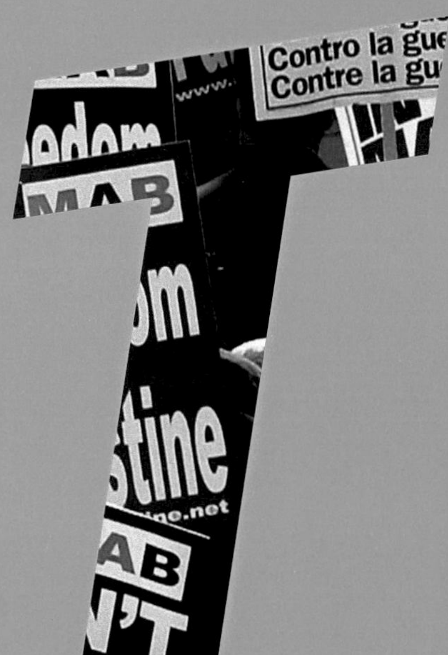
MAB

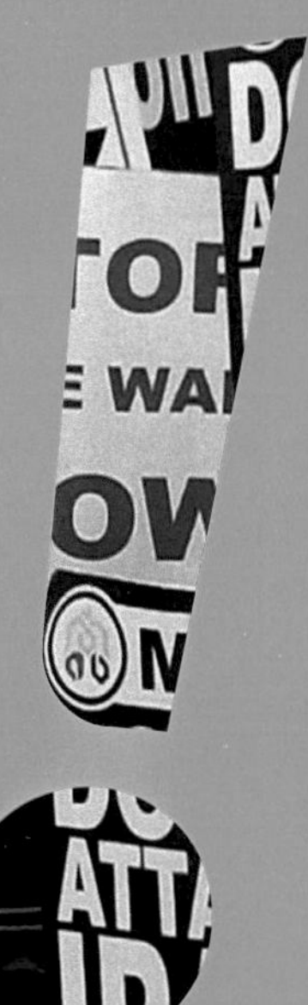

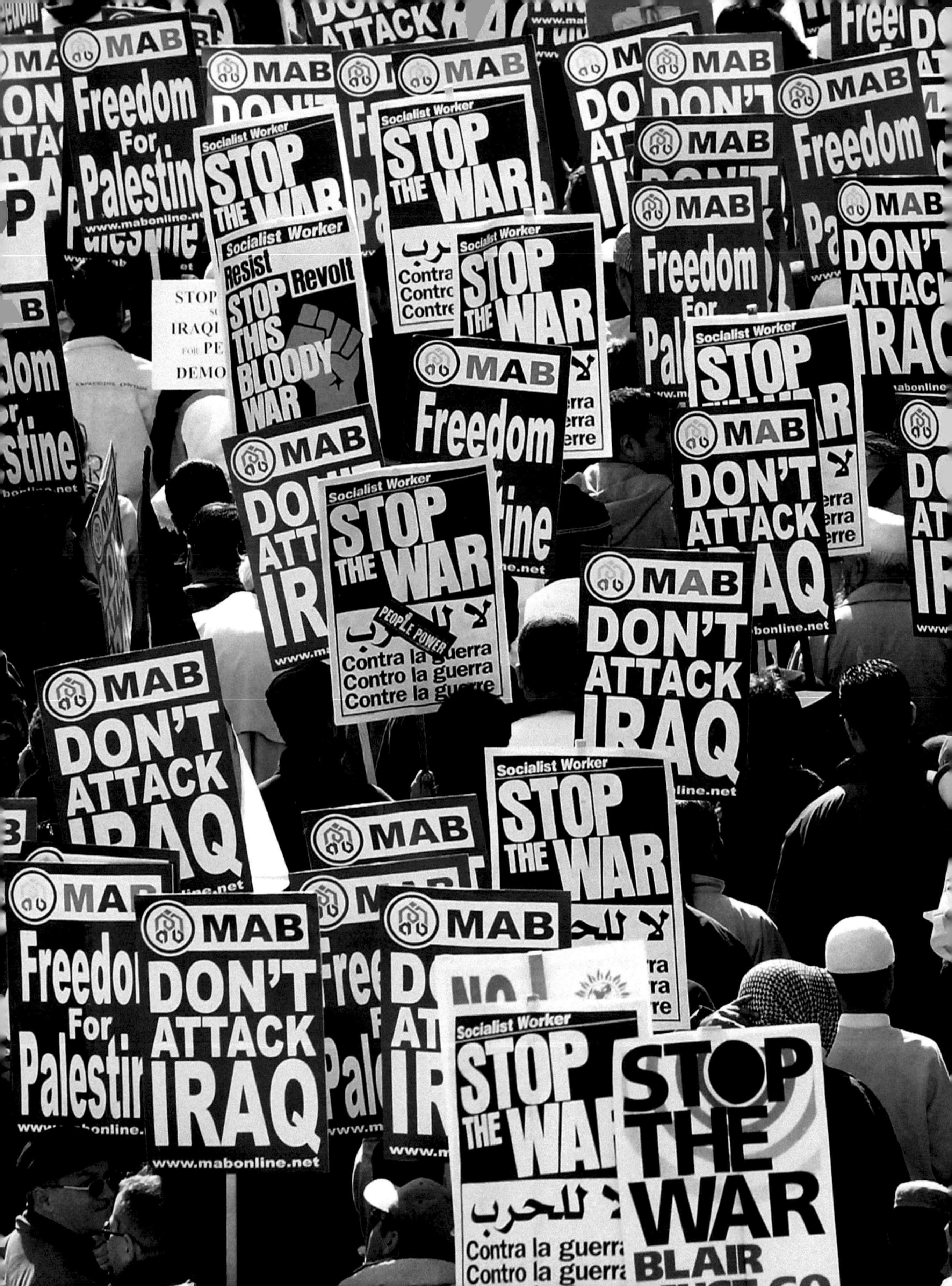

MAB
Freedom For Palestine
www.mabonline.net
Socialist Worker
STOP THE WAR
Socialist Worker
Resist
Revolt
STOP THIS BLOODY WAR
MAB
Freedom
MAB
DON'T ATTACK IRAQ
Socialist Worker
STOP THE WAR
PEOPLE POWER
لا للحرب
Contra la guerra
Contro la guerra
Contre la guerre
MAB
DON'T ATTACK IRAQ
MAB
DON'T ATTACK IRAQ
www.mabonline.net
Socialist Worker
STOP THE WAR
MAB
DON'T ATTACK IRAQ
www.mabonline.net
Socialist Worker
STOP THE WAR
لا للحرب
Contra la guerra
Contro la guerra
STOP THE WAR
BLAIR

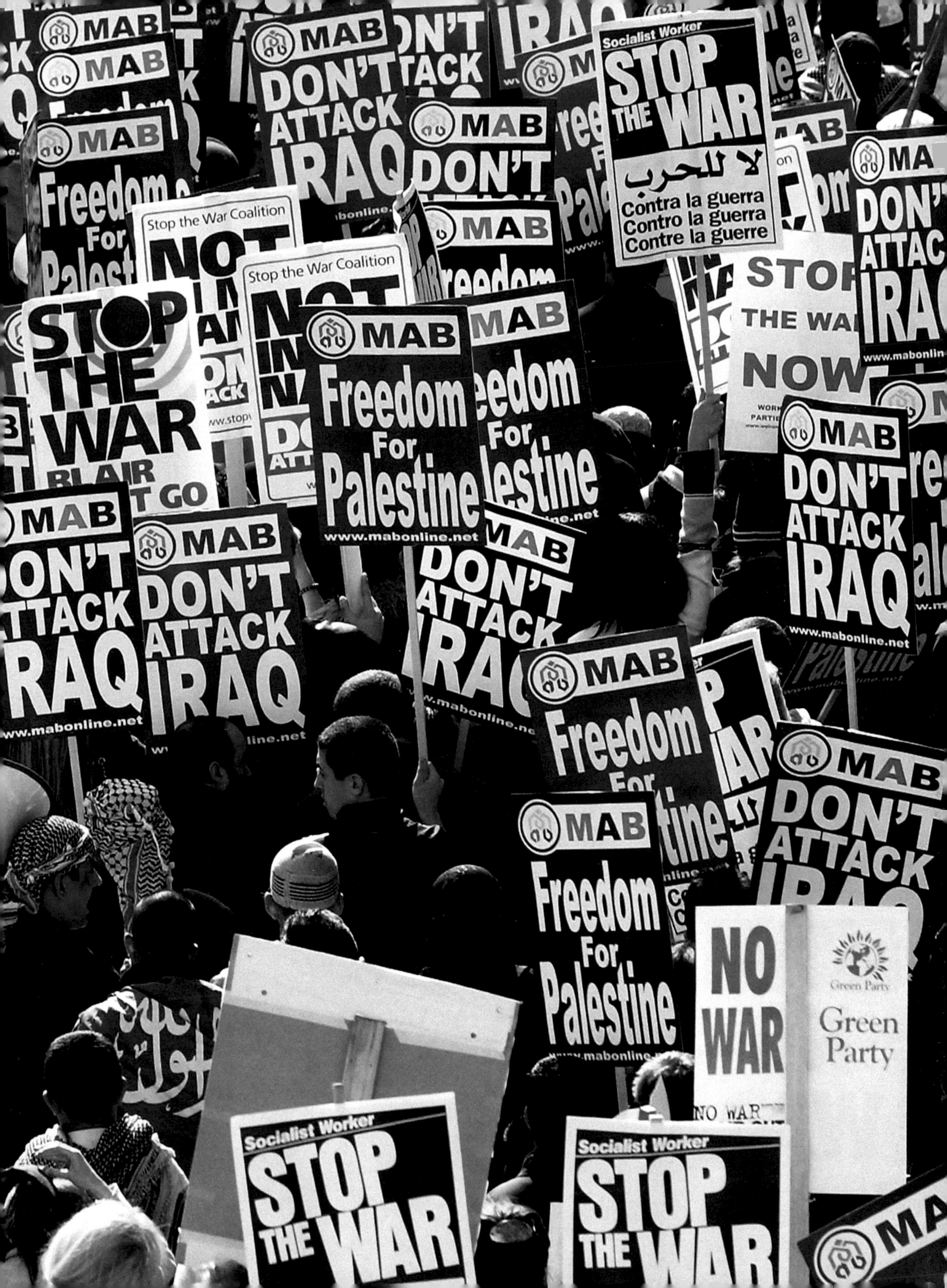
MAB
DON'T ATTACK IRAQ
Socialist Worker
STOP THE WAR
لا للحرب
Contra la guerra
Contro la guerra
Contre la guerre
MAB
DON'T
Stop the War Coalition
Stop the War Coalition
STOP THE WAR
MAB
Freedom For Palestine
www.mabonline.net
STOP
THE WAR
NOW
MAB
DON'T ATTACK IRAQ
www.mabonline.net
MAB
DON'T ATTACK IRAQ
www.mabonline.net
MAB
DON'T ATTACK IRAQ
MAB
Freedom
MAB
DON'T ATTACK
MAB
Freedom For Palestine
NO WAR
Green Party
Green Party
Socialist Worker
STOP THE WAR
Socialist Worker
STOP THE WAR

"Those who profess to favor freedom, and yet deprecate agitation, are men who want crops without plowing up the ground. They want rain without thunder and lightning. They want the ocean without the awful roar of its many waters. This struggle may be a moral one, or it may be a physical one, and it may be both moral and physical, but it must be a struggle. Power concedes nothing without a demand. It never did and it never will."

—Frederick Douglass, West India Emancipation speech, 1857

RESIST!

The history of protest is grounded in the continuing saga of struggle. In an 1857 speech to abolitionists that foreshadowed the American Civil War, Frederick Douglass invoked slave rebellions in Haiti and the larger West Indies that had resulted in emancipation in the early 1800s. For the Black orator and reformer, who had himself escaped involuntary servitude, the success of these revolts showed that freedom is never granted without defiance: "Who would be free, themselves must strike the blow."

More than 150 years later, Douglass's fiery call for resistance has been heard, heeded, and amplified thousands of times over. And versions of this message—built upon by activists working on behalf of civil rights, the antiwar movement, gender equality, LGBTQIA+ rights, environmentalism, and more—have found their way into the print materials used to rebut the status quo.

The graphics in this chapter rally around resistance, defined as a form of collective civil disobedience, and loosely interpreted to mean nonviolent protest. Beyond their use as signage in events like sit-ins, marches, and encampments, as well as public notices, posters, and publications for use in community organizing, they share a sense of urgency—an insistence on clear, rapid-fire delivery of often dire messaging.

Type and lettering are mission-critical to this communication. From nineteenth-century anti-slavery broadsides set in frenetic lines of mixed wood type to the anger-fueled handwritten signs of the Black Lives Matter marches two centuries later, the friction of resistance makes itself visible in typographic forms.

Along the way, the 1960s stand out as a watershed decade, in both its explosion of protest activity and its graphic output. The era's movements include massive anti-Vietnam sentiment, as expressed in *Q. And babies? A. And babies*, a 1968 poster that confirms the U.S. massacre of unarmed Vietnamese villagers. Civil rights were also a major flashpoint: In 1966, Bobby Seale and Huey P. Newton launched the indelible Black Panther Party, papering Black neighborhoods with posters, newspapers, and pamphlets that indicted white supremacy and spread word of the Party's pioneering social programs.

The Panthers inspired many, including members of OSPAAAL (Organization of Solidarity of the Peoples of Asia, Africa, and Latin America), a socialist group born in revolutionary Cuba that created protest graphics for decades, as well as the See Red Women's Workshop, a cooperative of printers, designers, and activists fusing radical feminist power with educational support in 1970s England.

As the twentieth century rounded into the twenty-first, resistance morphed to speak to new crises. The legendary graffiti zine *IGTimes*, designed by graffiti artist Phase 2 starting in 1986, melded hip-hop culture and a street-smart visual language to call out police brutality in 1980s New York. And in 2011, the Arab world erupted into demands for democratic reform, only to be met with military action, as expressed in the graphic portraits of wounded protesters by artist Ganzeer. A decade later, the mortal lessons of inequity carry on in Black Lives Matter protests, refueled all too often by new deaths of Black people at the hands of both white police and racist vigilantes. In one especially haunting artifact, calligrapher Hunter Saxony III pens the name of Nia Wilson (a young Black woman brutally murdered because of her race) in plumes of red ink over a vintage burnt portrait of a wealthy Southern white woman.

Centuries later, Douglass's twin refrains of struggle and progress continue to be printed, stenciled, and inscribed in fresh ink.

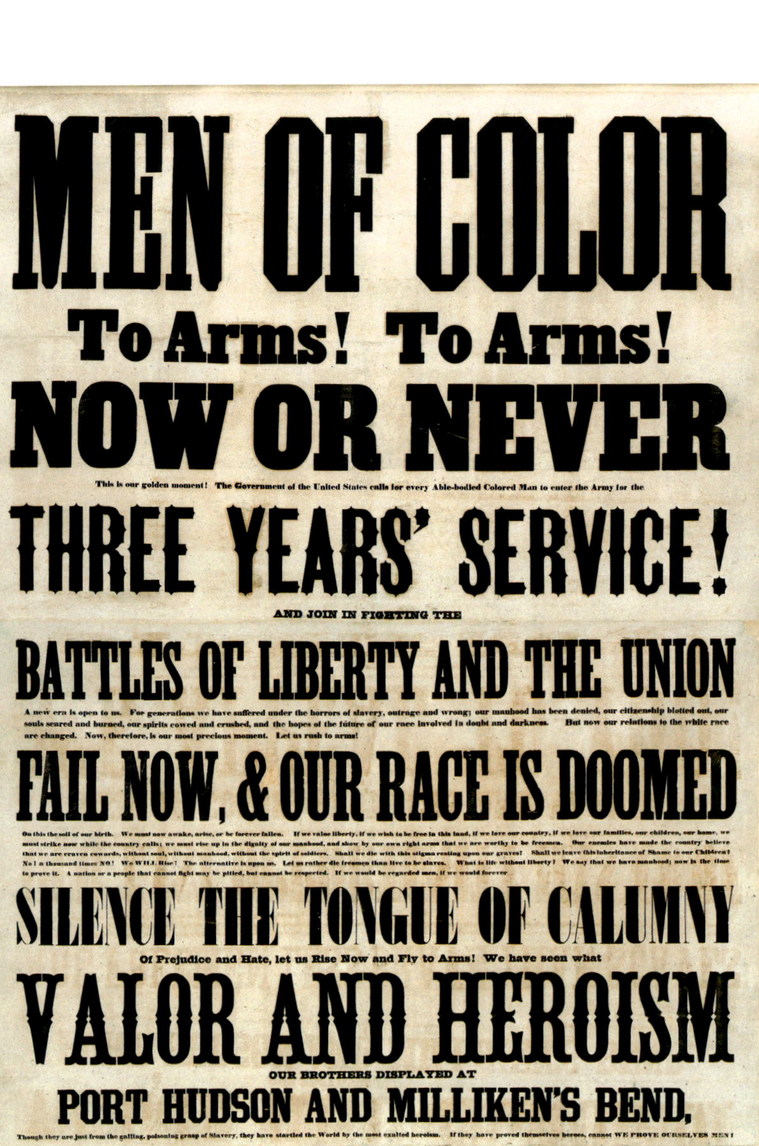
MEN OF COLOR
To Arms! To Arms!
NOW OR NEVER
This is our golden moment! The Government of the United States calls for every Able-bodied Colored Man to enter the Army for the
THREE YEARS' SERVICE!
AND JOIN IN FIGHTING THE
BATTLES OF LIBERTY AND THE UNION
A new era is open to us. For generations we have suffered under the horrors of slavery, outrage and wrong; our manhood has been denied, our citizenship blotted out, our souls seared and burned, our spirits cowed and crushed, and the hopes of the future of our race involved in doubt and darkness. But now our relations to the white race are changed. Now, therefore, is our most precious moment. Let us rush to arms!
FAIL NOW, & OUR RACE IS DOOMED
On this the soil of our birth. We must now awake, arise, or be forever fallen. If we value liberty, if we wish to be free in this land, if we love our country, if we love our families, our children, our home, we must strike now while the country calls; we must rise up in the dignity of our manhood, and show by our own right arms that we are worthy to be freemen. Our enemies have made the country believe that we are craven cowards, without soul, without manhood, without the spirit of soldiers. Shall we die with this stigma resting upon our graves? Shall we leave this inheritance of Shame to our Children? No! a thousand times NO! We WILL Rise! The alternative is upon us. Let us rather die freemen than live to be slaves. What is life without liberty? We say that we have manhood; now is the time to prove it. A nation or a people that cannot fight may be pitied, but cannot be respected. If we would be regarded men, if we would forever
SILENCE THE TONGUE OF CALUMNY
Of Prejudice and Hate, let us Rise Now and Fly to Arms! We have seen what
VALOR AND HEROISM
OUR BROTHERS DISPLAYED AT
PORT HUDSON AND MILLIKEN'S BEND,
Though they are just from the galling, poisoning grasp of Slavery, they have startled the World by the most exalted heroism. If they have proved themselves heroes, cannot WE PROVE OURSELVES MEN!
ARE FREEMEN LESS BRAVE THAN SLAVES
More than a Million White Men have left Comfortable Homes and joined the Armies of the Union to save their Country. Cannot we leave ours, and swell the Hosts of the Union, to save our liberties, vindicate our manhood, and deserve well of our Country. MEN OF COLOR! the Englishman, the Irishman, the Frenchman, the German, the American, have been called to assert their claim to freedom and a manly character, by an appeal to the sword. The day that has seen an enslaved race in arms has, in all history, seen their last trial. We now see that
OUR LAST OPPORTUNITY HAS COME
If we are not lower in the scale of humanity than Englishmen, Irishmen, White Americans, and other Races, we can show it now.
MEN OF COLOR, BROTHERS AND FATHERS!
WE APPEAL TO YOU!
By all your concern for yourselves and your liberties, by all your regard for God and humanity, by all your desire for Citizenship and Equality before the law, by all your love for the Country, to stop at no subterfuge, listen to nothing that shall deter you from rallying for the Army. Come Forward, and at once Enroll your Names for the Three Years' Service.
STRIKE NOW!
And you are henceforth and forever FREEMEN!
E. D. Bassett,
Wm. Whipper,
D. D. Turner,
Jas. McCrummell,
A. S. Cassey,
A. M. Green,
J. W. Page,
L. R. Seymour,
Rev. J. Underdue,
John W. Price,
Augustus Dorsey,
William D. Forten,
Rev. Stephen Smith,
N. W. Depee,
Dr. J. H. Wilson,
J. W. Cassey,
Frederick Douglass,
P. J. Armstrong,
J. W. Simpson,
Rev. J. B. Trusty,
S. Morgan Smith,
William E. Gipson,
Rev. J. Boulden,
Rev. J. Asher,
Rev. J. C. Gibbs,
Daniel George,
Robert M. Adger,
Henry M. Cropper,
Rev. J. B. Reeve,
Rev. J. A. Williams,
Rev. A. L. Stanford,
Thomas J. Bowers,
Elijah J. Davis,
John P. Burr,
Robert Jones,
O. V. Catto,
Thos. J. Dorsey,
I. D. Cliff,
Jacob C. White,
Morris Hall,
James Needham,
Rev. Elisha Weaver,
Ebenezer Black,
Rev. William T. Catto,
James R. Gordon,
Samuel Stewart,
David B. Bowser,
Henry Minton,
Daniel Colley,
J. C. White, Jr.,
Rev. J. P. Campbell,
Rev. W. J. Alston,
J. P. Johnson,
Franklin Turner,
Jesse E. Glasgow.
U. S. Steam-Power Book and Job Printing Establishment Ledger Buildings, Third and Chestnut Streets, Philadelphia.

From its onset, Black printing in the United States forged itself in active resistance to slavery. The nation's first Black-owned newspaper, *Freedom's Journal*, was published in 1827 by John B. Russwurm and Samuel Cornish in order to hit back against racist attacks on the newly formed abolitionist movement. It set the course for Frederick Douglass's the *North Star*, established in 1847 as the primary vehicle for abolitionist news, and Ida B. Wells's *Memphis Free Speech*, which in 1892 denounced the lynching epidemic in the American South.

Another key tool of abolitionists was broadsides (large proclamations, notices, or advertisements with printing on only one side). Inexpensive to produce, broadsides were one of the most common forms of printed material during the nineteenth century—and they are the ancestors to the protest posters of the twentieth and twenty-first. Their ubiquity in the streets made them pivotal in shifting public opinion leading up to the Civil War. For example, *The Man Is Not Bought!* (see page 37) decries the story of Anthony Burns, who escaped from bondage in Virginia only to be arrested in Boston and re-enslaved. (Abolitionists rioted and raised funds to buy back his freedom.) Ironically, oppressors also wielded the power of the broadside to advertise bounties placed on Black people who had fled slavery, listing their physical descriptions, last known whereabouts, and skills that could lead to their capture.

After the Emancipation Proclamation of 1863, broadsides became a critical instrument in recruitment for the Union Army. One printed with Douglass's text, "Men of Color! To Arms! To Arms!" urges Black men to fight for their race's freedom. The massive three-panel broadside was read aloud in meeting halls and adapted in newspapers and pamphlets.

Mainly printed with wood type (which was, compared to metal type, lighter and cheaper to produce at the large size required for posters), nineteenth-century broadsides typically feature an eclectic mix of loud and decorative types, including extrabold and chamfered gothics (sans serifs), heavy slabs, and display styles with ornamental elements, often called Tuscans. This approach meant printers could showcase various styles, and it proved attention-grabbing. But it was born out of necessity: Most printshops had a limited supply of wood type (usually only one or two sizes of each typeface), so they simply picked the font that had the right proportions to fill each line. Created before graphic design became an acknowledged field, these broadsides were laid out by the printers themselves, whose contributions to the abolitionist cause remain anonymous.

Unknown designer, Frederick Douglass (author), *Men of Color! To Arms!*, 1863, letterpress, 93¾ × 46¼ inches (238 × 117.5 cm), Philadelphia. Collection of the Smithsonian National Museum of African American History and Culture.

Union with Freemen--No Union with Slaveholders.

ANTI-SLAVERY MEETINGS!

Anti-Slavery Meetings will be held in this place, to commence on at in the

To be Addressed by

Agents of the Western ANTI-SLAVERY SOCIETY.

Three millions of your fellow beings are in chains--the Church and Government sustains the horrible system of oppression.

Turn Out!

AND LEARN YOUR DUTY TO YOURSELVES, THE SLAVE AND GOD.

EMANCIPATION or DISSOLUTION, and a FREE NORTHERN REPUBLIC!

HOMESTEAD PRINT, SALEM, OHIO.

Unknown designer, *Anti-Slavery Meetings! Turn Out!*, 1850, letterpress, 16 × 11 inches (40.5 × 28 cm), Salem, Ohio. Collection of the Library of Congress.

Unknown designer, *The Man Is Not Bought!*, circa 1854, letterpress, 39 × 24 inches (99 × 61 cm), Boston. Collection of the Boston Public Library.

THE MAN IS NOT BOUGHT!

HE IS STILL IN THE

SLAVE PEN

IN THE COURT HOUSE!

THE KIDNAPPER AGREED

Both Publicly, and in writing, to SELL HIM

FOR $1200!

The sum was raised by eminent citizens of Boston, and offered him. He then claimed more. The BARGAIN WAS BROKEN. THE

KIDNAPPER BREAKS HIS AGREEMENT!

Though even the UNITED STATES COMMISSIONER advised him to keep it.

BE ON YOUR GUARD AGAINST ALL LIES!

WATCH THE SLAVE PEN

Let Every Man attend the Trial!

1860 SLAVE

1900 NIGGER

1920 NEGRO

1940 COLORED

1960 BLACK

1990 AFRICAN AMERICAN

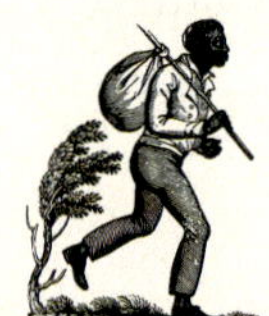

2000

WE'VE COME TOO FAR TO TURN AROUND.

Concept & Design / Archie Boston, Jr.

Archie Boston, *We've Come Too Far to Turn Around*, 1991, offset, 16 × 12 inches (40.5 × 30.5 cm), New York.

Unknown designer for the American Anti-Slavery Society, *Printers' Picture Gallery*, 1838, letterpress, 21⅞ × 14¾ inches (56 × 37.5 cm), New York. Collection of the Library of Congress.

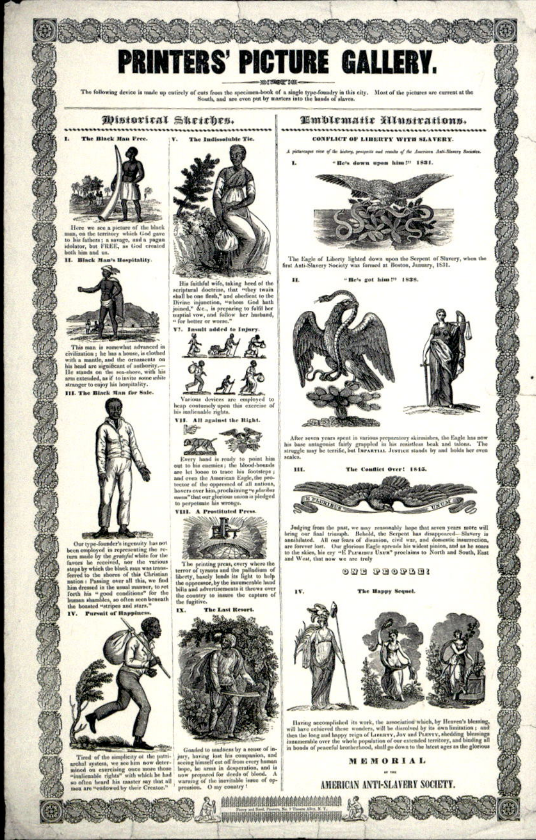

PRINTERS' PICTURE GALLERY.

The following device is made up entirely of cuts from the specimen-book of a single type-foundry in this city. Most of the pictures are current at the South, and are even put by masters into the hands of slaves.

Historical Sketches.

I. The Black Man Free.

Here we see a picture of the black man, on the territory which God gave to his fathers; a savage, and a pagan idolator, but FREE, as God created both him and us.

II. Black Man's Hospitality.

This man is somewhat advanced in civilization; he has a house, is clothed with a mantle, and the ornaments on his head are significant of authority.—He stands on the sea-shore, with his arm extended, as if to invite some *white* stranger to enjoy his hospitality.

III. The Black Man for Sale.

Our type-founder's ingenuity has not been employed in representing the return made by the *grateful* white for the favors he received, nor the various steps by which the black man was transferred to the shores of this Christian nation: Passing over all this, we find him dressed in the usual manner, to set forth his "good conditions" for the human shambles, so often seen beneath the boasted "stripes and stars."

IV. Pursuit of Happiness.

Tired of the simplicity of the patriarchal system, we see him now determined on exercising once more those "inalienable rights" with which he had so often heard his master say that all men are "endowed by their Creator."

V. The Indissoluble Tie.

His faithful wife, taking heed of the scriptural doctrine, that "they twain shall be one flesh," and obedient to the Divine injunction, "whom God hath joined," &c., is preparing to fulfil her nuptial vow, and follow her husband, "for better or worse."

VI. Insult added to Injury.

Various devices are employed to heap contumely upon this exercise of his inalienable rights.

VII. All against the Right.

Every hand is ready to point him out to his enemies; the blood-hounds are let loose to trace his footsteps; and even the American Eagle, the protector of the oppressed of all nations, hovers over him, proclaiming "*e pluribus unum*" that our glorious union is pledged to perpetuate his wrongs.

VIII. A Prostituted Press.

The printing press, every where the terror of tyrants and the palladium of liberty, basely lends its light to help the oppressor, by the innumerable hand bills and advertisements it throws over the country to insure the capture of the fugitive.

IX. The Last Resort.

Goaded to madness by a sense of injury, having lost his companion, and seeing himself cut off from every human hope, he arms in desperation, and is now prepared for deeds of blood. A warning of the inevitable issue of oppression. O my country!

Emblematic Illustrations.

CONFLICT OF LIBERTY WITH SLAVERY.

A picturesque view of the history, prospects and results of the American Anti-Slavery Societies.

I. "He's down upon him!" 1831.

The Eagle of Liberty lighted down upon the Serpent of Slavery, when the first Anti-Slavery Society was formed at Boston, January, 1831.

II. "He's got him!" 1838.

After seven years spent in various preparatory skirmishes, the Eagle has now his base antagonist fairly grappled in his resistless beak and talons. The struggle may be terrific, but IMPARTIAL JUSTICE stands by and holds her even scales.

III. The Conflict Over! 1845.

Judging from the past, we may reasonably hope that seven years more will bring our final triumph. Behold, the Serpent has disappeared—Slavery is annihilated. All our fears of disunion, civil war, and domestic insurrection, are forever lost. Our glorious Eagle spreads his widest pinion, and as he soars to the skies, his cry "E PLURIBUS UNUM" proclaims to North and South, East and West, that now we are truly

ONE PEOPLE!

IV. The Happy Sequel.

Having accomplished its work, the association which, by Heaven's blessing, will have achieved these wonders, will be dissolved by its own limitation; and then the long and happy reign of LIBERTY, JOY and PLENTY, shedding blessings innumerable over the whole population of our extended territory, and binding all in bonds of peaceful brotherhood, shall go down to the latest ages as the glorious

MEMORIAL

OF THE

AMERICAN ANTI-SLAVERY SOCIETY.

Call and Response

A hallmark of nineteenth-century printing was the use of metal or woodcut illustrations, which were repurposed between print jobs just like type. For news stories and broadsides that addressed slavery, these artworks—called *cuts*—proved problematic imagery for a Black press determined to represent its community on its own terms. In 1838, the American Anti-Slavery Society printed this broadside of cuts depicting Black enslaved people in stereotypical postures and acts, including a runaway with a bindle in tow. Scathing in its annotation, the text laments that the cuts "are even put by masters into the hands of slaves" to print with.

More than 150 years later, Black art director Archie Boston repurposed one of these cuts in a typographic timeline of racial epithets. Boston uses the different typefaces that were popular across U.S. history to set the names (often slurs) used by white people to describe Black Americans during those same times. Starting with *slave* in a display face called Jim Crow, first used in the United States around 1860, the following years are expressed in Caslon Antique (1900), Goudy Handtooled (1920), City (1940), Helvetica (1960), and ITC Novarese (1990). Boston annotates the most recent year (2000) with the antique cut, positioned so the man appears to run toward the future. It is followed by the text "We've come too far to turn around" set in Franklin Gothic—a standard choice for twentieth-century ad headlines, especially in the style often employed by Boston.

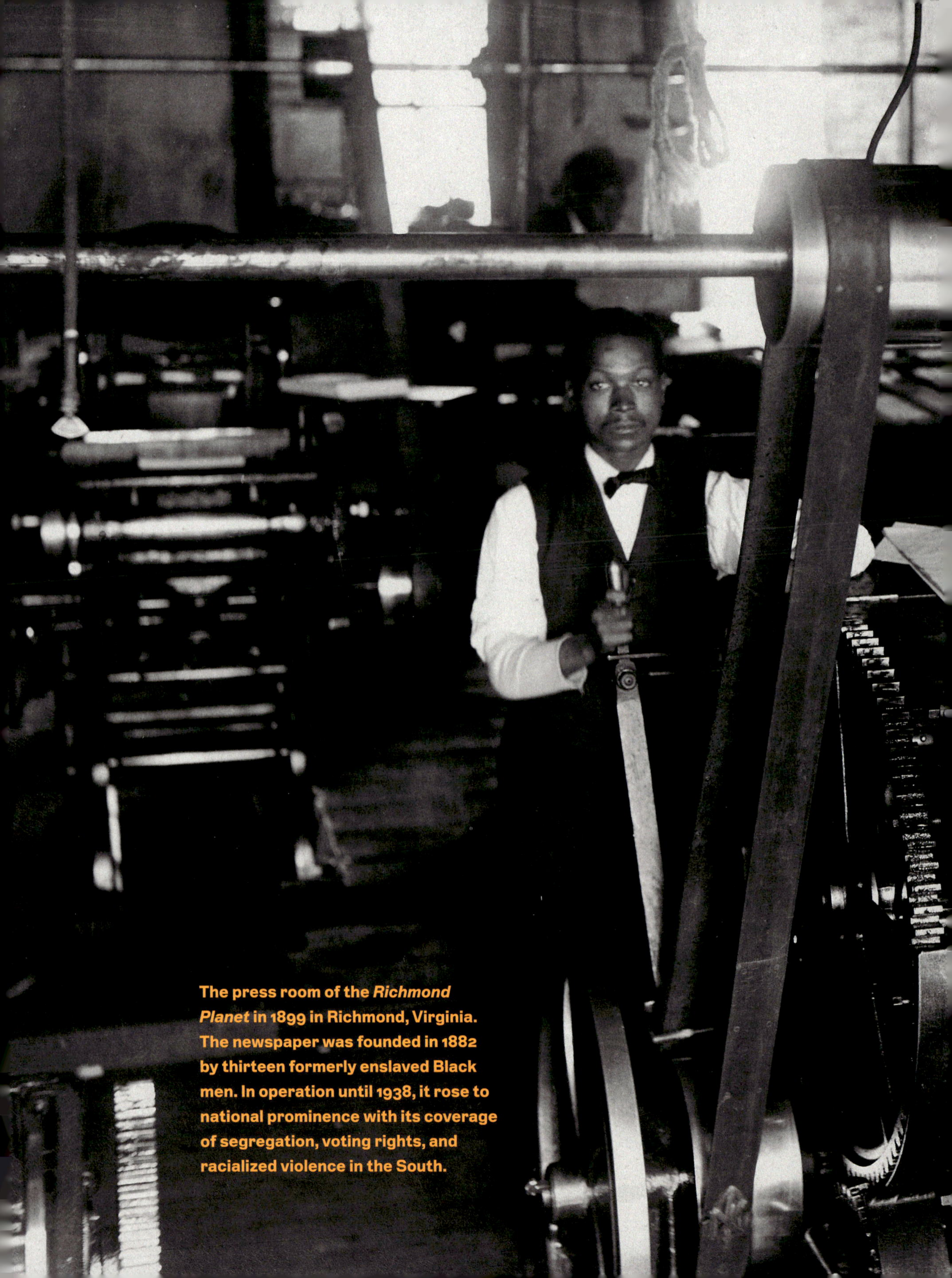

The press room of the *Richmond Planet* in 1899 in Richmond, Virginia. The newspaper was founded in 1882 by thirteen formerly enslaved Black men. In operation until 1938, it rose to national prominence with its coverage of segregation, voting rights, and racialized violence in the South.

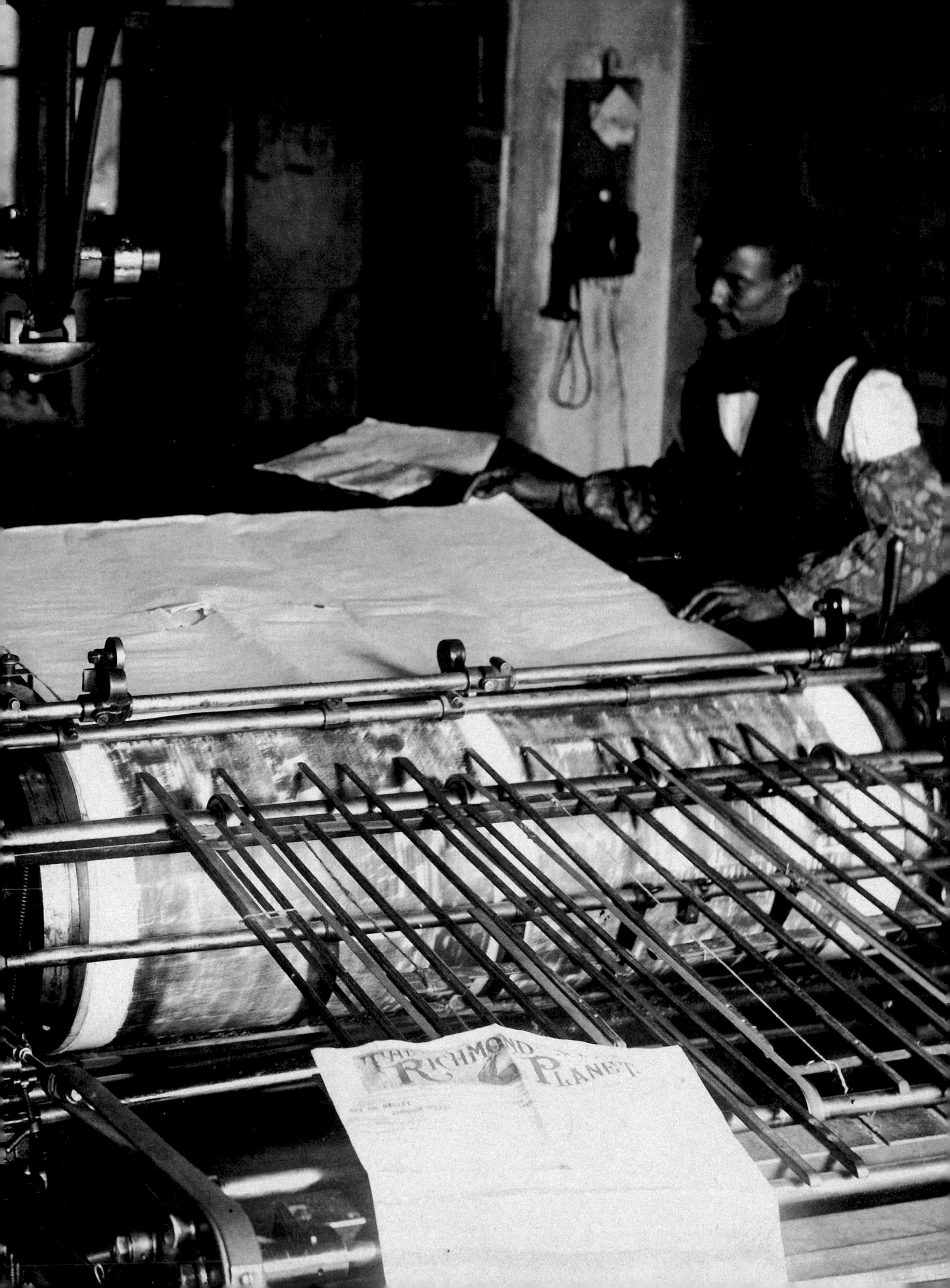
RICHMOND PLANET

"In [*The Crisis*'s] pages [were] the first encouragement of Negro writers and artists. Here [were] the first literary contests, the first section devoted to Negro children, the first presentation of Negro artwork, the first feature stories about successful Negroes . . . . Here were scathing denunciations and flaming defense . . . . Here for the first time with brilliance, militancy, facts, photographs and persuasiveness, a well-edited magazine [that] challenged the whole concept of white supremacy then nationally accepted."

—George Schuyler, *The Crisis* business manager, 1951

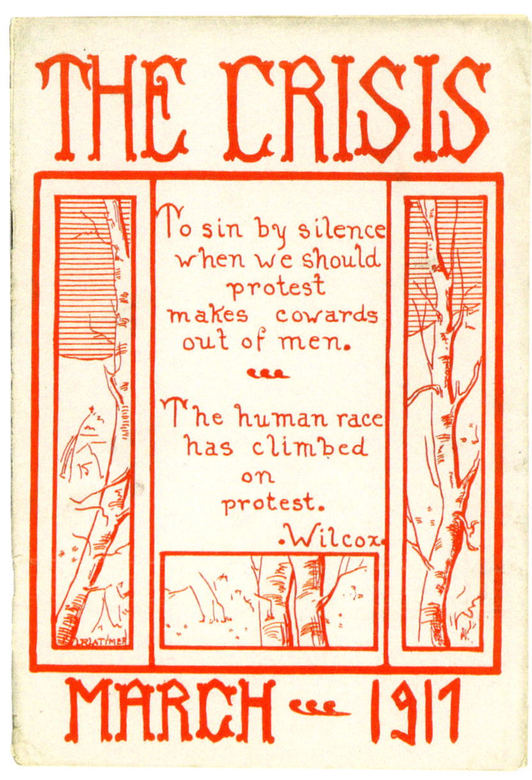

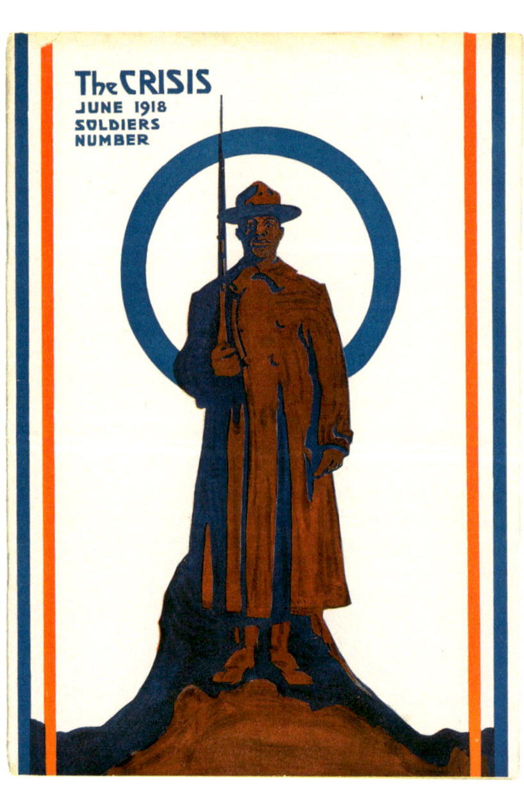

Louise R. Latimer (cover designer), W. E. B. Du Bois (editor), *The Crisis*, vol. 13, no. 5, March 1917, letterpress, 9¾ × 6⅞ inches (25 × 17.5 cm), New York.

Robert Edmund Jones (cover designer), W. E. B. Du Bois (editor), *The Crisis*, vol. 16, no. 2, June 1918, letterpress, 9⅝ × 6¾ inches (25 × 17.5 cm), New York.

Frank Walts (cover designer), W. E. B. Du Bois (editor), *The Crisis*, vol. 15, no. 5, January 1918, letterpress, 9⅞ × 6⅞ inches (25 × 17.5 cm), New York.

Collection of the Smithsonian National Museum of African American History and Culture (all).

The official publication of the National Association for the Advancement of Colored People (NAACP), *The Crisis* was founded in 1910 by W. E. B. Du Bois and is still in production today. These covers showcase unique lettering that is integrated with or otherwise plays off the illustration style.

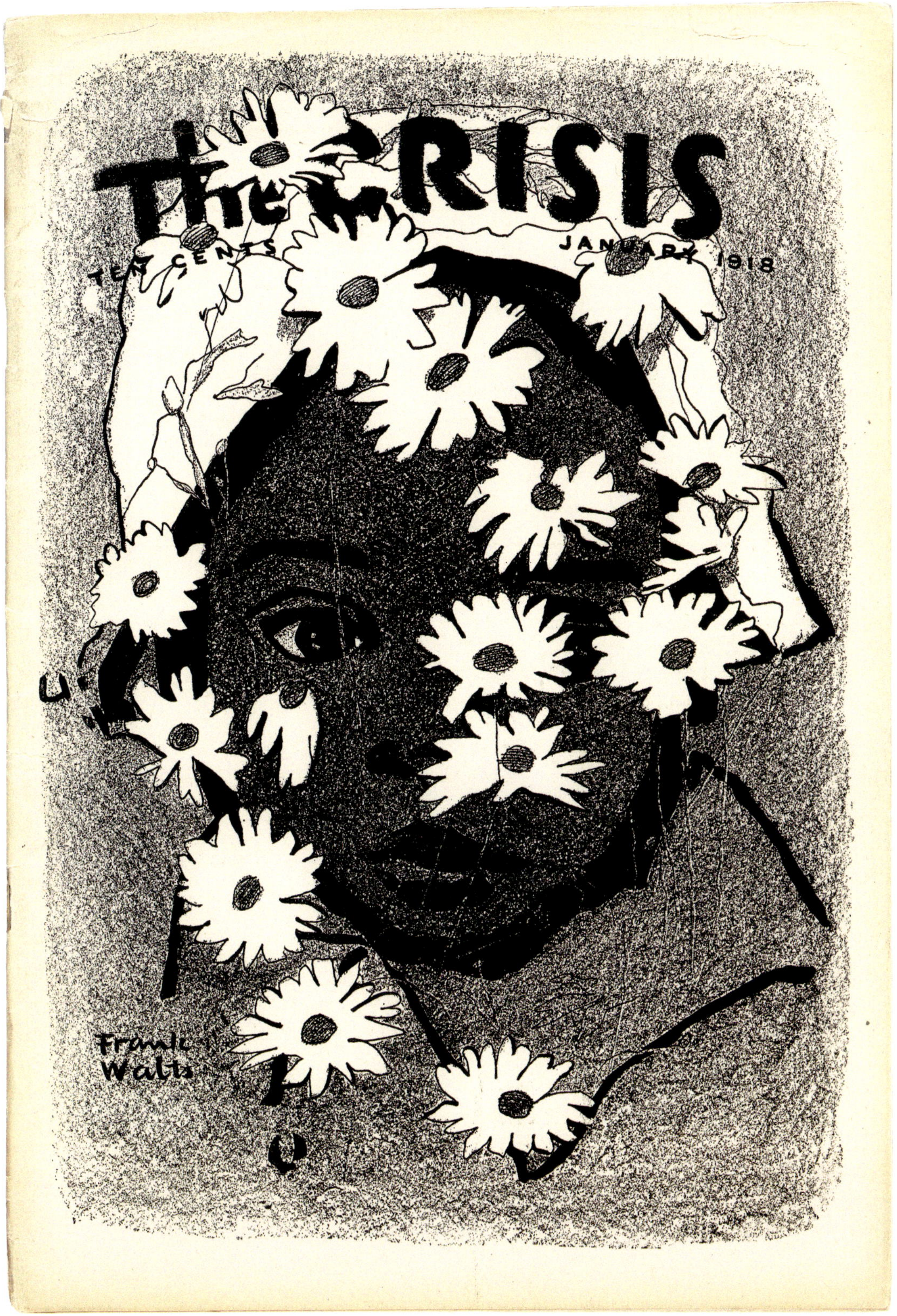
The CRISIS
TEN CENTS
JANUARY 1918
Frank Walts

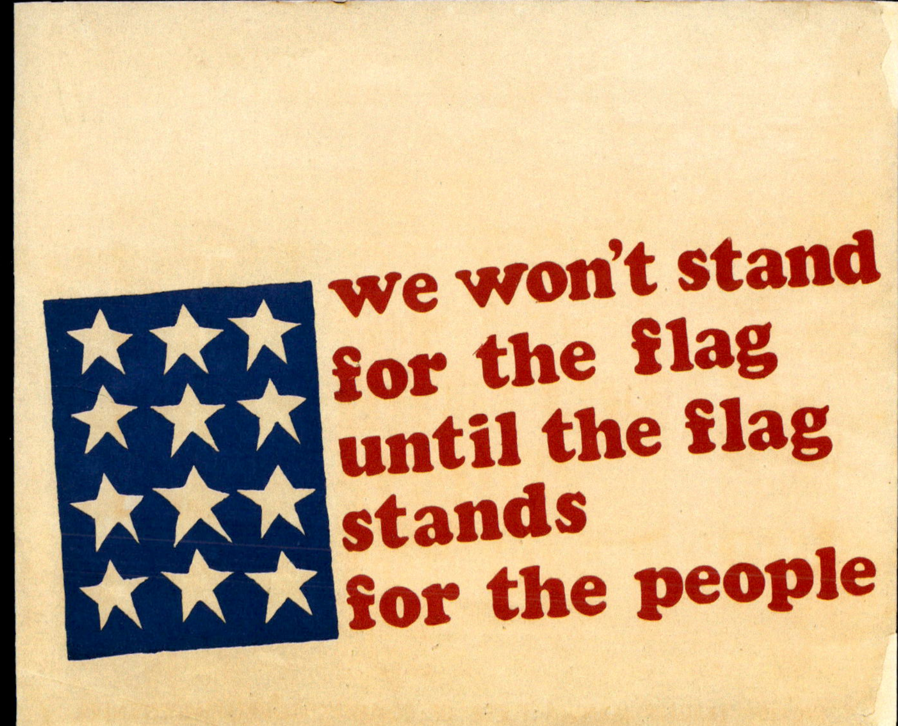

Call and Response

The American flag has long provided artists a canvas for protest. Its simple, graphic iconography serves as a foil for the nation's more complicated past and present. These two posters from the height of the 1960s antiwar movement rewrite the flag's meaning by replacing symbology with words. For "We won't stand . . ." in the screen print above, art-directed by American artist and photographer Bill Stettner, the hand-cut letters are based on Cooper Black, a typeface frequently seen in both commerce and counterculture. The use of lowercase text disrupts the traditionally even height of the flag's stripes, while the ragged right edge adds a tattered effect. The flipped *w* in *won't*—which indicates that type (rather than handlettering) was the source material—furthers the DIY aesthetic.

George Maciunas, a Lithuanian American whose family immigrated to New York in 1948, was the founder of the Fluxus art collective, whose avant-garde works often subverted political, social, and commercial conventions. On his flag at right, the stars are replaced with skulls and crossbones, while the stripes morph into lines of text comparing the United States's dark legacy to other examples of ethnic cleansing. The last line invites viewers to send away by mail to receive documentation of Maciunas's claims. His title, *U.S.A. Surpasses All the Genocide Records!*, appropriates the language of American exceptionalism, reframing dominance as a national scourge. Inserat-Grotesk, a popular poster typeface style of the 1960s, packs the statements into bold, continuous lines.

U.S.A. SURPASSES ALL THE GENOCIDE RECORDS!

KUBLAI KHAN MASSACRES 10% IN NEAR EAST

SPAIN MASSACRES 10% OF AMERICAN INDIANS

JOSEPH STALIN MASSACRES 5% OF RUSSIANS

NAZIS MASSACRE 5% OF OCCUPIED EUROPEANS AND 75% OF EUROPEAN JEWS

U.S.A. MASSACRES 6.5% OF SOUTH VIETNAMESE & 75% OF AMERICAN INDIANS

FOR CALCULATIONS & REFERENCES WRITE TO: P.O. BOX 180, NEW YORK, N.Y. 10013

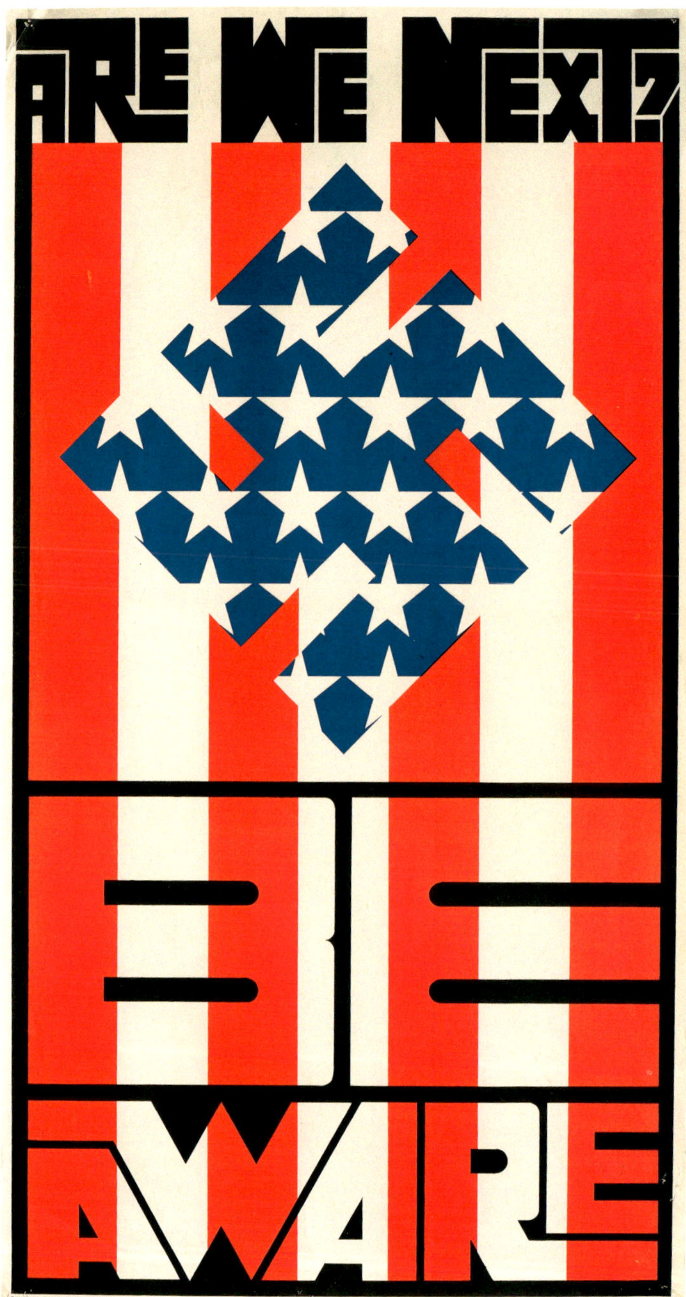

Wes Wilson, *Are We Next?*, 1965, offset, 35 × 19 inches (89 × 48.5 cm), San Francisco. Wilson, who later designed iconic concert posters for San Francisco's Fillmore Auditorium, created this poster—his first—in response to the Vietnam War. While his later work is more psychedelic, his trademark integration of letters into "word-images" is visible at this early stage. On his printer's recommendation, he added the words "Are we next?" to avoid any misinterpretation of the Nazi swastika.

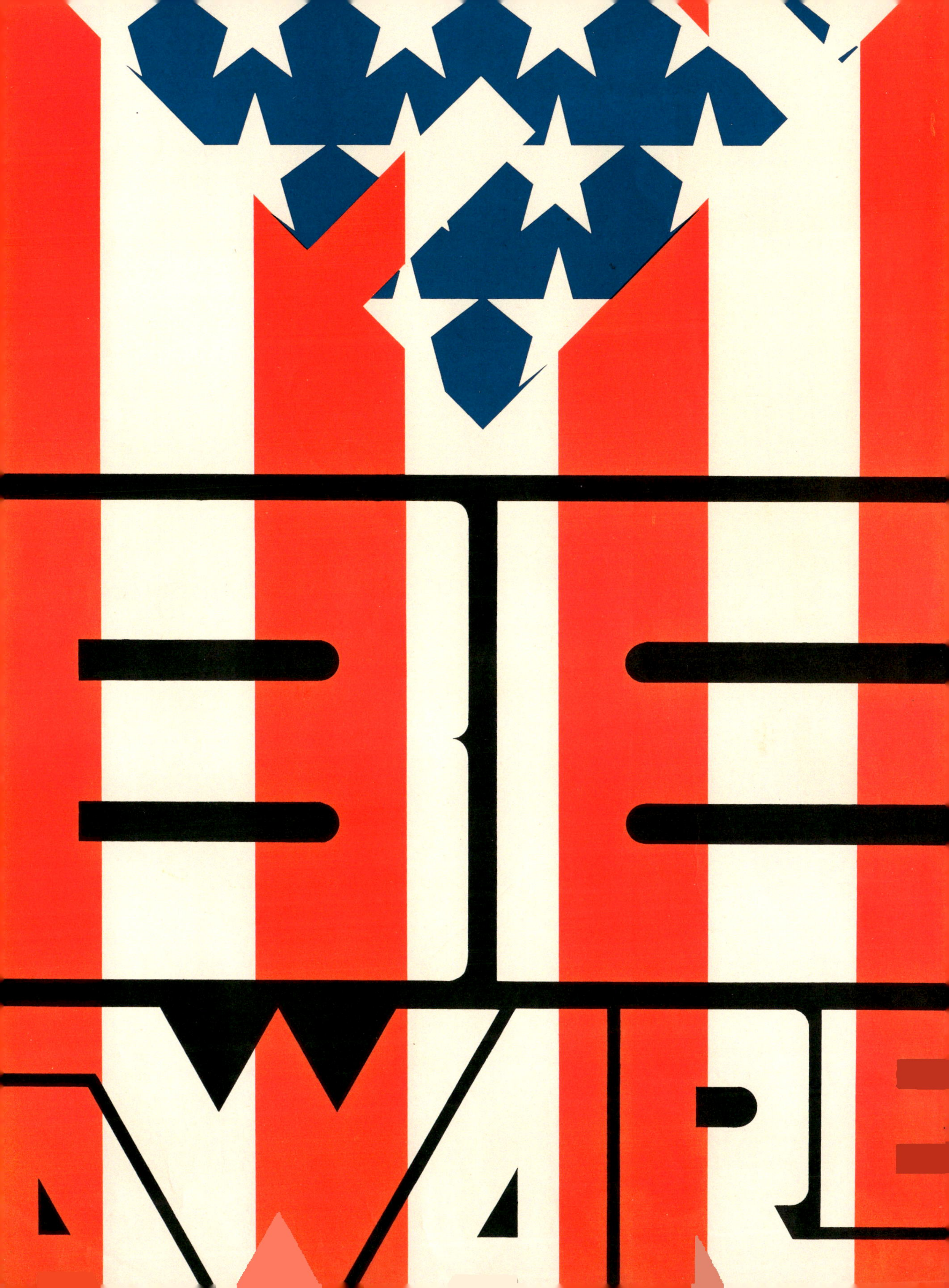

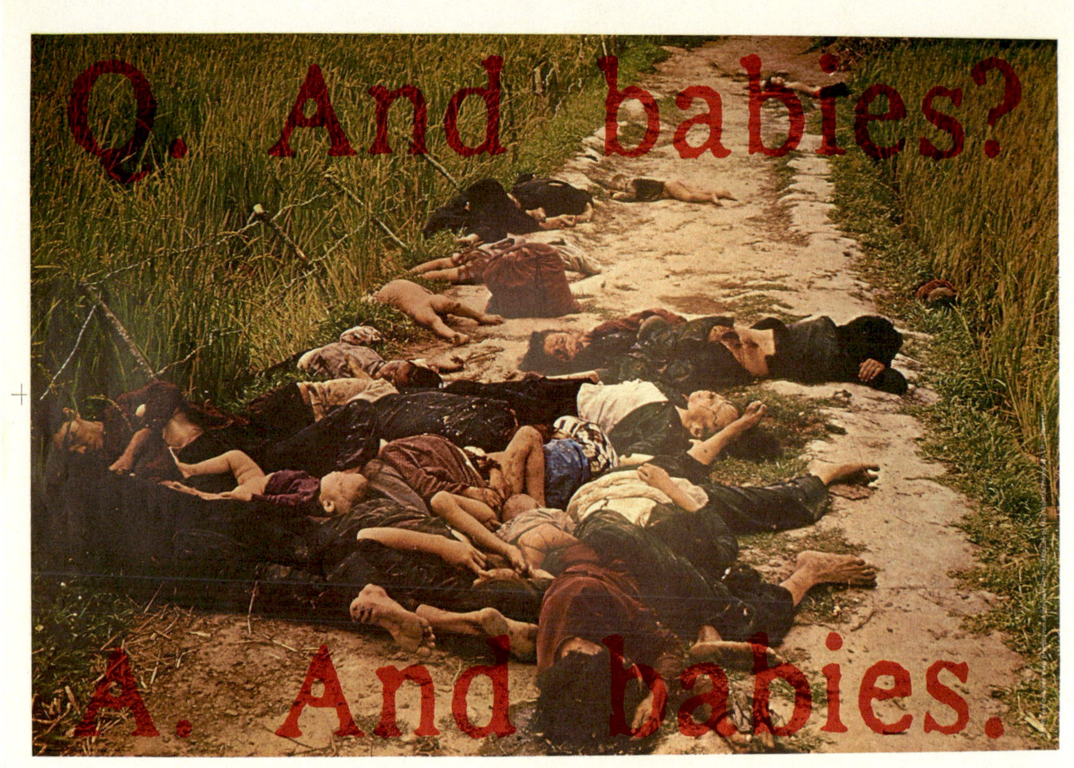

Broadly considered the most wrenching and effective antiwar poster of the Vietnam era, *Q. And babies? A. And babies* assaults viewers with evidence of the 1968 Mỹ Lai massacre, in which hundreds of unarmed Vietnamese citizens were mutilated and murdered under the orders of the Nixon administration. A follow-up to the iconic poster, *Four More Years?*, asked on the eve of the 1972 election if the United States could morally justify another Nixon term given its war crimes in Southeast Asia.

Army photographer Ronald L. Haeberle took the image with his personal camera, knowing that his official documentation would be subject to censorship, if not outright destroyed. After being discharged, he sold the photograph to *Life*; its publication outraged citizens and spurred Frazer Dougherty, Jon Hendricks, and Irving Petlin—members of an antiwar group called the Art Workers' Coalition—to create these political statements.

The Q&A styling of the first poster's text comes from a televised interview in which CBS news anchor Mike Wallace asked a soldier to confirm that, yes, "and babies" were also victims. Resembling dried blood, the poster's text was photographically reproduced off the *New York Times* transcript; the eroded edges caused by enlargement demonstrate that it is an accurate, if horrifying, quote. The second poster directly connects the most damning image of Nixon's presidency to his bid for re-election, using Times New Roman—the typeface of institutions—to make an all-caps indictment of his leadership, as well as to challenge the viewer/voter to stand up against it.

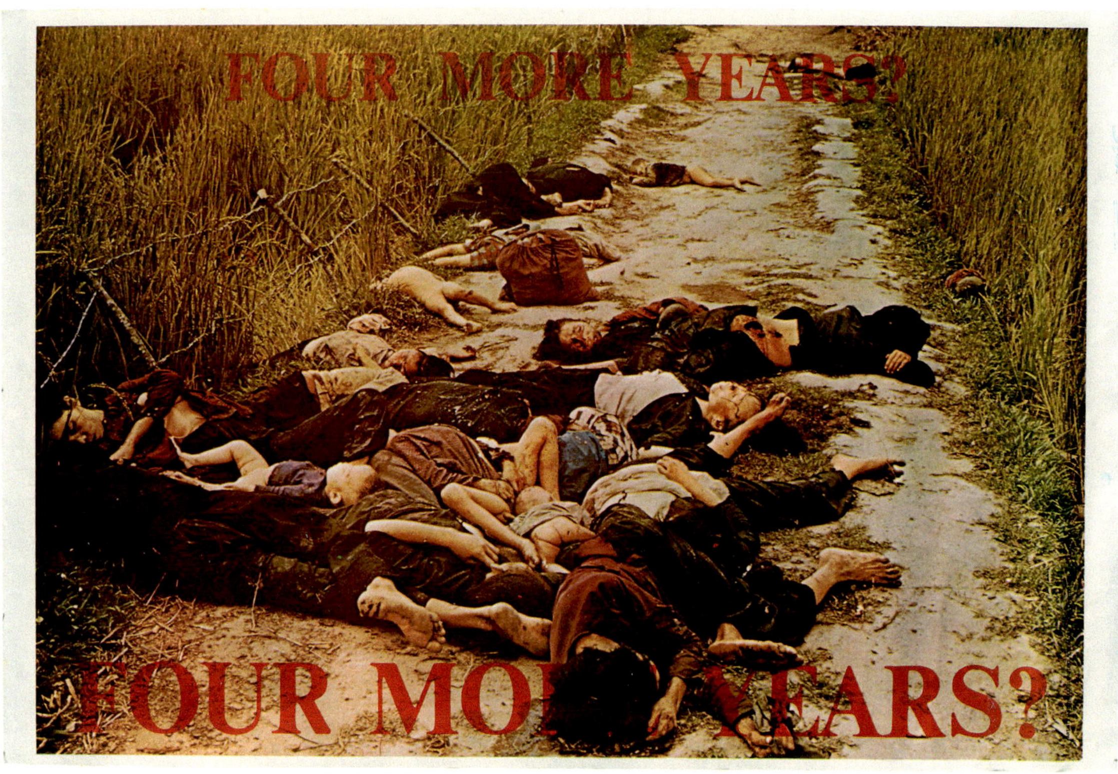

Frazer Dougherty, Jon Hendricks, and Irving Petlin (designers), Ronald L. Haeberle (photographer), offset, New York. *Q. And babies? A. And babies*, 1970, 27½ × 40⅝ inches (70 × 103 cm), and *Four More Years?*, 1972, 25 × 38 inches (63.5 × 96.5 cm). The first poster was initially a joint project with the Museum of Modern Art, which pulled its support before the poster went to press.

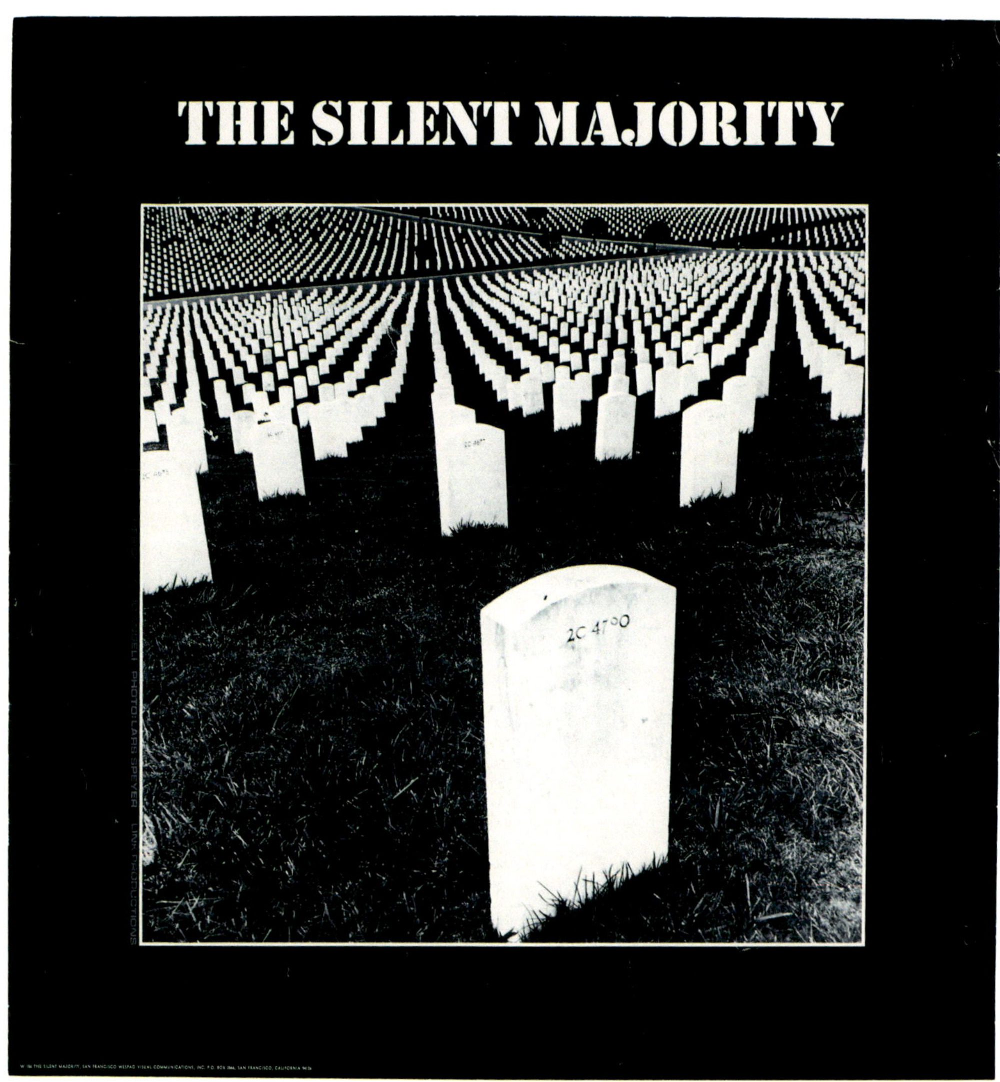

Primo Angeli (designer), Lars Speyer (photographer),
The Silent Majority, 1969, offset, 23 × 22 inches (58.5 × 56 cm), San Francisco. Distributed at a huge peace rally in San Francisco, Angeli's poster ironically pairs an image of a military graveyard with a quote from President Nixon in which he falsely claimed that the public's support for the Vietnam War was overwhelming, albeit silent. The poster was soon after remixed to include a wreath and text reading "No Christmas as Usual."

MARCH BECAUSE YOU HATE THE WAR
MARCH TO DEFEAT THE MAD BOMBER
NIXON MARCH BECAUSE YOU CAN'T
FIND A JOB MARCH BECAUSE NIXON'S
BOMBING THE DIKES IN VIETNAM
MARCH BECAUSE THEY KILLED
GEORGE JACKSON MARCH BECAUSE
THEY USE RACISM TO KEEP US APART
MARCH FOR THE VIETNAMESE 7 POINT PEACE
PLAN MARCH TO GET SMACK OFF THE
STREETS MARCH BECAUSE YOUR TAXES
ARE TOO HIGH MARCH FOR WOMEN TO BE FREE
MARCH BECAUSE VIETNAM WASN'T A "MISTAKE"
MARCH BECAUSE THE U.S. IS EATING UP THE WORLD
MORE OF THE SAME IS UNACCEPTABLE

DAY OF UNACCEPTANCE
AUGUST 24 11:30A.M. S.F. CIVIC CENTER
RALLY & MARCH TO NIXON HEADQUARTERS
AND SAIGON CONSULATE

APRIL 22 COALITION

Jane Norling, *Day of Unacceptance*, 1974, offset, 22½ × 17½ inches (57.5 × 44.5 cm), San Francisco. Norling created this poster for a march expressing rage against the war in Vietnam, as well as against racial, economic, and gender inequality and U.S. world domination. Its edge-to-edge hand-lettered list of reasons to march responds to student works of the same era, in which entire posters were filled with justifications to strike.

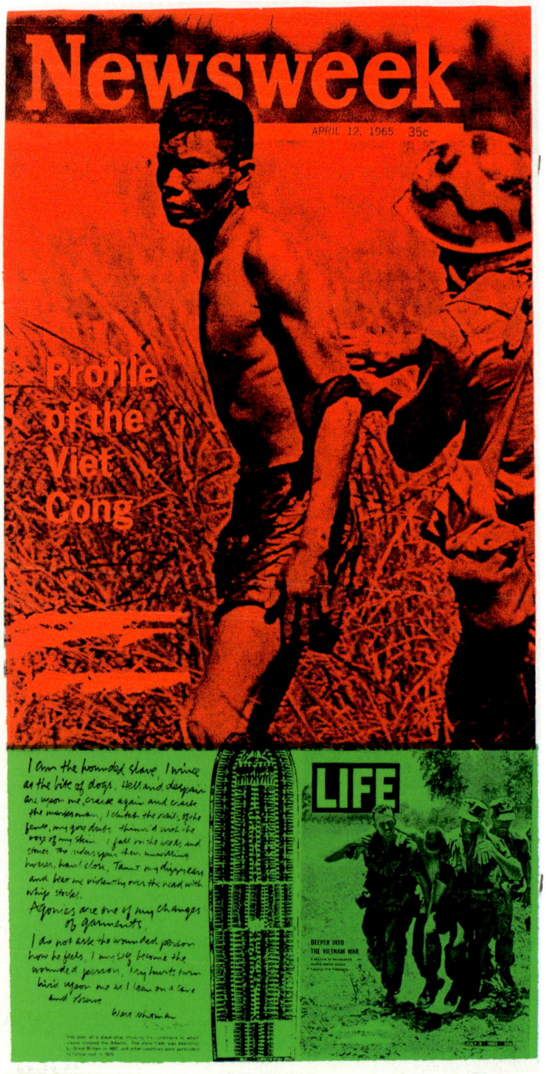

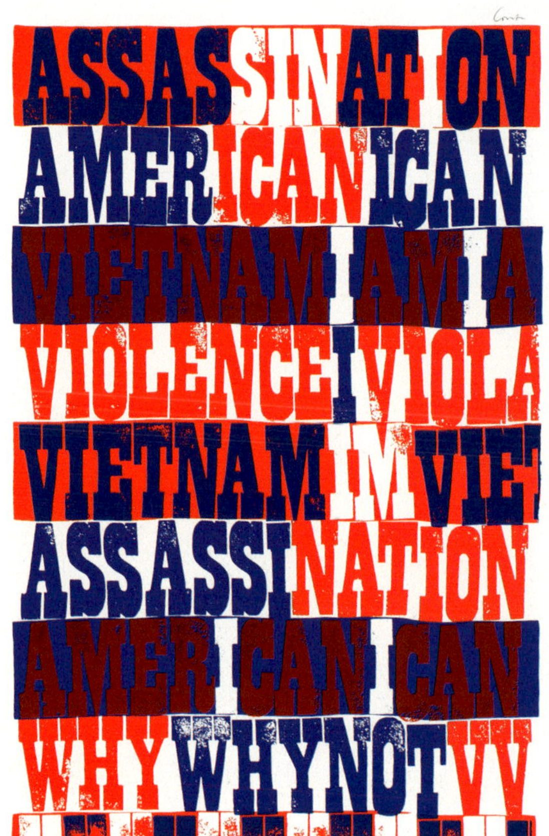

Corita Kent, from the *29 Heroes and Sheroes* series, 1969, screen print, 23 × 12 inches (58.5 × 30.5 cm), Boston. From left to right: *News of the Week*, *American Sampler*, *King's Dream*, *If I*. Collection of Corita Art Center.

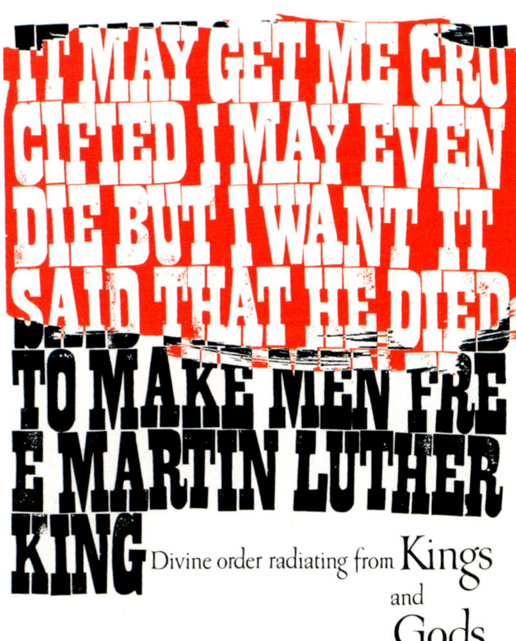
IT MAY GET ME CRU
CIFIED I MAY EVEN
DIE BUT I WANT IT
SAID THAT HE DIED
TO MAKE MEN FRE
E MARTIN LUTHER
KING
Divine order radiating from Kings
and
Gods
I have a dream that my four little children
will one day live in a nation
where they will not be judged
by the color of their skin
but by the content of their character.
With this faith we will be able
to transform the jangling discords
of our nation
into a beautiful symphony
of brotherhood.
With this faith we will be able to work
together
to pray together,
to go to jail together,
to stand up for freedom together,
knowing that we will be free one day.

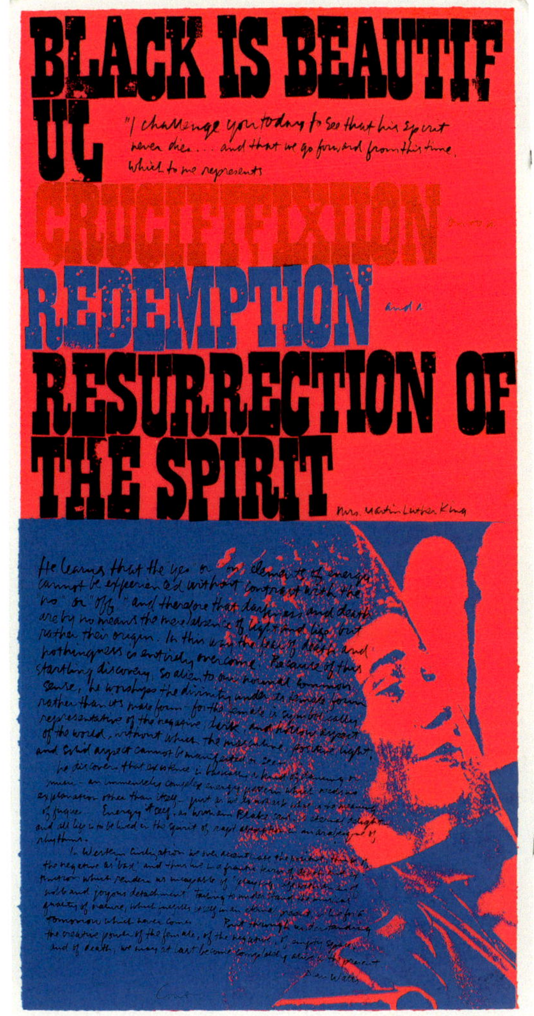
BLACK IS BEAUTIF
UL
"I challenge you today to see that his spirit
never dies... and that we go forward from this time,
which to me represents
REDEMPTION
RESURRECTION OF
THE SPIRIT

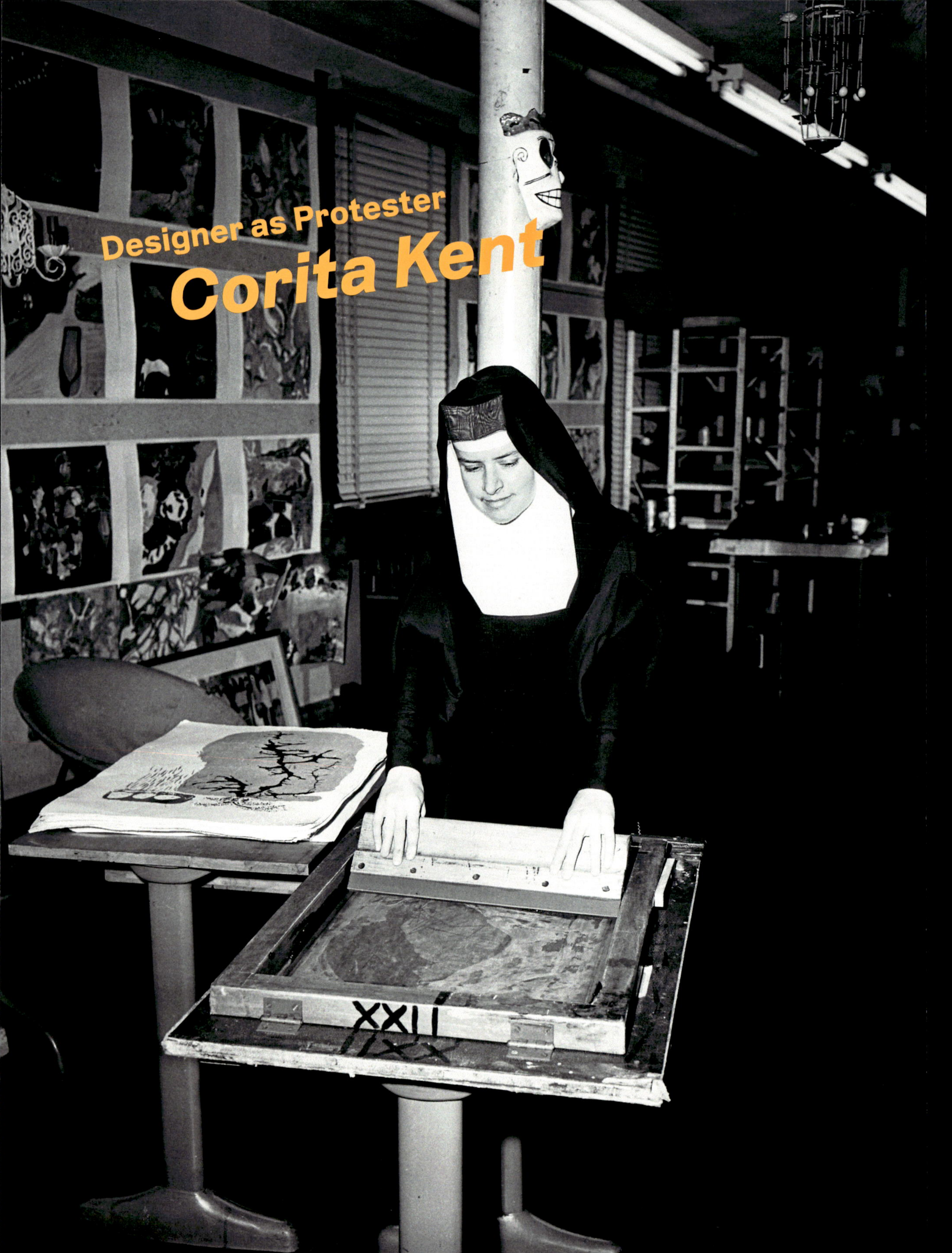

Designer as Protester

Corita Kent

"When art has changed, it's because the world was changing."

—Corita Kent

In 1936, an eighteen-year-old named Frances Elizabeth Kent joined the Sisters of the Immaculate Heart of Mary in Los Angeles. Taking the name Sister Mary Corita, she went on to become one of the twentieth century's most well-regarded pop artists, known for her vibrant screen-printed messages of social justice.

Sister Corita began teaching in the art department at Immaculate Heart College in 1947. After seeing an Andy Warhol show, she became drawn to *serigraphy* (silk-screening) for its ability to produce multiples that could spread spiritual teachings to more people, especially those outside of traditional religion. She worked hard at highlighting the sacred in the secular, which she did through photographing words and graphics from advertising and elevating them to the level of scripture in her prints. Under her hand, the bold blue cursive *G* of the General Mills logo gets reimagined as "The Big *G* Stands for Goodness," while the colored dots on Wonder Bread packaging become the Eucharist for the masses. Her unique take and generous pedagogy attracted artists including Saul Bass, Buckminster Fuller, Charles and Ray Eames, John Cage, and Alfred Hitchcock.

As the 1960s passed and the Immaculate Heart community around her became more progressive, Kent's printing became more overtly political. She also took over stewardship of the Mary's Day procession, a parade that aimed to make the Virgin Mary more relevant via modern spectacle. For the 1964 event, Kent made a screen print announcing that "Mother Mary is the juiciest tomato of all," which the Vatican misinterpreted as sexual—just one of the many skirmishes between the trailblazing Sisters and the church leadership. Ultimately, the Sisters of the Immaculate Heart of Mary were banned from teaching at Los Angeles Catholic schools, and Kent left the congregation in 1968, taking the name Corita with her.

After her Catholic service, Kent became further radicalized by the social justice issues of her time. Her *29 Heroes and Sheroes* prints (see pages 52–53) weigh in on the Vietnam War, the nuclear arms race, and the civil rights movement. These posters represent a major turning point in her career: Freed from the conservative eye of the cardinal, Kent pairs startling images—some torn from magazines such as *Life* and *Newsweek*—with text urging readers to "give a damn about their fellow man."

Regardless of message, text was always the central graphic of Kent's prints. While most of her works feature her own loose script, many pieces in her *29 Heroes and Sheroes* series also incorporate Playbill, a 1938 revival of a wood type style called French Antique that had been common on nineteenth-century theater broadsides. Playbill's bold shapes allowed Kent to easily reverse out of or overprint on top of images. She would also fold or rip her printed source material before photographing it to lend character to the letterforms in her final prints.

Before she died of cancer in 1986, Kent created a "Love" stamp for the U.S. Postal Service. Her blithe and colorful take on its enduring message sold more than 700 million stamps.

In 1966, after the murders of Black activist Malcolm X and unarmed Black San Francisco teenager Matthew Johnson, who was shot by the police, college students Bobby Seale and Huey P. Newton founded the Black Panther Party in Oakland, California. First called the Black Panther Party for Self-Defense, it advocated for armed citizens' patrols to challenge police brutality in Black communities. While known for its beret-wearing, rifle-toting image, the organization made a major impact through social programs and information campaigns, anchored by its weekly newspaper, *The Black Panther*.

At its height, from 1968 to 1971, as the Party expanded to offices in sixty-eight cities, *The Black Panther* was the most widely read Black newspaper in the United States. In fact, it had among the highest distributions of publications of any kind, reaching a weekly circulation of more than 300,000, rivaling the major papers of most cities. Each issue from the "Black Community News Service" (the newspaper's tagline) shone a light on Black struggle, worked to educate and organize the community, and promoted the Party's platform, the Ten-Point Program, which demanded full employment, decent housing, education, and health care. The Party also pioneered a free school breakfast program that was adopted around the United States. Despite its apparent machismo, the Party's membership was more than two-thirds women at its peak, and the paper was edited by a woman, Judy Juanita, who at the time was a college student at San Francisco State University.

The Party's insistence that the Second Amendment extend to all Americans—not just white ones—as well as its strengths in organizing and messaging, caught the FBI's attention. The Bureau launched a smear campaign in the press and a violent offensive in the streets, imprisoning leaders, like cofounder Huey P. Newton, and assassinating others, like national deputy chairman Fred Hampton. Posters like this one—designed by minister of culture Emory Douglas, with the iconic Black Panther logo on the bottom created by Lisa Lyons—reframed the incarceration of Black people as a political rather than criminal punishment and an abuse of government power.

As the FBI tactics chipped away at the Panthers' regard in the public eye, and as infiltrators sparked internal conflict that at times resulted in violence, the Party's power waned. It's still seen as one of the most impressive models of grass-roots organizing in history, an effort furthered by the savvy messaging of its newspaper.

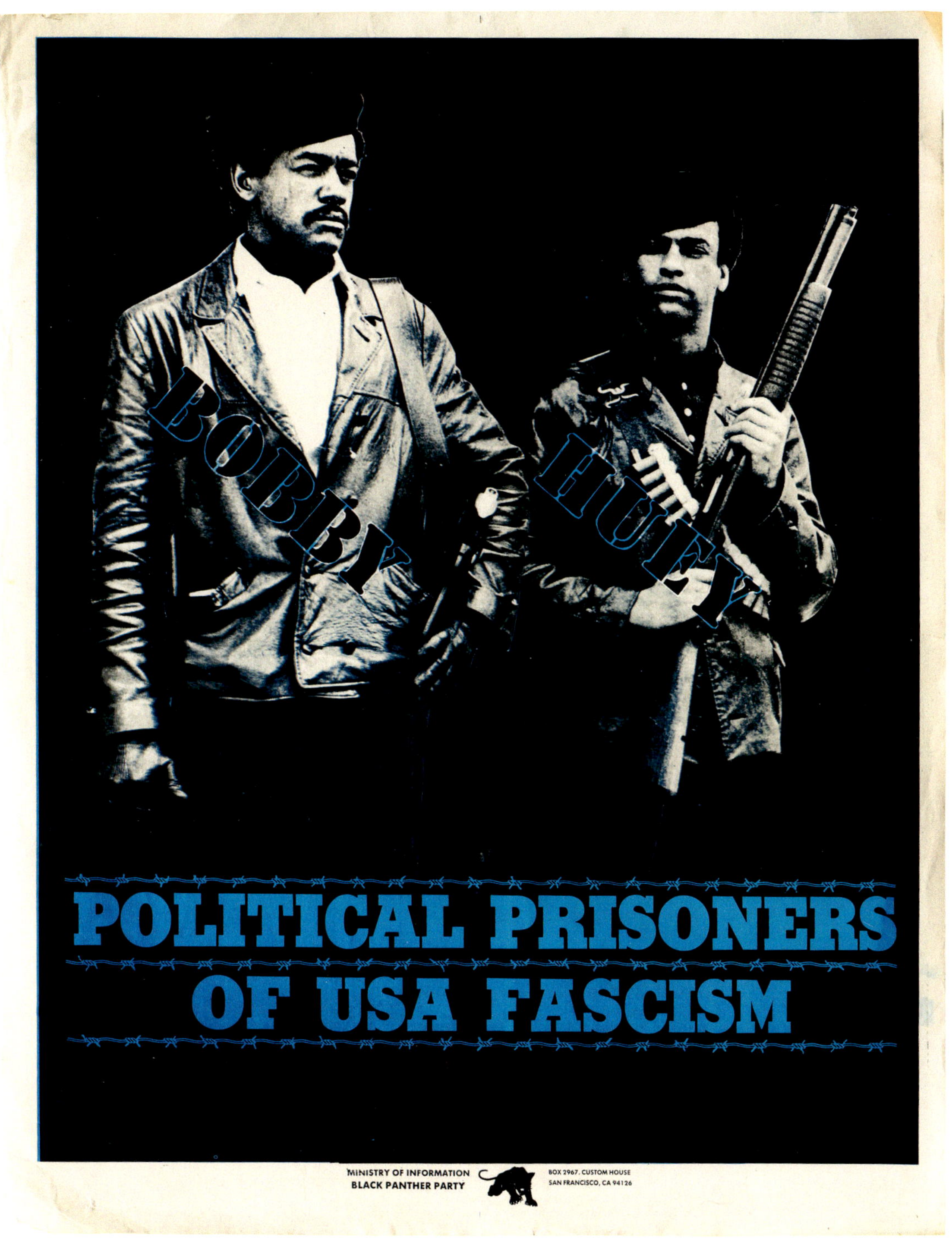

Emory Douglas, *Political Prisoners of USA Fascism*, circa 1970, offset, 28⅜ × 22½ inches (72 × 57 cm), Oakland, California.

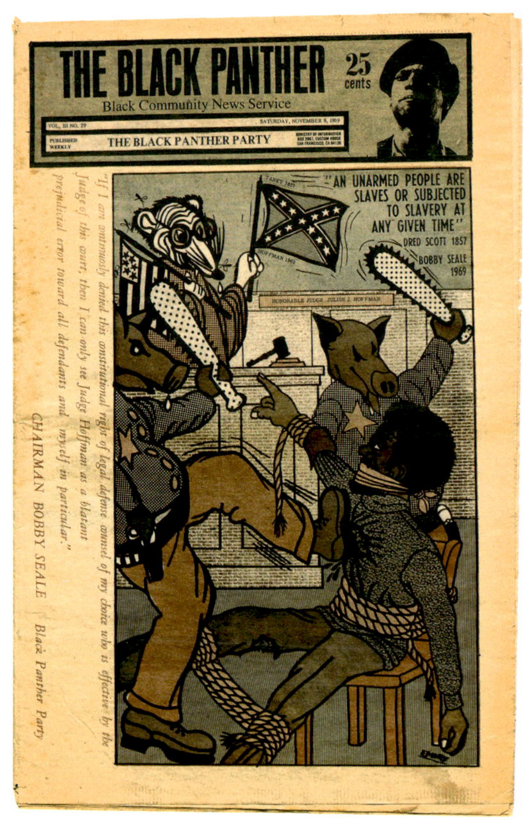
THE BLACK PANTHER 25 cents
Black Community News Service
SATURDAY, NOVEMBER 8, 1969
PUBLISHED WEEKLY THE BLACK PANTHER PARTY
"AN UNARMED PEOPLE ARE SLAVES OR SUBJECTED TO SLAVERY AT ANY GIVEN TIME"
DRED SCOTT 1857
BOBBY SEALE 1969
HONORABLE JUDGE JULIUS J. HOFFMAN
"If I am continuously denied this constitutional right of legal defense counsel of my choice who is effective by the judge of this court, then I can only see Judge Hoffman as a blatant prejudicial error toward all defendants and myself in particular."
CHAIRMAN BOBBY SEALE Black Panther Party

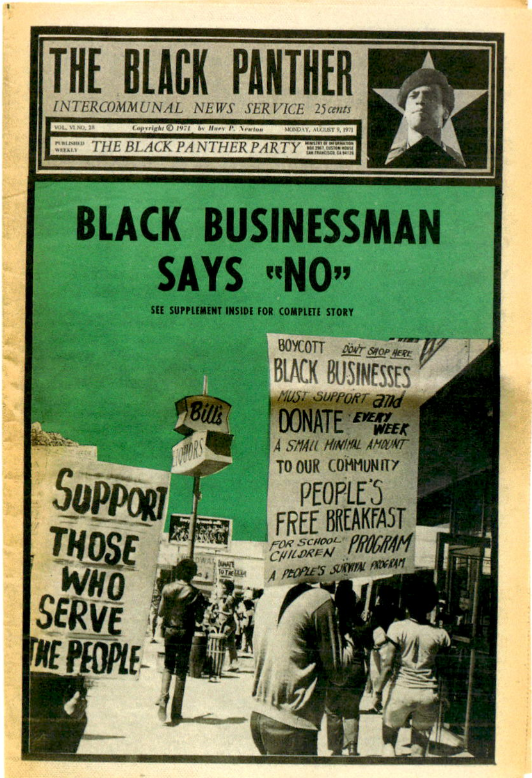
THE BLACK PANTHER
INTERCOMMUNAL NEWS SERVICE 25 cents
Copyright © 1971 by Huey P. Newton MONDAY, AUGUST 9, 1971
PUBLISHED WEEKLY THE BLACK PANTHER PARTY
BLACK BUSINESSMAN SAYS "NO"
SEE SUPPLEMENT INSIDE FOR COMPLETE STORY

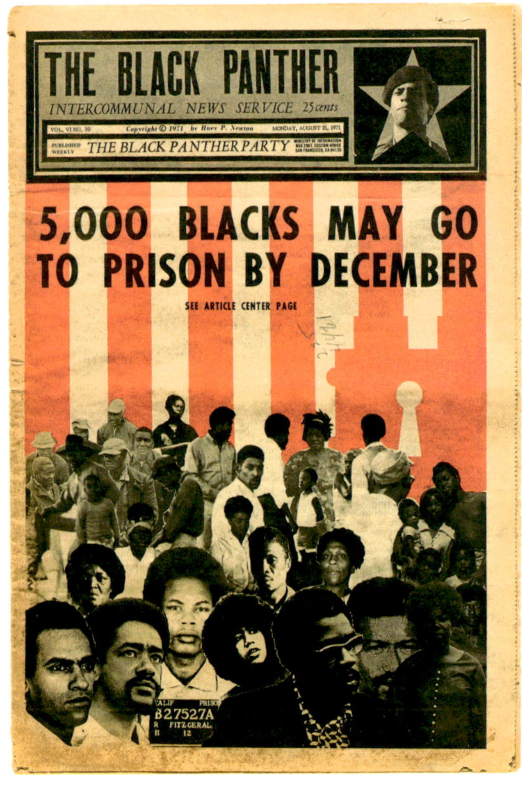
THE BLACK PANTHER
INTERCOMMUNAL NEWS SERVICE 25 cents
Copyright © 1971 by Huey P. Newton MONDAY, AUGUST 21, 1971
PUBLISHED WEEKLY THE BLACK PANTHER PARTY
5,000 BLACKS MAY GO TO PRISON BY DECEMBER
SEE ARTICLE CENTER PAGE

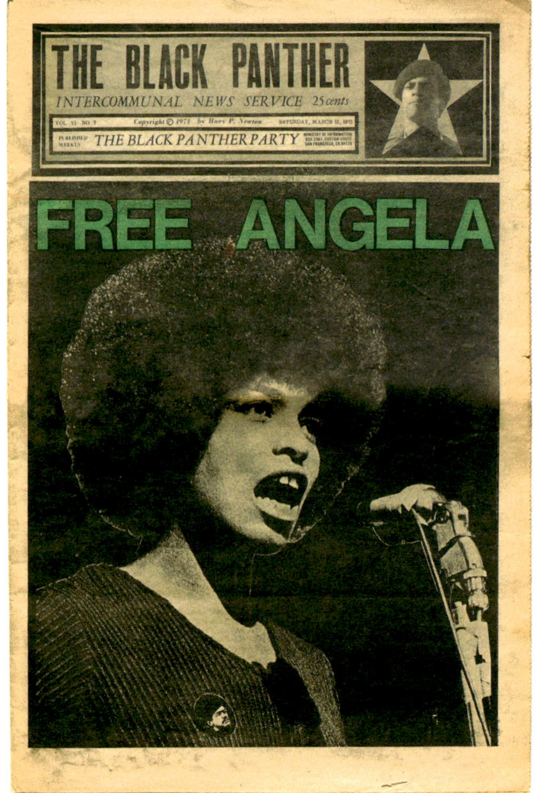
THE BLACK PANTHER
INTERCOMMUNAL NEWS SERVICE 25 cents
Copyright © 1971 by Huey P. Newton
PUBLISHED WEEKLY THE BLACK PANTHER PARTY
FREE ANGELA

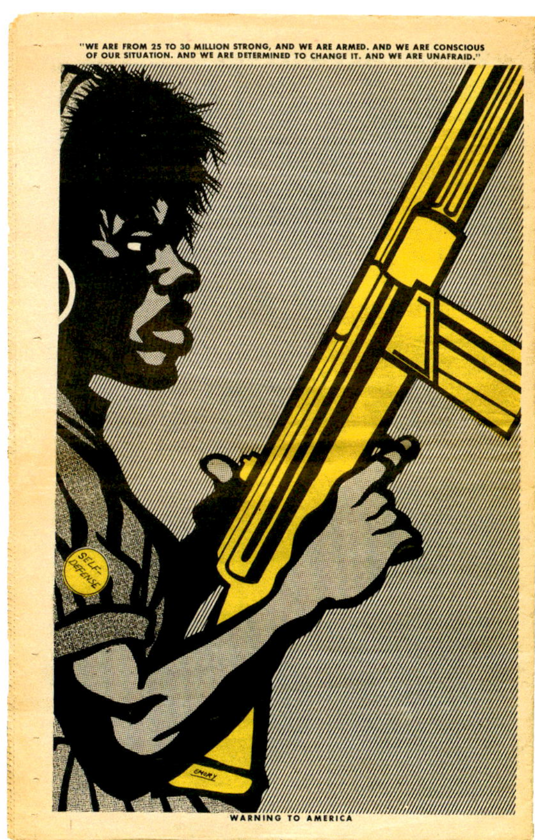

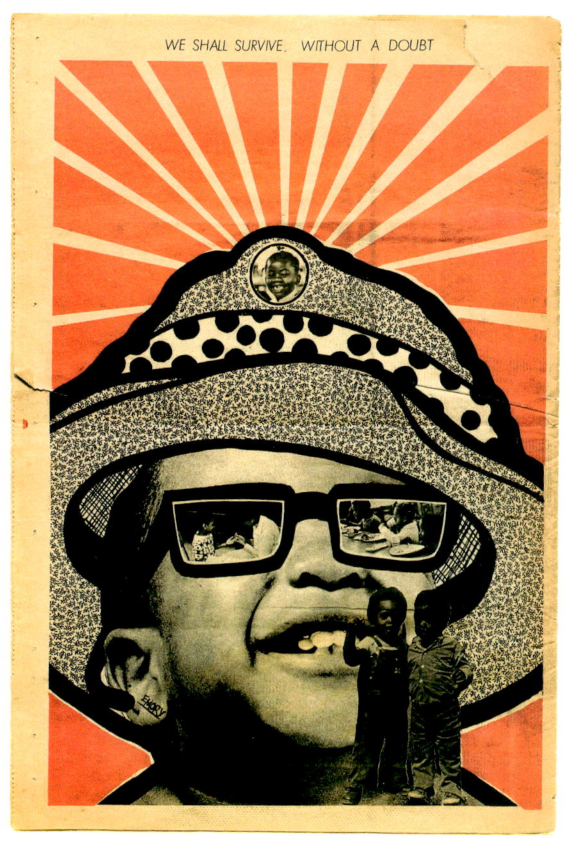

Emory Douglas, front and back covers of *The Black Panther*, offset, approximately 17 × 11½ inches (43 × 29.5 cm), Oakland, California. Clockwise from left to right: vol. 3, no. 29, 1969; vol. 6, no. 28, 1971; back cover of vol. 4, no. 30, 1970; back cover of vol. 6, no. 30, 1971; vol. 6., no. 7, 1971; and vol. 6, no. 30, 1971. Each issue features a photographic front cover and an illustrative back, printed in the same limited palette. The front cover at bottom far left, for instance, accompanies the back cover at right above.

Emory Douglas, back cover of *The Black Panther*, vol. 7, no. 5, 1971, offset, 17 × 11½ inches (43 × 29.5 cm), Oakland, California. Here is an example of a later, more detailed and delicate illustrative style from Douglas, with graphics repurposed from a previous issue (see page 58, top right). While perhaps a money- and time-saving measure, this tactic creates a visual callback as well, presenting the support of Black businesses that helped fund the Party's free school breakfast program as a key issue (a.k.a., the beat of the tambourine).

WE'RE GOING TO KEEP ON STRUGGLING FOR BRIGHTER DAYS
WE'RE GOING TO KEEP ON STRUGGLING UNTIL WE WIN YOUR LOVE.

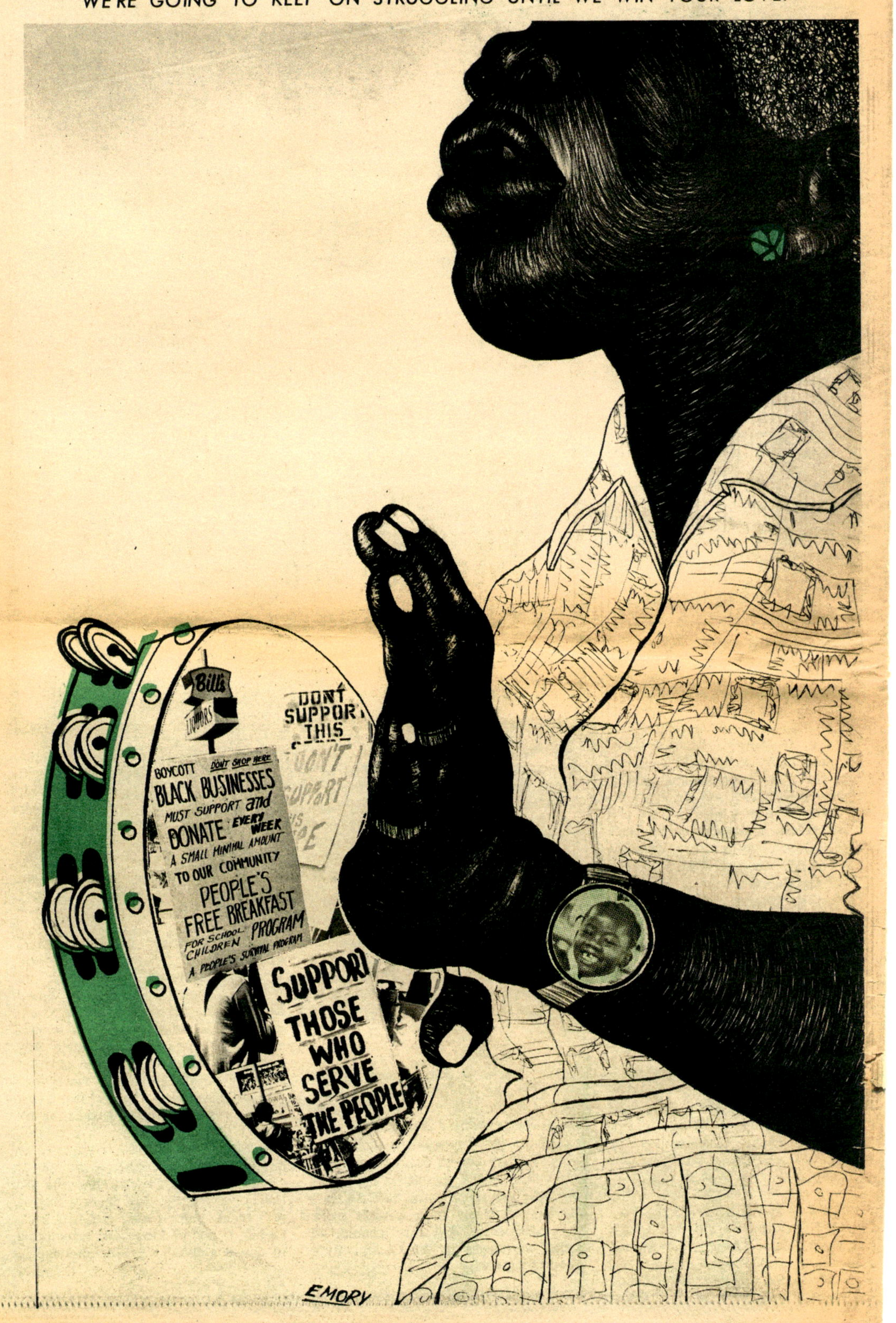

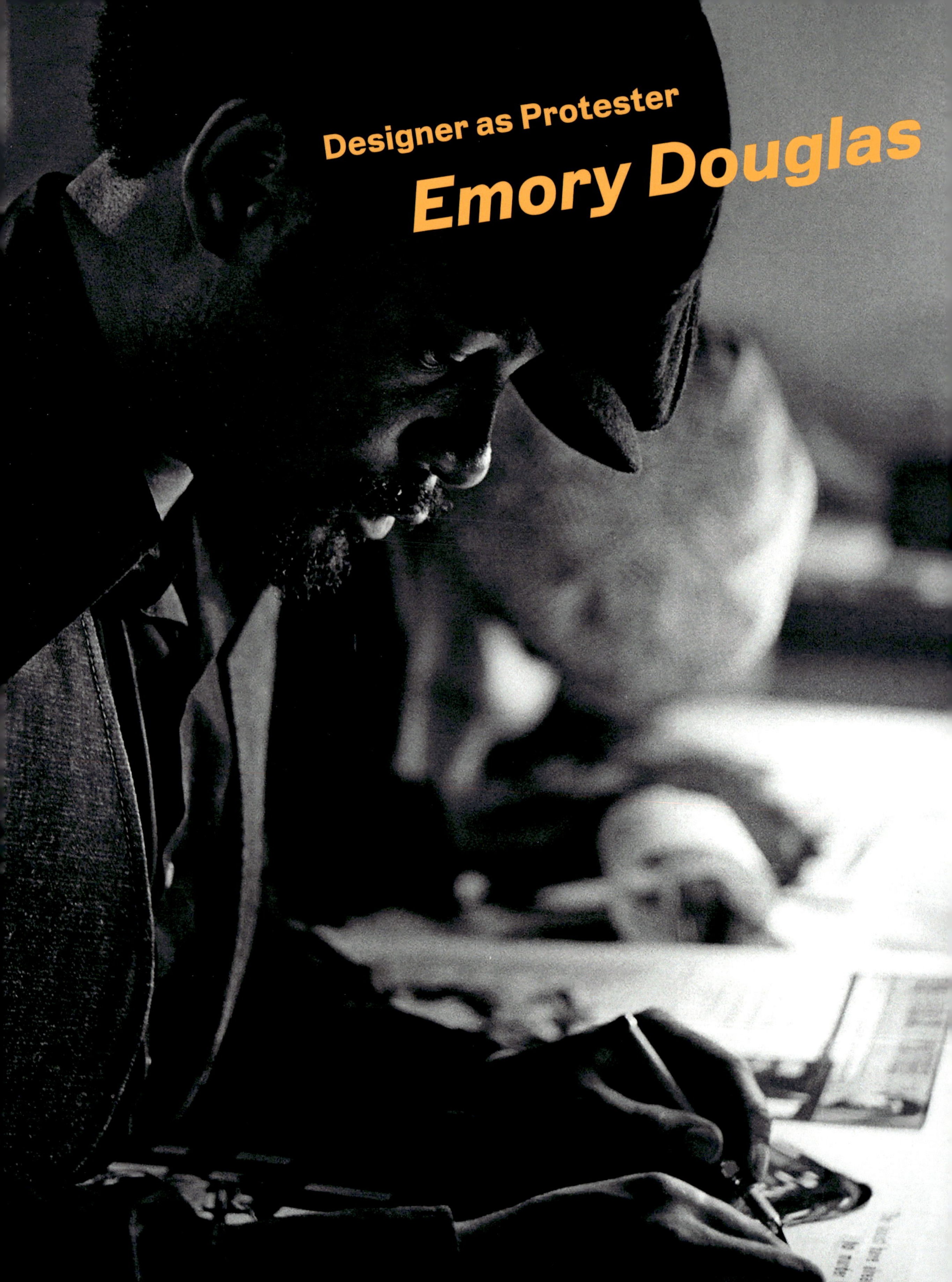

Designer as Protester

Emory Douglas

"The people saw themselves in the artwork. They became the heroes."

—Emory Douglas

Emory Douglas was twenty-three years old when, in January of 1967, he met Huey P. Newton and Eldridge Cleaver, respectively the ministers of defense and information of the Black Panther Party, and this moment set the course for his life in revolutionary art. Douglas, who had commercial art experience from San Francisco's free City College and a printing class he took while in juvenile detention, was soon conscripted to become the Party's minister of culture and its revolutionary artist, responsible for the production of *The Black Panther* newspaper, the posters wheatpasted on the streets of Oakland and San Francisco, and the leaflets and pamphlets distributed to communities around the country. His work was crucial in forging the visual identity of the Black Panther Party.

In his artwork for the newspaper and beyond, Douglas depicted those who abused their power—police and landlords—as pigs and rats, while Black people were shown as proud revolutionaries defending their right to exist. Many of the images might strike some viewers as militant, but the objective was to convey the Party's belief in organized armed resistance as part of the solution to cop-sanctioned murder.

Douglas's resourceful use of affordable and accessible tools allowed *The Black Panther* to be produced quickly and cheaply, and this practice also came to define its visual style. The thick marker lines of Douglas's woodcut-inspired drawings are not only graphically appealing, they also mask imperfect printing registration. His use of rub-down tints and patterns adds texture to the artwork and made for an effective, low-cost alternative to multicolor printing, as most issues were printed in either black or black plus one color. For type, Douglas favored basic, readable typefaces—Century for body text (set with an IBM Selectric typewriter), and Futura, Helvetica, and various gothics for headlines and posters. He used transfer type for headlines—specifically Formatt, a cheaper, reusable version of Letraset. While these production choices were made out of necessity, they focused and amplified the paper's messaging, giving it an aesthetic of urgency. This message was also under threat by the FBI: Lawyers had to accompany each print run to the airport to ensure the issues made it into circulation, and the Bureau even surveilled Douglas's Pantone selections.

Douglas recruited other Black artists to *The Black Panther* and taught them to integrate social justice into their work. He recalls, "Our philosophy was [the African proverb] 'Each one, teach one.' Some of them had even greater artistic skills than I, but they didn't understand the political content. So [mentoring them] was my responsibility."

Douglas's universally powerful graphics perpetually influenced agitprop design long after the Black Panthers' heyday, and he continues to mentor, lecture, teach workshops, and collaborate with artists and political activists around the world. In 2015, the American Institute of Graphic Arts awarded him an AIGA Medal in recognition of his fearless and powerful use of graphic design in the struggle for civil rights.

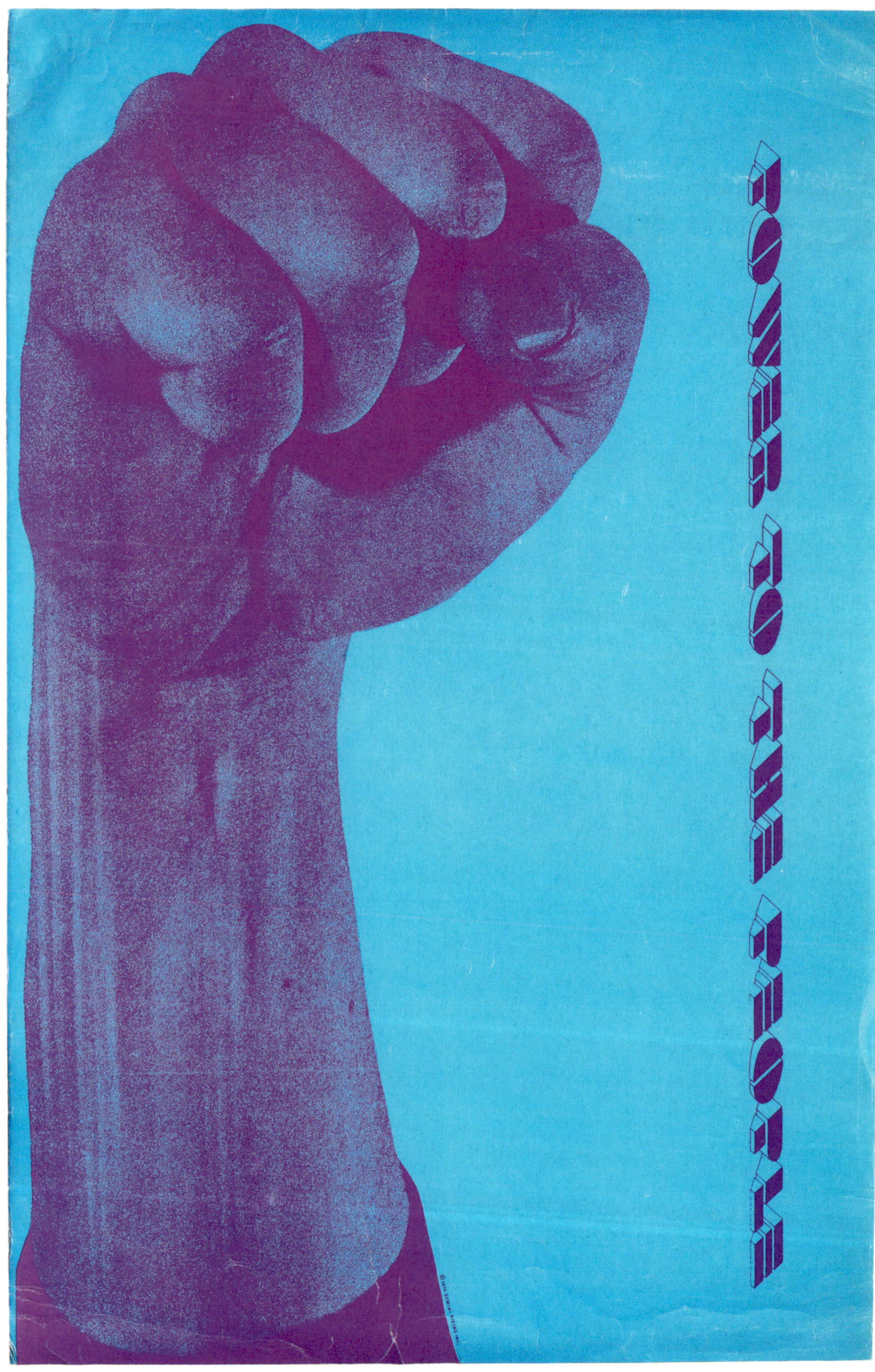
POWER TO THE PEOPLE

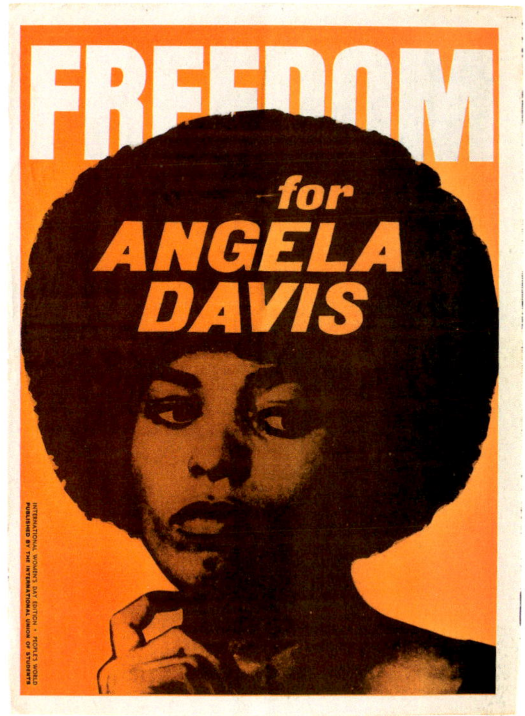

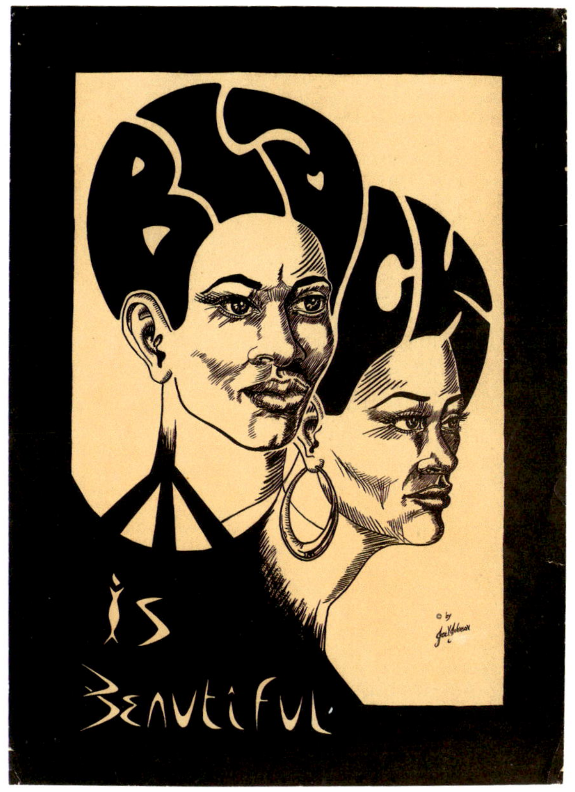

Unknown designer for Gemini Rising Inc., *Power to the People*, 1970, screen print, 35½ × 23½ inches (90 × 59.5 cm), New York. This poster on blue paper features the wedge-shaped dimensional font Cenotaph, a typeface sometimes seen in album art for Black musicians of the era.

José Vasquez Johnson, *Black Is Beautiful*, circa 1971, offset, 23 × 17 inches (58.5 × 43 cm), San Francisco. This poster champions natural hair using completely original lettering, with "Black" spelled out in Afro hairstyles and "is beautiful" rendered in letterforms composed of repeating minimalist arcs.

International Union of Students, *Freedom for Angela Davis*, 1971, offset, 22½ × 17 inches (57 × 43 cm), San Francisco. Created for an International Women's Day issue of the socialist publication *People's World*, this poster urges the release of activist Angela Davis, who was imprisoned for over a year after guns she purchased were used by others in a courthouse shootout.

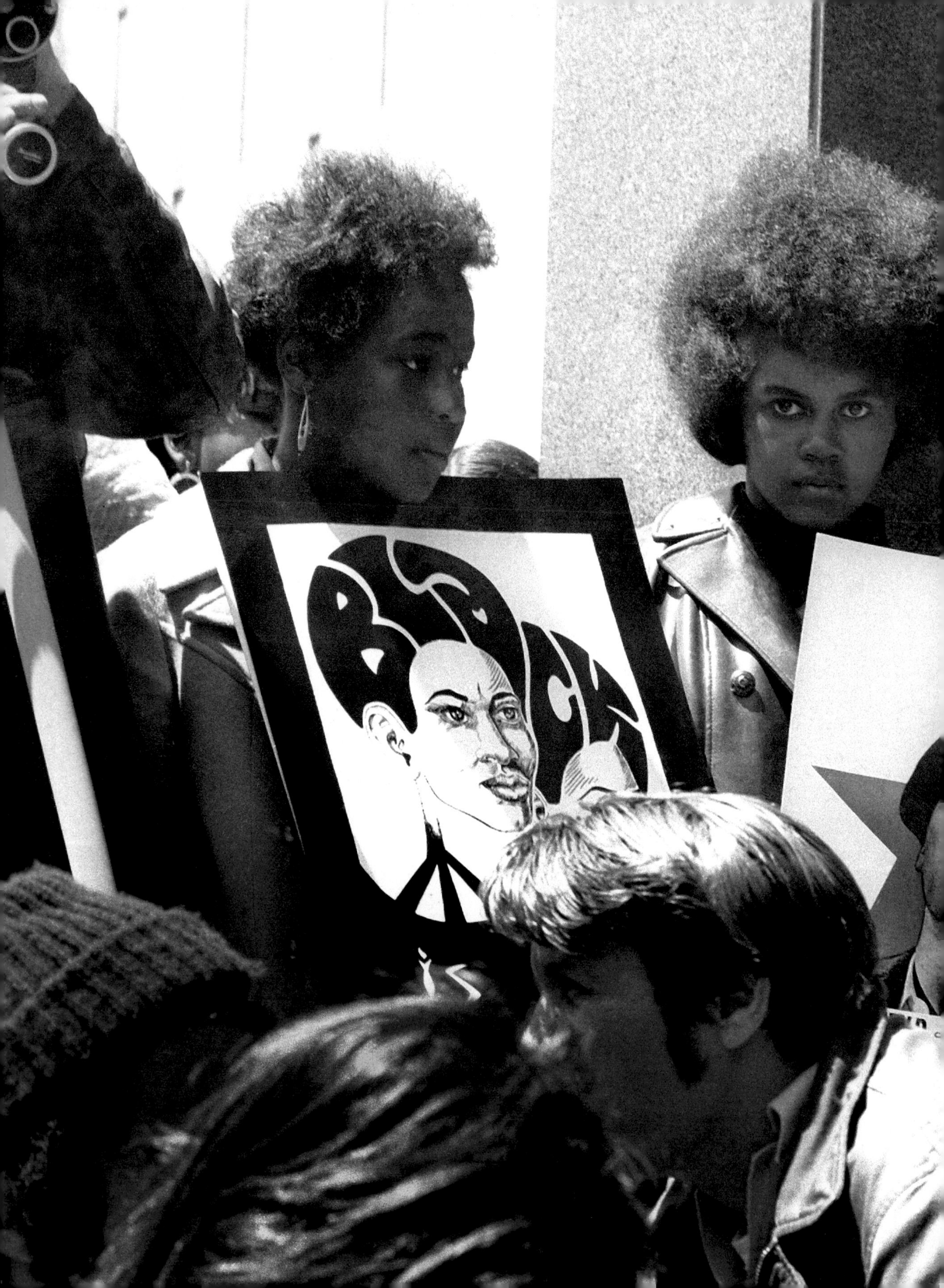

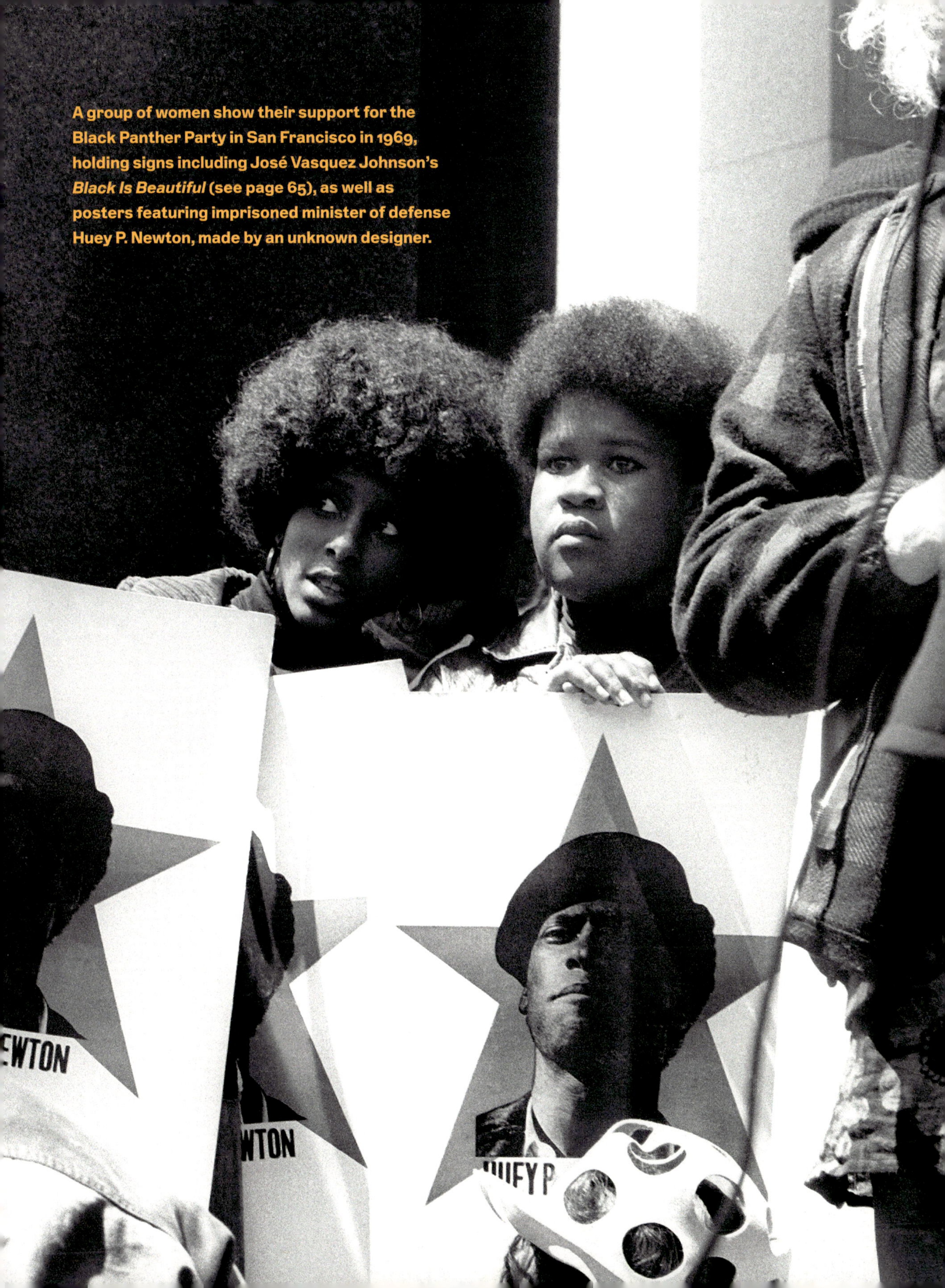

A group of women show their support for the Black Panther Party in San Francisco in 1969, holding signs including José Vasquez Johnson's *Black Is Beautiful* (see page 65), as well as posters featuring imprisoned minister of defense Huey P. Newton, made by an unknown designer.

"[The U.S. embargo on Cuba] helped [artists] in the quest for our own forms of expression . . . . This had limited the arrival of design materials, and hence, from the need to solve our own material problems, we began to discover new forms."

—Alfredo Rostgaard, OSPAAAL creative director

In 1966, delegates from more than eighty nations gathered in Cuba to form OSPAAAL, the Organization of Solidarity of the Peoples of Asia, Africa, and Latin America. To combat American neocolonialism on the three continents, the group started *Tricontinental*, a revolutionary magazine with a covert poster insert that, once unfolded, could be displayed to help spread the group's ideas. Building on a rich Cuban poster tradition, dozens of artists created more than three hundred works, each of which amplifies a human rights issue and includes a simple message of solidarity in English, French, Spanish, and Arabic. Graphically, they are united by bold color and an image-centric, nearly wordless approach that communicates without requiring literacy or fluency. An example, *Day of the Heroic Guerrilla*, is one of the first known uses of a now-iconic image—taken by Alberto Korda—of Argentine revolutionary Che Guevara, who in 1967 was assassinated by CIA-backed operatives in Bolivia. Created by Cuban artist Elena Serrano, the poster repeats the portrait over the shape of South America in vibrating colors and at telescoping sizes, casting its socialist message in the op art style of the 1960s.

Tricontinental was issued until 2019, despite the U.S. embargo, which cut off supplies like ink and paper to Cuba. Its designers made do with this shortage of materials by printing on old newspapers and collaging letters and photos cut from magazines into layouts. At its height, *Tricontinental* had a global circulation of 50,000.

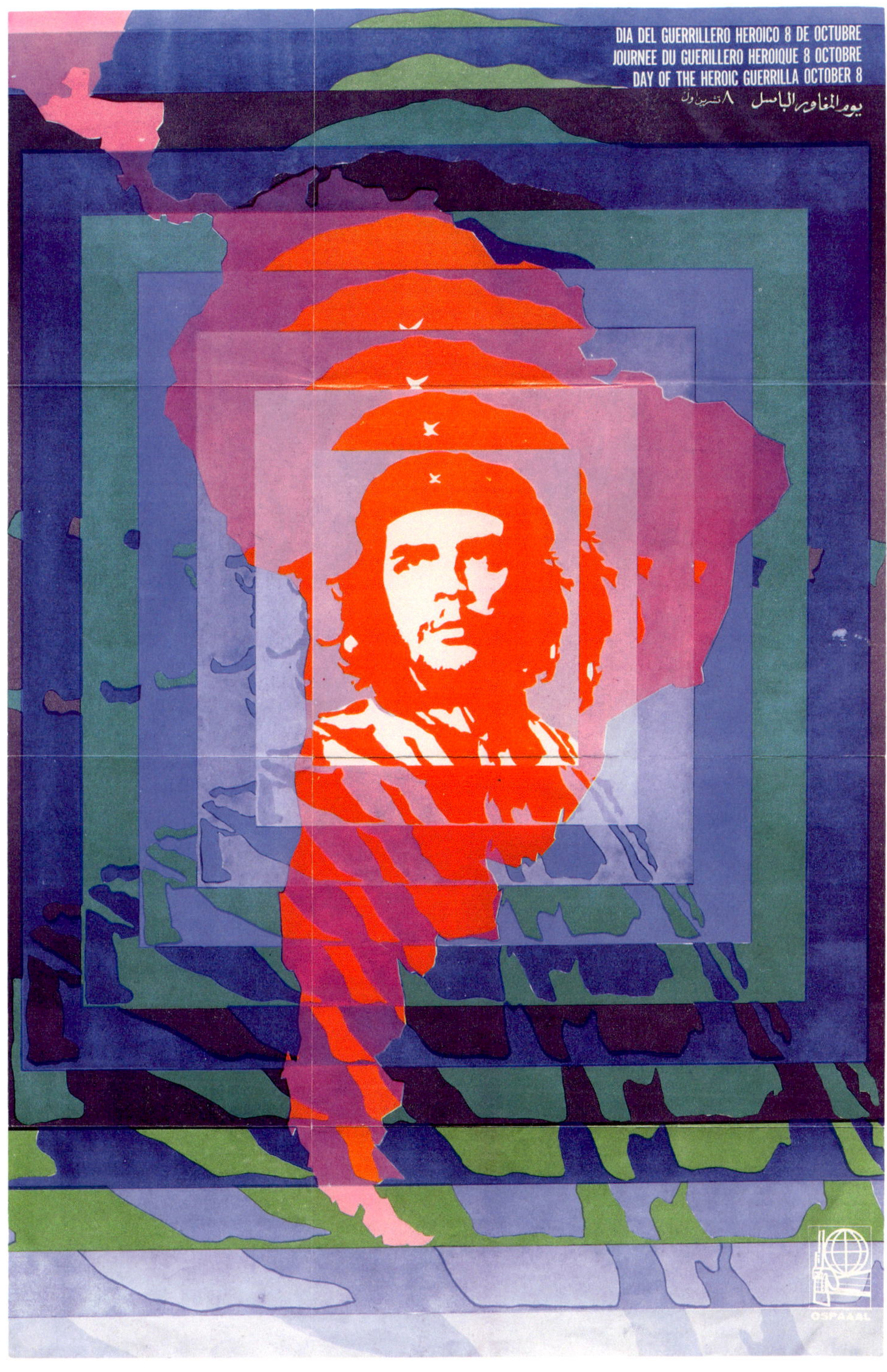

Elena Serrano for OSPAAAL, *Day of the Heroic Guerrilla*, 1968, offset, 19⅝ × 13⅛ inches (49.5 × 33.5 cm), Havana.

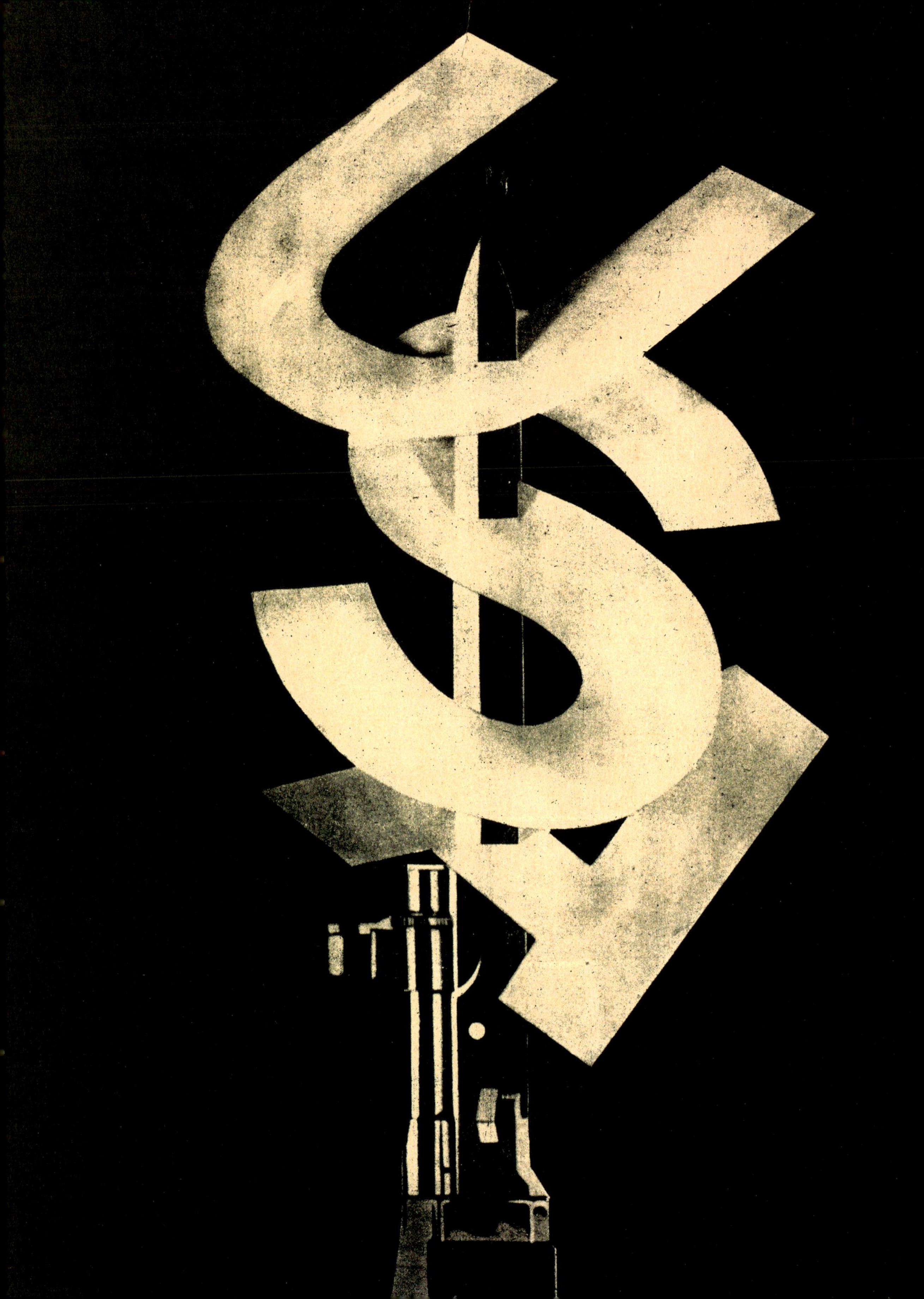

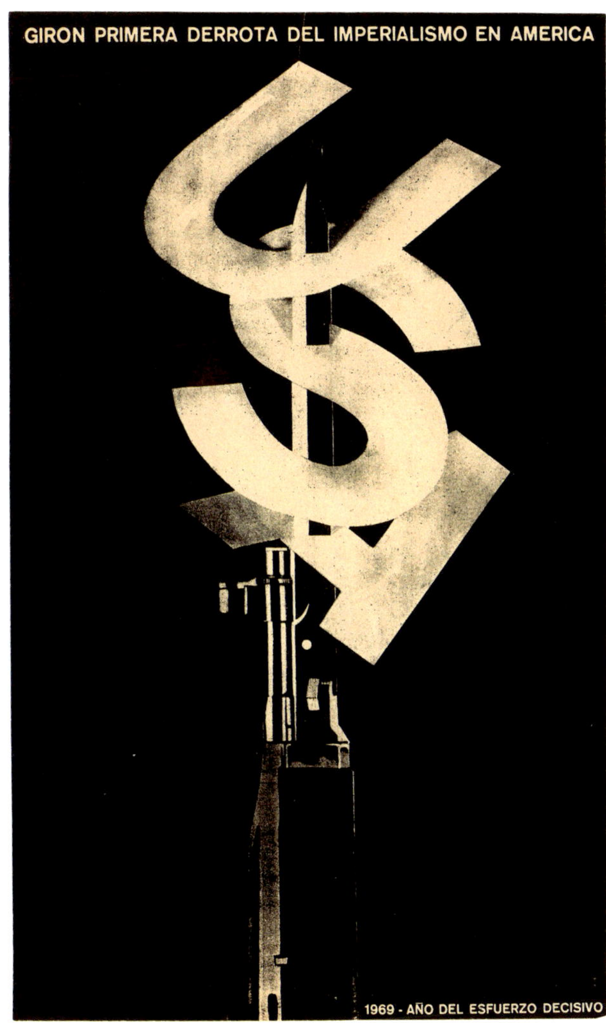

Felix Beltran, *Giron Beach First Defeat of Imperialism in America, 1969* (*Giron Primera Derrota del Imperialismo en America, 1969*), 1969, offset, 23¼ × 14⅛ inches (59 × 36 cm), Havana. This Cuban military propaganda poster celebrates the failure of the 1961 CIA-backed Bay of Pigs invasion (one of the landing spots of which was Giron Beach), with "USA" set in Standard, the American version of Akzidenz-Grotesk, and skewered by a bayonet.

CUBA gramma

o DE US $ do lar sabe

de açucar

O BRA SIM

yes só
eua
yes
oea
yes
eua
yes
oea
yes
eua
como SAL VE sugar yes A AMÉRICA
oea
yes
eua
açucar yes
oea
yes
SIL O BRA SIL
men

uma hiena só

entre dez al IAN ça

mo

es molas
trelas

para o progr esso

O BRASIL DIZ QUE NÃO

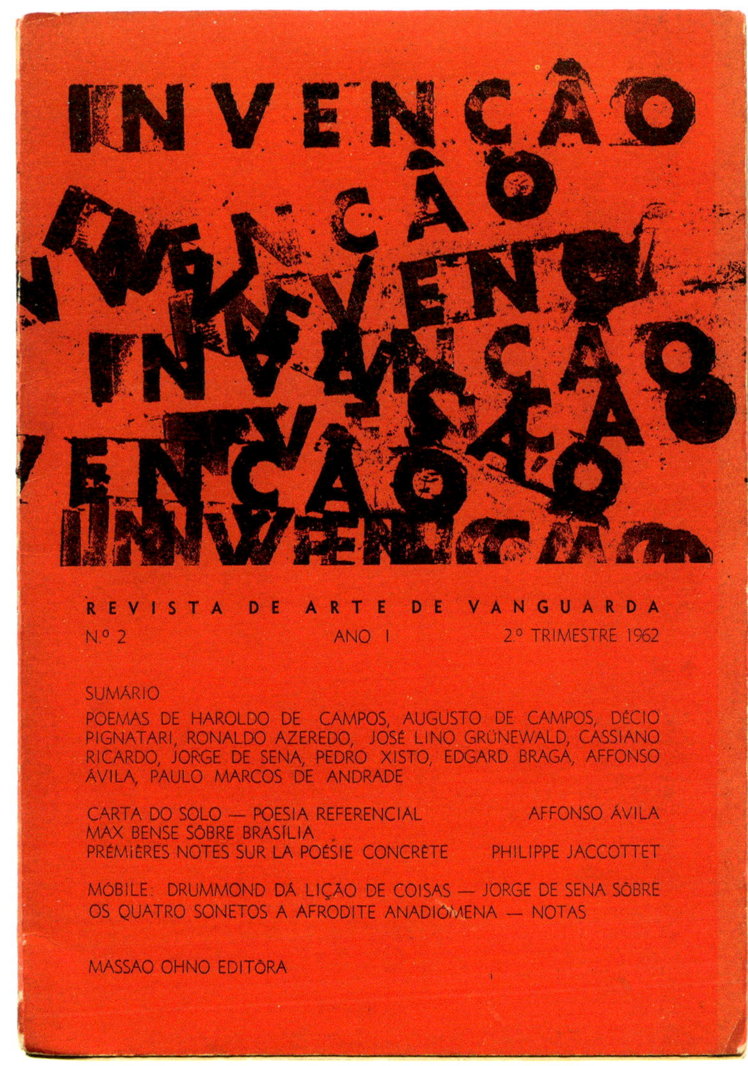

Décio Pignatari (cover designer/editor), Augusto de Campos (contributor), cover and interior page of *Invention: Avant-garde Magazine* (*Invenção: Revista de arte de vanguarda*), vol. 1, no. 2, 1962, offset, 10 × 7⅛ inches (25.5 x 18 cm), São Paulo. This Brazilian concrete poetry magazine, with the title stamped repeatedly on the cover (above) in Futura Bold, contains de Campos's poem "Cubagramma" (left), a color-coded typographic grid (consisting of Futura and other straightforward sans serifs) that critiques U.S. intervention in South American trade and politics.

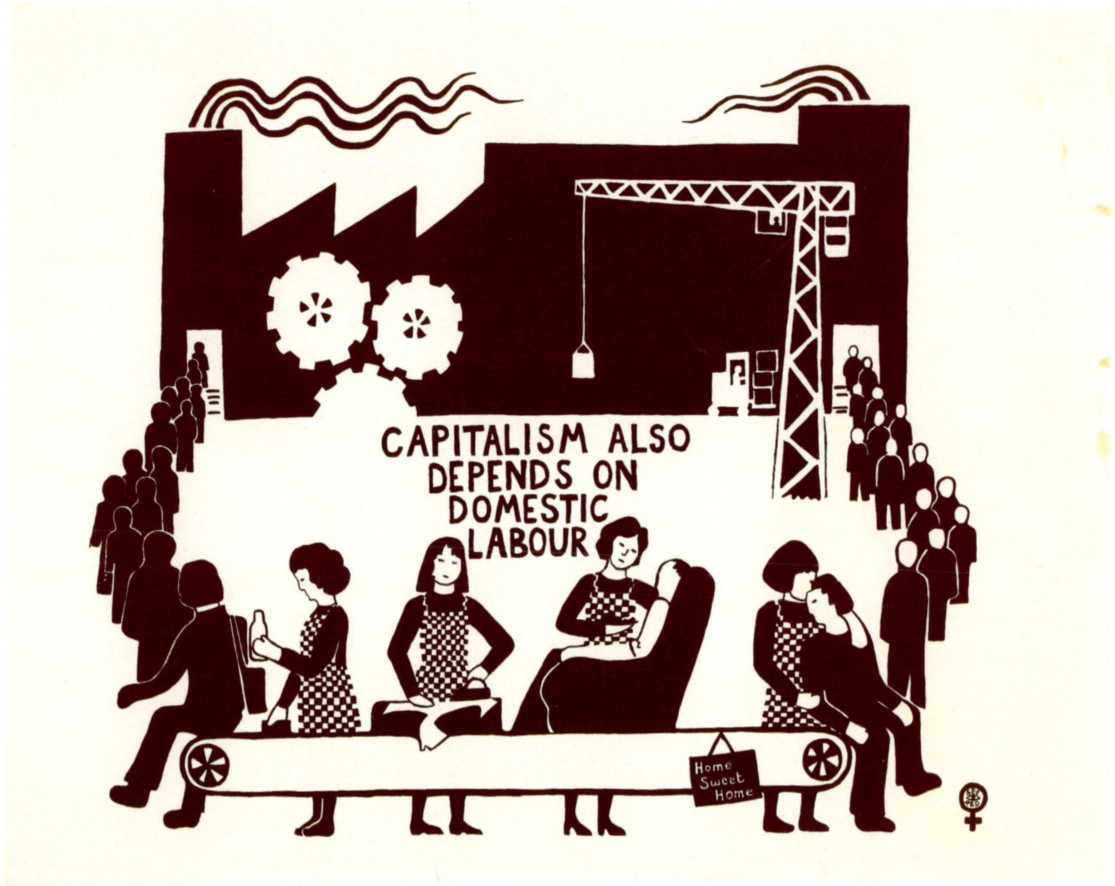

In 1974, a group of artists founded the See Red Women's Workshop to express the challenges of women's experiences and to further the women's liberation movement. Over sixteen years, the London collective put women through its workshops, supported social programs to aid and educate women in need, and spoke out against oppression via wheatpasting and sticker-bombing. Its legacy is most visible in the prints its members produced, each with a carefully crafted message to a world that has long undervalued women's sacrifices and societal contributions. The posters address gender discrepancies in pay, capitalism's reliance on unpaid labor in homekeeping and childrearing, sexist depictions in advertising, and the importance of women uniting against racism. They are screen-printed in one or two inks with simplified line art or collaged photography, often with hand-lettered rallying cries or typefaces that reference pop culture, such as Flash Bold, which is reminiscent of comic books, in *Girls Are Powerful* at right.

The outspoken women's collective was seen as a threat by some right-wing extremists, such as the National Front, who repeatedly vandalized their shop, forcing them to relocate. Despite such opposition, the See Red Women's Workshop operated until 1990.

See Red Women's Workshop, screen print, London. *Capitalism Also Depends on Domestic Labour*, 1975, 21 × 27⅛ inches (53.5 × 69 cm), and *Girls Are Powerful*, 1979, 31 × 21¼ inches (79 × 54 cm). Courtesy of See Red Women's Workshop.

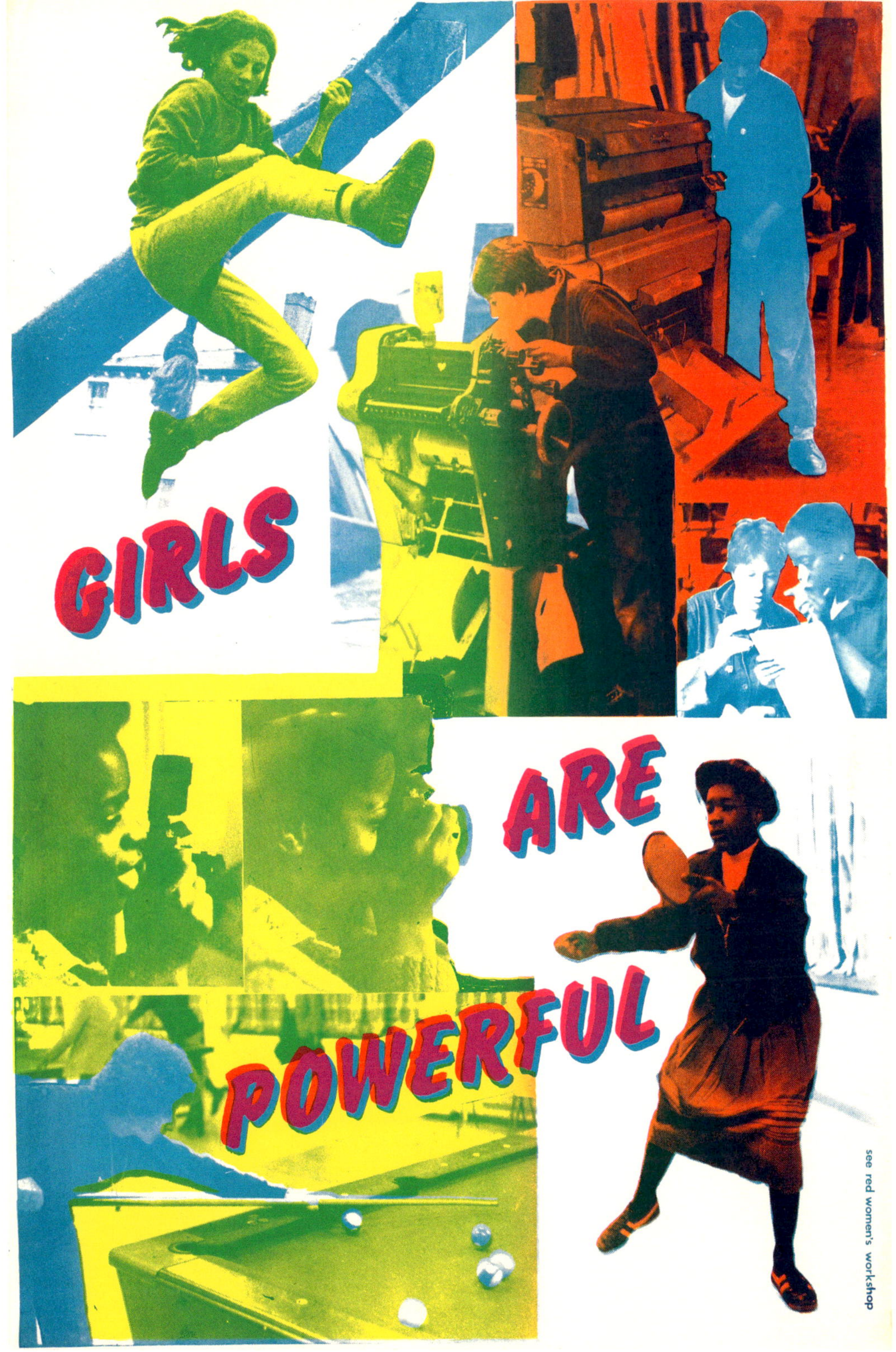
GIRLS
ARE
POWERFUL
see red women's workshop

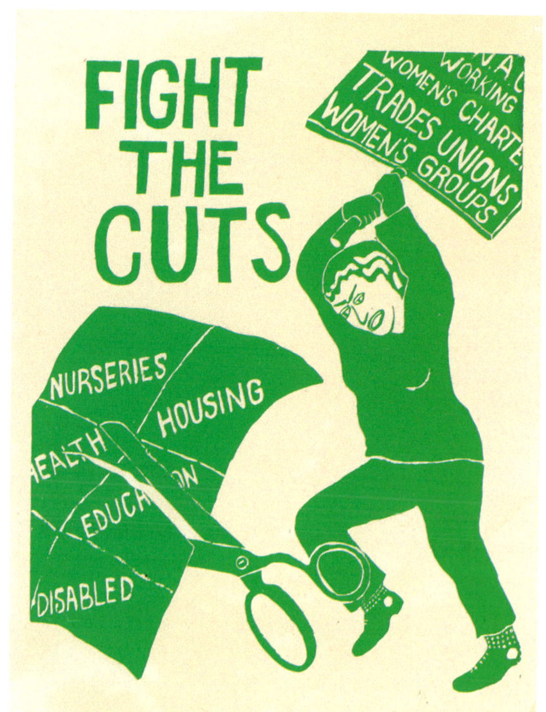
FIGHT
THE
CUTS
TRADES UNIONS
WOMEN'S GROUPS
NURSERIES
HOUSING
DISABLED

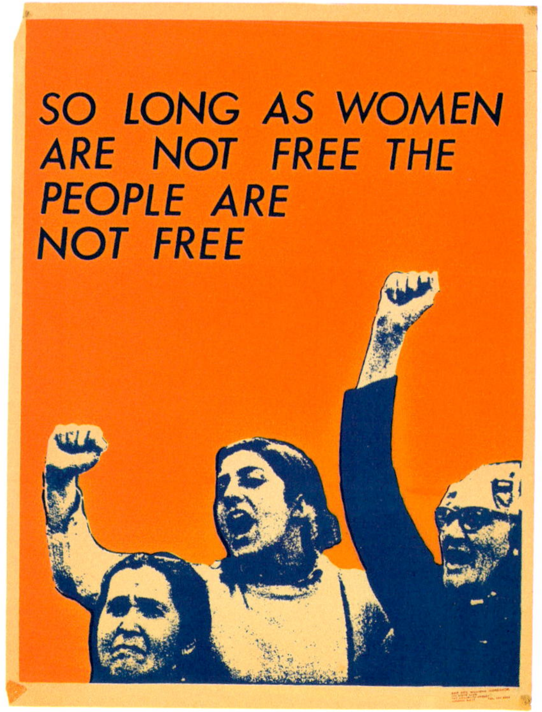
SO LONG AS WOMEN
ARE NOT FREE THE
PEOPLE ARE
NOT FREE

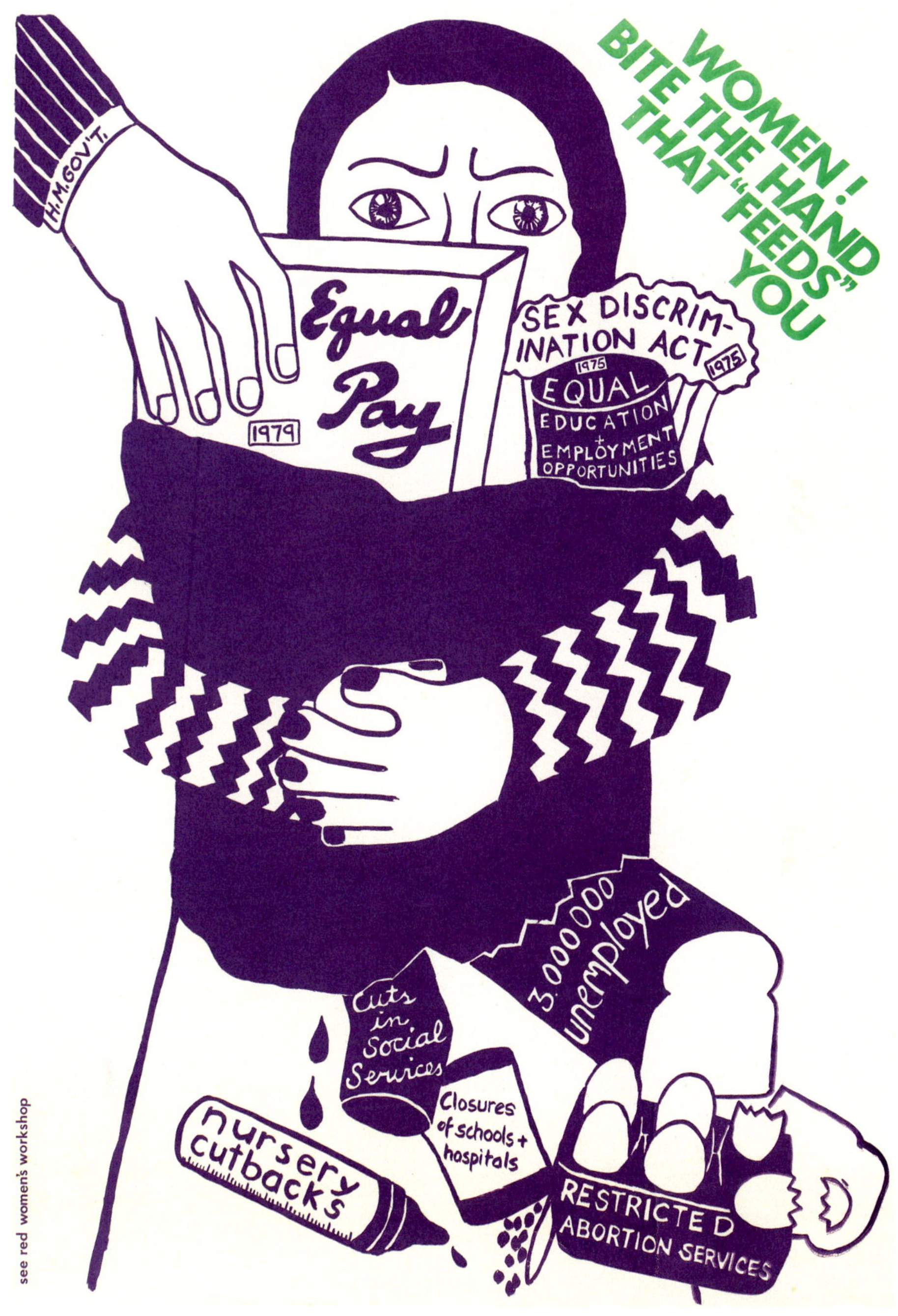

See Red Women's Workshop, screen print, London. From left to right: *Fight the Cuts*, 1975, 27⅜ × 21¼ inches (69.5 × 54 cm); *So Long as Women Are Not Free*, 1978, 25¼ × 17¾ inches (64 × 45 cm); and *Bite the Hand*, 1978, 25⅛ × 17¾ inches (64 × 45 cm). Courtesy of See Red Women's Workshop.

An underground publication capturing an underground culture, *IGTimes* was the first periodical devoted to New York street and subway art. Appearing under various names (*International Graffiti Times*, *International Get-Hip Times*, *Tight*, and *IGT*, to name a few), the zine was founded in 1984 by David Schmidlapp, an artist and photographer who came from outside the insular graffiti community but forged relationships with its players.

One of these was Phase 2, a young Bronx graffiti writer, DJ, rapper, break-dancer, and designer. The author of the now-iconic bubble lettering style called *softies* that took off in the early 1970s, Phase 2 went on to be known for his photocopied fliers promoting jam events at the dawn of hip-hop culture later in the decade. He joined *IGTimes* in 1986 for volume 8, bringing to the zine's grid-breaking layouts his lively, improvisational style, which included transfer lettering, thick marker, early digital type (such as Susan Kare's Chicago, developed for the Macintosh), and dense collages of full-color photography. *IGTimes* covered writers and their *tags* (simple stylized signatures in one color), their *throw-ups* (larger signatures in multiple hues), and their *pieces* (elaborate works that take up an entire wall, short for *masterpieces*), intercut with texts such as updates on South African apartheid and a call to arms against police brutality. In short, *IGTimes* translated what was going on in the streets to the page.

Graffiti began as a way to speak back to the urban development and redlining policies gutting inner-city, often Black neighborhoods in the 1970s and 1980s. While today the art world has capitalized on graffiti, Phase 2 and other early writers were criminalized and labeled vandals in the press. NYC police arrested them based on the broken windows theory, which posited that minor property damage was a precursor to more serious, even violent, offenses—a tactic widely criticized today for overpolicing communities of color.

As New York City gentrified, efforts like the 1989 Clean Train Movement threatened to erase the collective "I am here" layered onto the landscape by a generation of disenfranchised urban youth. *IGTimes* risked police persecution to publish artists' pieces before they were buffed away, using print to resist the whitewashing of a vital cultural legacy.

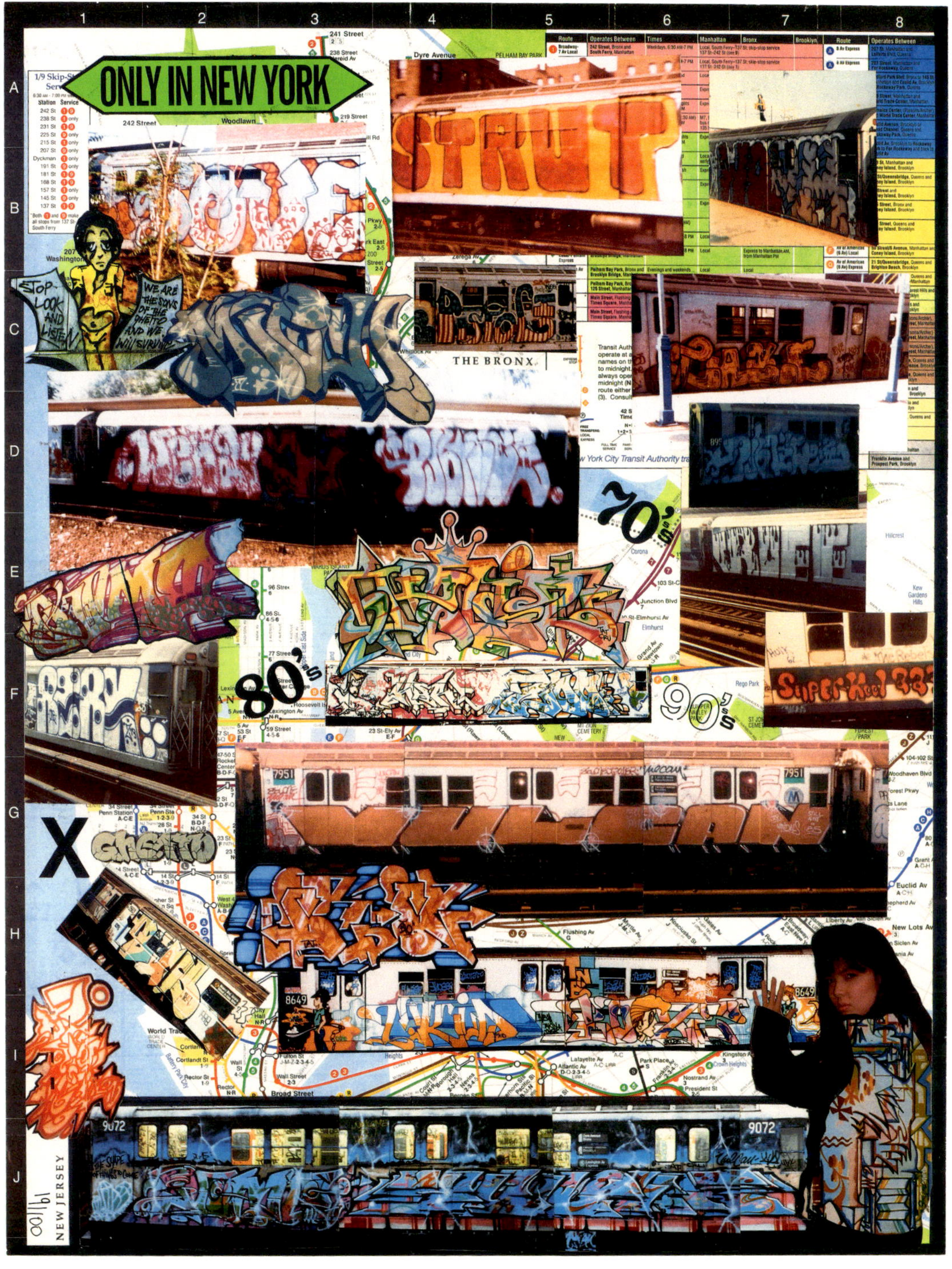

Phase 2 (designer/editor), *IGTimes*, vol. 12, 1991, offset, 22 × 17 inches (56 × 43 cm), New York. Pages 80–81: vol. 14, 1993, offset, 16⅞ × 22 inches (43 × 56 cm), New York.

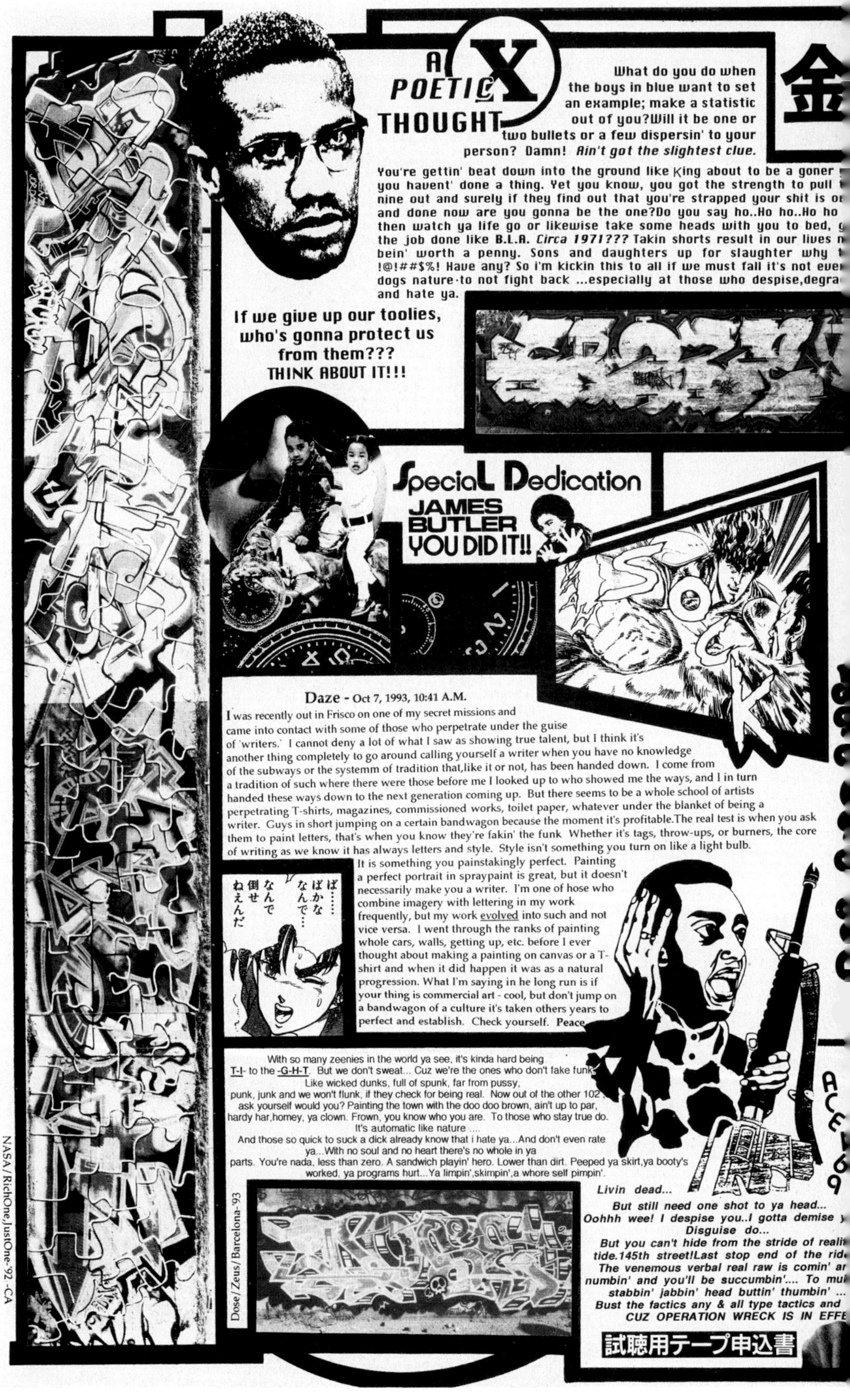

A POETIC X THOUGHT

What do you do when the boys in blue want to set an example; make a statistic out of you?Will it be one or two bullets or a few dispersin' to your person? Damn! *Ain't got the slightest clue.*

You're gettin' beat down into the ground like King about to be a goner you havent' done a thing. Yet you know, you got the strength to pull nine out and surely if they find out that you're strapped your shit is o and done now are you gonna be the one?Do you say ho..Ho ho..Ho ho then watch ya life go or likewise take some heads with you to bed, the job done like B.L.A. *Circa 1971???* Takin shorts result in our lives bein' worth a penny. Sons and daughters up for slaughter why !@!##$%! Have any? So i'm kickin this to all if we must fall it's not eve dogs nature·to not fight back ...especially at those who despise,degra and hate ya.

If we give up our toolies, who's gonna protect us from them??? THINK ABOUT IT!!!

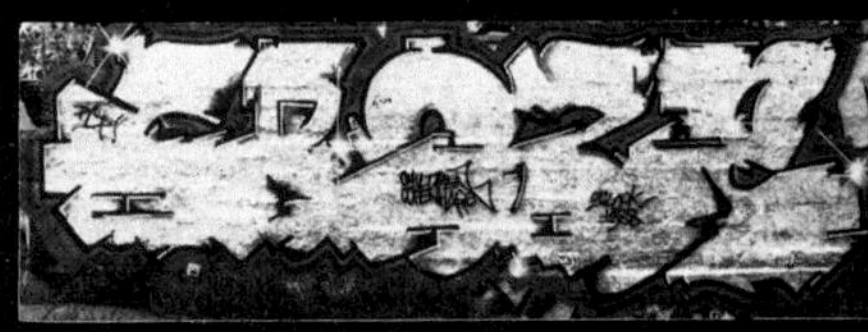

Special Dedication
JAMES BUTLER
YOU DID IT!!

Daze - Oct 7, 1993, 10:41 A.M.

I was recently out in Frisco on one of my secret missions and came into contact with some of those who perpetrate under the guise of 'writers.' I cannot deny a lot of what I saw as showing true talent, but I think it's another thing completely to go around calling yourself a writer when you have no knowledge of the subways or the systemm of tradition that,like it or not, has been handed down. I come from a tradition of such where there were those before me I looked up to who showed me the ways, and I in turn handed these ways down to the next generation coming up. But there seems to be a whole school of artists perpetrating T-shirts, magazines, commissioned works, toilet paper, whatever under the blanket of being a writer. Guys in short jumping on a certain bandwagon because the moment it's profitable.The real test is when you ask them to paint letters, that's when you know they're fakin' the funk Whether it's tags, throw-ups, or burners, the core of writing as we know it has always letters and style. Style isn't something you turn on like a light bulb. It is something you painstakingly perfect. Painting a perfect portrait in spraypaint is great, but it doesn't necessarily make you a writer. I'm one of hose who combine imagery with lettering in my work frequently, but my work evolved into such and not vice versa. I went through the ranks of painting whole cars, walls, getting up, etc. before I ever thought about making a painting on canvas or a T-shirt and when it did happen it was as a natural progression. What I'm saying in he long run is if your thing is commercial art - cool, but don't jump on a bandwagon of a culture it's taken others years to perfect and establish. Check yourself. Peace

ば……
ばかな
なんで……
なんで
倒せ
ねえんだ

With so many zeenies in the world ya see, it's kinda hard being
T-I- to the -G-H-T. But we don't sweat... Cuz we're the ones who don't fake funk
Like wicked dunks, full of spunk, far from pussy,
punk, junk and we won't flunk, if they check for being real. Now out of the other 102
ask yourself would you? Painting the town with the doo doo brown, ain't up to par,
hardy har,homey, ya clown. Frown, you know who you are. To those who stay true do.
It's automatic like nature ....
And those so quick to suck a dick already know that i hate ya...And don't even rate
ya...With no soul and no heart there's no whole in ya
parts. You're nada, less than zero. A sandwich playin' hero. Lower than dirt. Peeped ya skirt,ya booty's
worked, ya programs hurt...Ya limpin',skimpin',a whore self pimpin'.

ACE 69

Livin dead...
But still need one shot to ya head...
Oohhh wee! I despise you..I gotta demise
Disguise do...
But you can't hide from the stride of reali
tide.145th street!Last stop end of the rid
The venemous verbal real raw is comin' a
numbin' and you'll be succumbin'.... To mu
stabbin' jabbin' head buttin' thumbin' ...
Bust the factics any & all type tactics and
CUZ OPERATION WRECK IS IN EFF

試聴用テープ申込書

NASA/ RichOne, JustOne-'92-CA

Dose/ Zeus/ Barcelona-'93

E STATE OF YOUR STATE......

Who run *tings* in the aerosol dominion? We? Dem? Ask yourself or be one gives a fuck not. With all the representation and representatives of the art being used to be ,wanna be, was, a watered down on of the real thing or some shit that resembles something other than the real thing.

If you really do give a damn about the culture...would have to wonder. You gots the "nigga who started ages ago who failed to ion he wasn't jack shit til years later (if he did in fact start when he said he did) syndrome". Then you've got the frequent funk fucko who's forte is .... *well, just that*. Being fake.

there's the quasi-mode-o art gallery goo goo that every misled adolescent wants to emulate and every retarded adult swears is el above any thing you'd actually consider authentic because all they can relate to is Ren and Stimpy or Daffy and Buggs.

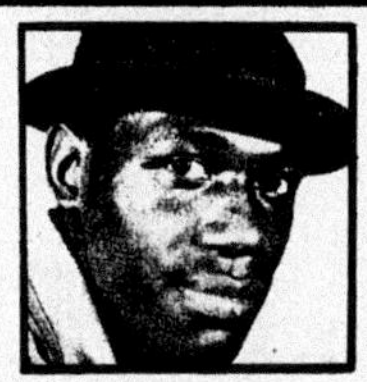

Are you following me gee?

Where does this leave.. The Real Nigs???

Oh, we forgot to mention those little devilish so called experts who got all of the above riding their dildos for some "fame". *Yo!True-pers better start thinking.*

The longer this shit continues the more the art suffers. Wether we ever give a fuck one way or another if the mainstream "accepts" this culture, is *a dog of a different donut.*

Why if any of "this" is gonna get some public exposure should it be the pure d' bullshit and not the hardest of the hardest live and direct real shit? The booty wipe? That shit is madness. When the fuck are we gonna start rocking and stop jocking? Yep...We is doing this and we is doing that, but by whose guidelines? Whose ideology? It's either some Columbus ass sucker discovering how credible this shit is or us kickin' the ballistics using their logistics.

Enslaved You, Never Gave You, And Ain't Gonna Save You.

We is always waiting around for somebody to put us on instead of putting ourselves on, or we think that this thing can live on the art itself and needs no explaining, that it is an entity that exists solely because niggas is painting and that's it. But that's not it. Standing up for the culture isn't gonna happen simply because you are nice or you are up, because in the meantime some dick head is writing the script and defining... Technically redefining your past, present, and future. Friends who are enemies and enemies who are friends. So whose call is it? Whose job is it to totally wreck shit from a to z in this domain? You'd better get with it and peep the scenario. You can keep believing that some otha' negroe is going to take care of your shit for you....But in the mean time the house is gettin' funkier and funkier and we ain't talkin George Clinton.

So......What cha gonna do about it???

"WORD TO HERB"

Don't let that "where were you in 73' shit" fool you.
Some who claim to have been down were either : crayon kings, super duper toys, or not even down at all and are just tryin to give themselves credibility they never earned. To "jock-ey" for position you're not in line for is the ultimate weak wack. If you were there the proofs in the mix. If you weren't....Don't even try it... Beware and fuck a funk fakin' faggot! To dope zines...Don't deal with dopes.

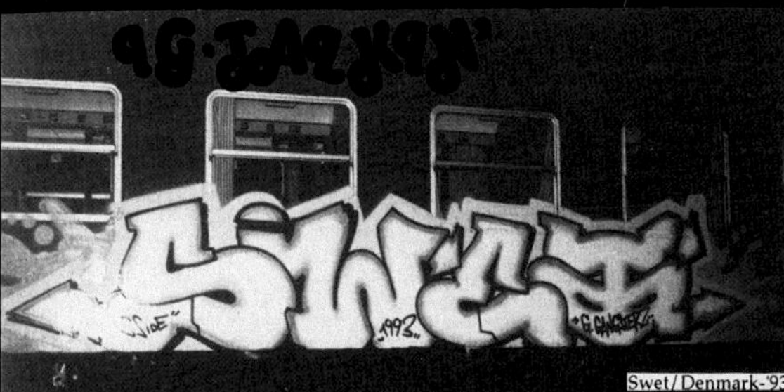

Swet/Denmark-'93

AEROSOL ENDEAVORS

So if you ask some of the so called writers in old New York, they'd say you "subway trainless writers" on earth are in no way writers at all. What an intelligent deduction! More like ignorant, considering the fact that tons of the art which exists (even in New York), country & worldwide and keeps the art alive is portrayed on the walls. Ignorance is the one factor that "killed" the art in N.Y.C. and more ignorance like this *mickey mouse theory of who's who* will only further suppress & stagnate the progress & visibility of the aerosol culture. The whole idea is to paint...somewhere, someplace. If that doesn't happen, the art is dead. Obviously, how such a statement got by in a magazine in a city where "walls rule" is subject to question. We need to push this culture wherever & however we can, to bring the credibility it already has to a wider audience. All the books that claim to be "the definitive" documentive sources, fall far short of educating , and only serve as a mythical dramatization of the true facts that surround its birth & evolution. Hopefully the time will come when some folks with some real integrity will put something together, from the first hand experience and not like most "American History" books, which serves as a false record of someone else's reality.

EDEC / Miami Fl-'93

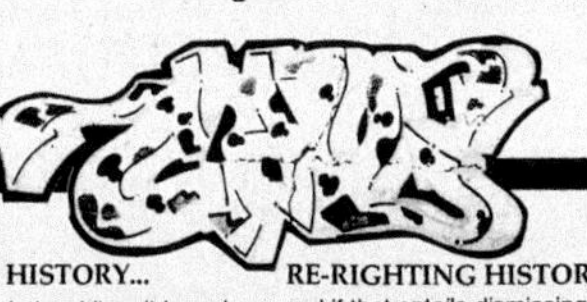

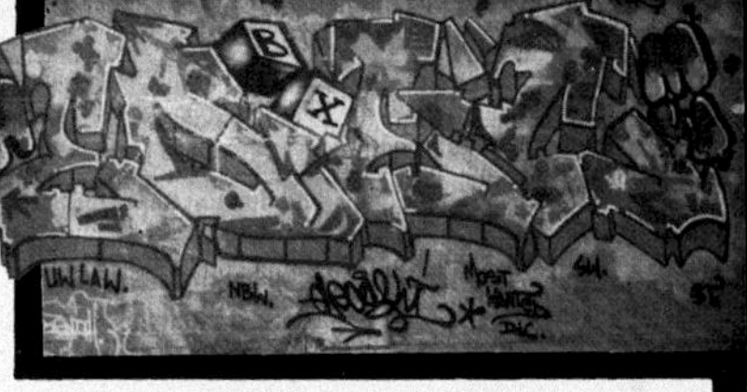

DA' REAL HISTORY... RE-RIGHTING HISTORY 101

Our job is to kick the shit as it is and was and if that entails dismissing some other publications "rendition of the facts" wether intentional or an over sight ,then so be it. Contrary to what was written in the current **Flashbacks**, let it be known that **TAKI 183** himself said that his seeing the name **JULIO 204** around is what inspired him; and though Taki initiated marker tagging on the subways, it is without question the acts of those who took that to a "whole nother" level {i.e.. Hitting sides of trains and using spray paint,bombing.} That "created " the culture in the light we see it today. The main criticism is the insinuation that the first top to bottom whole cars {not trains} being initiated in 1979. This is totally false. The concept of painting a top to bottom/whole car was initiated by **SUPERKOOL 223** in 1972, followed by **LIL HAWK 149**...{According to who you talk to either or} and without question **HONDO ONE**. did a top to bottom, end to end. Between that time and 1976 you had **COMET, BLADE** and a host of others doing tons of whole cars and "double whole cars". That concept was executed by all **JIVE 161** who used two coupled cars to complete his whole title. Technically speaking long before **CAINE 1** and **THE FABULOUS FIVE, JAPAN 1** did ten top to bottoms on one train. {INDS}. Despite them not being quite as elaborate is another story. The fact is that he did it first. The bottom line is that if your gonna write about roots and the facts you should know them or at least explain them in the right context.

...ast thing want to do is be at war with our contemporaries ...BUT

SOUTH AFRICA UP DATE

The recent election is a historical victory for the massive of South Africans, yet it is an easy mirage for the so-called democratic peoples of the world. The repressive state apparatus is still in tact, the white minority still has the right to veto, and of course, the De Beers are still pushing diamonds off the backs of the poor. (How else do you think the multi-nationals balance their books?) The ANC government will lead struggles to correct the constitution and to improve the living conditions of the masses, yet there are no guarantees. The international capitalist situation will take credit more jobs, as the word is out that "*there are only black faces in white places.*" The trump up tribes and the white volkstaat fascist will try to de stablize any democratic gains.

Don't be mistaken about the descents of the mighty Zulus who commented carnage on the British empire the same time as the Sioux wiped out Custer. If you know your history, it was the white Afrikaners who took advantage of the situation, defeated the British, eventually bought out the Zulus and thus created the apartheid state. In today's globe bloodlines can only take credit for your sorry-ass looks. Believe it or not, it's culture, a world-wide, motherfucking, fighting, peoples' culture, that is needed. Give foundations (leave the props at home) to the Zulu hip hop international. Check out the movement returning to the land where it all started. Hip hop has its inroads on the cape among the children of the so-called coloreds, whom the media claim supports the white nationalist party Send $4 for an issue; $48 for 12 of South African hip hop zine: Da Juice. T.E.A.C.H.Project, PO. Box 31184, Grassy Park 7945, Capetown 8000, South Africa. Send a hip communiqué':fax(021) 475385

EMILE Y X ?

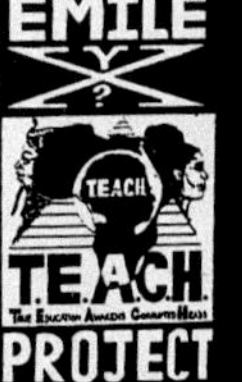

PROJECT

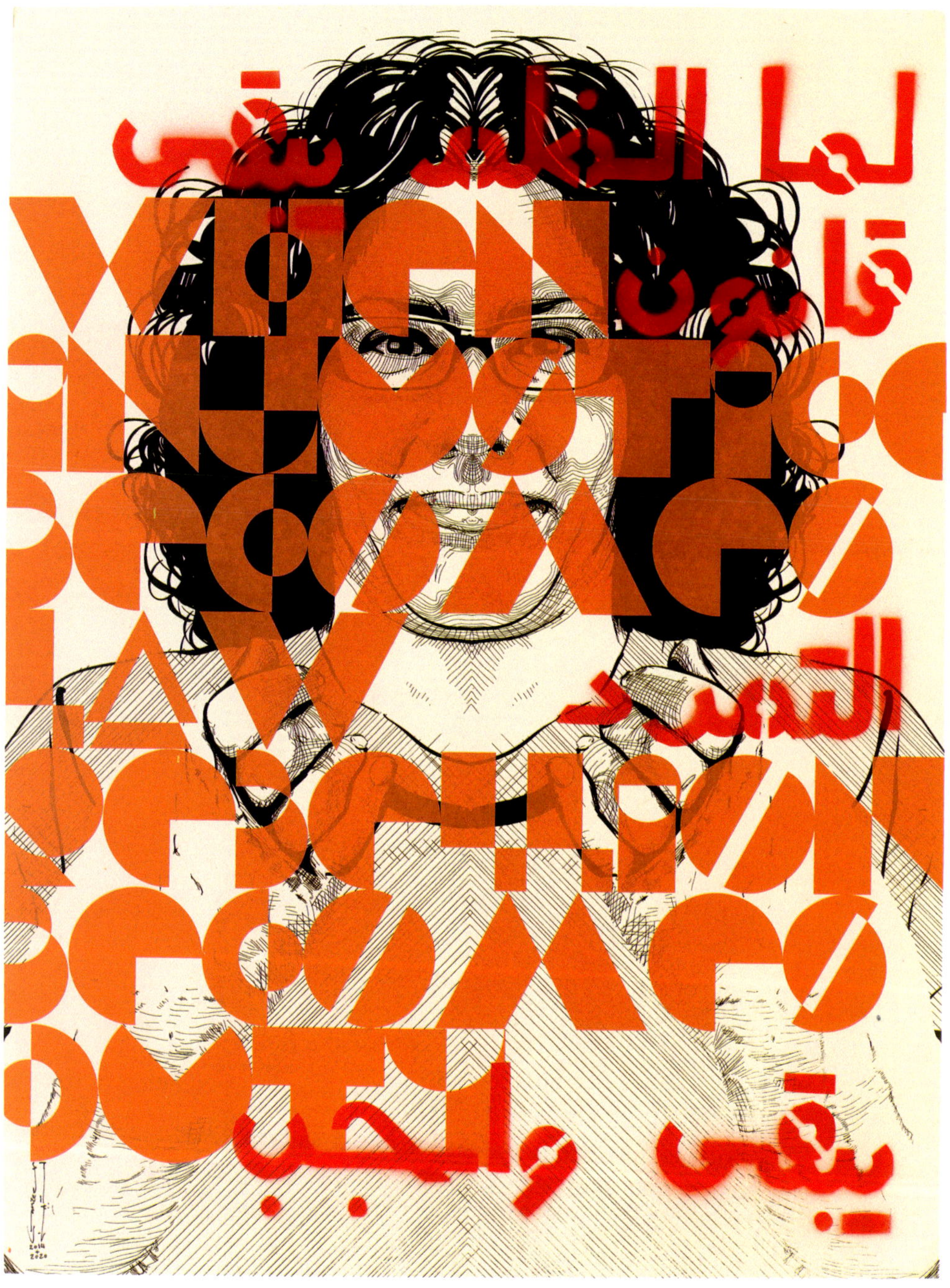

Ganzeer, *Justice for Mona*, from the *Of Course the Army Protected the Revolution* series, 2020, Houston. From left to right: final print, spray paint on screen print, 25 × 19 inches (63.5 × 48.5 cm), and sketch with ink and colored pencil (top) and hand-cut stencil with spray paint (bottom), both 11 × 17 inches (28 × 43 cm).

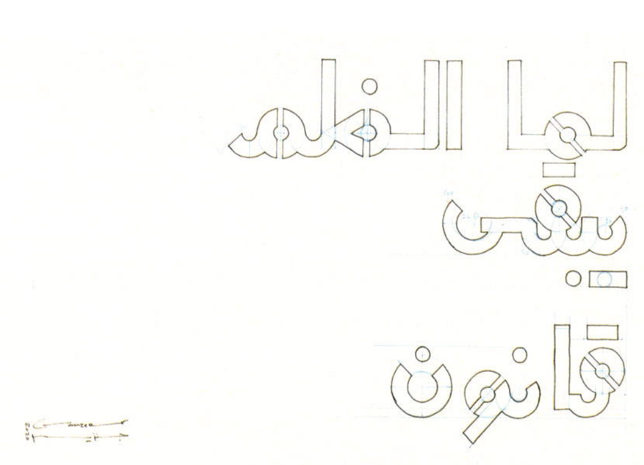

In *Of Course the Army Protected the Revolution*, Egyptian-born muralist and activist Ganzeer presented a series of posters featuring portraits of four Egyptian citizens, each of whom had been brutalized by police during the 2011 uprising against President Hosni Mubarak now known as the January Revolution. The victims depicted are Mona Eltahawy (whose arms were both broken); Ahmed Harara (who lost both eyes to shotgun wounds in separate protests; see page 12); Emad Effat (a popular sheik who was shot and killed); and the Blue Bra Lady, an anonymous woman who was tragically beaten and forcibly exposed, as documented in a media image that enraged thousands online.

Each poster features the phrase "When injustice becomes law, rebellion becomes duty" spray-painted in Arabic and silk-screened in English. Ganzeer created the Arabic text with a custom hand-cut stencil. It is a very contemporary interpretation of the oldest of Arabic calligraphic scripts: Kufic, prevalent starting in the seventh century and known for its rectilinear qualities, as well as Naskh, a round script that originated around the same time. Ganzeer screen-printed the English translation in geometric, almost modular forms, echoing graphic ornamental motifs that are visual pillars in Arab art and culture. The layering of orange and red, and the near obfuscation of the subjects' faces with text, heightens the sense of urgency and warning—as well as the responsibility called for in the message.

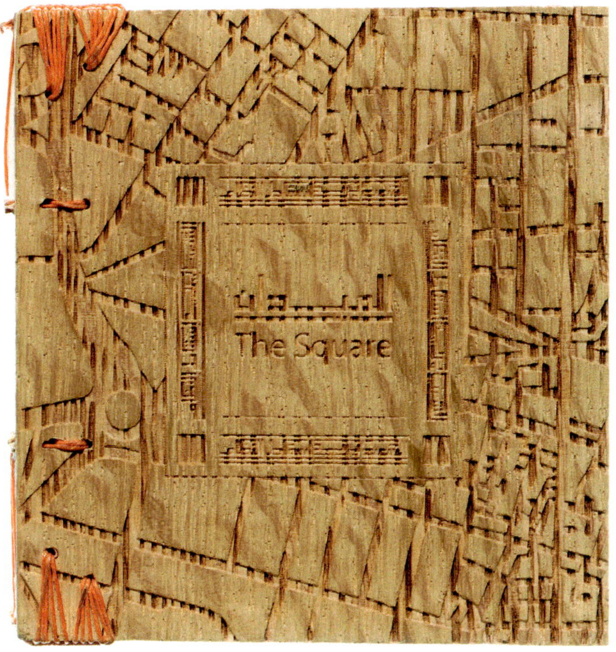

Islam Aly, *The Square* (*Al Midan*), 2014, laser-etched wood with coptic binding and laser-cut paper, 4½ × 4½ × 2⅞ inches (11.5 × 11.5 × 7.5 cm), Iowa City, Iowa. This artist book is named after Cairo's Tahrir Square, the site of the 2011 Egyptian uprising. Aly etched a map of Cairo into the wood cover and laser-cut the chant "The people want to bring down the regime" ("al-sha'b yurid isqat al-nizam") in Kufic script into the book's pages (see pages 86–87).

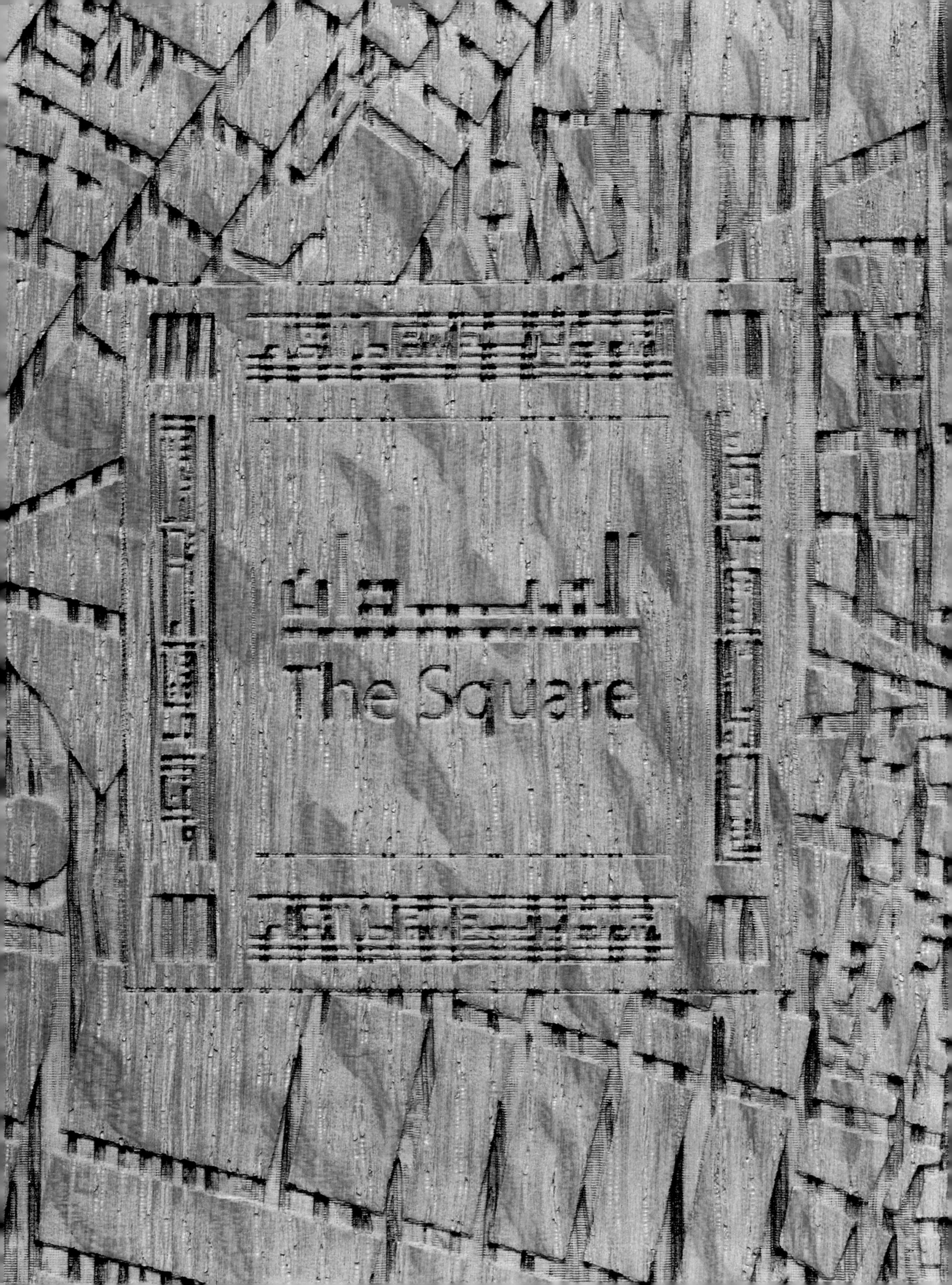
The Square

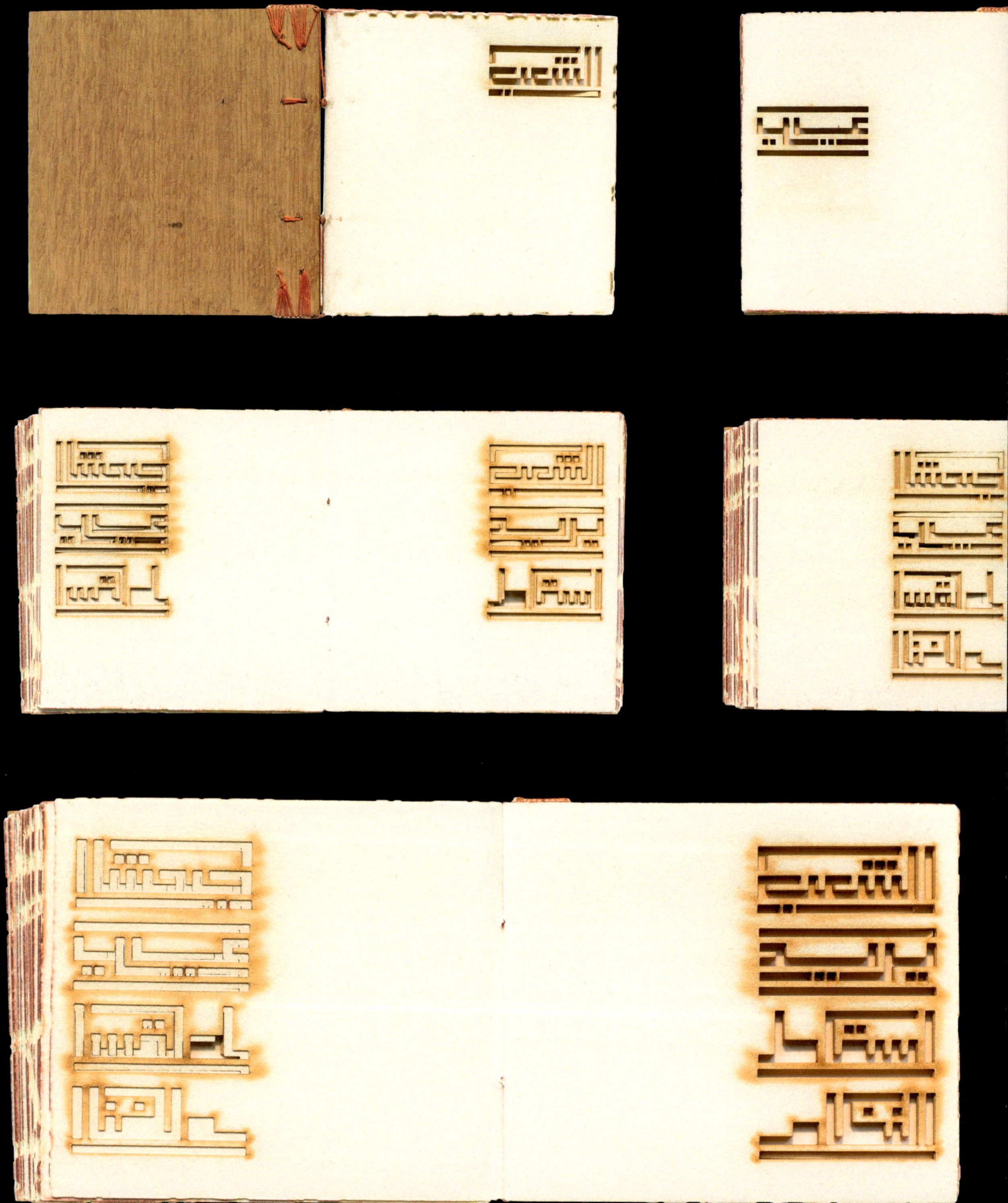

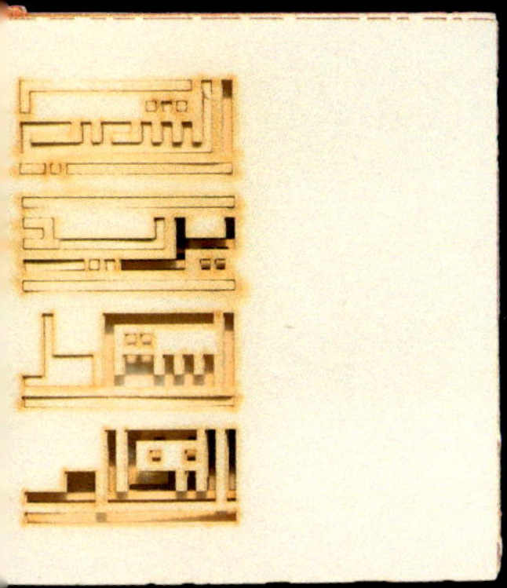

“The book is a documentation of the chant ‘The people want to bring down the regime.’ Lasercutting the words gives them a faded effect, which mimics the voices. At the end, the chant fills up the whole page.”

—Islam Aly on his book *The Square*, 2022

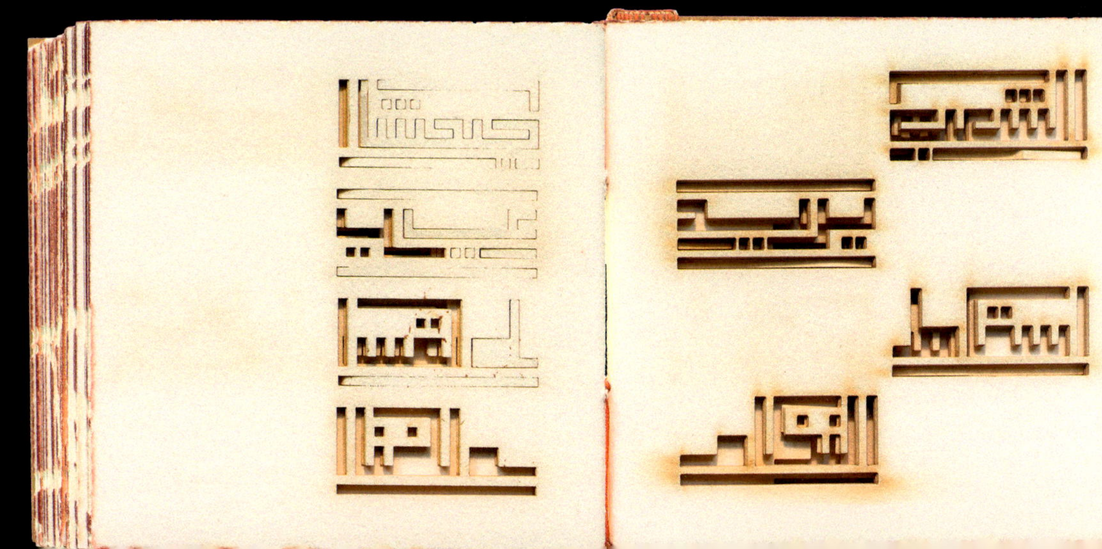

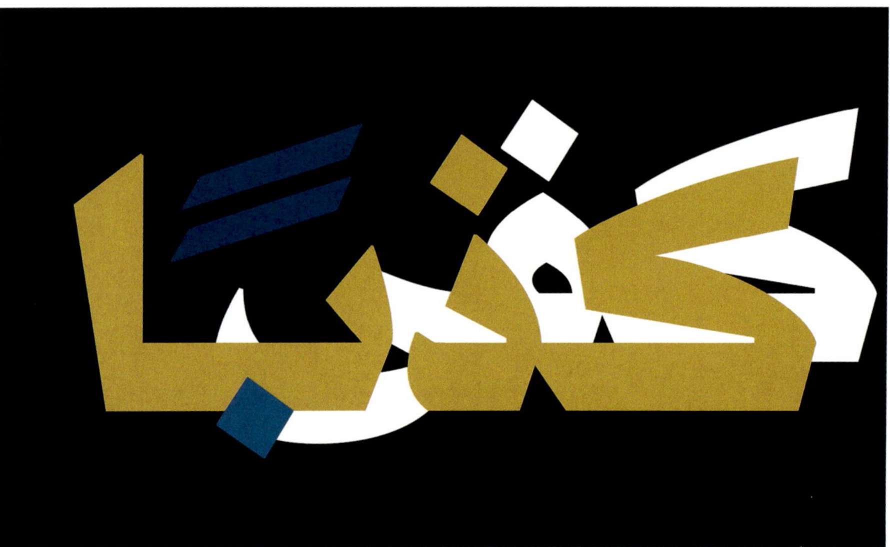

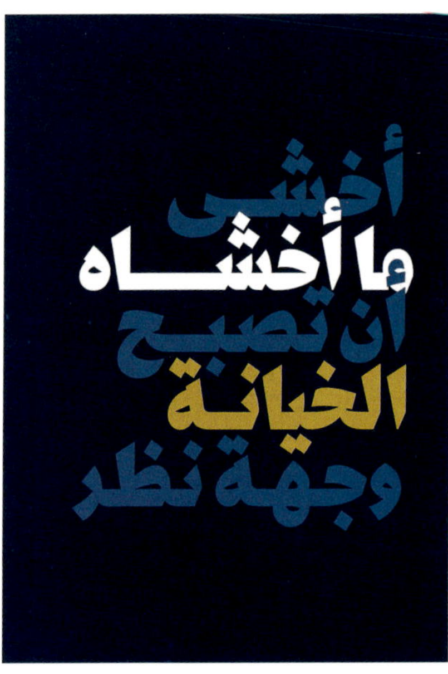

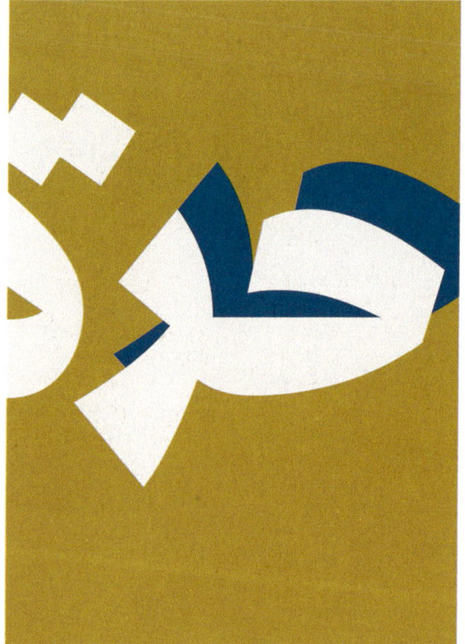

Nadine Chahine, digital samples of Kafa, Arabic Type Foundry, 2018, digital font, London. With a name that means *enough* in Arabic, Kafa joins a recent trend in Arabic type design, in which the script is pushed to extrabold extremes, in this case to echo the shouts of protest. Created in response to President Trump's xenophobic statements, it was distributed for free for use on protest signage.

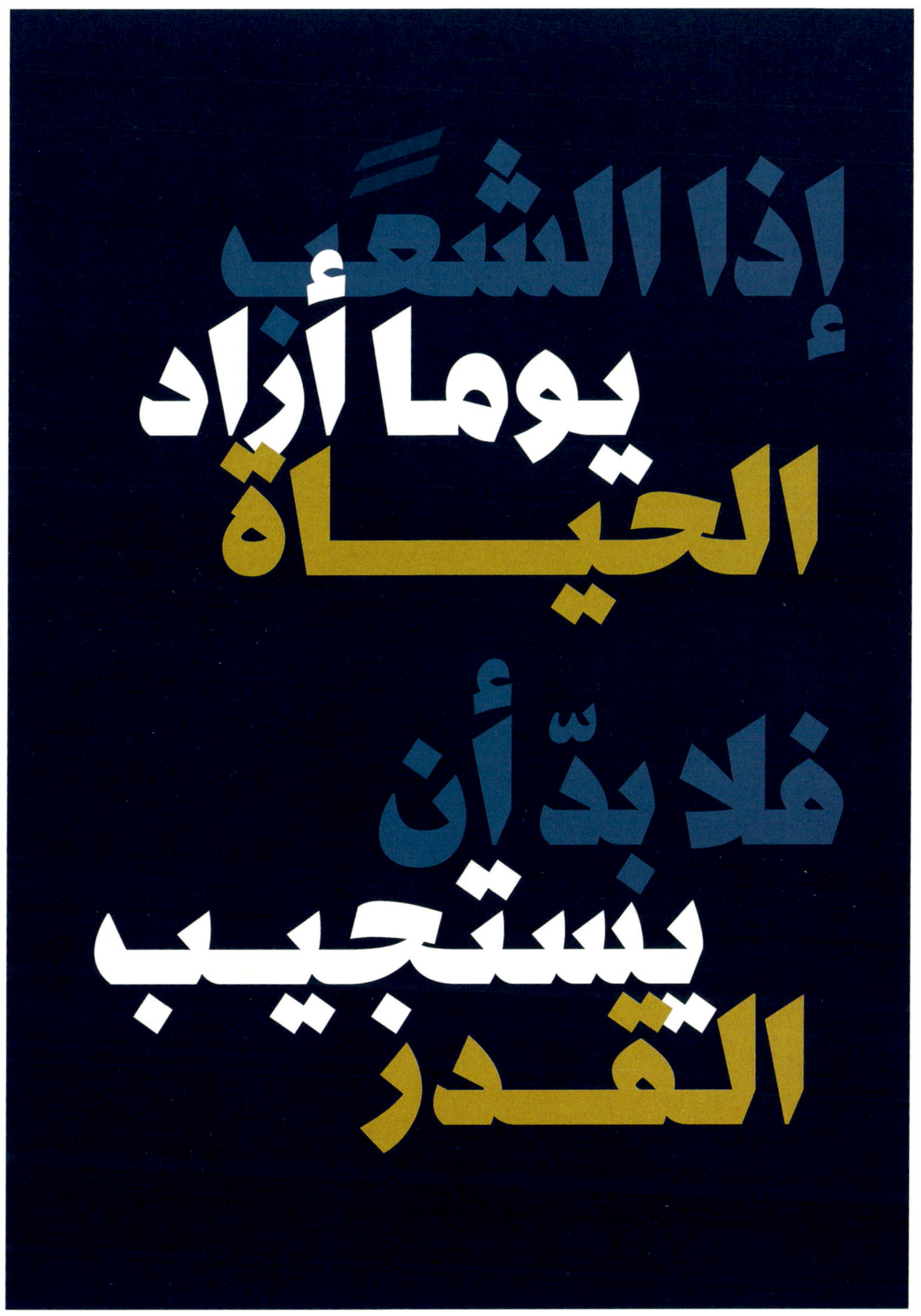
إذا الشعب
يوما أراد
الحياة
فلا بدّ أن
يستجيب
القدر

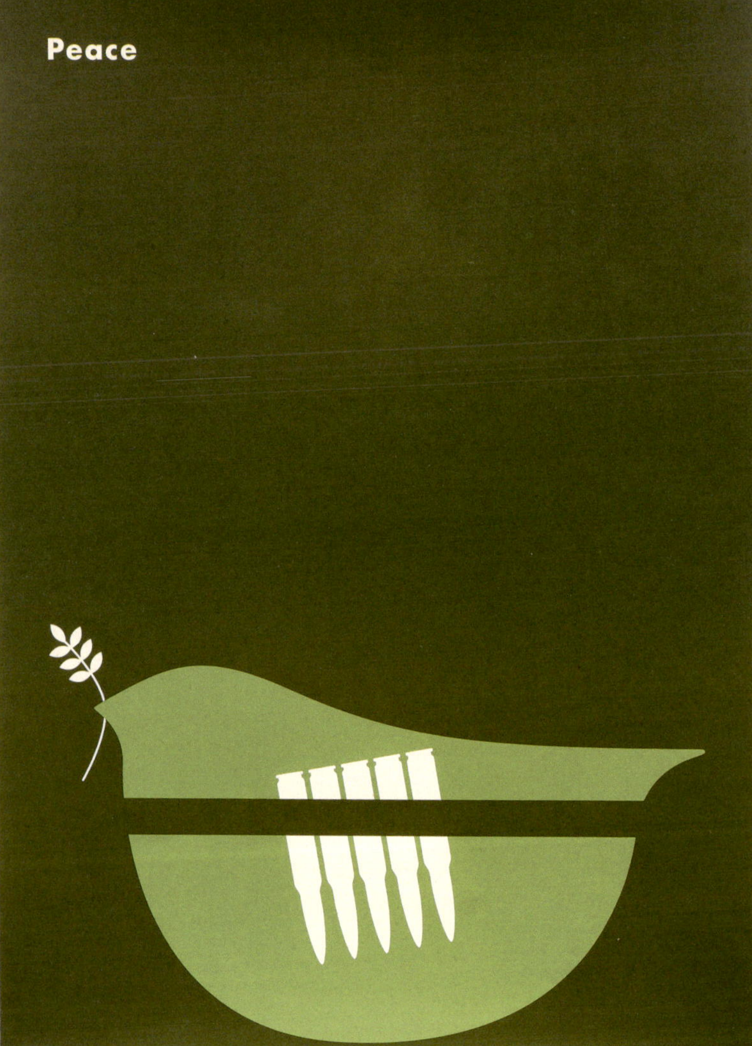
Peace

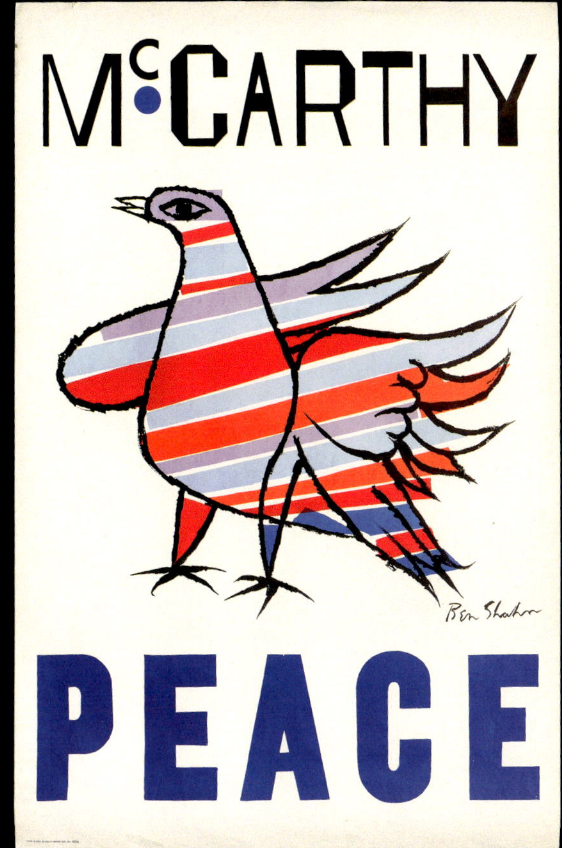

Call and Response

When Eugene McCarthy ran for the Democratic nomination in the 1968 presidential election, his platform was antiwar—he was going to get the United States out of Vietnam. Ben Shahn, the Lithuanian-born American artist best known for his social realist work, created this campaign poster for McCarthy with an illustration of a dove, the international symbol for peace. The name McCarthy appears in Shahn's signature hand style, with its irregular sizes and chaotic placement of thick and thin strokes—except for the curious intrusion of a typeface for the superscript *C*, which is set in Futura. Shahn likely

While Shahn's political poster was anti-Vietnam, Jason Munn's understated 2012 poster is more generally antiwar. Similar to Shahn, Munn employs both an illustration of a dove and the word *peace* (this time set completely in Futura). Working with a palette reminiscent of military fatigues, he turns a classic army helmet upside down to create the bird's silhouette—with an ammunition belt forming its wing—as a metaphor for laying down weapons. When asked about this art, Munn replied, "To me it also represents that the answer is always in the problem—it just depends how you look at it."

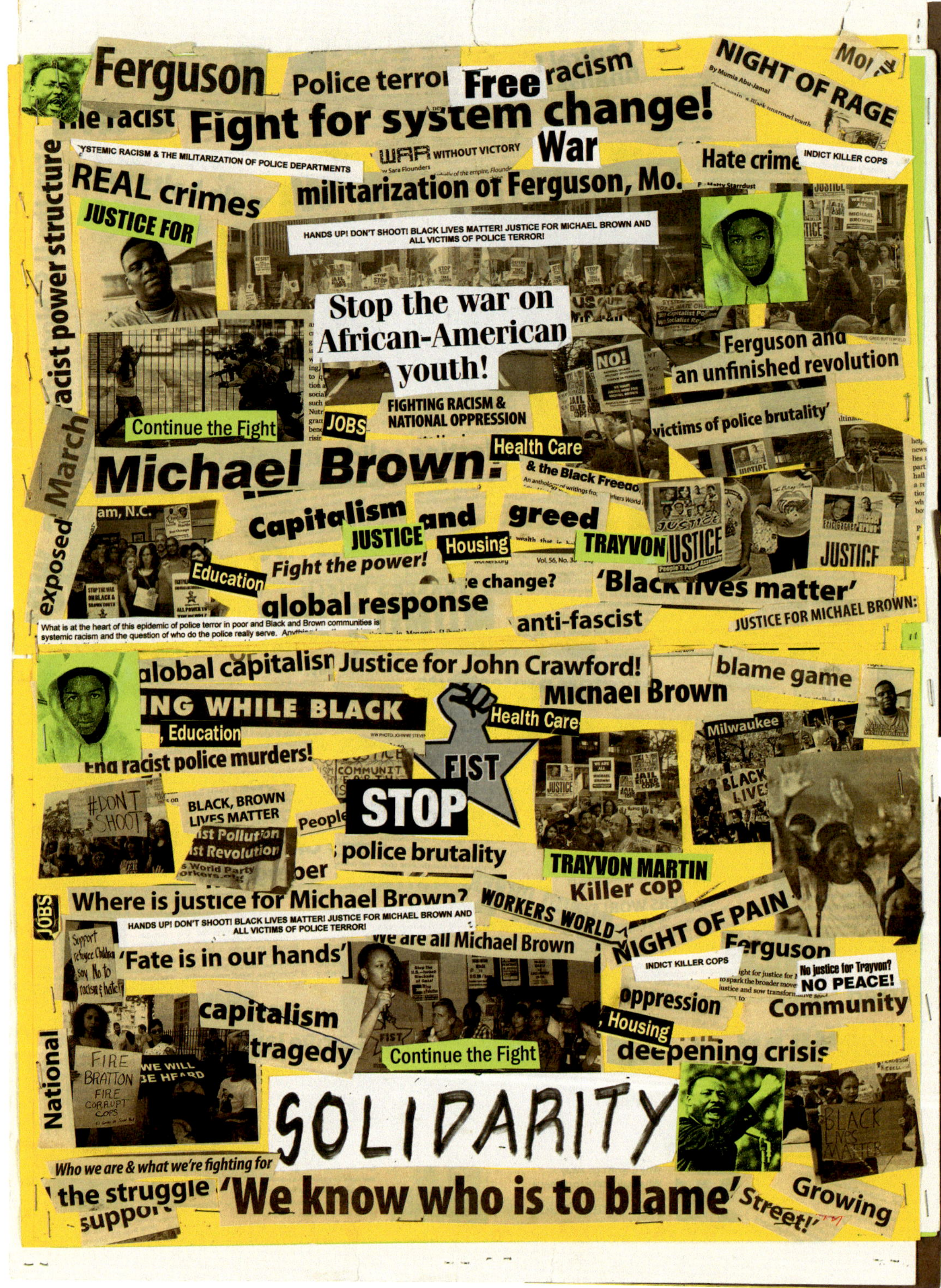
Ferguson
Police terror
Free
racism
NIGHT OF RAGE
By Mumia Abu-Jamal
Fight for system change!
War
SYSTEMIC RACISM & THE MILITARIZATION OF POLICE DEPARTMENTS
WAR WITHOUT VICTORY
Hate crime
INDICT KILLER COPS
REAL crimes
militarization of Ferguson, Mo.
racist power structure
JUSTICE FOR
HANDS UP! DON'T SHOOT! BLACK LIVES MATTER! JUSTICE FOR MICHAEL BROWN AND ALL VICTIMS OF POLICE TERROR!
Stop the war on African-American youth!
Ferguson and an unfinished revolution
FIGHTING RACISM & NATIONAL OPPRESSION
JOBS
Continue the Fight
victims of police brutality'
March
Health Care
Michael Brown:
& the Black Freedom
Capitalism
and
greed
JUSTICE
Housing
TRAYVON
JUSTICE
exposed
Education
Fight the power!
change?
'Black lives matter'
global response
anti-fascist
JUSTICE FOR MICHAEL BROWN:
What is at the heart of this epidemic of police terror in poor and Black and Brown communities is systemic racism and the question of who do the police really serve.
global capitalism
Justice for John Crawford!
blame game
Michael Brown
ING WHILE BLACK
Health Care
, Education
End racist police murders!
FIST
STOP
#DON'T SHOOT
BLACK, BROWN LIVES MATTER
People
police brutality
Milwaukee
BLACK LIVES
TRAYVON MARTIN
Killer cop
JOBS
Where is justice for Michael Brown?
WORKERS WORLD
NIGHT OF PAIN
HANDS UP! DON'T SHOOT! BLACK LIVES MATTER! JUSTICE FOR MICHAEL BROWN AND ALL VICTIMS OF POLICE TERROR!
We are all Michael Brown
'Fate is in our hands'
Ferguson
INDICT KILLER COPS
No justice for Trayvon? NO PEACE!
oppression
Community
capitalism
, Housing
tragedy
Continue the Fight
deepening crisis
National
FIRE BRATTON FIRE CORRUPT COPS
WE WILL BE HEARD
SOLIDARITY
BLACK LIVES MATTER
Who we are & what we're fighting for
the struggle
support
'We know who is to blame'
Street!'
Growing

In October of 2014, hundreds of protesters gathered in St. Louis to march 12 miles to Ferguson, Missouri, to honor the life and protest the death of Michael Brown, who was murdered by police while unarmed in August of that year. The event was dubbed the "Weekend of Resistance," and it attracted protesters from across the country, including Sara E. Benjamin, a young Black mother of a five-year-old daughter named Imari.

Starting in Baltimore, Benjamin and her child carpooled with other protesters for more than 800 miles on a budget of $100 to demonstrate with fellow activists. When they arrived at the Justice for All Rally at the end of the march, news broke that yet another young St. Louis Black man, Vonderrit Myers, Jr., had been fatally shot by a white police officer.

Benjamin's handmade poster is frenetic, dynamic, and layered, using typographic and photographic clippings from a series of newspaper articles. She layers these with digital prints on fluorescent green paper over bright yellow posterboard, with her own lettering in felt-tip marker along the bottom: SOLIDARITY. Widely accessible fonts, like Impact and Myriad, referencing the public-generated messages of internet memes and social media posts, mix with the headlines of established press.

In her collage, Benjamin includes the name and image of Trayvon Martin, a Black seventeen-year-old who was murdered in Florida in 2012. The acquittal of his killer, George Zimmerman, who claimed self-defense although Martin was unarmed, spawned the first use of a now historic hashtag: Black Lives Matter. Coined by Black activists Alicia Garza and Patrisse Cullors, the phrase has become the rallying cry for a loose coalition of activists demanding an end to racially motivated police brutality. In 2020, after the state murders of Breonna Taylor and George Floyd, these words found their way onto the signs of more than 15 million protesters.

Benjamin's considerable personal labor and long pilgrimage reflect demonstrators' commitment to voicing their heartbreak and outrage. As we continue to grapple with the failures of our justice system, her sign suggests that the design process can perhaps provide catharsis. In aggregating the endless headlines into a tool against racism, one may find solace and power.

Sara E. Benjamin, untitled poster for a Black Lives Matter protest, 2014, newsprint and digital print collage on paperboard with metal staples, 24 × 18 inches (61 × 46 cm), Baltimore. Collection of the Smithsonian National Museum of African American History and Culture.

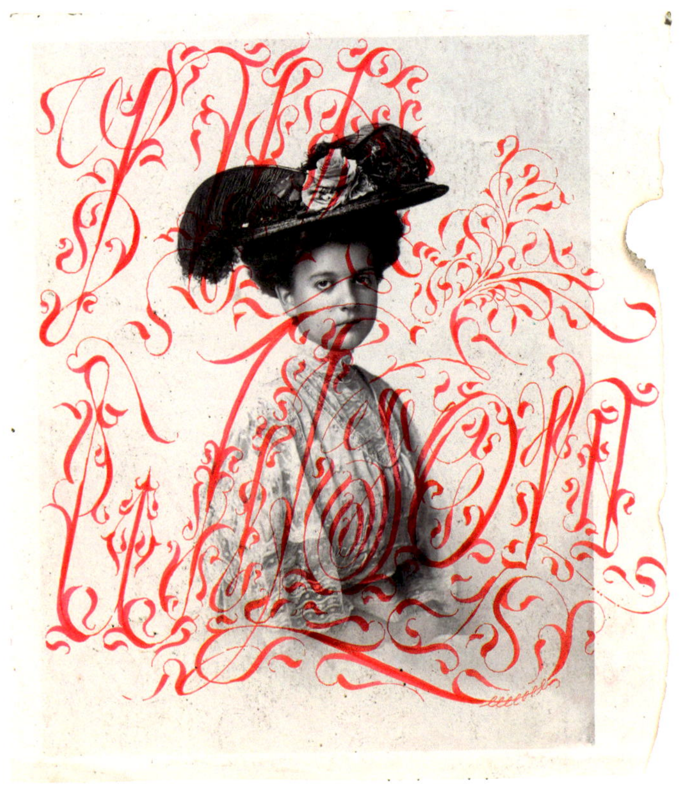

Hunter Saxony III, a.k.a. the Last Black Calligrapher in SF, untitled work from the series *Nia Wilson/Say Her Name/No Silence*, 2020, ink on vintage magazine paper, 9¾ × 8⅝ inches (25 × 22 cm), San Francisco. Saxony created this piece in response to the 2018 racially motivated murder of eighteen-year-old Nia Wilson at a transit station in Oakland, California. Her name appears in nineteenth century–style red calligraphy over a burned image of a wealthy Southern woman, taken during the post-slavery Reconstruction era.

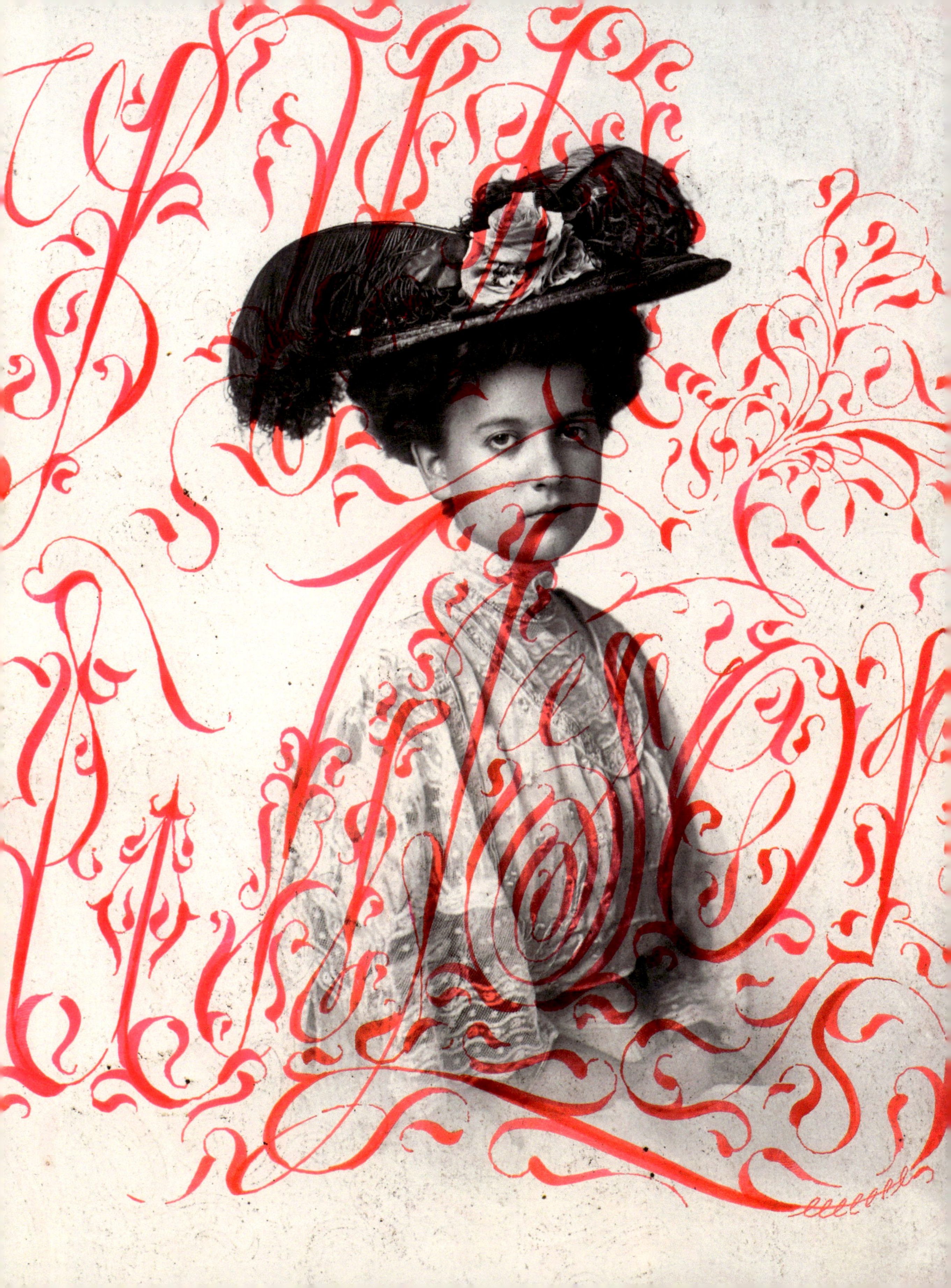

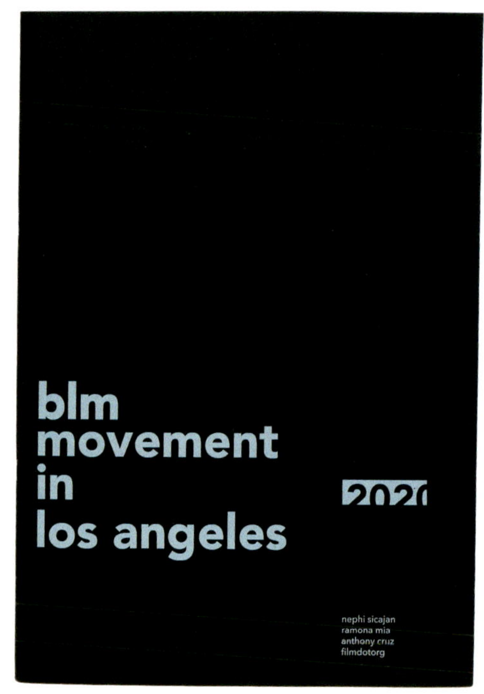
blm
movement
in
los angeles
2020
nephi sicajan
ramona mia
anthony cruz
filmdotorg

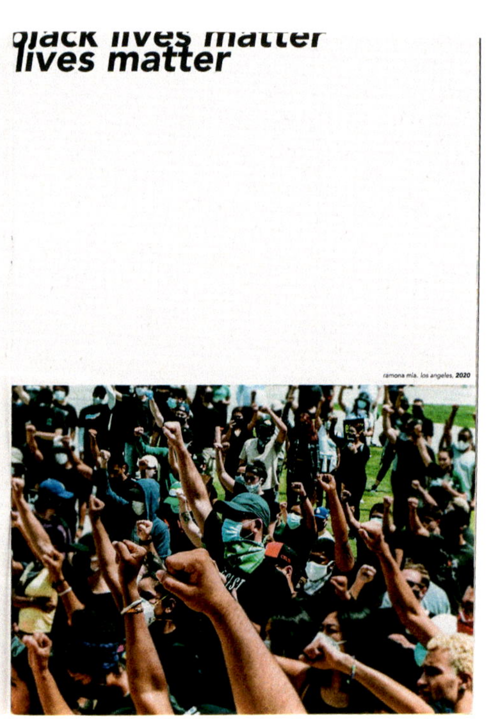
lives matter
ramona mia. los angeles, 2020

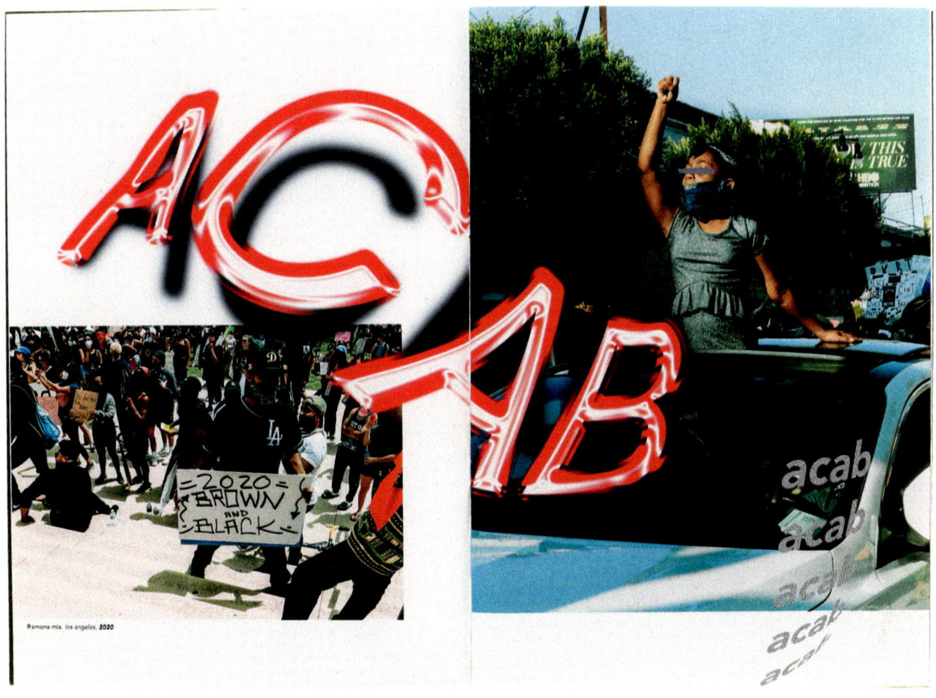

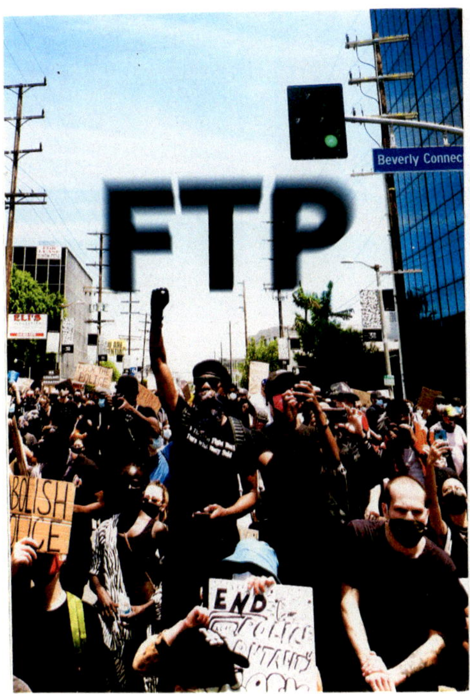

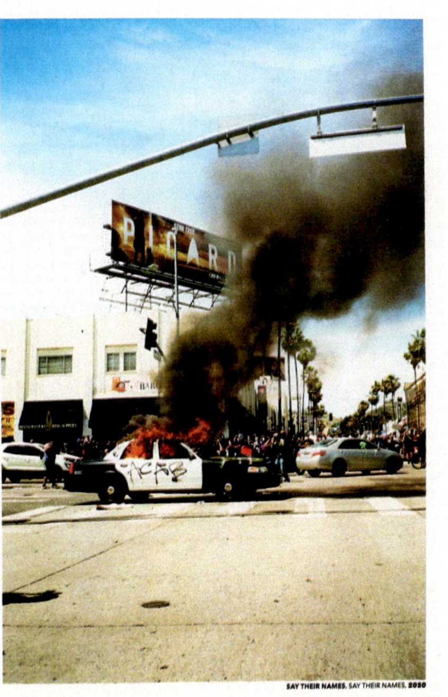

Nephi Sicajan (designer), Ramona Mia, Anthony Cruz, and Michael Sandoval (photographers), *BLM Movement in Los Angeles*, 2020, digital printing, 11⅝ × 8¼ inches (29.5 × 21 cm), Los Angeles. This zine overlays protest photos with digitally manipulated type that amplifies slogans from the crowd.

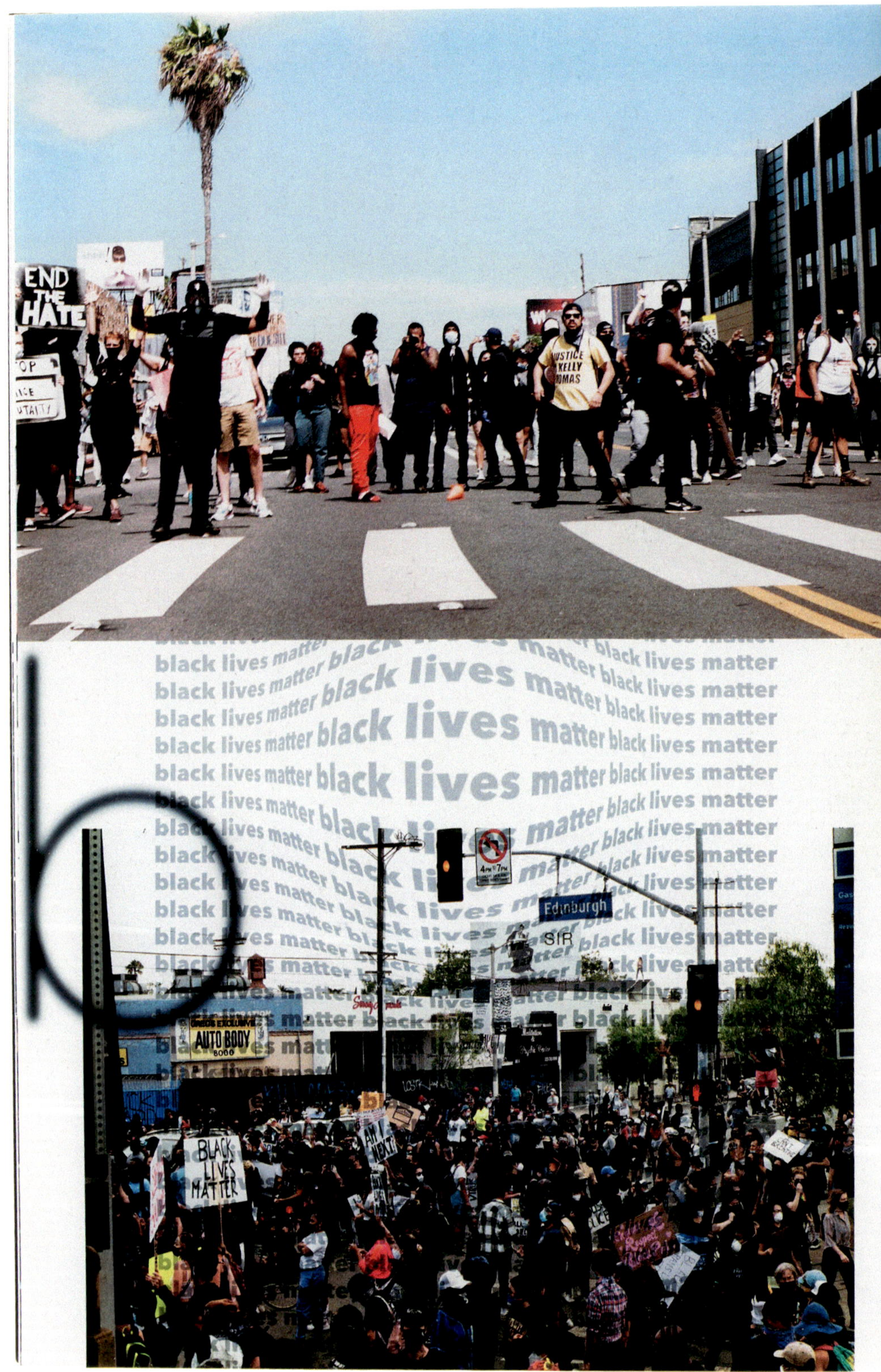
END THE HATE
JUSTICE KELLY THOMAS
black lives matter
Edinburgh
SIR
AUTO BODY
BLACK LIVES MATTER
AM I NEXT?

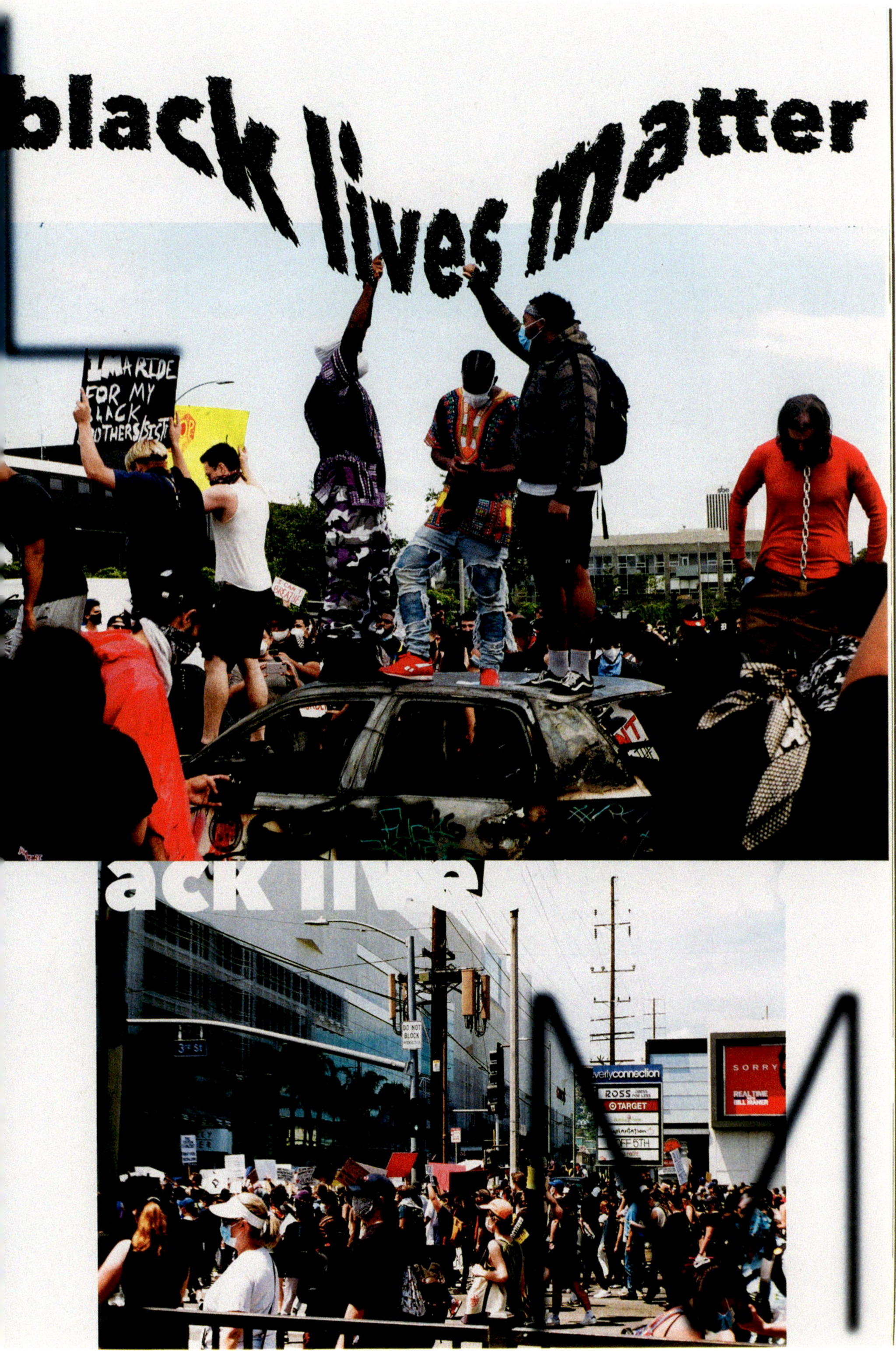
black lives matter
I'M A RIDE
FOR MY
BLACK
BROTHERS/SISTE
SORRY
REAL TIME
BILL MAHER
ROSS
TARGET
3rd St
DO NOT BLOCK

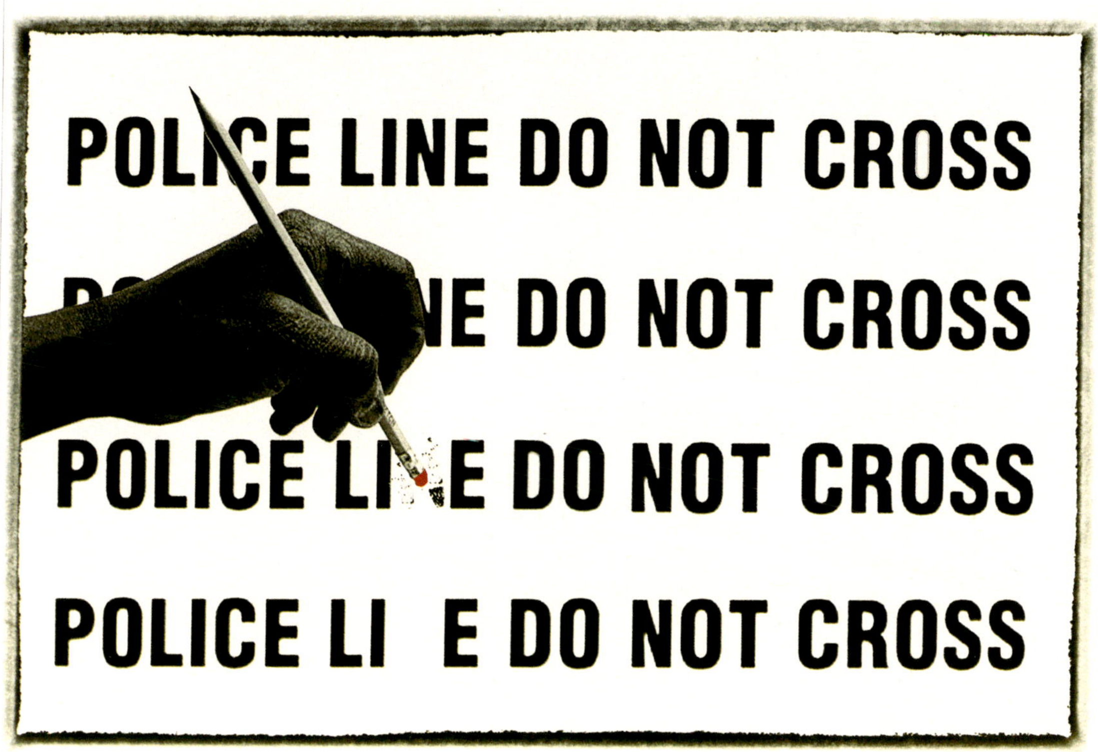

Chip Thomas, *Police Lie*, 2016, digital print, 16 × 24 inches (40.5 × 61 cm), Flagstaff, Arizona. This poster protests the disproportionate number of Black people who die at the hands of U.S. police, showing a pencil eraser transforming the common crime-scene message from "Police line" to "Police lie."

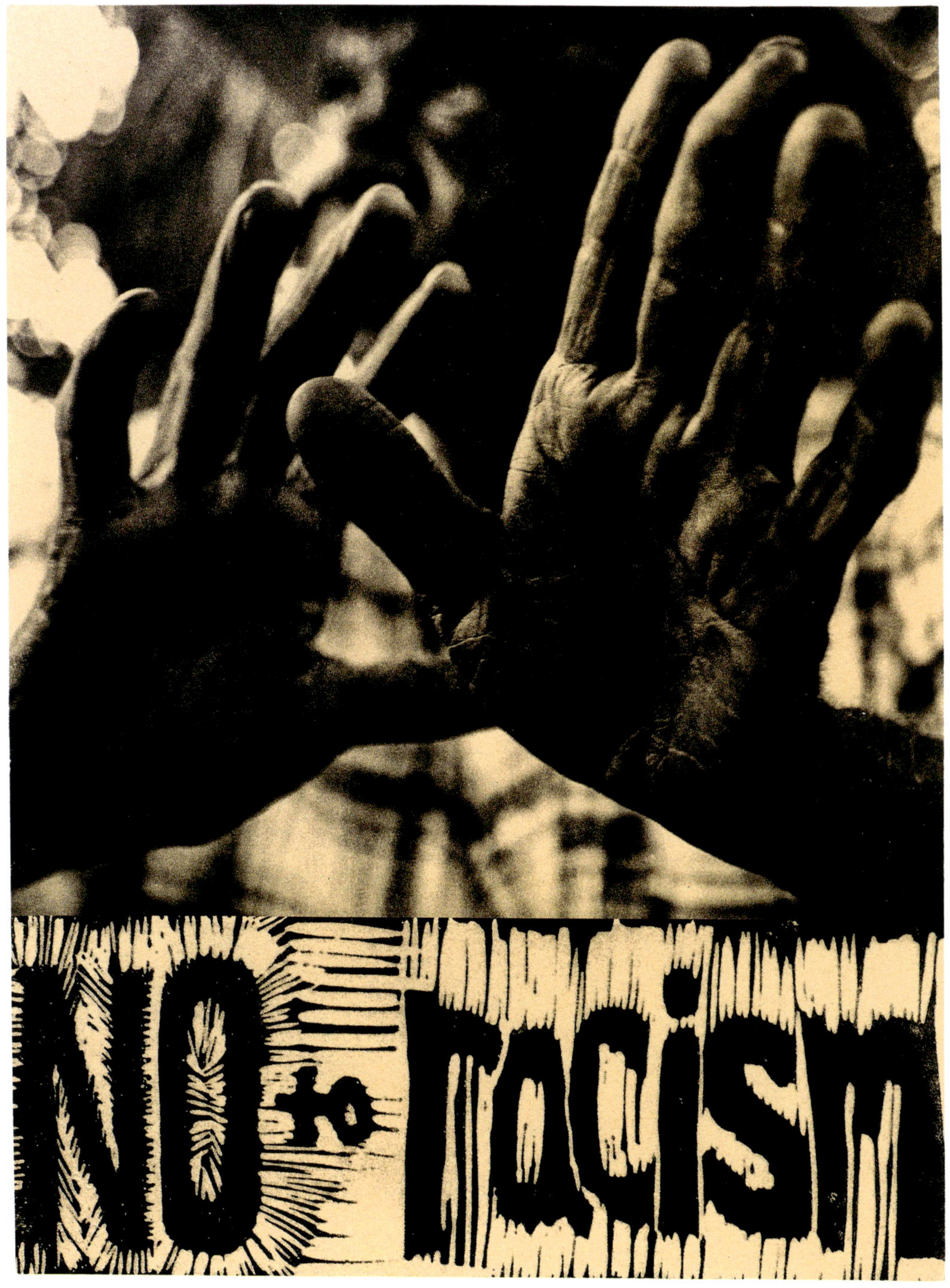

Chip Thomas (designer and photographer), Thea Gahr (linocut artist and printer), *No to Racism*, 2018, screen print, 23⅞ × 18 inches (61 × 45.5 cm), Chicago. In this collaboration designed by Thomas for the Social Medicine Consortium, Gahr cut in the letterforms within a pattern of hand-carved lines that echo the lines of the hands in the photograph.

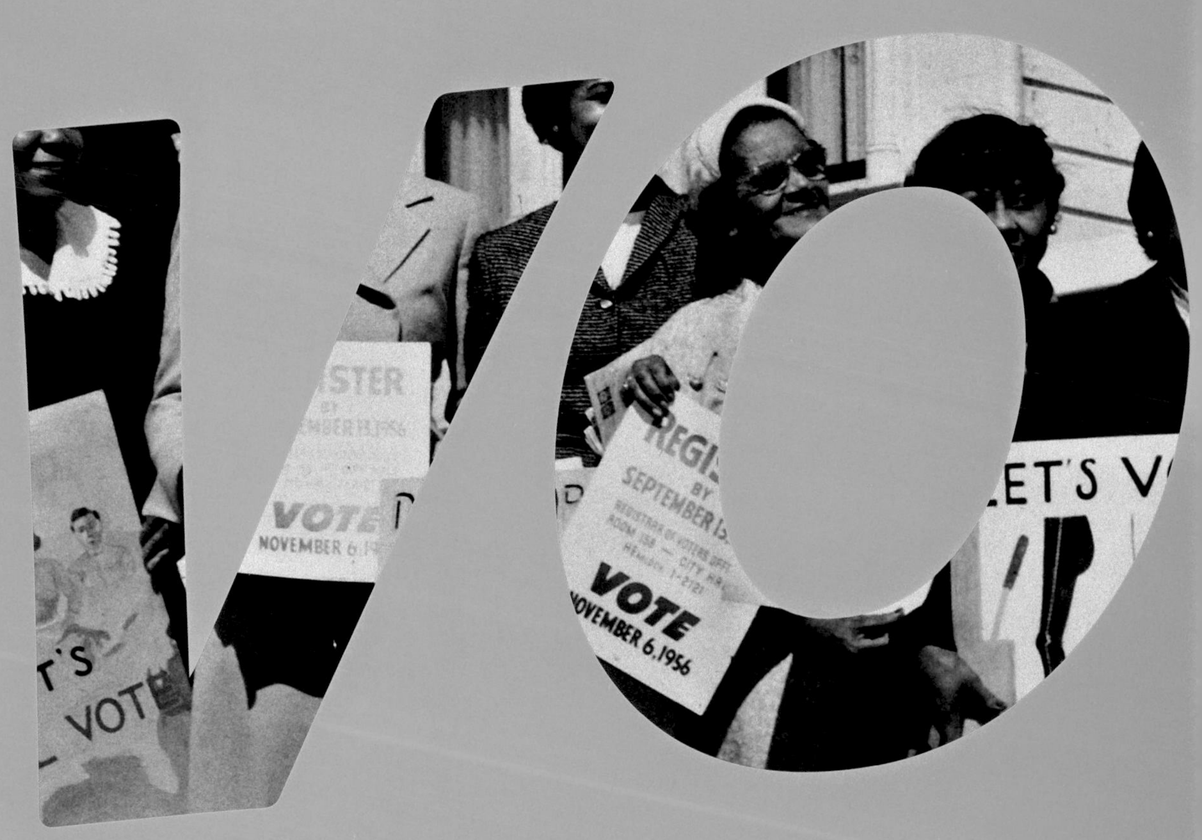
VOTE
BY
VOTE
NOVEMBER 6,1956
LET'S

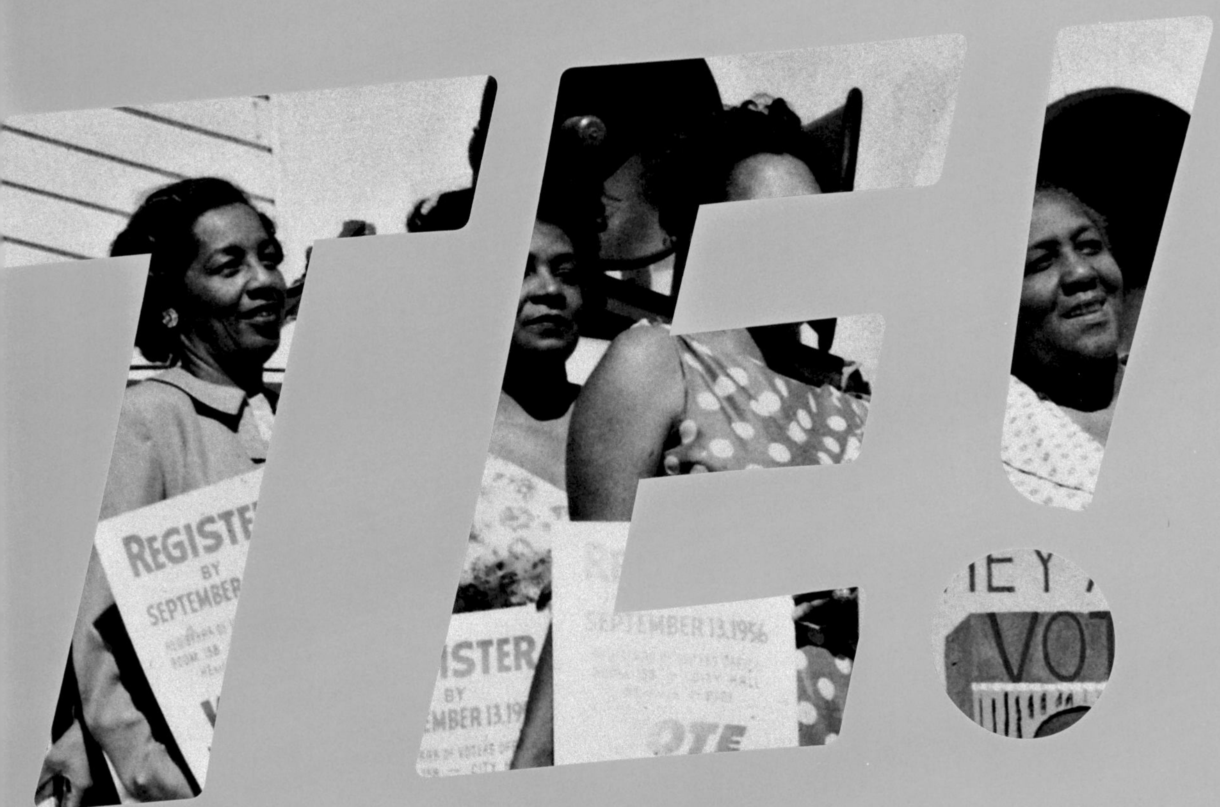
TE!
REGISTE
BY
SEPTEMBER
ISTER
BY
EMBER 13,195
SEPTEMBER 13,1956
VOT

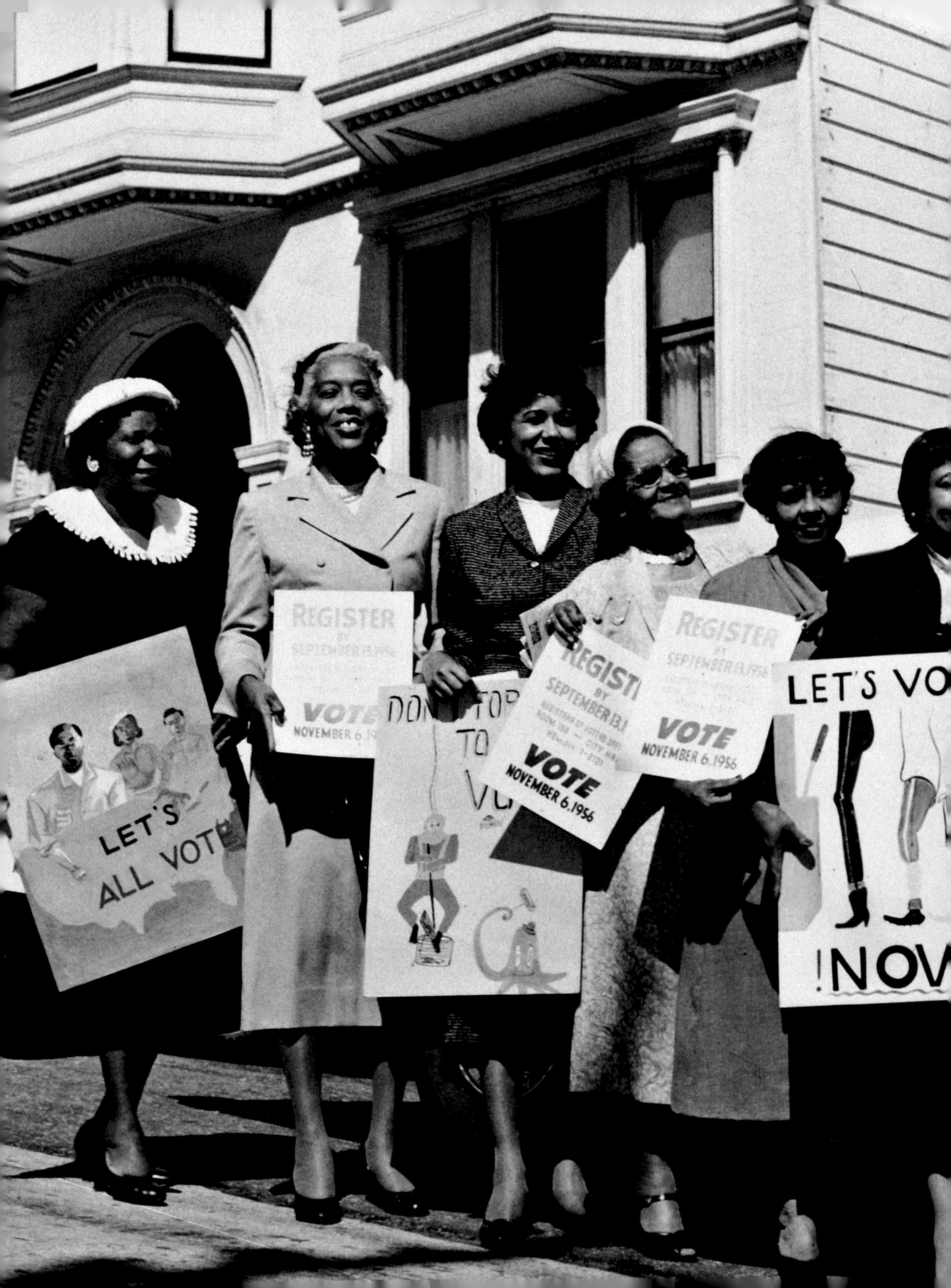
LET'S
ALL VOT
REGISTER
BY
SEPTEMBER 13, 1956
VOTE
NOVEMBER 6, 19
DON
FOR
TO
REGISTI
BY
SEPTEMBER 13,
VOTE
NOVEMBER 6, 1956
REGISTER
BY
SEPTEMBER 13, 1956
VOTE
NOVEMBER 6, 1956
LET'S VO
!NOV

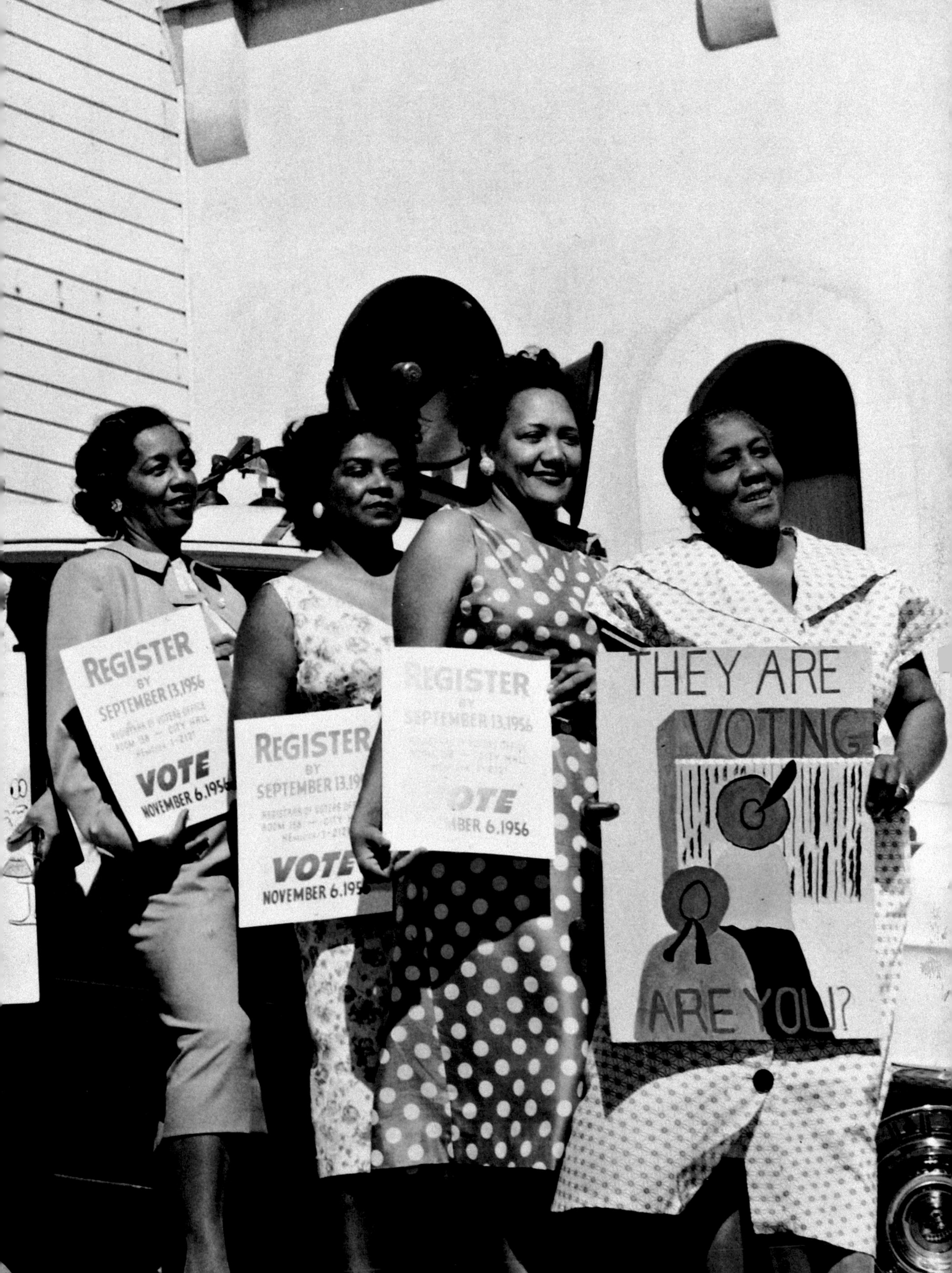

REGISTER
BY
SEPTEMBER 13,1956
VOTE
NOVEMBER 6,1956
THEY ARE
VOTING
ARE YOU?

"From limiting original voting rights to white men, to the elitist and racist origins of the electoral college, American democracy has always left people out of participation by design."

—Stacey Abrams, *Our Time Is Now*, 2020

VOTE!

The quest for equal voting rights in America has sadly been glacial. Since the nation's founding nearly 250 years ago, power and its distribution have been tied to those holding the colonial purse strings. When the U.S. Constitution was ratified in 1789, only landowning white men could vote; from the 1820s on, poor white men were gradually allowed to cast ballots. The Fifteenth Amendment granted Black men the vote in 1870, followed fifty years later by the Nineteenth's extension of voting rights to women. And the 1924 Snyder Act granted citizenship to Indigenous peoples—a painful irony considering they have been on so-called U.S. soil the longest.

These inequities did not result from casual political detour. Meeting in secret in 1787, the nation's founders deliberately wove them into the Constitution. In addition to limited voting rights, the Fugitive Slave Clause allowed for the pursuit of people who had escaped bondage across state lines, while the Three-Fifths Compromise valuated the lives of enslaved people at a mere fraction of those of free citizens. The mathematical imbalance still reverberates today.

If voting rights at the federal level were slow to come to all, state and local entities were fast in canceling them once they were made law. Almost immediately after Black men obtained suffrage, Southern states enacted Jim Crow policies to suppress their votes, including literacy tests, poll taxes, and primaries in which only white men could participate. In the late 1800s, white mobs massacred Black people in Southern towns, including Opelousas, Louisiana, and Wilmington, North Carolina, to punish them for participating in democracy. And in 1965, Alabama troopers attacked six hundred demonstrators marching for Black voting rights in Selma. Citizens of all races and genders could not effectively vote until the Voting Rights Act passed later that year.

We open this chapter with a proud relic from the Black suffragist movement: a badge from the

1914 convention of the National Association of Colored Women. It was worn by Mamie Williams, one of the many Black women to light the torch carried by modern-day organizers such as Stacey Abrams. Shortly thereafter, working in post–WWI Germany, John Heartfield—a pioneer of typographic activism—urged voters to turn out against Nazism's rise with one of his trademark political montages. Ben Shahn and Herb Lubalin (both of Jewish lineage) forged a graphic allyship with underrepresented communities—the former in his posters encouraging people to unite for worker rights in the 1940s, the latter in his designs for magazine editorials covering the racial strife and political conflict of the 1960s.

Printing fifty years later, Amos Paul Kennedy, Jr., reminds us of the sacrifices made for our democracy with *Someone Died for Your Right to Vote!* Kennedy prints, over a highway map, the story of an assassinated Selma protester with the words "Murdered in Alabama" resembling a bloody government stamp on the soil below. This layered intensity recurs in Ward Schumaker's *Trump Papers*, a collection of typographic compositions that hiss with the oppressive rhetoric of former U.S. president Donald Trump.

It is perhaps no surprise that many of the pieces in this chapter speak directly to the Trump presidency. Design is Play, the collective of Mark Fox and Angie Wang, riffs on Trump's pompous corporate branding to hold him graphically accountable for his lies. Meanwhile, Favianna Rodriguez reminds us of the power of women voters with brazen, all-caps sex positivity: "I AM A SLUT. I VOTE. SO DOES EVERYONE I SLEEP WITH." Rodriguez, Fox and Wang, Schumaker, and Kennedy all tap into a lineage of big, bold type expressing equally big and bold statements.

There are anonymous designers, too, working deep within their causes to spread the word. One example of unattributed protest art, a round green sign reading "ERA YES," has long been a mainstay in the fight to pass the Equal Rights Amendment. It reminds us that civic engagement is not limited to the individual vote; it consists of many levers, one of which is lobbying representatives to demand change.

Centuries after the country's founding, we still know how fragile a democratic election can be. After a misinformation campaign insisted that Trump won the 2020 U.S. presidential contest, "stop the steal" protesters breached the Capitol on January 6, 2021, and several states passed laws to turn back the clock on voting rights for minorities. The work in this chapter energizes us to keep up the fight for all Americans to be fully represented at the ballot box.

"We need to talk over not only those things which are of vital importance to us as women, but also the things that are of special interest to us as colored women."

—Josephine St. Pierre Ruffin, address at the First National Conference of Representatives of Black Women's Clubs, 1895

In 1896, Black women from around the United States, including abolitionists and suffragists Harriet Tubman, Ida B. Wells, Josephine St. Pierre Ruffin, and Mary Church Terrell, gathered in Washington, D.C., to form the National Association of Colored Women (NACW). The year before, Ruffin had first called for a national convention when James Jacks, the white president of the Missouri Press Association, wrote a letter denigrating Black women as prostitutes and thieves. In response, Black women met to advocate for better lives for all Black people, calling for antilynching legislation, the purging of Jim Crow laws, and increasing access to education and opportunities for their children. They adapted the motto "Lifting as we rise."

Chief among their concerns was suffrage for Black women. While Black and white women had worked together in the abolitionist and suffragist movements of the mid-1800s, many white women ceased to include Black women in their campaign for the vote after the Civil War. Members of the NACW also organized to protect the votes of Black men, whose right to cast a ballot—granted in 1870—had been eroded by racist terrorism in the South.

One of the NACW members, Mamie Williams, whose 1914 delegate badge appears here, went on to become one of the first African American women appointed to the Republican National Committee, as well as the first to speak at a Republican National Convention. After women gained the right to vote, Williams registered and mobilized women voters in her native state of Georgia, and she established the National League of Republican Colored Women.

Made of white and purple ribbon (the colors of the suffragist movement), with a brass pin and a gold medallion stamped with the face of Mary B. Talbert, the organization's president at the time, Williams's delegate badge reveals the newly found—or, more accurately, long-denied—pride taken by Black women in their ability to organize for their own political representation on a national stage.

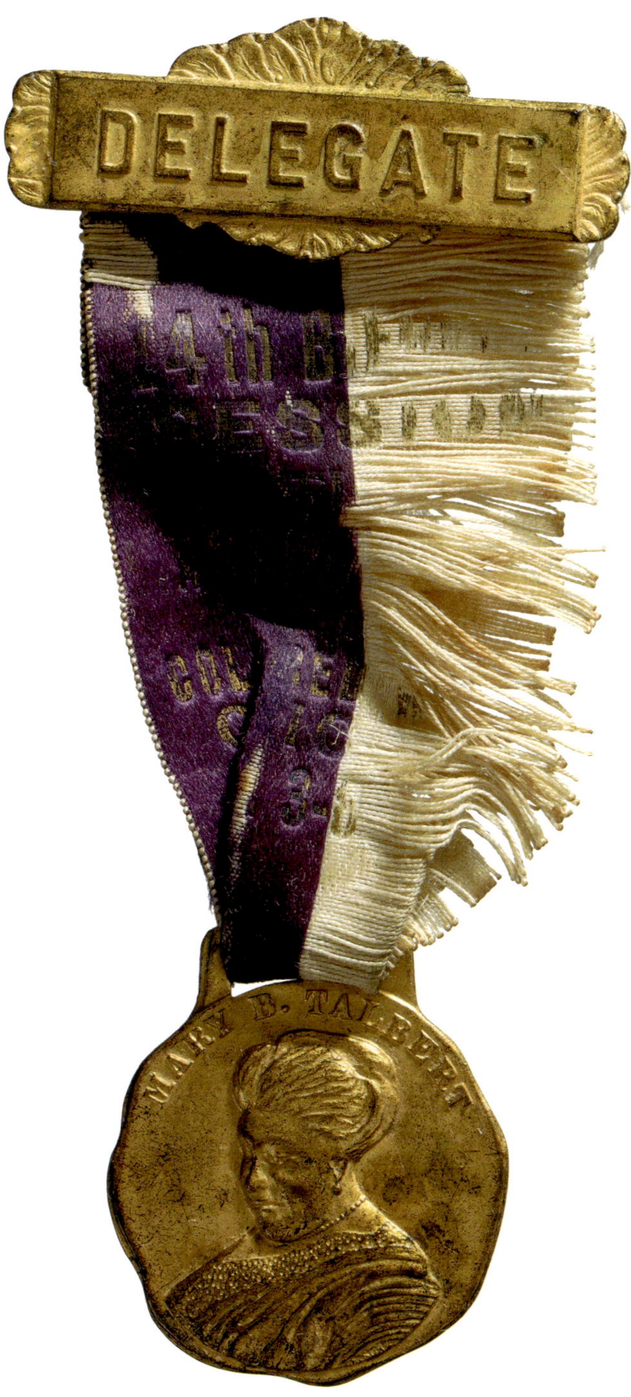

Unknown designer for the National Association of Colored Women's Clubs, delegate badge worn by Mamie Williams, 1913 or 1914, gold, brass, and now-fraying ribbon, 4¼ × 2 inches (11 × 5 cm), Washington, D.C. Collection of the Smithsonian National Museum of African American History and Culture.

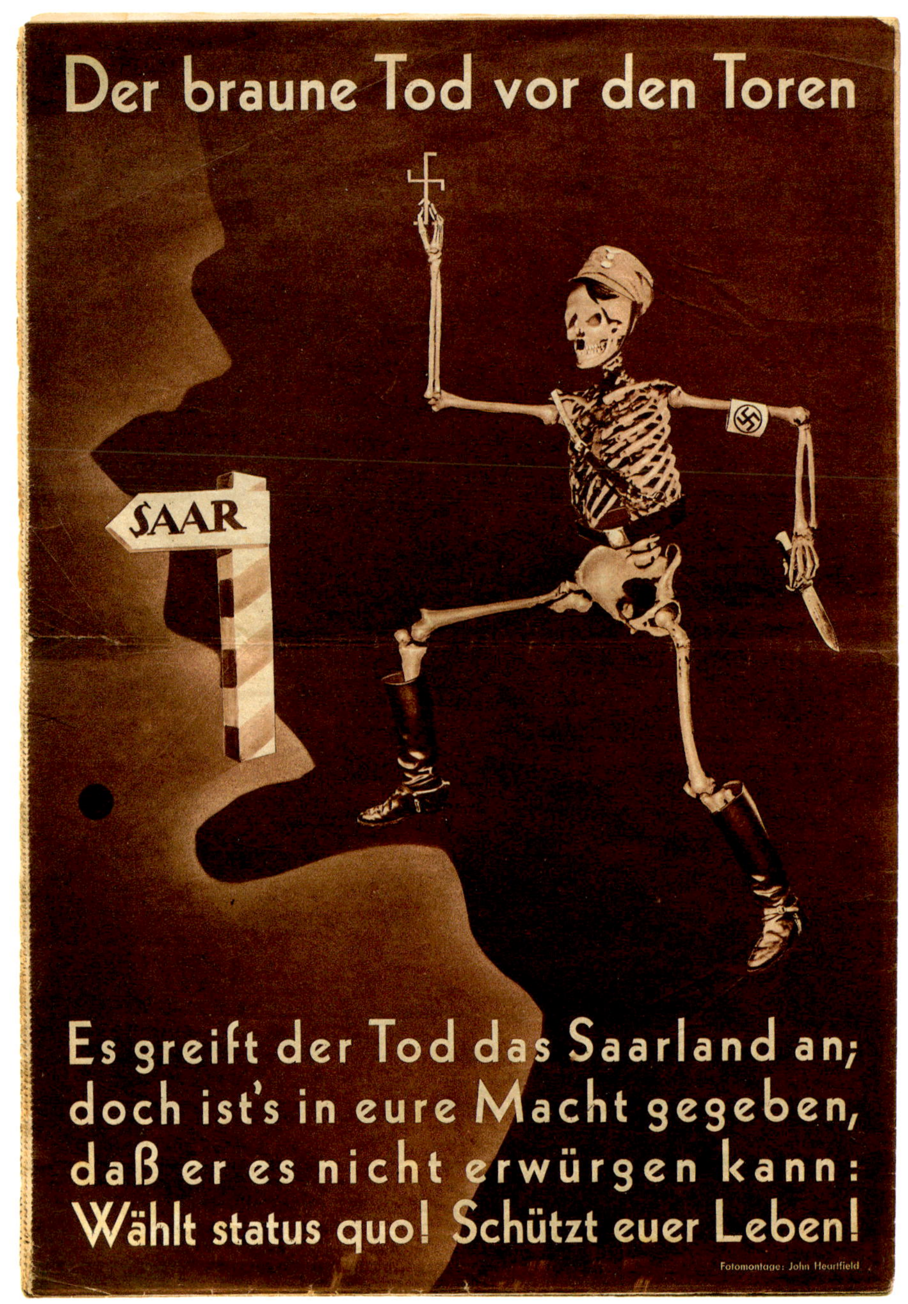

John Heartfield, photomontage with the headline "The Brown Death at the Gates" ("Der braune Tod vor den Toren"), back cover of *AIZ*, vol. 14, no. 2, 1935, offset, 15 × 10⅝ (38 × 27 cm), Prague.

The name John Heartfield itself is a protest. Born in Berlin in 1891, Helmut Herzfeld anglicized his name during World War I as a way of objecting to anti-British sentiment in Germany. Heartfield was a pioneer of photomontage, particularly in political messaging, and used it frequently in his illustrations for the popular communist weekly *AIZ* (*Arbeiter-Illustrierte-Zeitung*, or *Worker's Illustrated Newspaper*). On the back cover of the 1935 issue shown here, he made one of his most chilling and direct appeals for civic engagement, warning voters about the consequences of returning the Saar territory—administered by the League of Nations, a peace-keeping coalition assembled after World War I—to German (and thus Nazi) power. His text, including the call to action "Death is attacking Saarland, but you have the power to prevent him from strangling it: Vote status quo! Protect your lives!", is set starkly in Kabel, one of a few geometric sans-serif typefaces that were just becoming popular. Its use was antithetical to the Nazis' preference for Germanic Fraktur type, also commonly referred to as blackletter.

Heartfield lived in Berlin until April 1933, when the Nazi Party took power and he fled to Czechoslovakia by walking over the Sudeten Mountains. He eventually rose to number five on the Gestapo's most-wanted list.

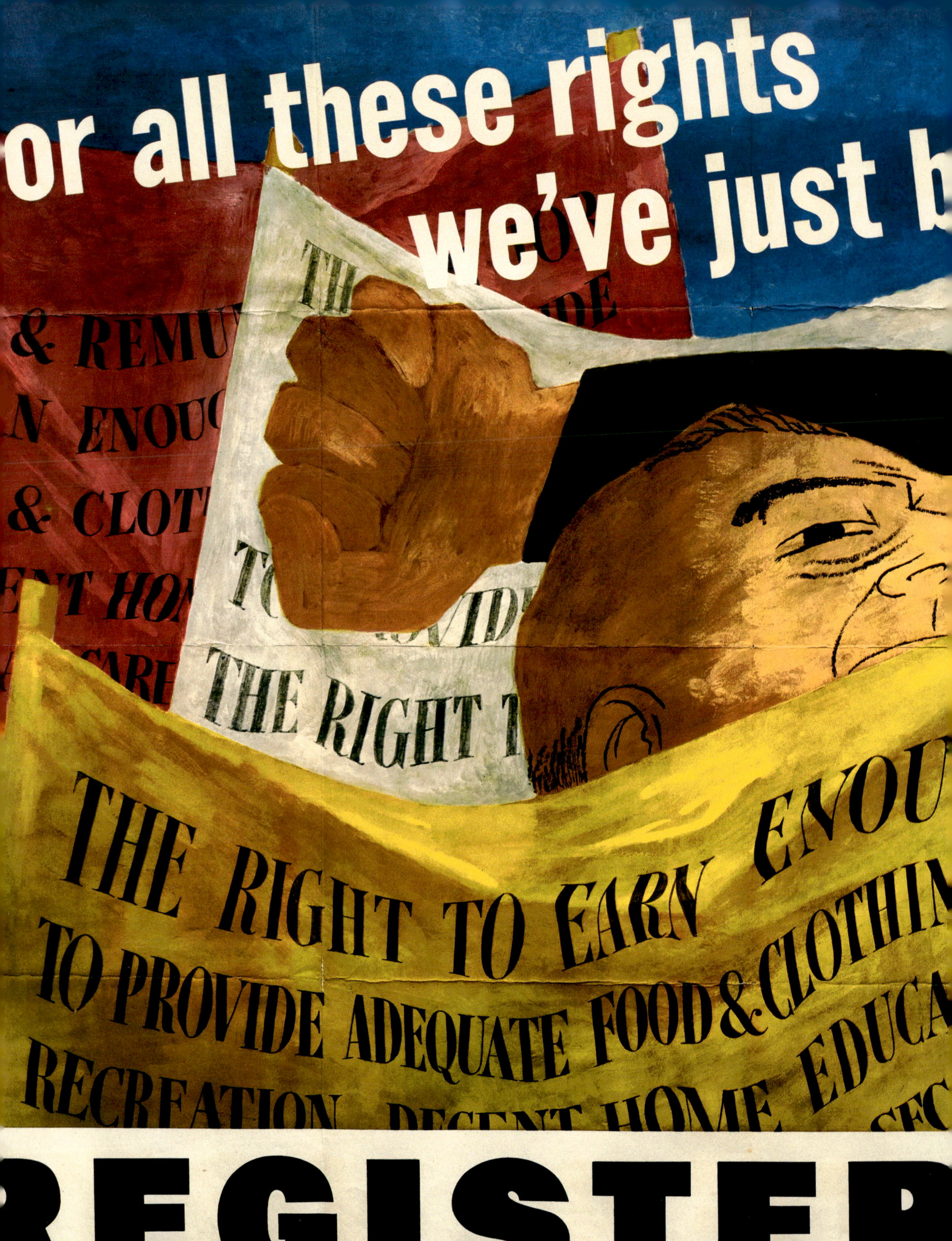

or all these rights
we've just
THE RIGHT
THE RIGHT TO EARN
TO PROVIDE ADEQUATE FOOD &
RECREATION
REGISTER

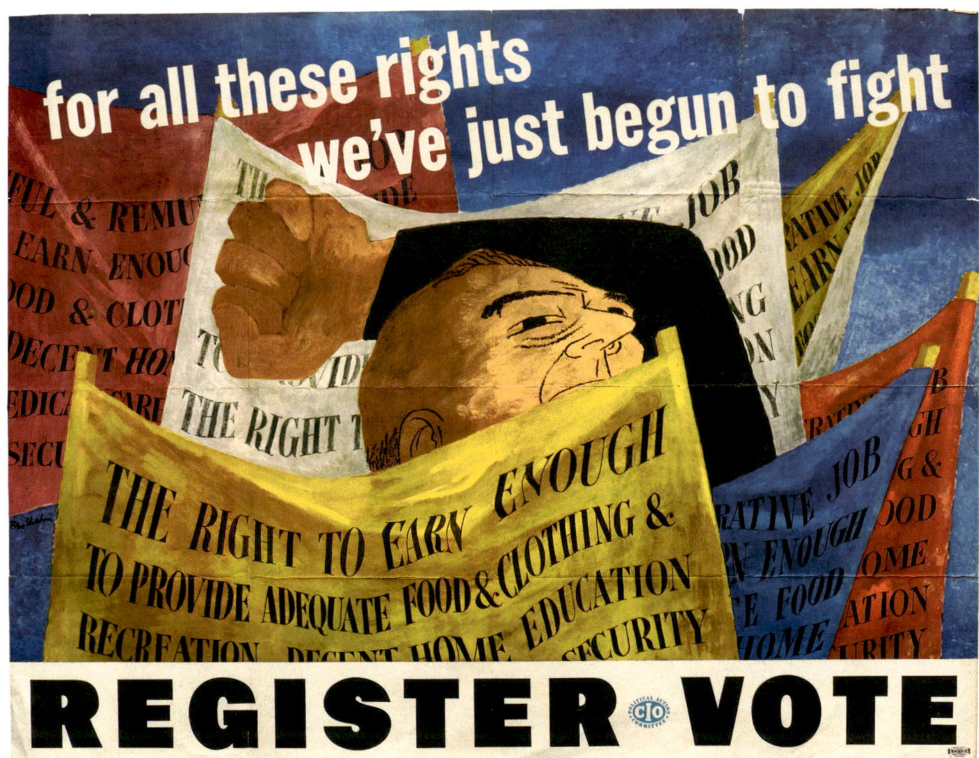

Ben Shahn, *For All These Rights We've Just Begun to Fight*, 1946, offset, 28⅞ × 38⅝ inches (73.5 × 98 cm), New York. This poster for the Congress of Industrial Organizations Political Action Committee (CIO-PAC) was issued as a rallying cry a year after the death of President Franklin D. Roosevelt, who had campaigned, for his fourth term, on extending the progressive consumer and worker protections of the New Deal.

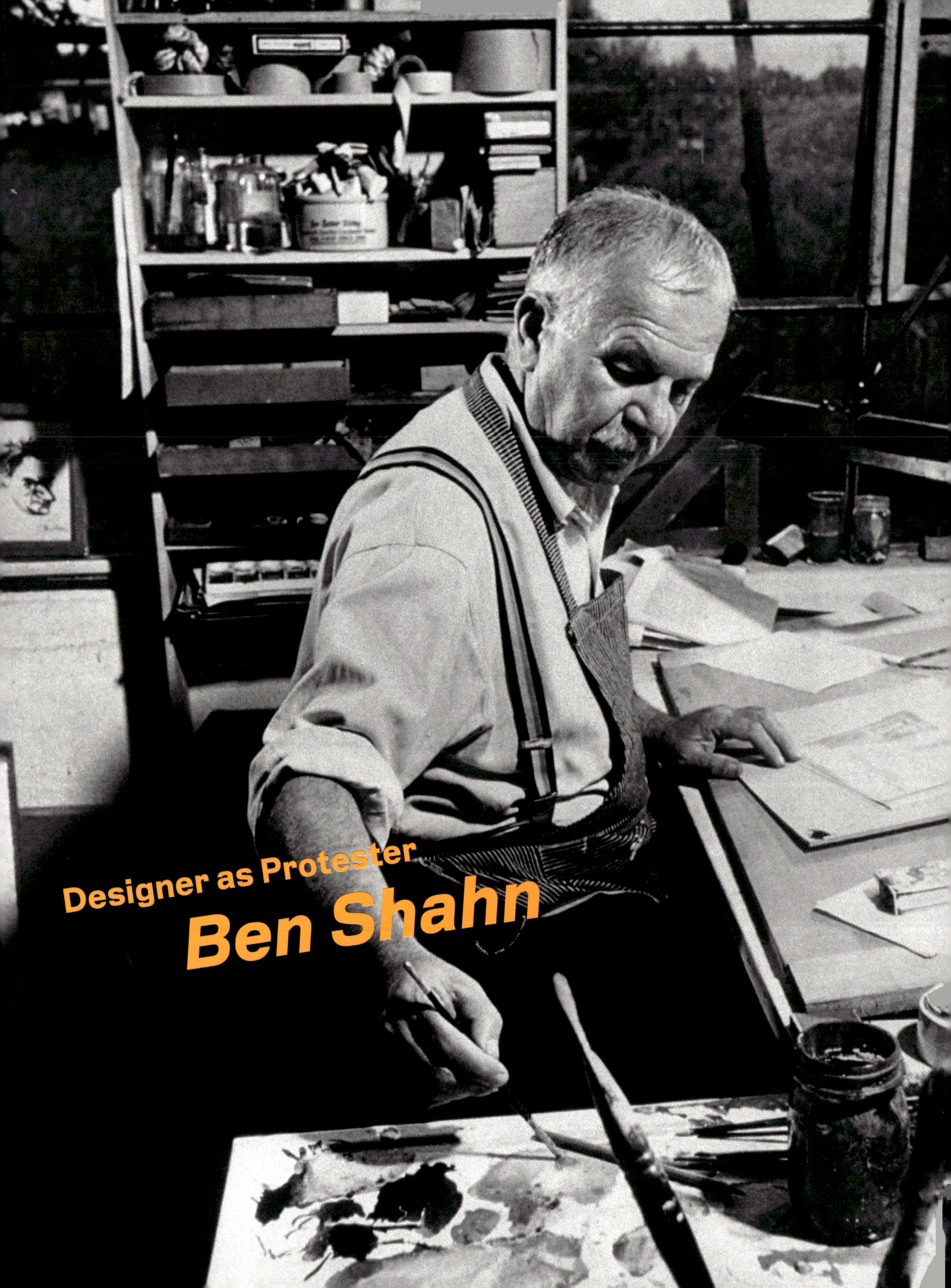

Designer as Protester

Ben Shahn

"Whatever one has rejected is in itself a tangible shaping force."

—Ben Shahn

The early memories of Ben Shahn, who was born in Lithuania to Jewish parents, were colored by anti-Semitism and the arrest and exile of his leftist father. After moving as a child to Brooklyn in 1906, he experienced economic hardship firsthand and, at fifteen, began an apprenticeship with a lithographer in Manhattan to help support his family. Working long hours while attending high school via night classes, Shahn painstakingly practiced commercial lettering and drawing—skills he later put to use in his lifelong opposition to injustice.

His artistic breakthrough occurred in 1932 and 1933, with two series of gouache paintings depicting a pair of unfair trials and convictions: those of immigrant anarchists Nicola Sacco and Bartolomeo Vanzetti in Massachusetts, and of the radical labor leader Tom Mooney in San Francisco. These paintings introduced a realist style that combined expressive outlines with flat color, rendering scenes with directness, sympathy, and satire. Shahn's unique social realism soon translated to large-scale murals celebrating working-class America, as well as many posters and prints supporting organized labor and the progressive ballot.

For nearly ten years during the Great Depression, Shahn worked as a graphic artist and photographer for agencies set up through President Franklin D. Roosevelt's New Deal, a program of public employment, government planning, and welfare designed to combat the anguishes of the 1930s. Shahn's commitment to New Deal liberalism informed his work for the Committee for Industrial Organization (CIO; today called the Congress of Industrial Organizations), a federation of unions that became the second-largest organizing body for labor in the United States. In *For All These Rights We've Just Begun to Fight* (pages 112–113), created for a 1946 campaign encouraging workers to vote Democrat, a worker with a raised fist emerges from a sea of colorful banners. These bear the words of Roosevelt's unrealized Second Bill of Rights, proposed in 1944 as a guarantee of full employment, "the right to earn enough to provide adequate food and clothing and recreation," healthcare access, and social welfare. With a stately condensed serif resembling the Bodoni-style type used in official documents, Shahn's handlettering combines with the poster's workmanlike sans-serif type to drive home its message about the power of organized labor in politics.

When it comes to his handstyle, Shahn may be best known for his angular letterforms (possibly inspired by the vernacular signage he studied as a photographer), with their uniquely syncopated thick and thin strokes. This lettering appears in *McCarthy Peace* (page 91), a poster that encourages voters to back Eugene McCarthy for the 1968 presidential ticket with a one-word promise that implies the end of U.S. military involvement in Vietnam. Designed in the last months of Shahn's life, its pop-styled peace dove shares unmistakable features with the American eagle, symbolizing the possibility of change he found in the democratic process.

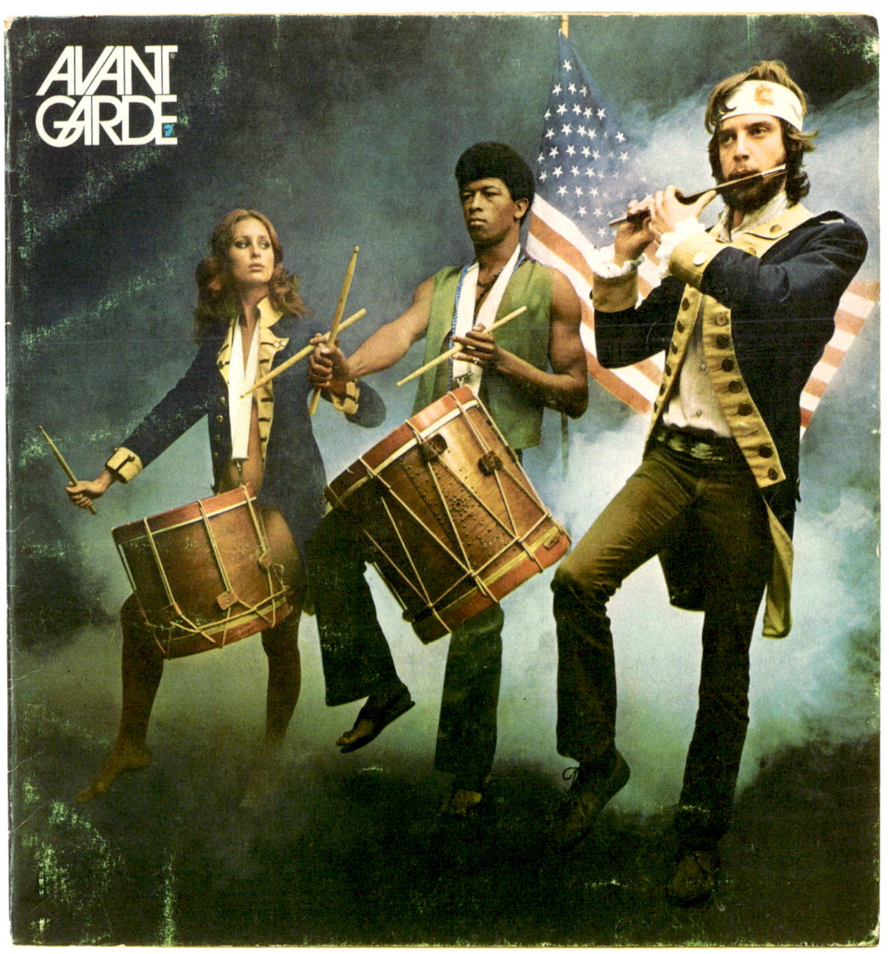

Herb Lubalin (designer), Ralph Ginzburg (editor), Carl Fischer (photographer), *Avant-Garde*, no. 7, 1969, offset, 11¼ × 10⅞ inches (28.5 × 27.5 cm), New York. This cover photo modernizes A. M. Willard's 1875 painting *The Spirit of '76*, but instead of showing minutemen marching in the American Revolution, "it depicts the heroes of America's present revolution—the avant-gardists who are struggling for sexual freedom, racial equality, and an end to war," as stated in the cover story.

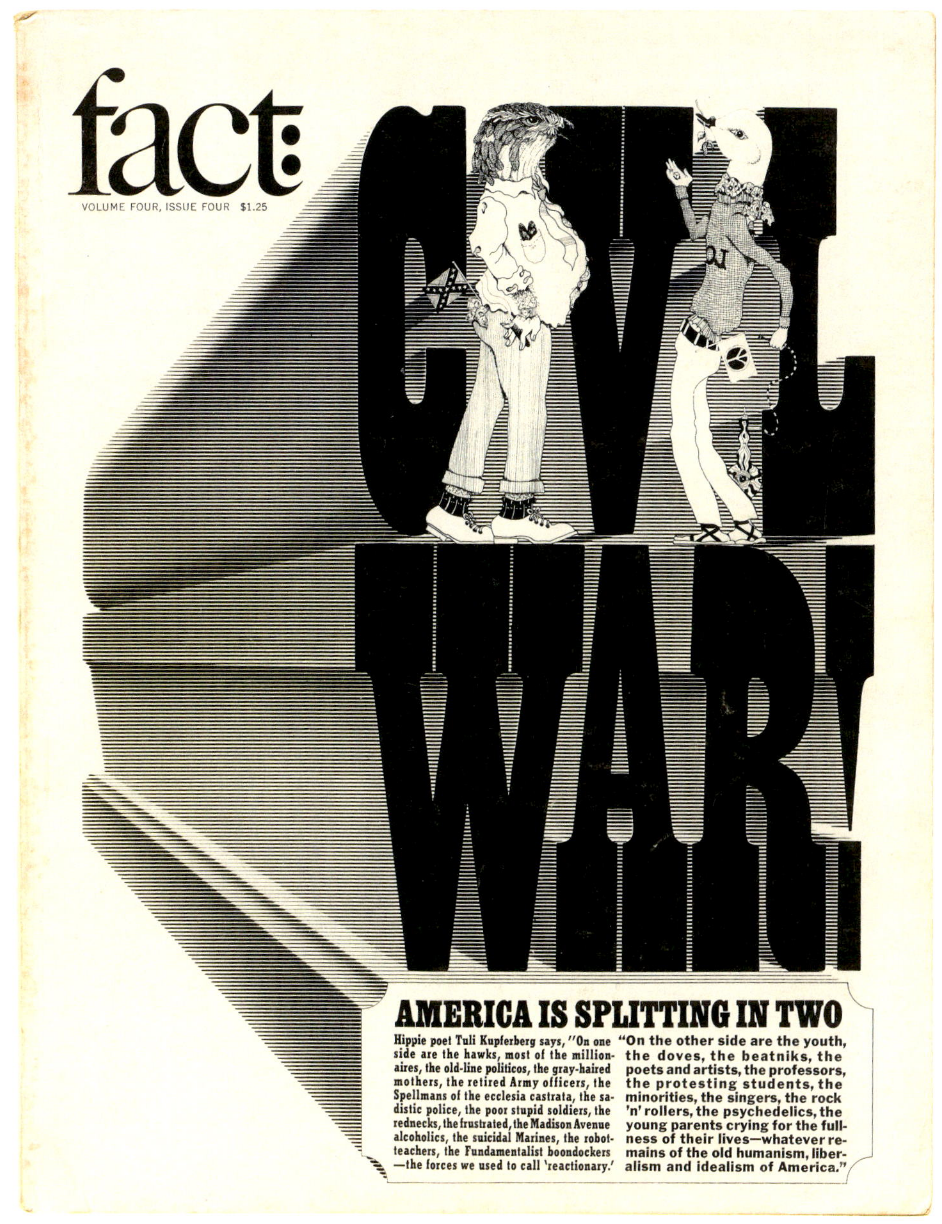

Herb Lubalin (designer), Ralph Ginzburg (editor), *Fact*, vol. 4, no. 4, 1967, offset, 10⅞ × 8½ inches (27.5 × 21.5 cm), New York. Lubalin uses French Clarendon on this cover of an issue exploring the polarized politics of late-1960s America. The nineteenth-century wood type—revived in the sixties in reaction to the clean lines of Swiss modernism, the dominant style at the time, and set here as if blasting from the past—links the era's upheaval to the opposition of the U.S. Civil War.

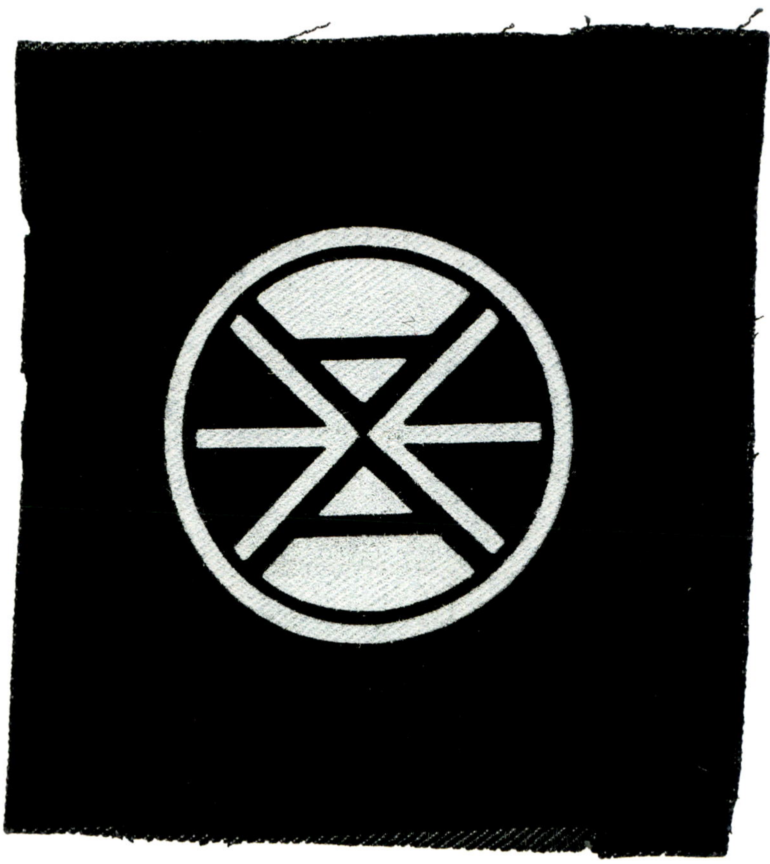

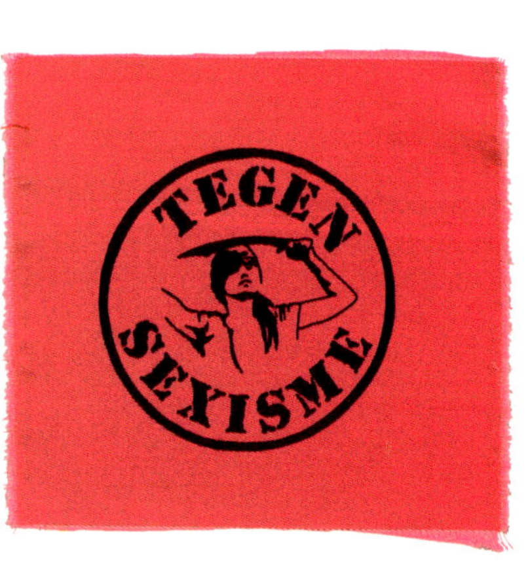

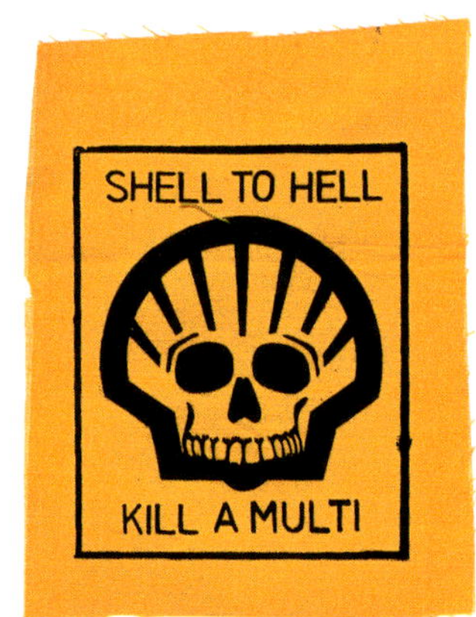

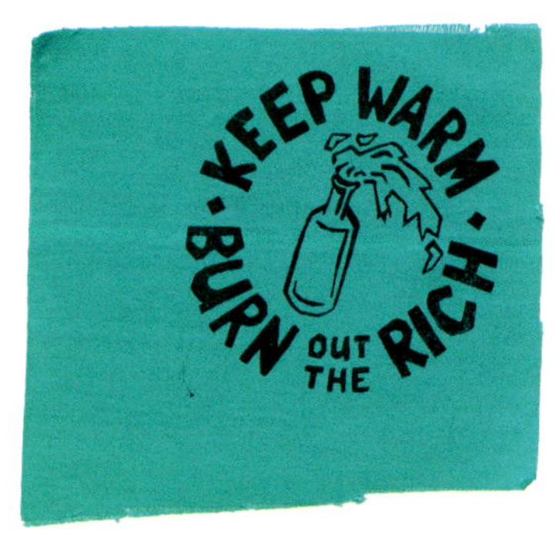

Clifford Harper (bottom right, this page), Seth Tobocman (top left, opposite page), and other unknown designers, political patches, circa 1980s, screen print on fabric, various sizes and locations. (See page 277 for more information.)

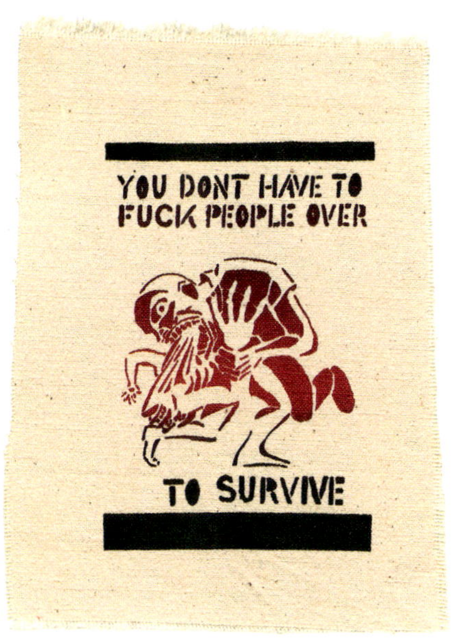

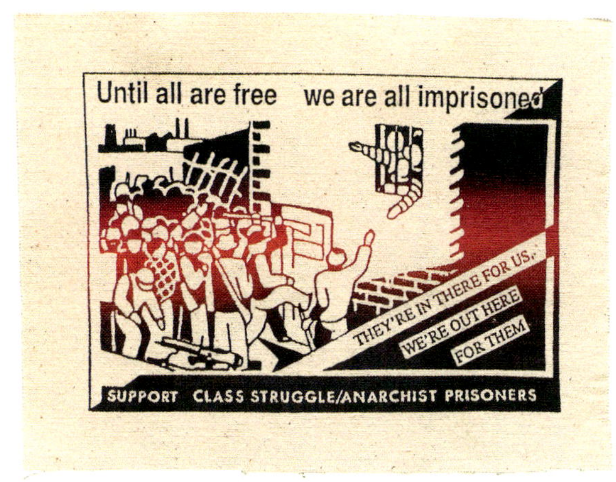

Fabric patches became omnipresent in countercultural movements starting in the 1960s, functioning as both a fashion choice and an overt political statement that signaled solidarity. The selection here, all from the 1980s, demonstrates a shift from the brightly colored, often flowery embroidered patches of the hippie generation to the proudly lo-fi, inexpertly screen-printed aesthetic of the punk scene. Stapled, sewn, and safety-pinned to jackets and jeans, the patches became an emblem of a sociopolitical identity that rejected the state and sneered at the naivety of its beatnik predecessors.

Unsurprisingly, there is no reverence for typographic tradition here. These patches rely mainly on roughly cut stencil lettering and bold sans-serif typefaces that can withstand screen-printing on fabric and quickly get the point across. When used, the typefaces themselves, often Impact, Helvetica, or Futura, are typically stretched and mangled to fit the illustration. The ideology has an especially typographic symbol: the letter *A* enclosed in a circle, which dates to the 1960s, when a group in Paris first introduced the design by Spanish anarchist Tomás Ibáñez. His mark proved general enough to be shared by all expressions of anarchism but also simple enough to be easily spray-painted and cheaply reproduced.

A frequent misconception of anarchy is that it only wishes to sow chaos, proposing a free-for-all style of governance with no rules or structure. With roots tracing back to the seventeenth century, anarchism emerged as a philosophy that repudiates established hierarchies, which can be found across racism, capitalism, fascism, and sexism. Many anarchists advocate for shared access to material resources, collective power in unions and cooperatives, and a direct model of democracy in which all individuals get a vote.

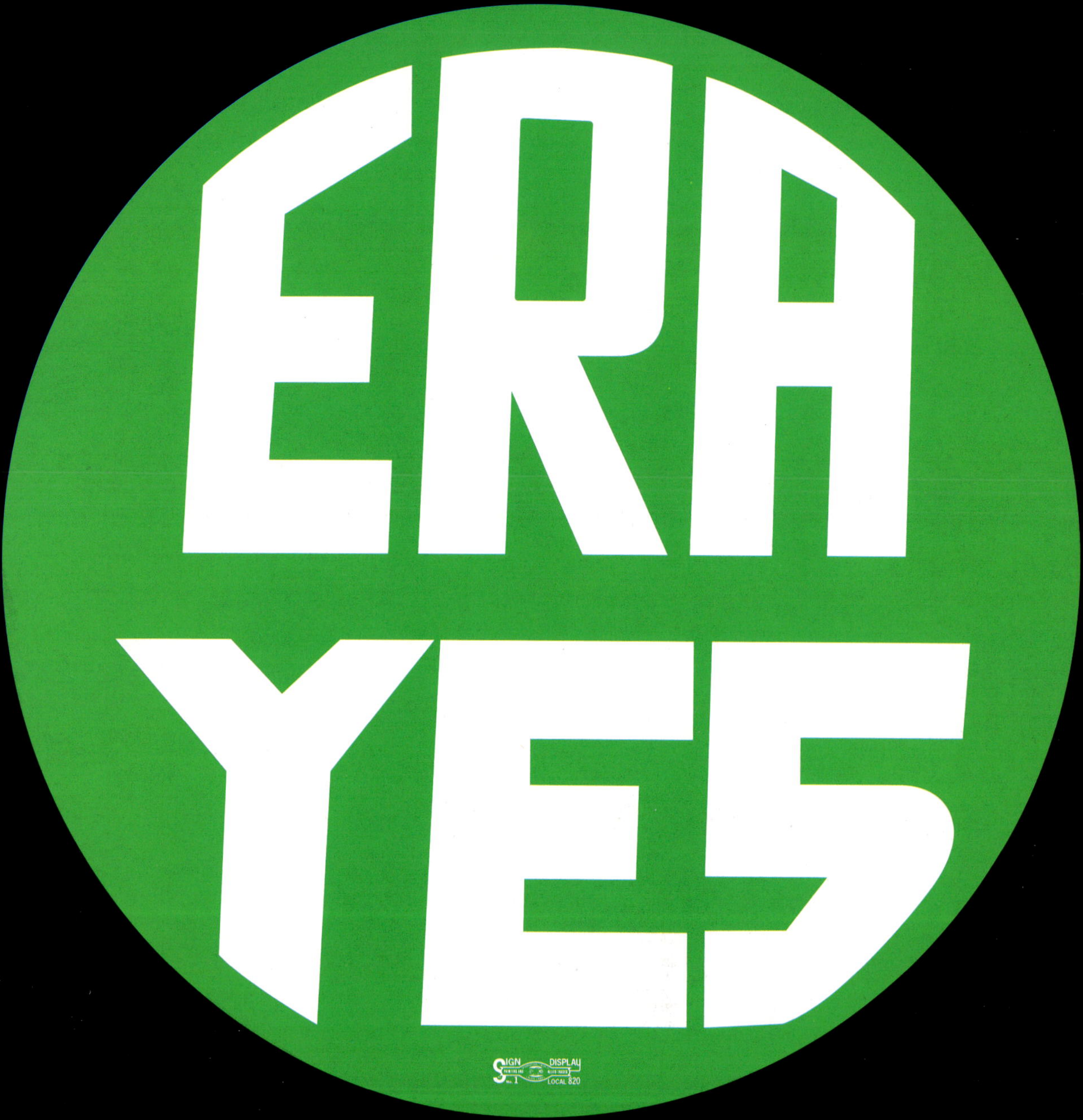

Unknown designer, Feminist Majority Foundation reissue of the 1979 protest sign for the ERA Yes movement, 2021, screen print, 22 × 22 inches (56 × 56 cm), Kansas City, Missouri. A tiny logo at the bottom identifying a local branch (called a "union bug") indicates that the sign was made by a unionized manufacturer.

If women are already equal, why is it such an event whenever one happens to be elected to Congress . . . . Women do not have the opportunities that men do. And women that do not conform to the system, who tried to break with the accepted patterns, are stigmatized as "odd" and "unfeminine."

—Shirley Chisholm, Equal Rights Amendment speech, 1969

The ERA Yes sign is iconic for its bright green color, unique circular shape, and bold white letterforms, contorted to fit the round. While the sign was designed in the 1970s, the battle for its namesake, the Equal Rights Amendment, actually began in 1923, when the bill authored by American suffragettes Alice Paul and Crystal Eastman was first presented in Congress. After winning the vote for women, they saw the ERA as a critical next step in securing women's economic independence. It called for legal equality in issues of property ownership, employment, and more. The effort lost momentum in part due to fears that it would end protections for women in the workplace.

Fast-forward nearly fifty years, when second-wave feminists reintroduced and passed the ERA in the House and Senate. The sign appeared in the rallying cry for thirty-eight states to ratify the bill to make it a constitutional amendment. The creator—a young woman who was volunteering for the cause but whose name has since been lost—had no experience in design, and its concept was simple: a green circle to counter the red octagon used by the "Stop ERA" campaign. Its idiosyncratic lettering is the effective result of an unskilled hand. Seen on the street, it caught on and became the movement's default logo (though its creation story is antithetical to the usual corporate branding process). As an ergonomic bonus, the sign's roundness enables the demonstrator to easily hold it overhead with one hand. The Feminist Majority Foundation—one of the bill's main proponents, along with the National Organization for Women—produced the sign for rallies across the nation.

In 1979, at the end of the ratification window imposed by Congress, the ERA fell short in its bid by three states. In 2022 (another fifty years after the bill was first passed), Congress voted to remove the time limit on ratification. In the meantime, three more states adopted the measure, fueled by the #MeToo movement and a new wave of women elected officials who declare that "there is no time limit on equality." While hurdles remain, after one hundred years, the ERA may someday become law.

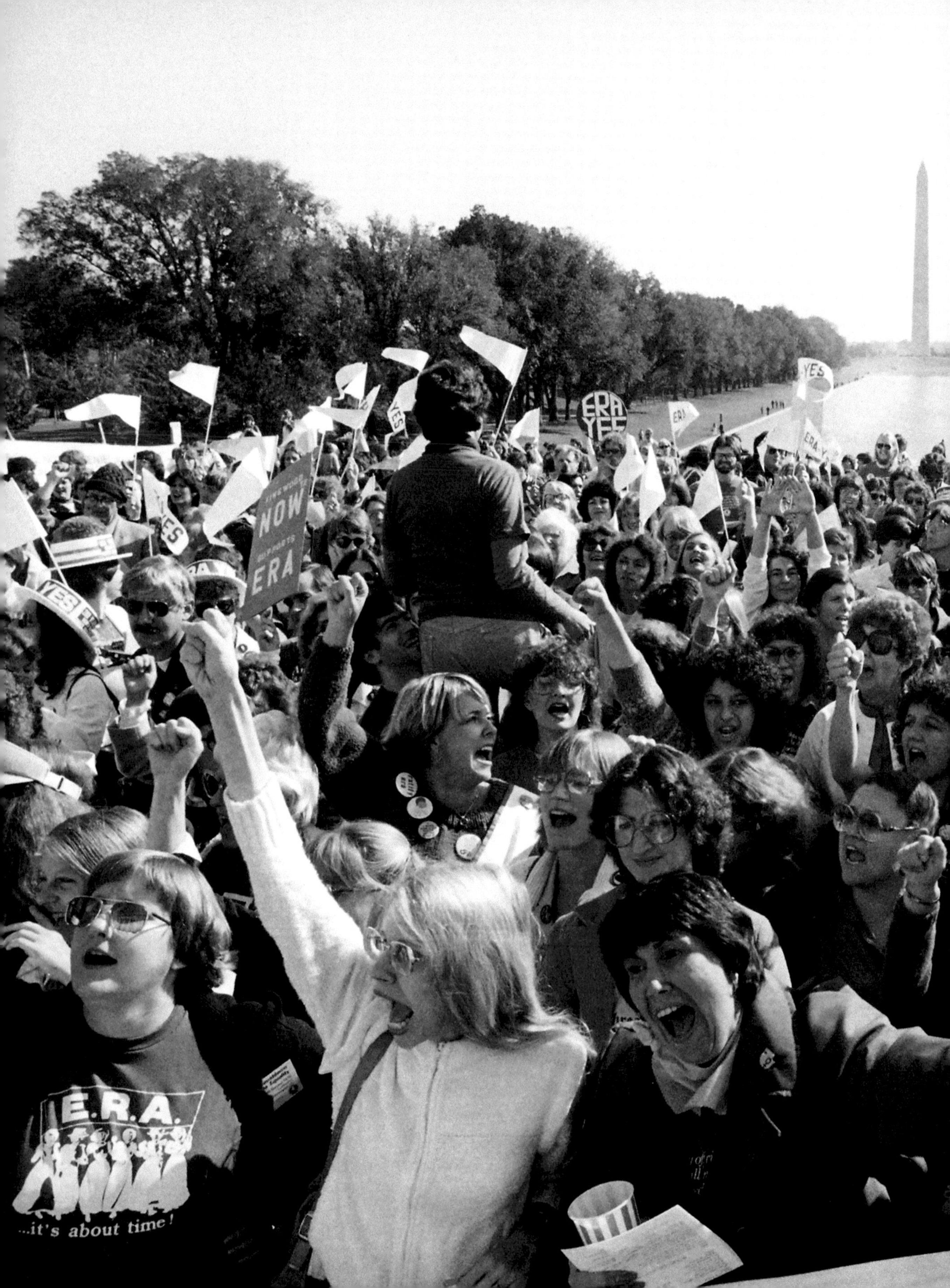
ERA
YES
NOW
ERA
YES
E.R.A.
...it's about time!

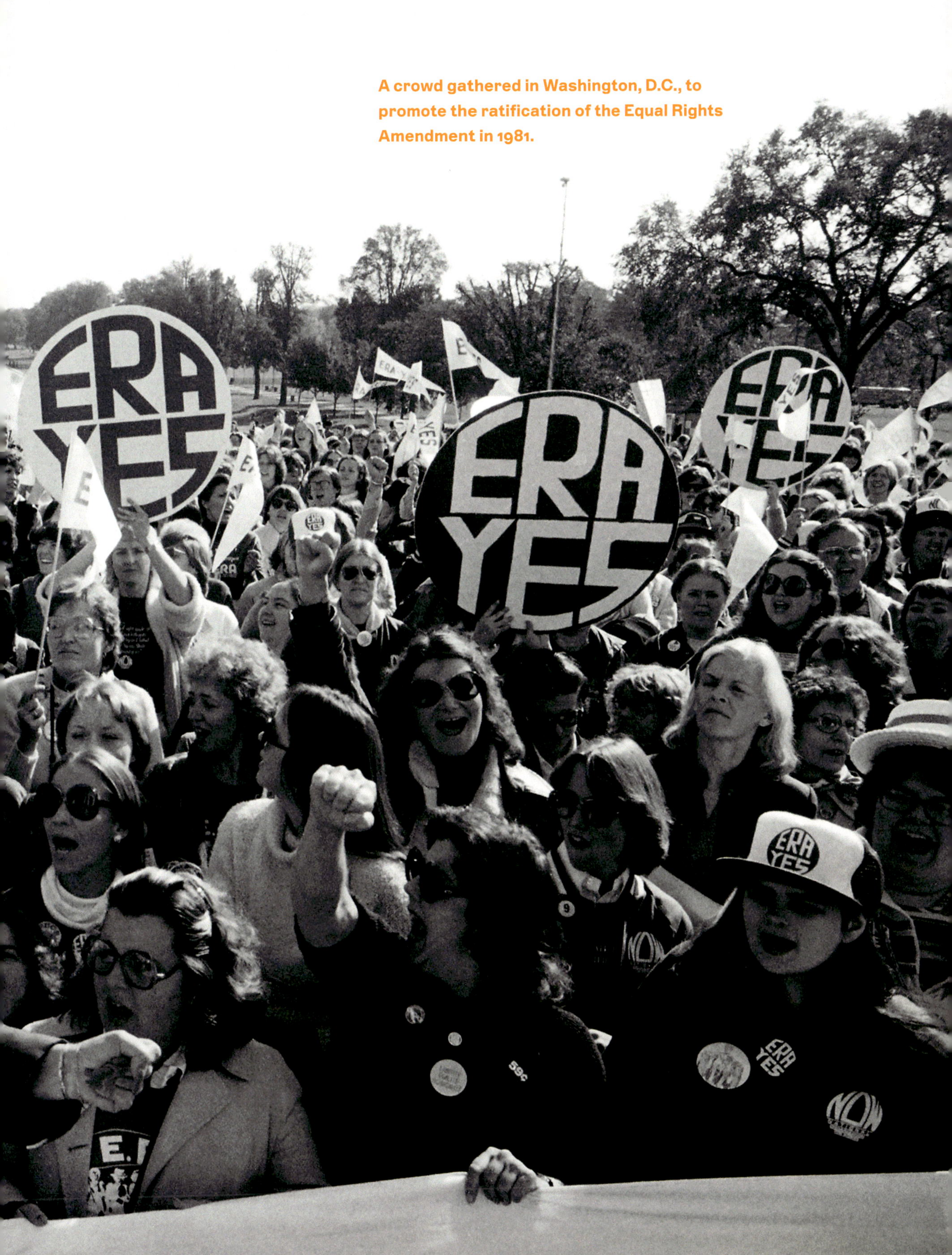

A crowd gathered in Washington, D.C., to promote the ratification of the Equal Rights Amendment in 1981.

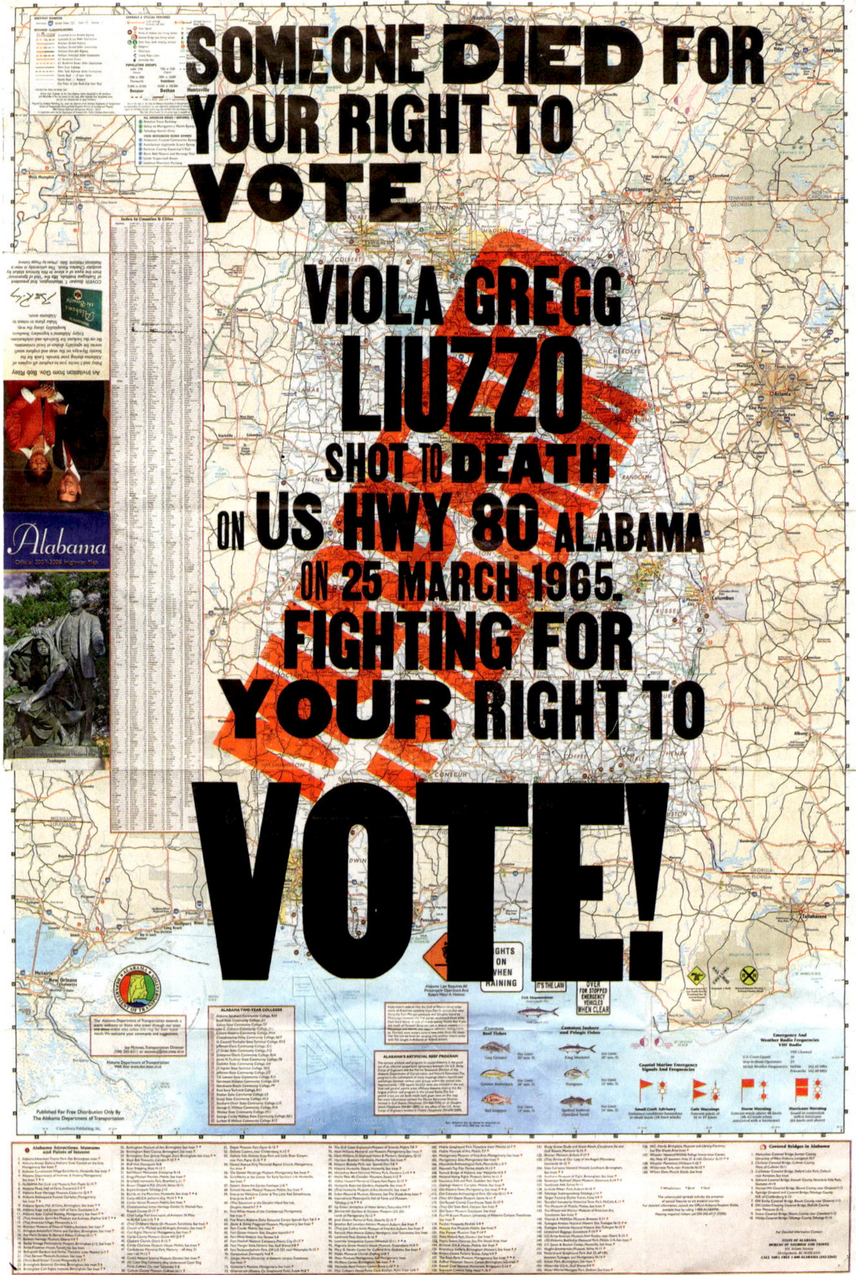

Amos Paul Kennedy, Jr., *Someone Died for Your Right to Vote!*, 2018, letterpress on a map of Alabama, 43½ × 29⅞ inches (110.5 × 76 cm), Detroit. This poster memorializes Viola Liuzzo, a white civil rights activist shot to death by members of the Ku Klux Klan under the watch of the FBI after she assisted in the 1965 marches for voting rights in Selma, Alabama.

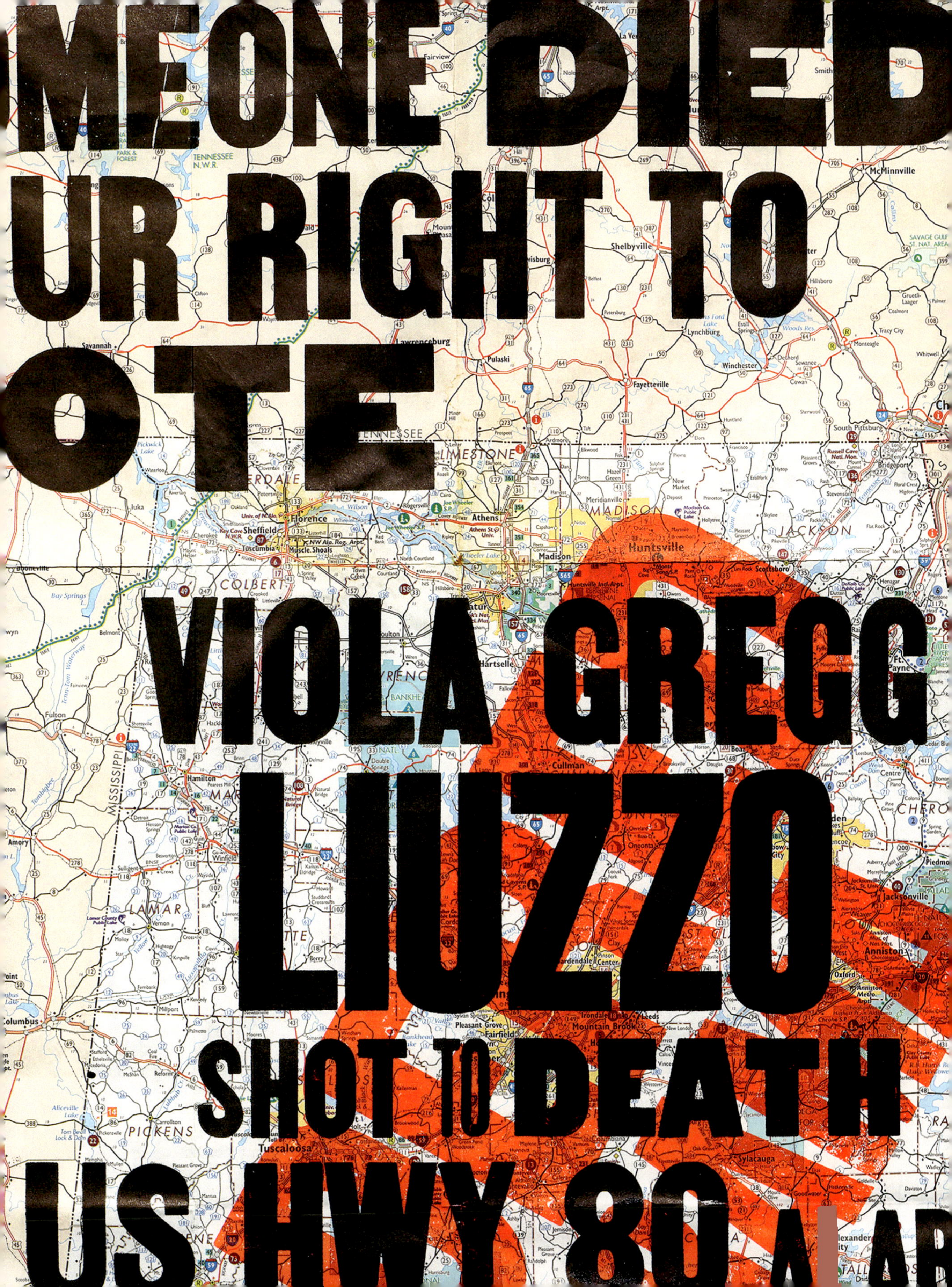
MEONE DIED
UR RIGHT TO
OTE
VIOLA GREGG
LIUZZO
SHOT TO DEATH
US HWY 80

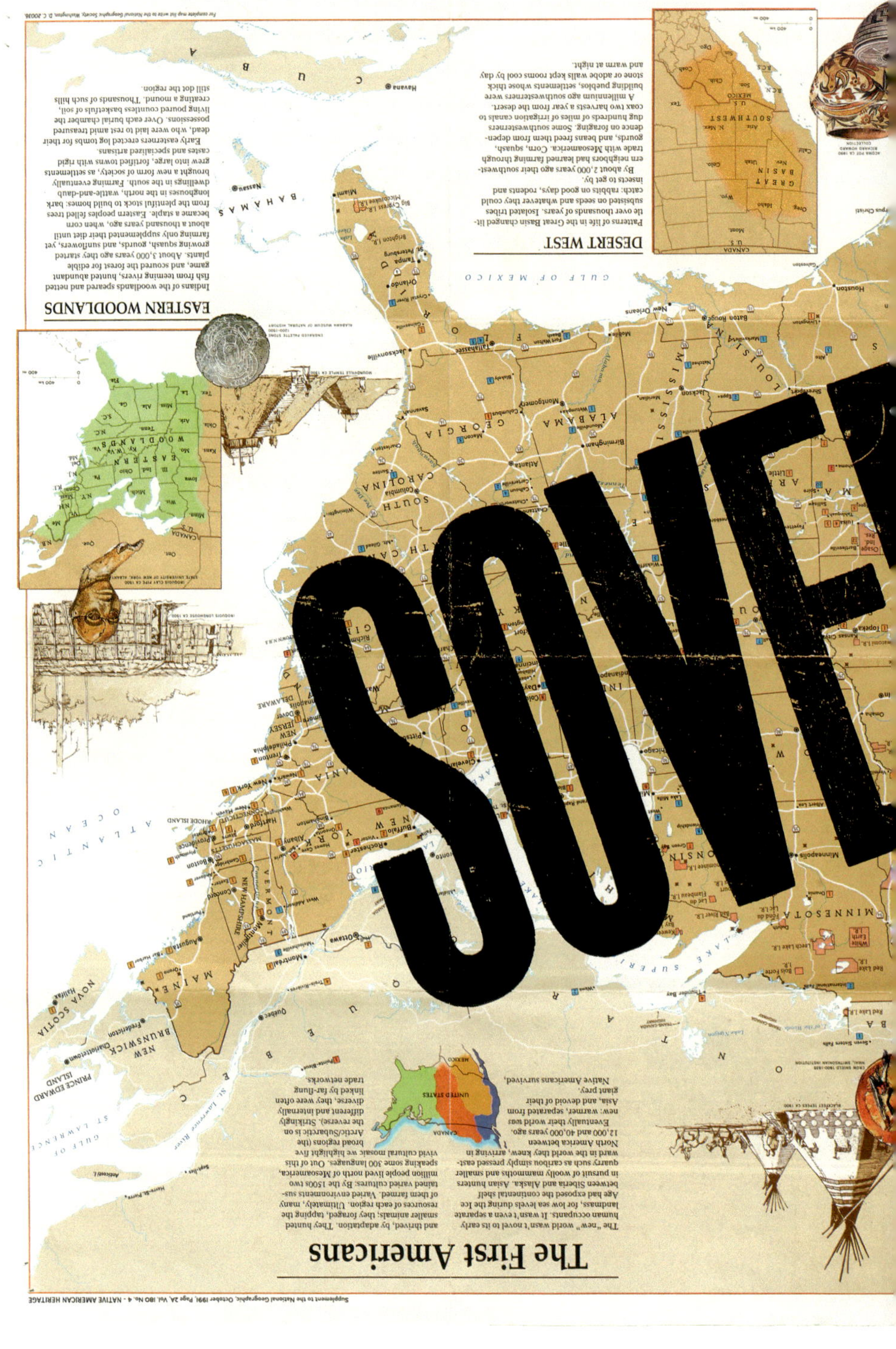
SOVE
The First Americans
EASTERN WOODLANDS
DESERT WEST

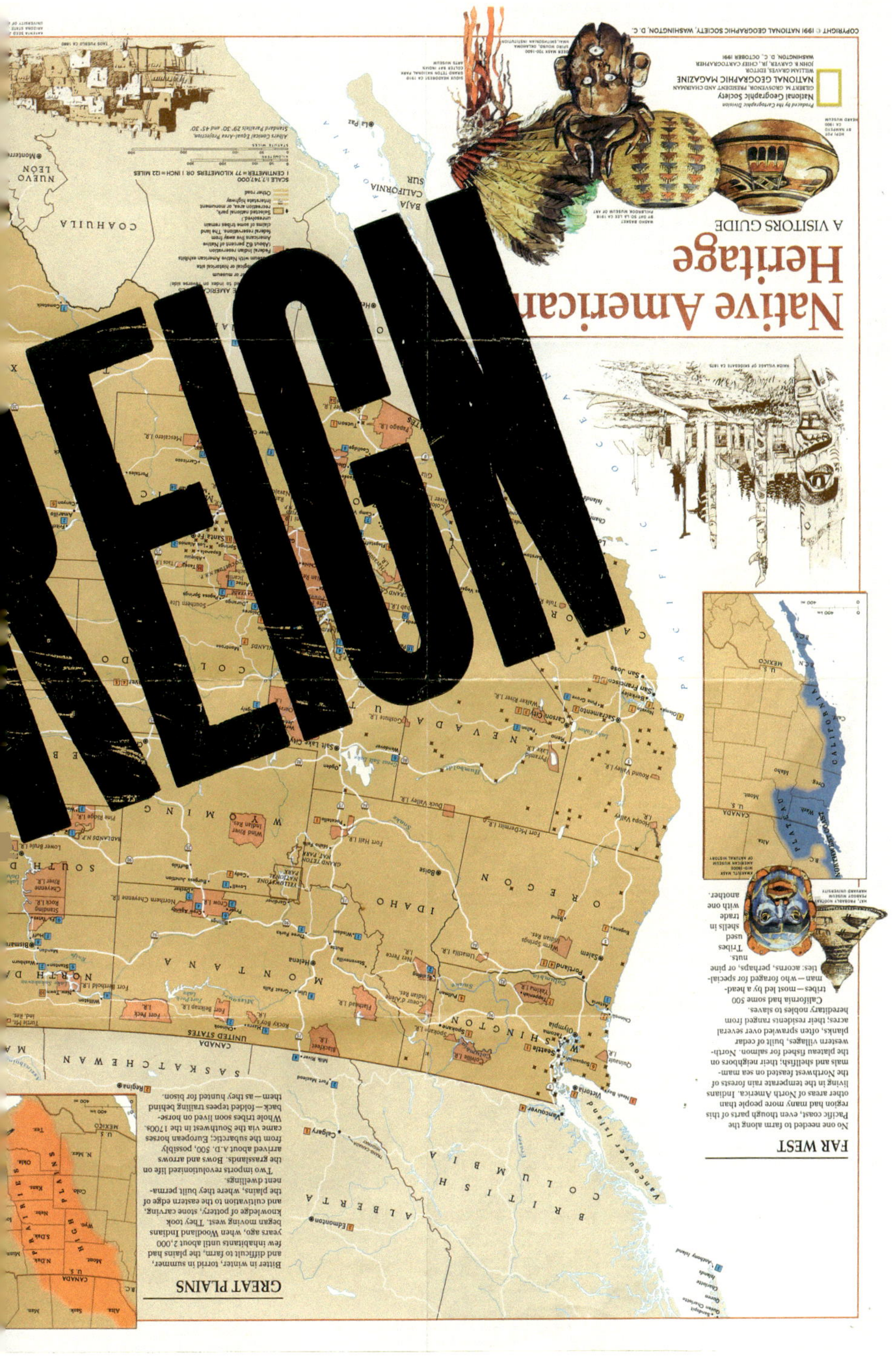

Amos Paul Kennedy, Jr., *Sovereign*, 2018, letterpress, 20½ × 29 inches (52 × 73.5 cm), Detroit. Kennedy printed a statement of solidarity with the Indigenous tribes and nations on this supplemental map from *National Geographic*'s October 1991 "Native American Heritage" issue.

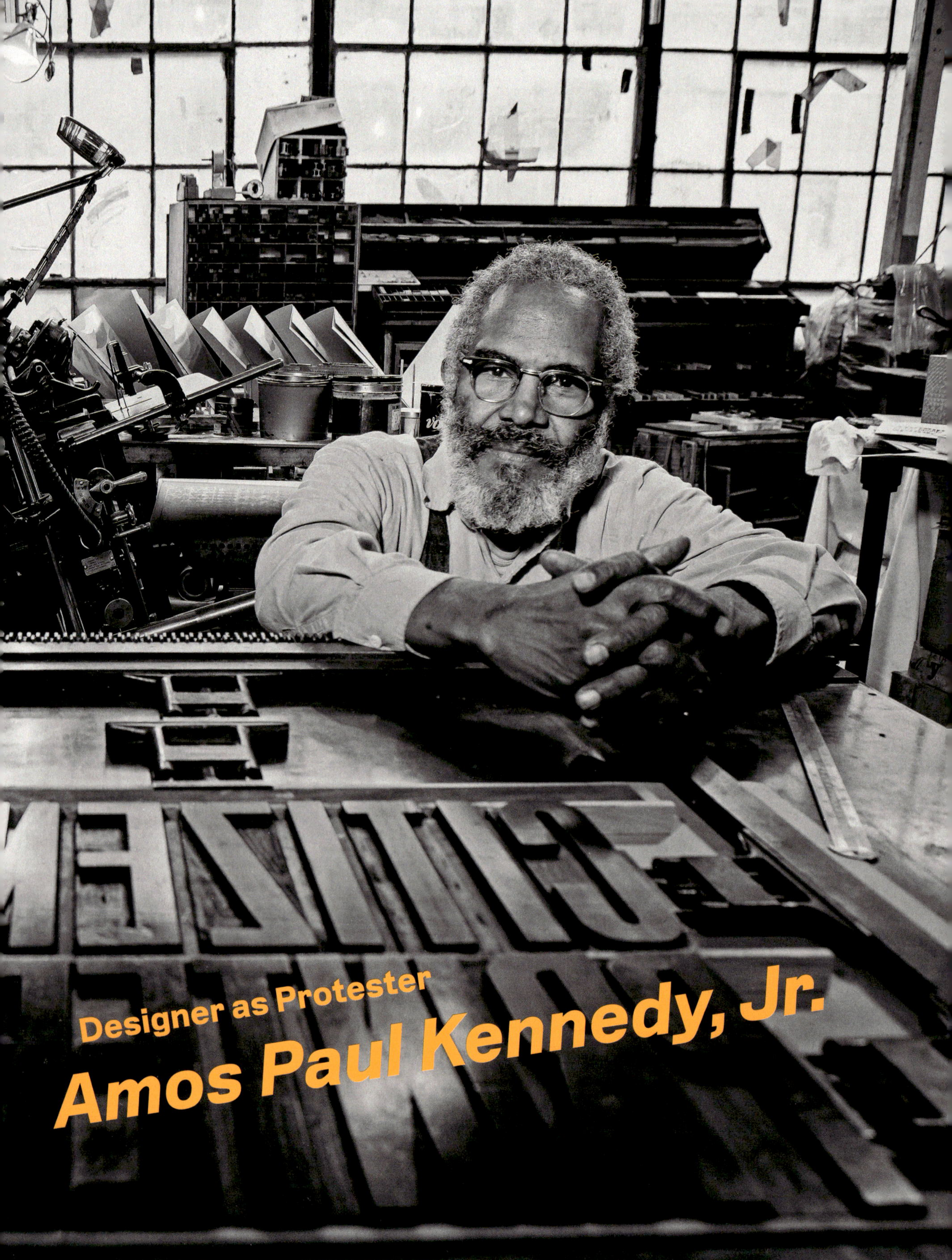

Designer as Protester

Amos Paul Kennedy, Jr.

"Put the message in the hands of the people and move on."

—Amos Paul Kennedy, Jr.

Amos Paul Kennedy, Jr., first encountered printing on a Cub Scout trip to a Louisiana newspaper in the late 1950s. Thirty years later, while working a corporate job at AT&T, he rediscovered printing on yet another tour—this time of a letterpress printshop in Colonial Williamsburg. He devoted himself to the craft, earning an MFA at the University of Wisconsin–Madison and then teaching at Indiana State University. He now operates Kennedy Prints! in Detroit, a communal letterpress center with a passionate following.

Borrowing words from social justice heroes Fannie Lou Hamer, Frederick Douglass, Sojourner Truth, and others, Kennedy layers bold statements on race, capitalism, history, and political advocacy in exuberant, colorful posters and *handbills* (small printed advertisements distributed by hand). He situates himself within a legacy of Black printing that includes Black pressmen making abolitionist broadsides and presses established at historically Black colleges and universities. Often self-uniformed in a pink button-down shirt and denim overalls, Kennedy upturns racial stereotypes of an earlier era when he refers to himself as "just a humble Negro printer." All the while, he provides an example of how we as citizens can seize the means of production to speak truth to power.

One of these levers is political action—or, as Kennedy puts it, "agitation." With text overprinted on a large-format map of Alabama, his *Someone Died for Your Right to Vote!* (see page 124) reminds viewers what our predecessors went through to defend voting rights for all. And in a portfolio of prints, he presents Rosa Parks's account of her 1955 refusal to vacate a bus seat for a white person (an act that launched the Montgomery bus boycott) by printing her story in her own words: "The only tired I was, was tired of giving in."

These bold stories and sayings find equal expression in Kennedy's presswork. Printing predominantly with salvaged ink, he stacks text in mismatched sizes of Cooper Black (a workhorse typeface beloved for its counterculture appeal), with differences in weight and width lending emphasis to key words. Sometimes he uses a wash of a single color as a background; other times he positions the text over irregular geometric patterns in multiple hues. Or he builds up a dense texture using type itself, reconfiguring the letterforms and inking the rollers with different colors between each pass on the press.

Kennedy's chosen text is by turns serious ("Just as Americans know little about who is executed and why, they are unaware of the dangers of executing an innocent man") and playful ("I knew God was Black but I didn't know they were trans!"). It is colloquial ("I am as southern as cornbread") and erudite ("Man builds no structure that outlives a book"). It is also instructive, urging viewers to do their part in the experiment of citizenry ("Vote, damn it!") and in life itself ("Ladies, no fighting in the bathroom!").

Above all, Kennedy's work is hopeful, as evinced by a quotation from a seventh-grade student, printed in all caps against deep, lush green: "Every day I dream of Black freedom and pride."

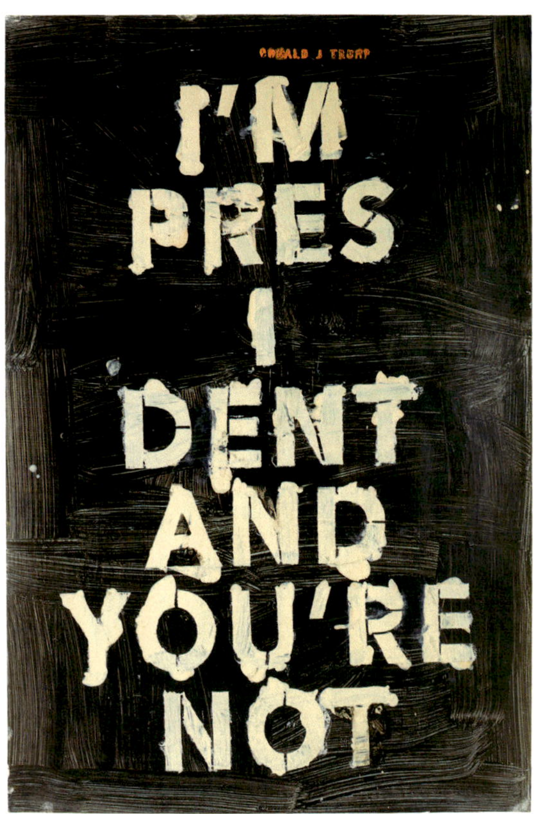

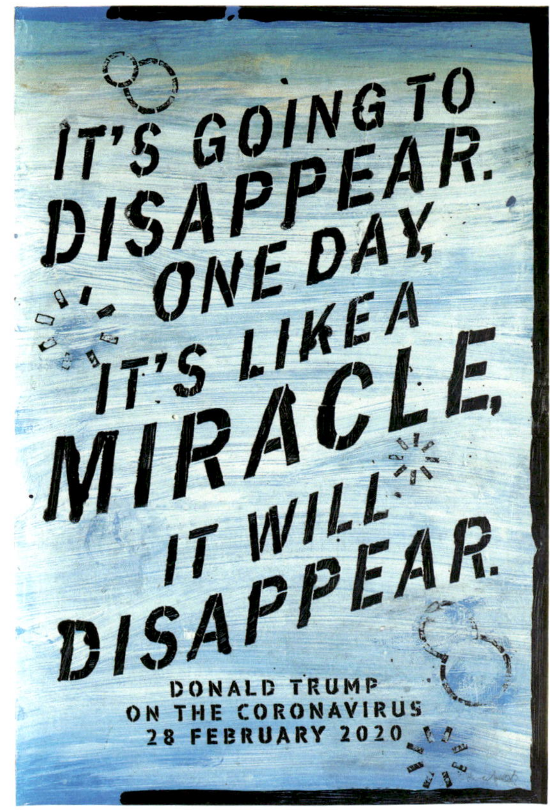

San Francisco–based painter and book artist Ward Schumaker has long incorporated found text into his pieces. Prior to 2016, his depicted words typically came from spiritual lines or quixotic instructions, rendered in rough calligraphy or unrefined stencil lettering. After the election of Donald Trump to the U.S. presidency, however, Schumaker found himself unable to ignore the downshift in national discourse. He filled two artist books with direct quotations from Trump, ranging from racist hate speech to misinformation about the COVID-19 pandemic. With his source material far from exhausted, Schumaker then created more than 300 one-of-a-kind posters called *Trump Papers*.

In both his artist books and broadsides, Schumaker presents the former president's language in artfully crude letterforms, achieved by distorting his chosen quotation in Photoshop, then hand-cutting a printout into a stencil. For the stencil, he uses a thin, woody paper that rarely lifts off intact, leaving shredded fiber that roughs up the otherwise clean all-caps messaging. Schumaker furthers this effect by mixing his acrylic paint with a medium used in bookbinding called methyl cellulose. When applied as a background, its slapdash wheatpaste texture recalls the broadside's history in political rallying—as well as underlines the hastiness of Trump's more erratic utterances. The letters themselves somehow retain an industrial effect, despite their organic, handpainted final form.

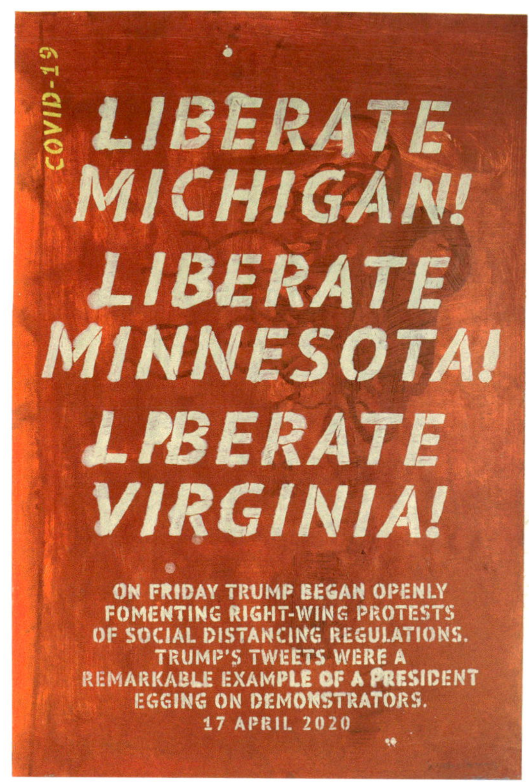

Ward Schumaker, posters from the series *Trump Papers* (*Hoisted by His Own Petard*), 2018, acrylic and paste on paper, 37 × 25¼ inches (94 × 64 cm), San Francisco. From left to right: *I'm President and You're Not*, *Disappear*, *Impeached*, *Liberate*.

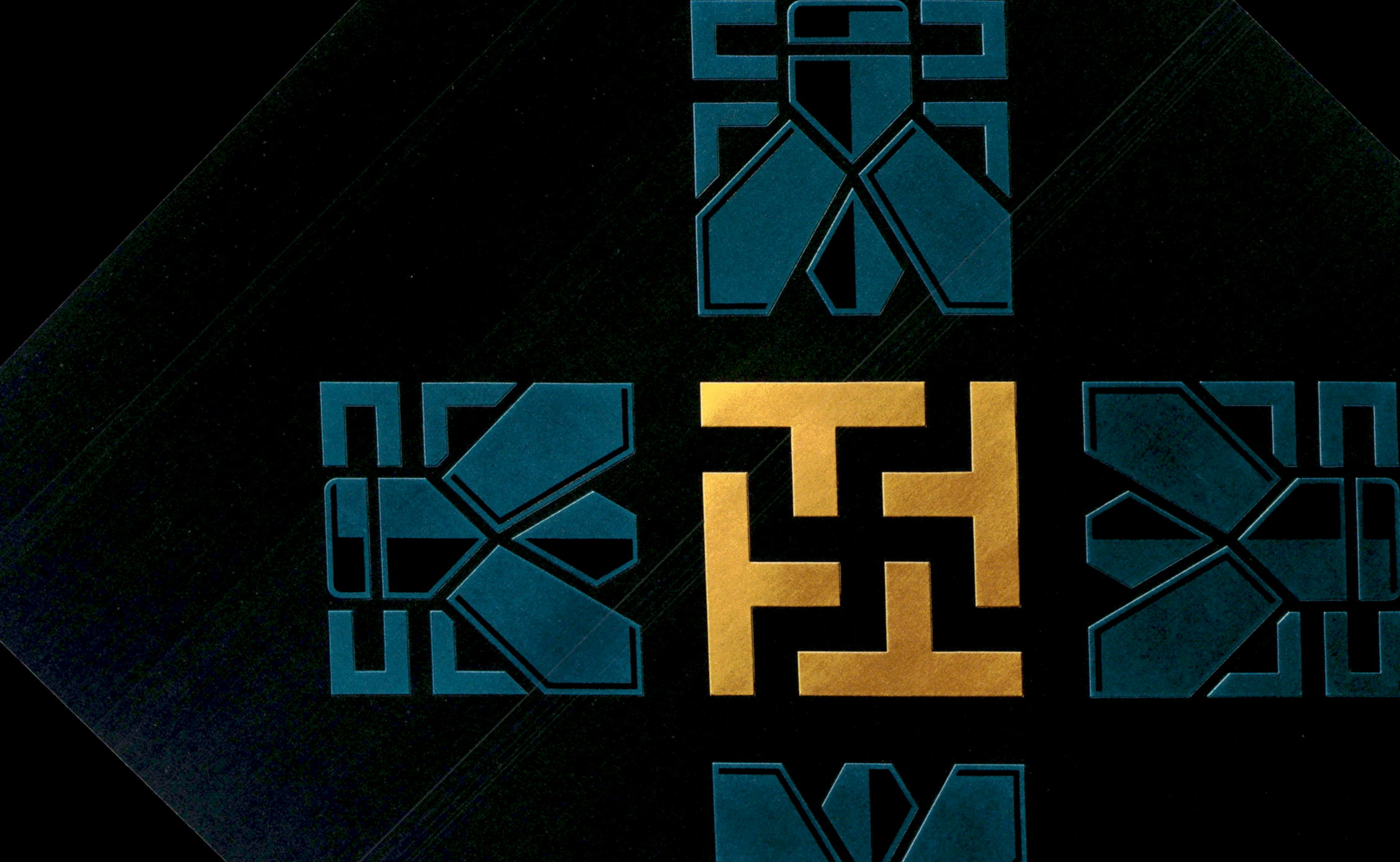

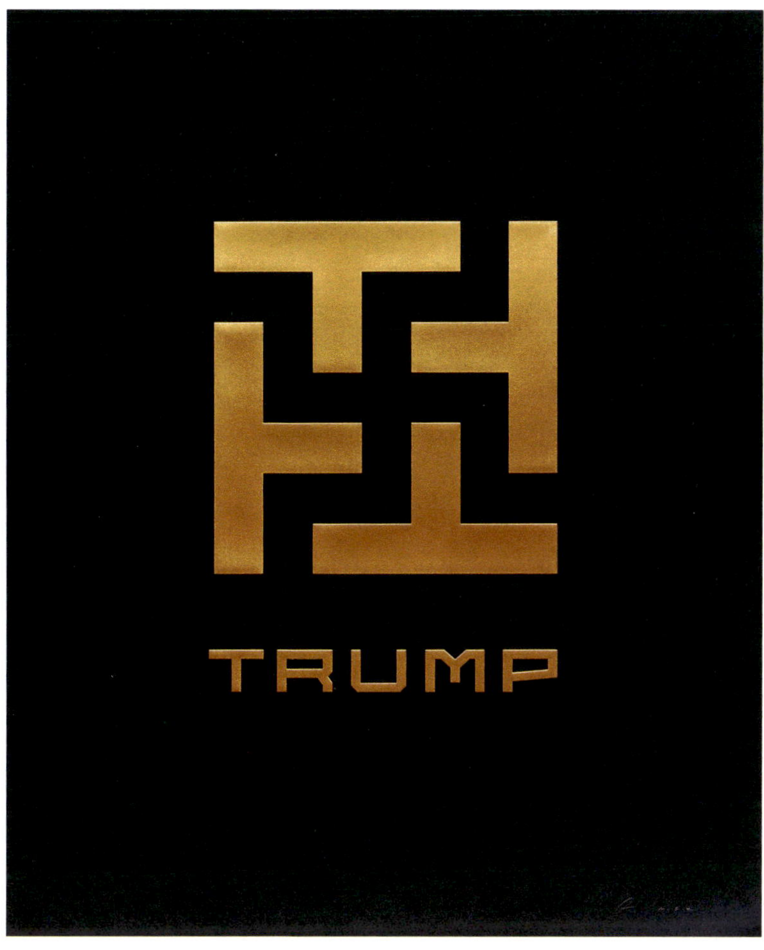

Design is Play (Mark Fox and Angie Wang), *Trump: Lord of the Lies*, 2020, and *Trump 24K Gold-Plated*, 2016, embossed and foil stamped, 22½ × 18⅞ inches (57 × 48 cm), San Francisco. This two-poster series repeats and rotates the *T* in Trump's name to turn the negative space into a swastika, here used as a symbol of hate speech. The text is set in Oblong, a typeface that smacks of both corporate empire and comic book villain.

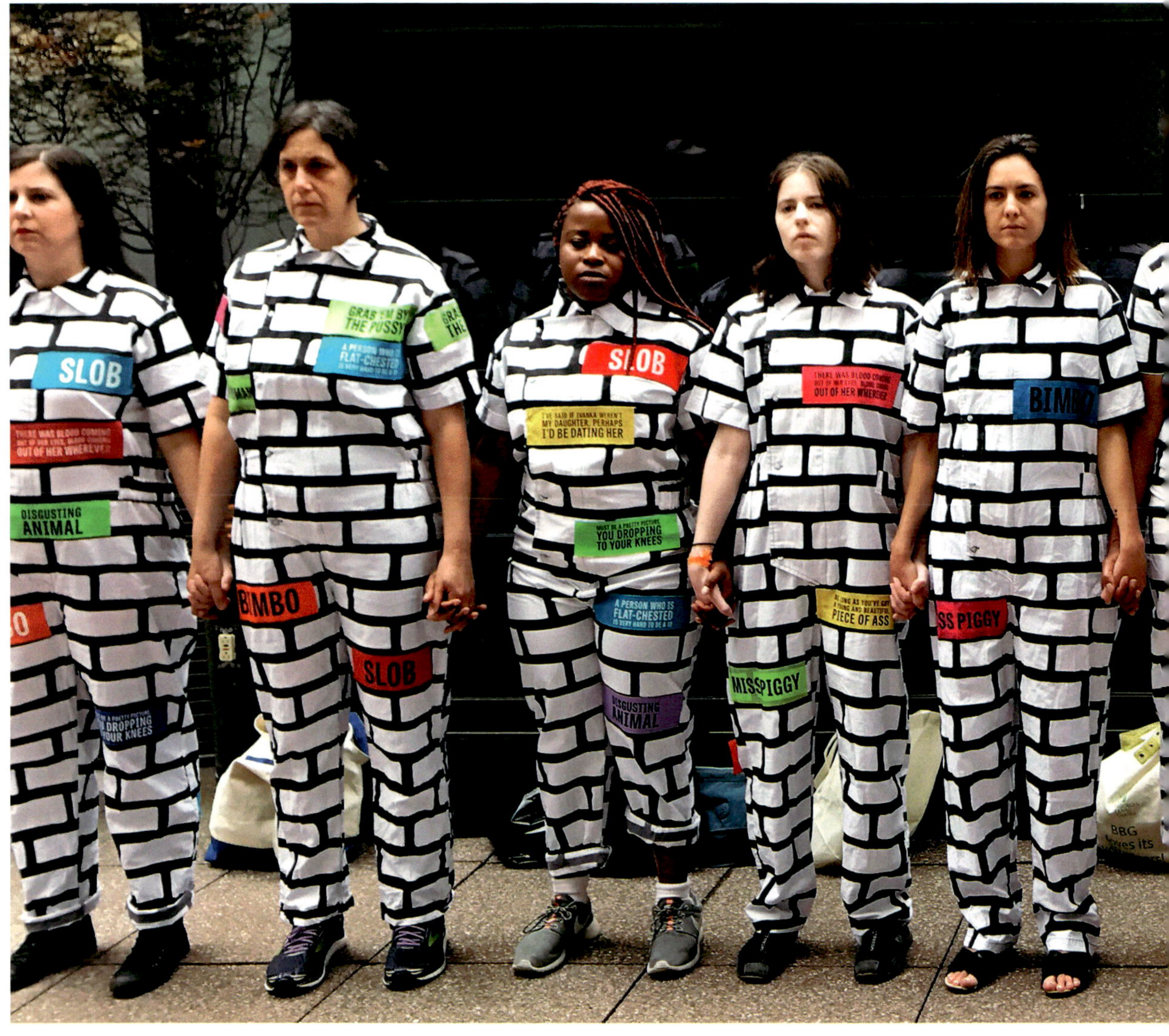

Formed in response to the 2016 U.S. presidential election, the performance art group Brick x Brick builds human walls against misogyny and xenophobia. Its participants wear jumpsuits printed with black-and-white brick outlines punctuated by colored blocks bearing slurs spoken by former president Trump. Set in a condensed gothic typeface that is stacked and justified to fill the rectangles, these words—among them "bimbo," "Miss Piggy," and, of course, "Grab 'em by the pussy," Trump's infamous brag about leveraging his power to sexually assault—are startling to see as labels on the participants, many of whom are women. The wall they form with their bodies—intersectional across race, ethnicity, age, and sexuality—stands in symbolic opposition to the one along the Mexican border partially constructed by the Trump administration. In their appearance at the 2017 Women's March in Washington, D.C., and at other demonstrations around the country, including at Trump Tower in Manhattan (seen here), Brick x Brick wields typography to exhibit strength against bigotry.

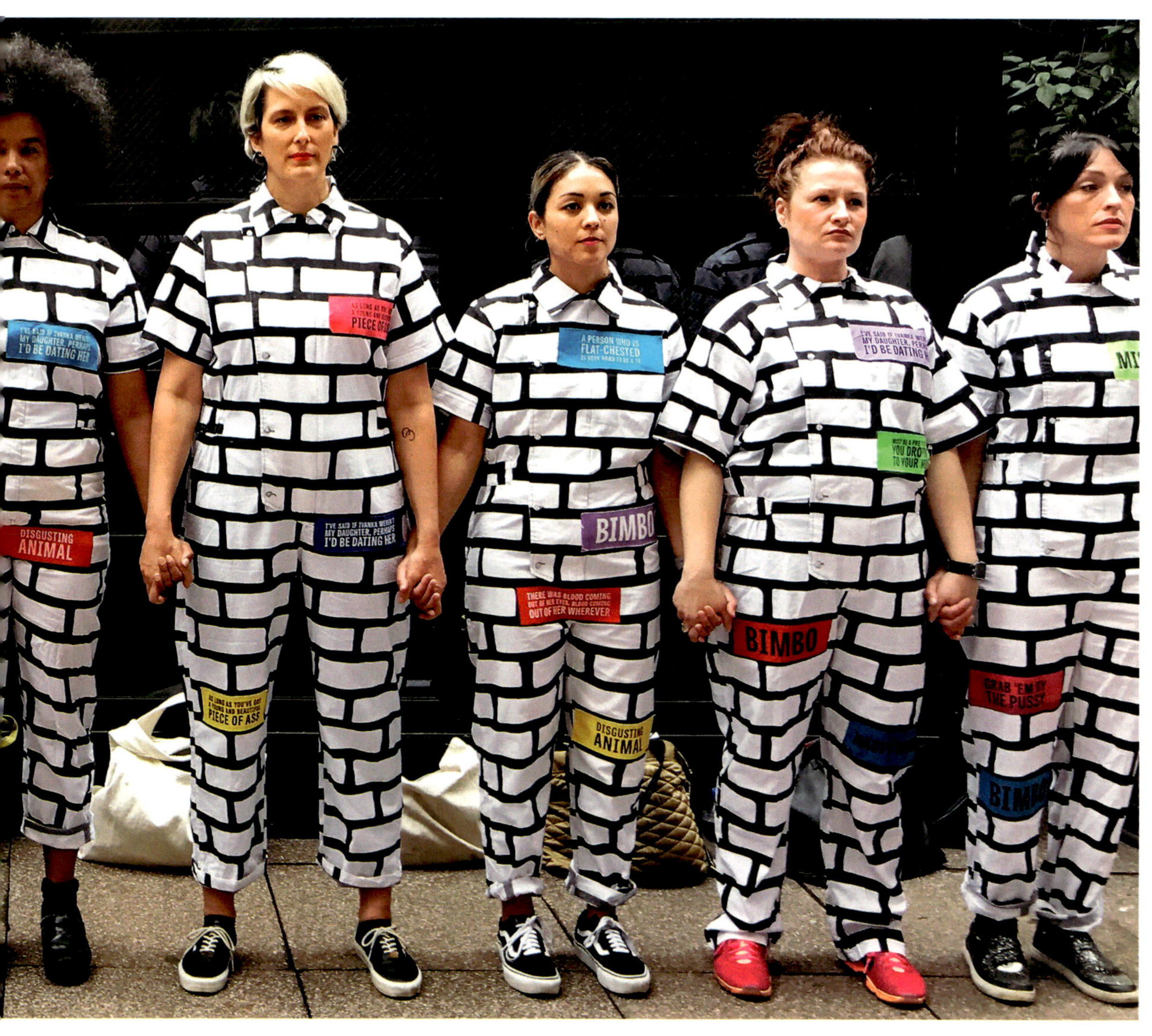

Brick x Brick (organization), Kyra Gaunt (creative strategist), Nikki Juen (co-director), Andrea Lauer and Sarah Sandman (co-directors and printers), Joey Ellis (garment-maker), jumpsuits for human wall demonstrations, 2017, screen print on cotton fabric, 59 × 36 inches (150 x 91.5 cm), Brooklyn.

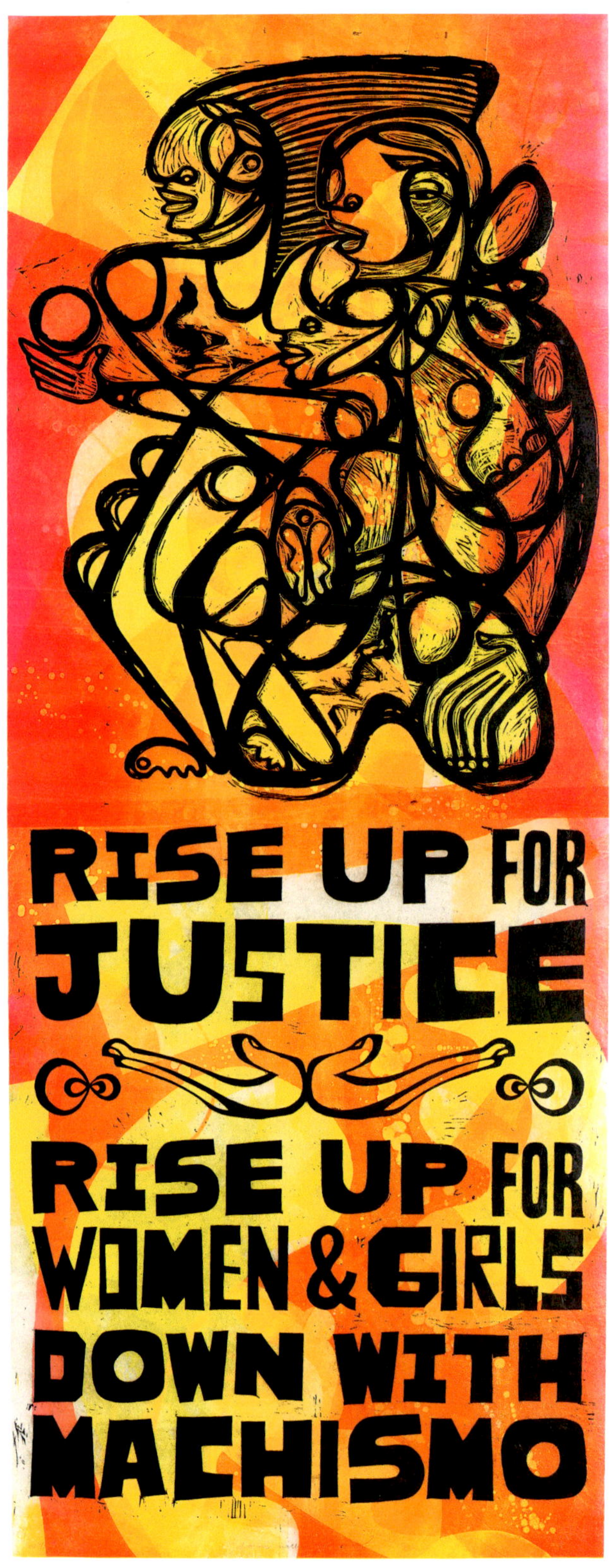
RISE UP FOR
JUSTICE
RISE UP FOR
WOMEN & GIRLS
DOWN WITH
MACHISMO

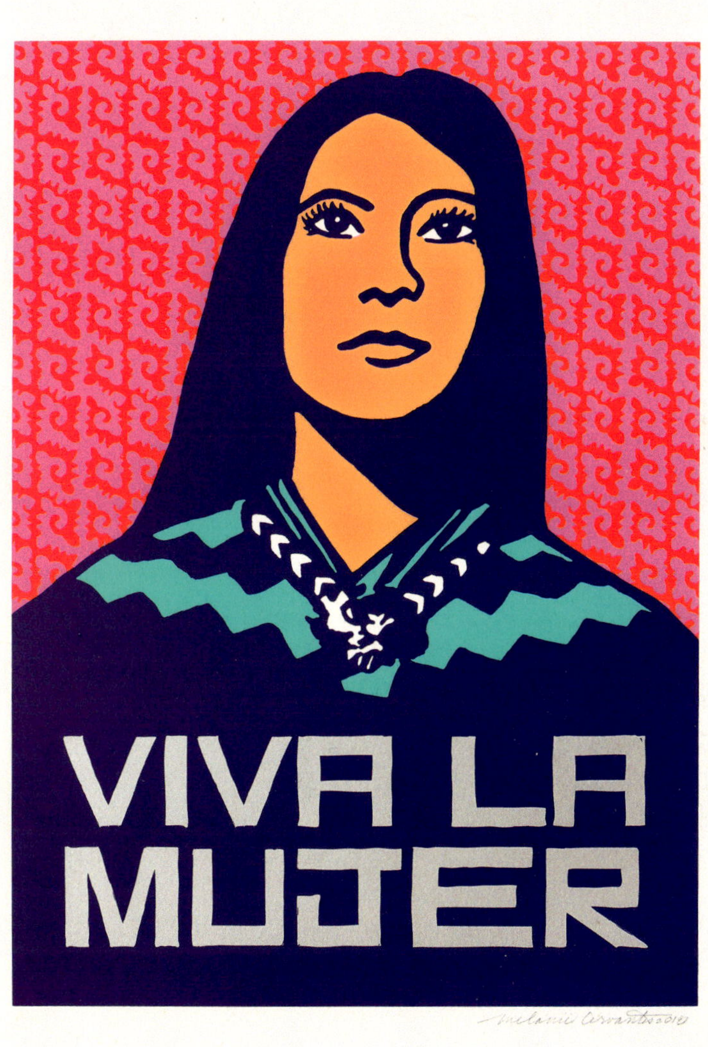

Favianna Rodriguez, *Down with Machismo*, 2014, monotype and woodblock, 60 × 24 inches (152.5 × 61 cm), Oakland, California. This poster was created in reaction to the abduction that year of hundreds of teenage girls from their school in northeastern Nigeria by the terrorist group Boko Haram.

Melanie Cervantes (designer), Jesus Barraza (pattern designer), *Long Live the Woman* (*Viva La Mujer*), 2020, screen print, 24 × 18 inches (61 × 45.5 cm), San Leandro, California. The background in this portrait of a Xicana woman is based on a three-thousand-year-old Olmec cosmological stamp.

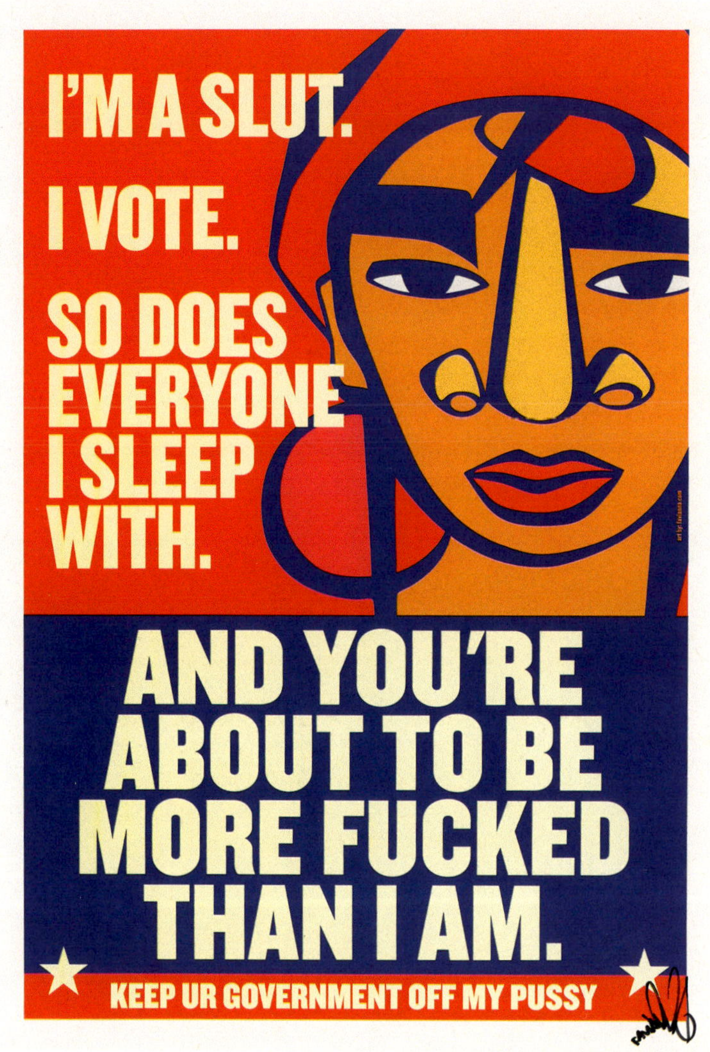

Favianna Rodriguez, *I'm a Slut*, 2012, digital print, 17 × 12 inches (43 × 30.5 cm), Oakland, California. This poster uses the typeface Knockout to convey its undaunted message, inspired by the ongoing political fight for access to healthcare, birth control, and safe, legal abortions.

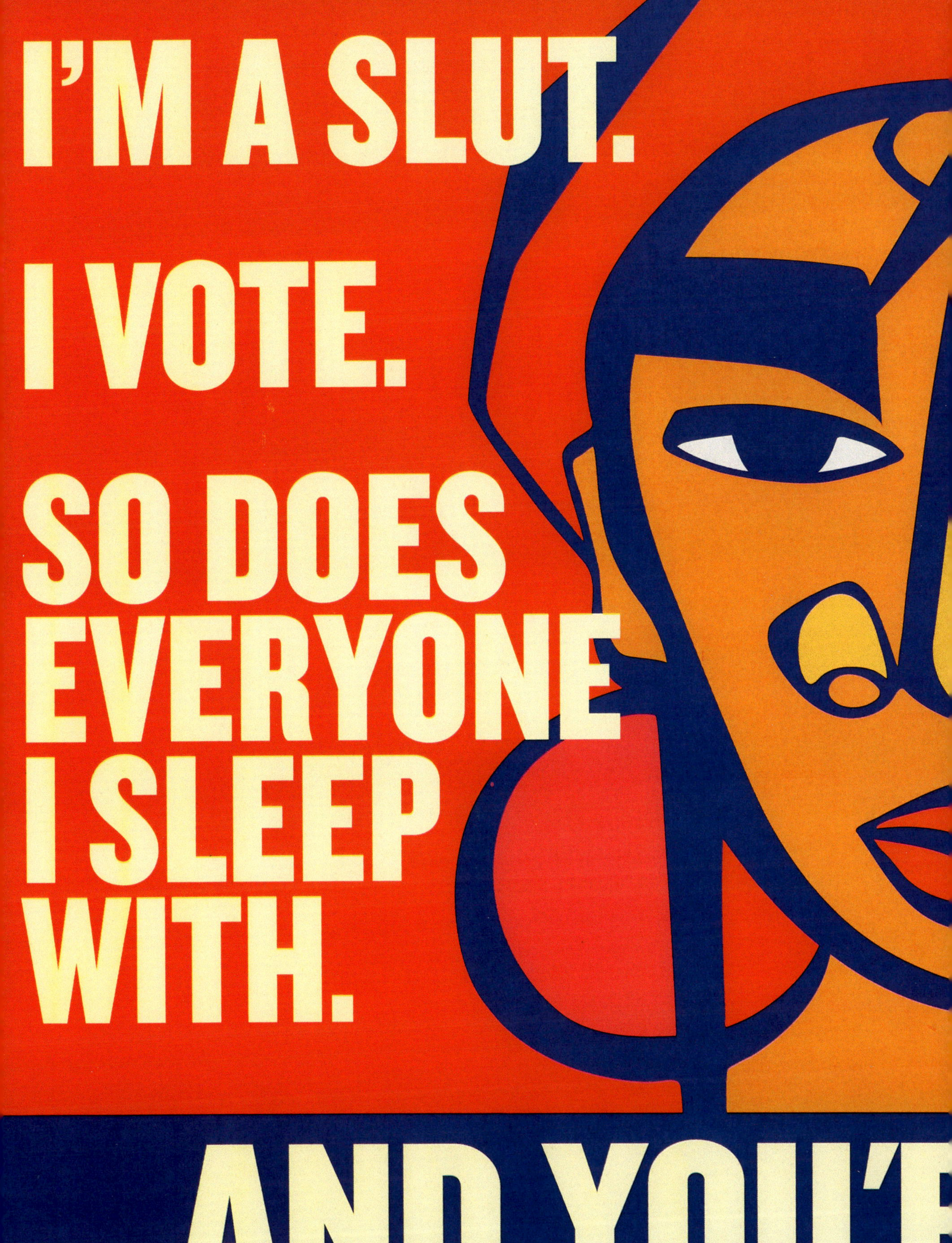
I'M A SLUT.
I VOTE.
SO DOES EVERYONE I SLEEP WITH.
AND YOU'

Designer as Protester

Favianna Rodriguez

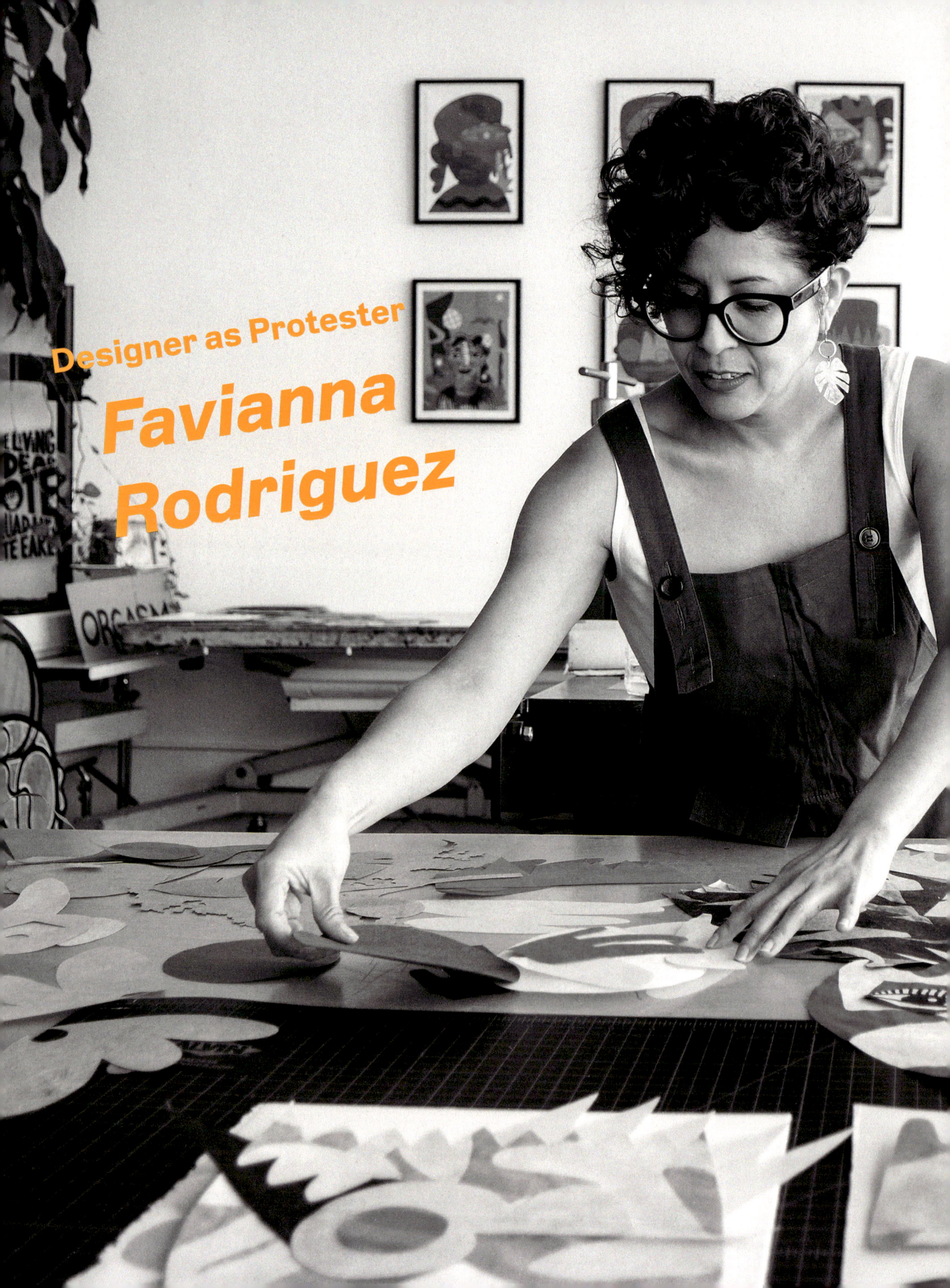

"Come out. Share your story. Break the silence."

—Favianna Rodriguez

For social justice artist and activist Favianna Rodriguez, there is no one single artistic medium for speaking out—just as there is no one single crucial political issue. Working at the intersection of sexual liberation, environmentalism, immigration, and racial and gender equality, Rodriguez's artwork demonstrates a multidisciplinary approach that involves screen print, linocut, woodblock, monotype, collage, murals, and more. One of her most celebrated works, *Migration Is Beautiful*, presents a migratory monarch butterfly with kaleidoscopic wings composed of two Indigenous faces to remind us what we gain through cultural cross-pollination. Other works, such as *Down with Machismo* (see page 136), made in response to the 2014 abduction of Nigerian schoolgirls by terrorist group Boko Haram, foregrounds the abuse of women and girls in a global trafficking economy that sees them as less than human.

Born in Oakland, California, to Peruvian immigrants in the late 1970s, Rodriguez came of age in a moment of tremendous social change. As a crack epidemic raged and gangs clashed in her neighborhood, she witnessed firsthand the police profiling of Black and Latinx people under the U.S. government's war on drugs.

Art provided an early sanctuary. She took her first printmaking class at the age of eight, where she encountered Chicano artists and organizers reshaping her community via bold artwork and direct action. She soon thereafter discovered the power of political murals in Mexico City, where she spent her early teenage years. While greatly inspired by the Mexican art she absorbed there, she also came up against the traditional gender roles often found in Latin culture.

When Rodriguez returned to Oakland for high school, she was galvanized by Proposition 187, a 1994 anti-immigration initiative that sought to bar undocumented individuals from access to California public schools, health care, and social services. She responded by leading a walkout and creating her first political flyers. Later, while pursuing degrees in architecture and ethnic studies at the University of California, Berkeley, Rodriguez experienced an unwanted pregnancy. After an abortion, she sojourned at the Self Help Graphics & Art center in Los Angeles, where she met artists such as print maker Yolanda Lopez, and came away with a new vision for her future.

Ten years after leaving school to make art in service of social justice, Rodriguez created the 2012 poster *I'm a Slut* (see page 138) as part of her series *Slut Power*, which responds to conservative politicians' efforts to restrict women's reproductive rights. She pairs exuberant, sophisticated portraits of Black and brown women—abstracted in bright colors and boldly outlined—with proud texts like "Keep Ur Government Off My Pussy" to both celebrate and defend the sexuality of women of color. For Rodriguez, the full experience of pleasure—sexual and otherwise—is one of the most potent ways to speak back to oppression.

And so is direct action, of course. Rodriguez is cofounder and president of the Center for Cultural Power, where she helps the next generation find ways to wield art that tells stories and makes lasting change.

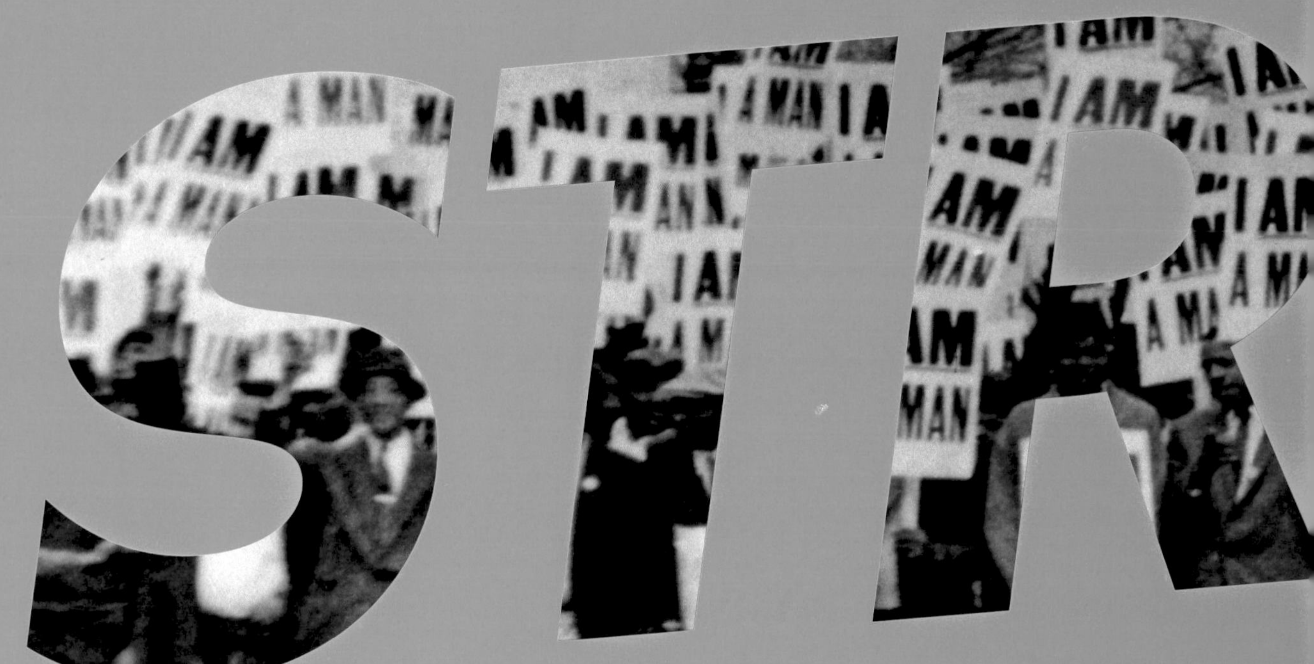
STR
I AM
A MAN

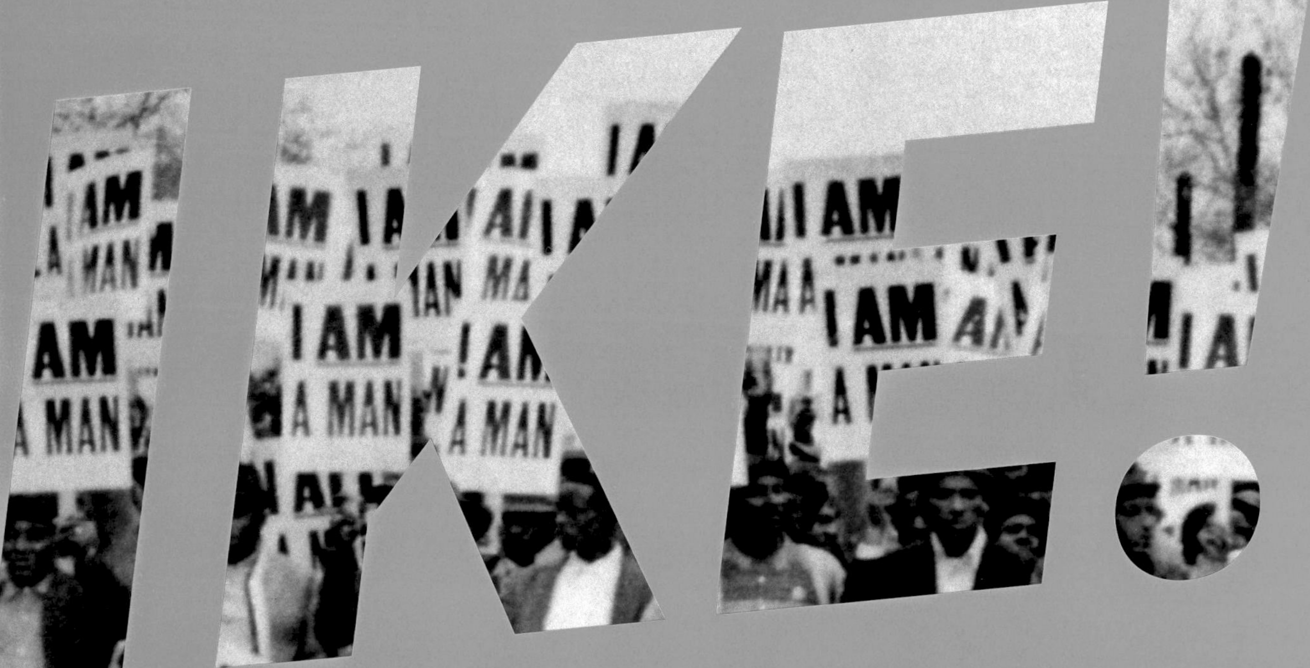
IKE!
I AM
A MAN

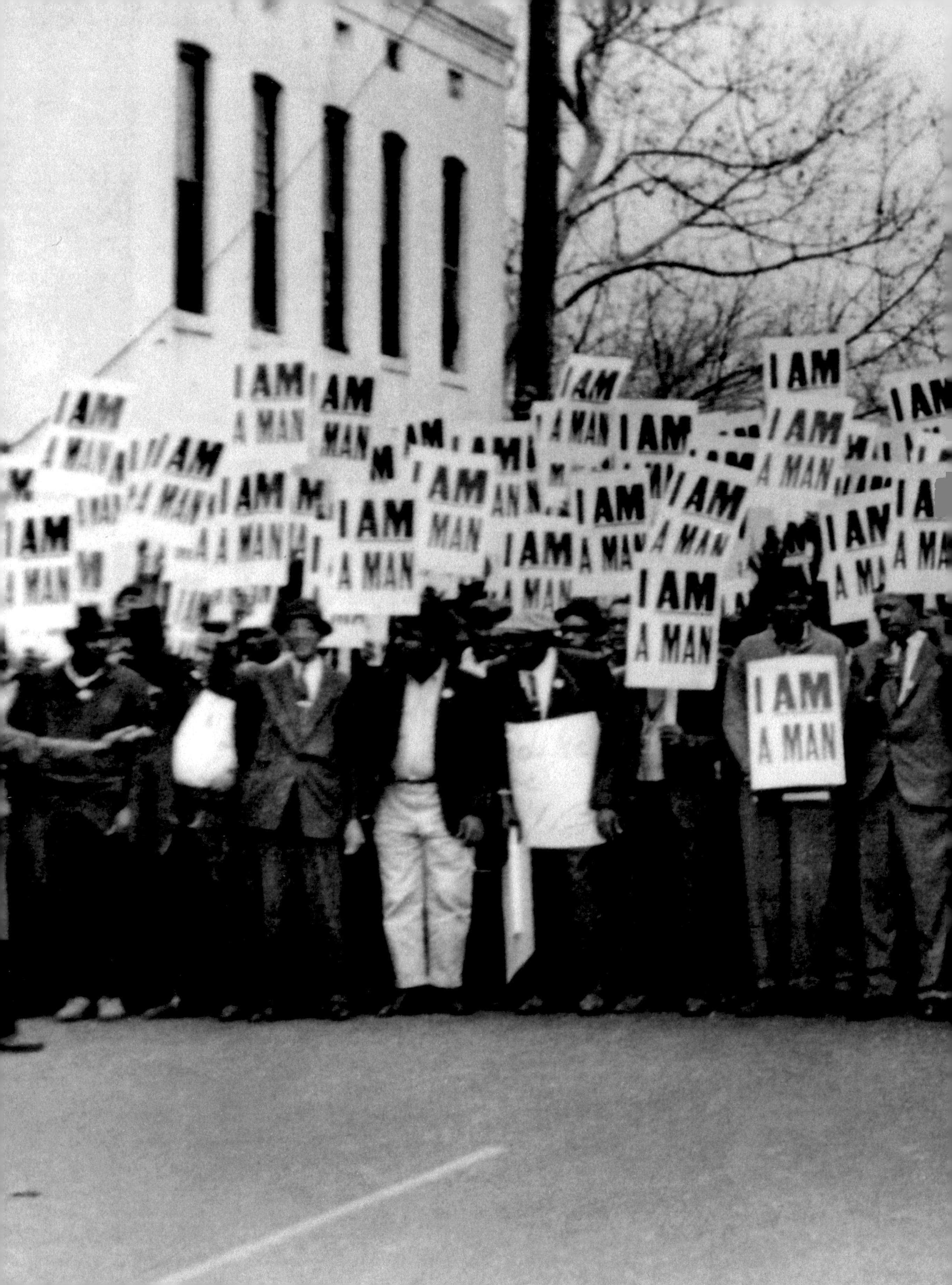
I AM
A MAN
I AM
A MAN

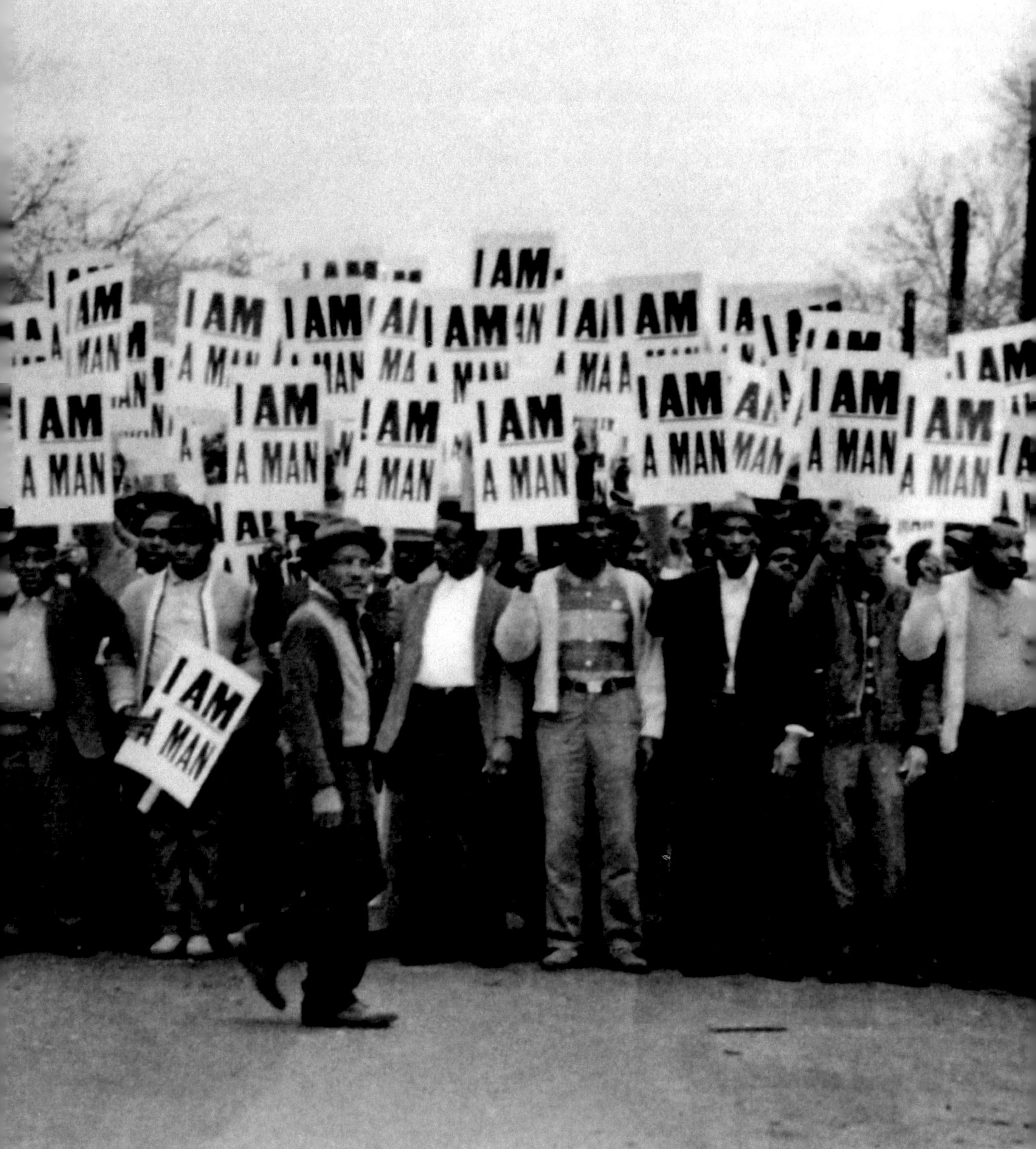
I AM
A MAN

"Lightning makes no sound until it strikes."

—Dr. Martin Luther King, Jr., *Why We Can't Wait*, 1964

STRIKE!

Recorded on an ancient papyrus, the first known labor strike occurred in the twelfth century BCE, when Egyptian artisans laid down their tools after the pharaoh missed payroll one too many times. Ever since, workers at various stages in history have walked off the job in protest, leveraging their collective power to create real and lasting change—from wage increases to enforced standards in workplace safety to the eight-hour workday to paid sick leave.

The fight that led to many of these more recent improvements began during the Industrial Revolution, as its dangerous factories, around-the-clock shifts, and unchecked demands on child and immigrant labor created a dire need for organizing. The Great Depression added to this need: In 1933, more than 12 million citizens (a quarter of the workforce) were out of a job. At the end of World War II, after federal policies permitted a surge in organizing across industries, more than the same number of people held unionized jobs, and unions became a powerhouse in the political landscape.

In the United States, the history of labor often intersects with major moments in civil rights. We begin this chapter with *I Am a Man*, one of the most iconic protest signs of the twentieth century. It was created in 1968 in Memphis to support a strike initiated by Black sanitation workers after two were crushed to death in a malfunctioning garbage truck and the city cruelly denied their families compensation. The sign's bold declaration in large letterpress type belies the complexity of what should be a simple ask: that its bearer be treated like a human being. As attention to the Memphis movement gained national attention, Dr. Martin Luther King, Jr., came several times to march in solidarity with the 1,300 striking workers. Tragically, King was assassinated during his third visit. In death, however, MLK inspired additional protest signs that read "Honor King, End Racism" in the same typographic style, as well as souvenir printings of the original *I Am a Man* design. The Memphis workers eventually got their due, but not until they went on strike again months later to force the city to follow through on its promises.

Across the country, another lengthy labor struggle was under way. Lasting from 1965 to 1970, and led by Dolores Huerta, Cesar Chavez, and Larry Itliong, the Delano Grape Strike would become one of the most notable campaigns in union history. Two posters in this chapter present different approaches to rallying support for the cause. *Don't Eat Grapes*, by the legendary American designer Milton Glaser, helped turn public opinion against the farm owners with a visual pun that equates nonunion fruit with a radioactive skull. Meanwhile, *¡Viva La Huelga!*, by an anonymous designer working with the United Farm Workers union, which organized the strike, proudly displays the battle cry of the migrant workers in their own language, accompanied by a graphic illustration of an Aztec bird overlaid onto a triumphant red-and-gold sunburst.

The works of Chicano poet, artist, and organizer Carlos Cortez also often highlight the contributions of immigrant or migrant workers. Cortez was a proud Wobbly—a member of the Industrial Workers of the World (IWW)—who lionized grassroots heroes of labor in his linocut portraits. Subjects of his tributes include Lucy Parsons, a Black anarchist who co-led the first May Day parade on the eve of the 1886 Haymarket affair in Chicago, and Joe Hill, a Wobbly folksong writer and itinerant worker who was wrongly put to death in 1915.

This chapter also includes posters by Atelier Populaire—a group of art students who helped spark a nationwide strike in France in 1968—and artwork from the 1969 pan-tribal Indigenous occupation of Alcatraz Island, which sought to reclaim stolen land for Native use. Together, the pieces in this section illustrate what organized solidarity can do.

We end with examples of how currency can be used as a vehicle for economic protest, particularly as rampant income inequality, predatory lending practices, and runaway corporate profits conspire against present and future generations.

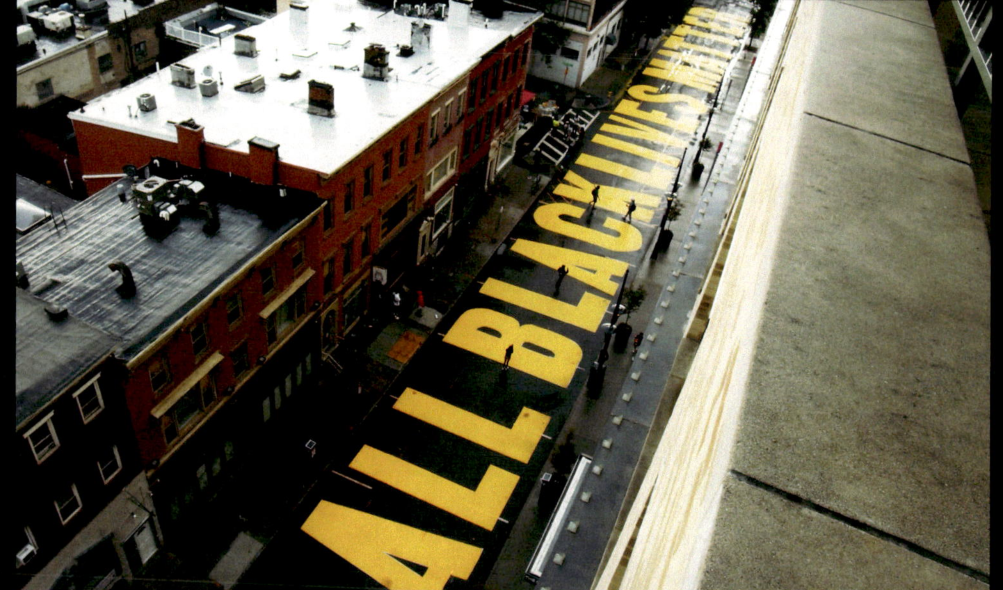

Call and Response

“I am a man”: These four short words compress four hundred years of Black men’s resilience and anger in the face of racial, economic, and social persecution. Made for Memphis sanitation workers striking over the deaths of two Black laborers, the sign pictured at left derives its power from a typographic approach that is as stark and insistent as its message. Its text was set in Plain Gothic No. 6243 (a wood type from the Hamilton Manufacturing Company), with “am” emphatically underlined, and printed by a local pastor in an edition of a few hundred. It revives the question posed by abolitionists in the previous century: “Am I not a man and a brother?”

Reprinted in a run of thousands as the strike wore on, the sign also draws power from its multiplicity: When held aloft, it reads as a visual chant, gaining in volume across the crowd. It also engages in a form of typographic call and response, not just with abolitionists but also with the nation’s founders, who put forth that “all men are created equal” but then drafted a Constitution that excluded many of them.

Black type designer Tré Seals, creator of the foundry Vocal Type, built on the sign’s legacy with his digital font revival Martin. Based on the letters on the sanitation workers’ signs, Martin allows a new generation to typographically honor its civil rights legacy—as well as continue the fight, as shown by its use above in a street mural for a 2020 Black Lives Matter demonstration. Seals conducts meticulous photo research of protesters and their signs to craft his typefaces, which include Marsha, named for gay liberation and trans activist Marsha P. Johnson; Carrie, based on banners used in a 1915 suffragist march led by Carrie Chapman Catt; and Bayard, named for Bayard Rustin, an openly gay Black man who worked with Dr. Martin Luther King, Jr., to plan the 1963 March on Washington for Jobs and Freedom.

I AM
A
MAN

Tré Seals, the typeface Martin, 2017, digital font, Washington, D.C. Here, Seals's digital revival appears painted on a street for the 2020 Murals for Justice project, a collaboration between the city of Newark, New Jersey; Rutgers University; and a local group of creative leaders and artists.

Unknown designer for the American Federation of State, County, and Municipal Employees (AFSCME), *I Am a Man!*, 1968, letterpress, 21½ × 14 inches (54.5 × 35.5 cm), Memphis, Tennessee. Collection of the Smithsonian National Museum of African American History and Culture.

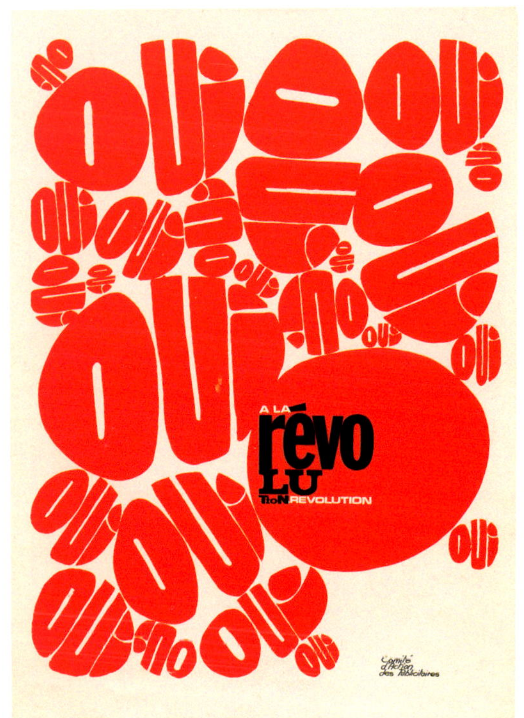

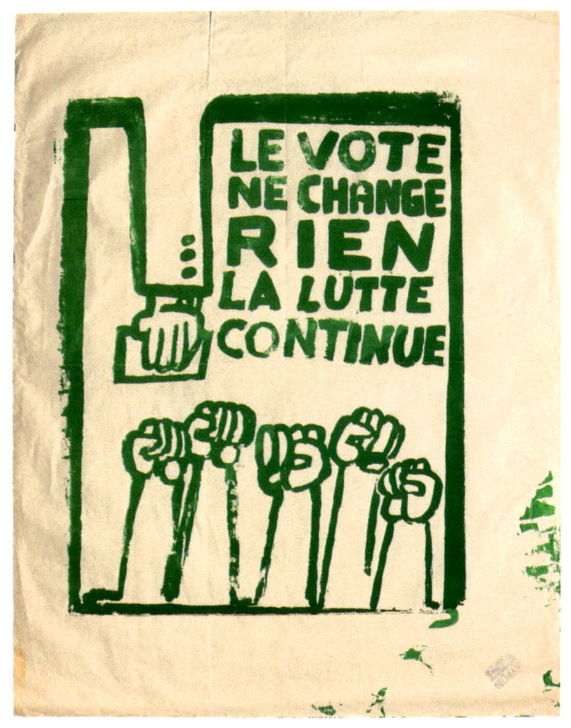

Atelier Populaire, 1968, screen print on newsprint, Paris. Clockwise from top left: *Yes to the Revolution!* (*Oui à la révolution!*), 24½ × 18 inches (62 × 45.5 cm); *The Vote Changes Nothing—The Struggle Continues* (*Le vote ne change rien—la lutte continue*), 37¾ × 29⅞ inches (96 × 76 cm); *The Police Are Also Men. The Proof? They Rape Women in the Stations* (*Les CRS sont aussi des hommes. La Preuve? Ils violent les filles dans les commissariats*), 27⅞ × 19⅞ inches (71 × 50.5 cm); *Solidarity with Flins* (*Solidaires de Flins*), 25¾ × 18¾ inches (65.5 × 47.5 cm); *Stop the Expulsion!* (*Halte à l'expulsion!*), 25⅞ × 22⅛ inches (65.5 × 56 cm); *Workers, Students, People: Effective Meeting Flins* (*Ouvriers, étudiants, population: Liaison effective Flins*), 31½ × 23⅝ inches (80 × 60 cm). Here are just a few of Atelier Populaire's more than six hundred poster designs, which include those created in solidarity with the workers at the Renault automotive factory in Flins, France.

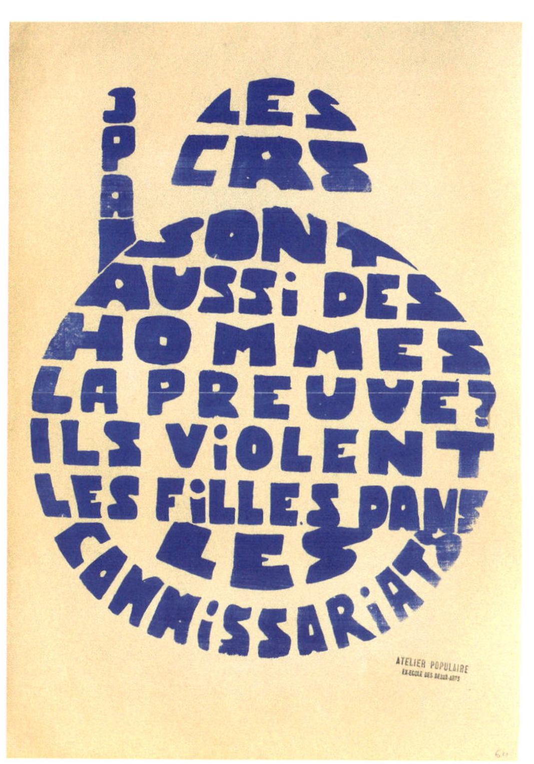
LES
CRS
SONT
AUSSi DES
HOMMES
LA PREUVE?
ILS ViOLENT
LES FiLLES DANS
LES
COMMiSSARiATS
ATELIER POPULAIRE

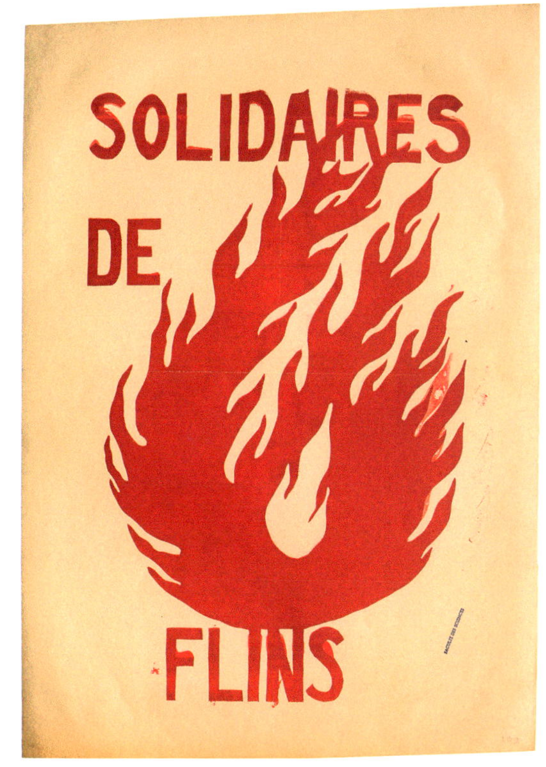
SOLIDAIRES
DE
FLINS

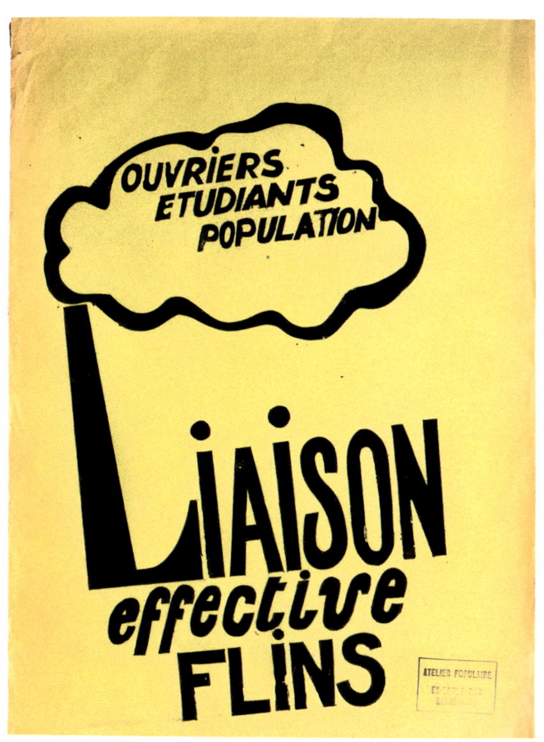
OUVRIERS
ETUDIANTS
POPULATION
LiAiSON
effective
FLiNS
ATELIER POPULAIRE

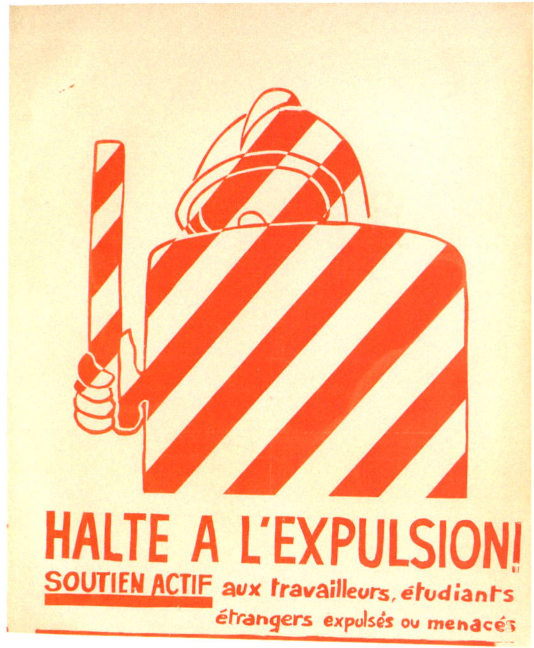
HALTE A L'EXPULSION!
SOUTIEN ACTIF aux travailleurs, étudiants
étrangers expulsés ou menacés

Designer as Protester

Atelier Populaire

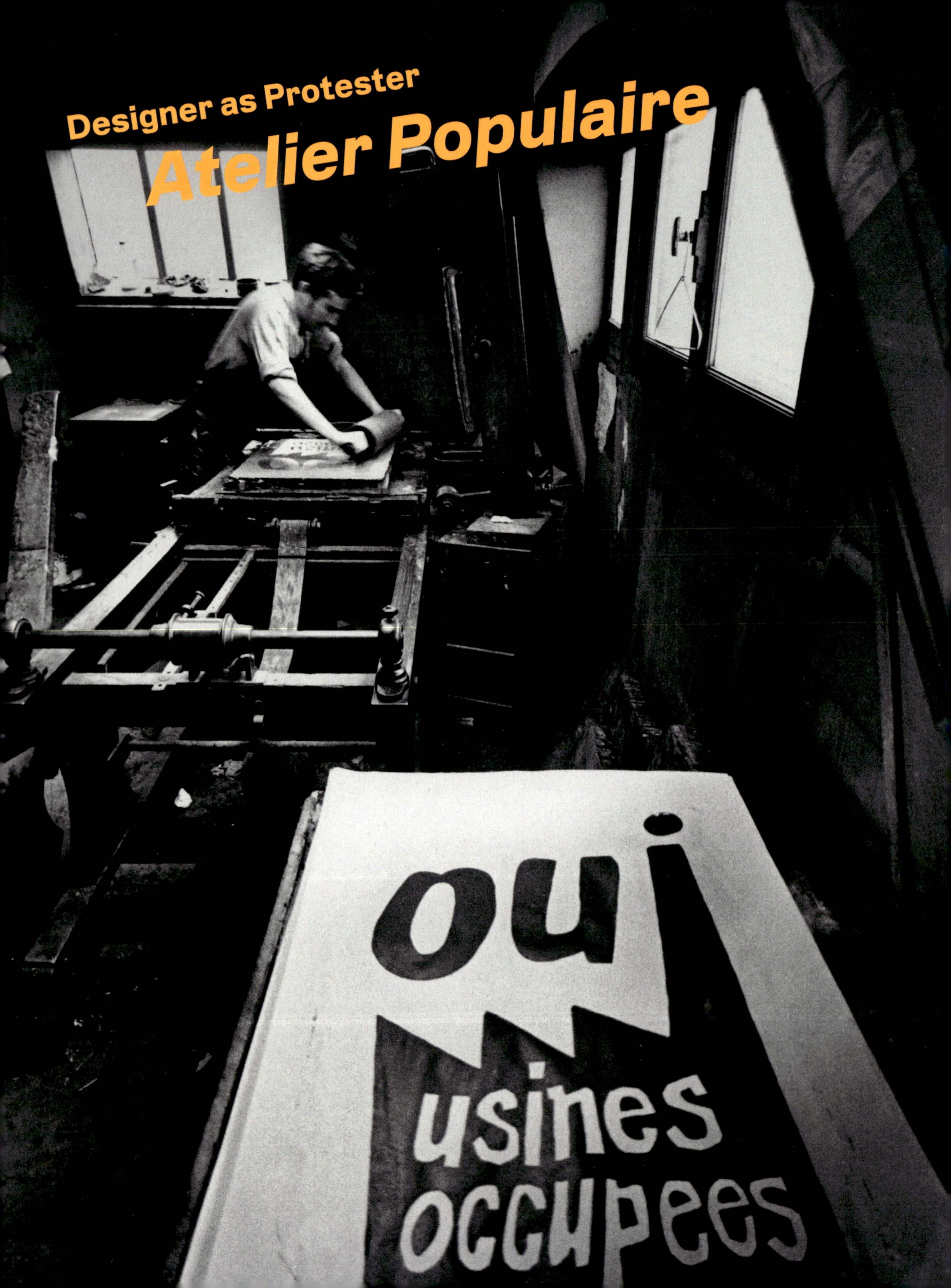

"The posters . . . are weapons in the service of the struggle and are an inseparable part of it."

—Atelier Populaire

In Paris in May of 1968, twenty thousand students, teachers, and supporters marched to the Sorbonne, France's most prestigious school, in protest of class discrimination within the university system. As they approached the campus, police beat them back with batons and tear gas. After days of barricades, fires, and arrests, French workers—angry over unemployment and poverty under President Charles de Gaulle—went on strike in solidarity with the students and faculty. Ultimately, 11 million people—more than 20 percent of France's workforce—joined in the actions. The nation ground to a halt.

To spread the message of the students and strikers, a collective of artists overtook the lithography workshop at the nearby École des Beaux-Arts. They renamed it Atelier Populaire ("popular workshop") and printed thousands of posters, with slogans like "Stop the expulsion!" and "The vote changes nothing!" (see pages 150–51). Charmingly irreverent in execution but dead serious in messaging, the posters forged a weaponized exuberance against the conservative de Gaulle presidency.

Many of the pieces feature organic, childlike handlettering, often arranged into *calligrams* (illustrations in which the placement of the words is inspired by the shape of their subject). For example, *The Police Are Also Men . . .* uses the shape of a cop's circular shield and helmet to tell the brutal story of police raping women at headquarters. And in *Yes to the Revolution!*, a chorus of "*Oui*" in red bubble letters of various sizes mimics the affirmative cries of a crowd. Most are printed in a single bold color for a naive effect that belies the sophistication of the group's message.

The students used silk-screening as a cheaper, more efficient production method than stone lithography. Since it wasn't taught at the school, they posted instructions in the pressroom. Out of solidarity with workers and befitting the group's first slogan, "*Usine—Université—Union*" ("Factory—University—Union"), the students worked in assembly lines and voted on which designs to print. In the same spirit, they often signed them as a collective with a stamp instead of with individual artists' names.

Atelier Populaire members did not want their posters sold by collectors or hung in galleries. Instead, they believed that their "rightful place is in the centers of conflict . . . in the streets and on the walls of the factories," as quoted in an introduction to a book on their work. "Even to keep them as historical evidence of a certain stage in the struggle is a betrayal, for the struggle itself is of such primary importance that the position of an 'outside' observer is a fiction which inevitably plays into the hands of the ruling class." Acknowledging this conundrum, we present them to raise awareness of Atelier Populaire.

The students were expelled from the workshop in June of 1968, after only six weeks. But the strikes, which ended later that summer, forever changed French notions of culture and hierarchy.

"We are holding the island of Alcatraz in the true names of freedom, justice, and equality . . . . WE HOLD THE ROCK!"

—*Indians of All Tribes* newsletter, vol. 1, no. 1, 1970

On November 20, 1969, nearly one hundred American Indians landed on Alcatraz, the site of a once-notorious island prison in the San Francisco Bay. Calling themselves the Indians of All Tribes, they asserted that, under an 1868 treaty, any surplus federal land must be returned to Native people. They offered what the Dutch supposedly paid the Lenape people for Manhattan in 1626: $24 in beads and cloth.

Over the year and a half of the occupation, which at times included as many as six hundred people, the island became home to a school, a clinic, and a communal kitchen. Led by LaNada Means (now LaNada War Jack), Richard Oakes, and John Trudell (of the Shoshone-Bannock, Mohawk, and Santee Dakota tribes, respectively), the group sought the deed to the island, with the intention of turning it into a cultural center. While the occupation fell short of its goal, it drew national attention and was a key event for the pan-tribal Red Power movement.

To educate the public about Native concerns (including the theft of ancestral lands and poor water quality on reservations), the Indians of All Tribes printed a newsletter. For one issue, fourteen-year-old Paiute member and Alcatraz resident Elvin Willie carved a woodblock that reads "This Is My Land, All of It" on an arching baseline. His irregular letters graphically link the silhouette of Alcatraz, the jagged San Francisco skyline, and an outline of the United States.

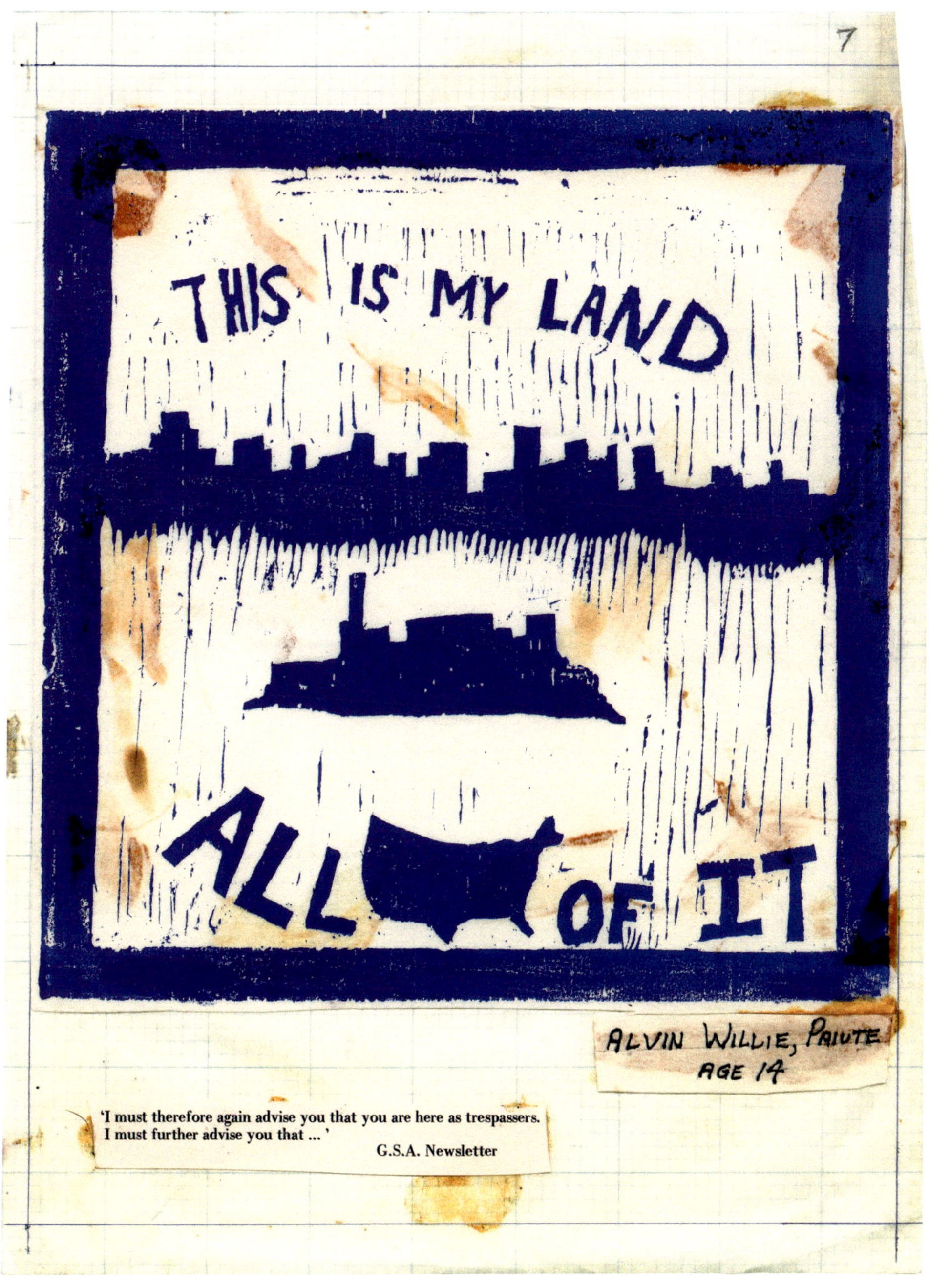

Unknown designer, mechanical for vol. 1, no. 1 of the *Indians of All Tribes* Alcatraz newsletter, featuring *This Is My Land, All of It*, by Elvin Willie (spelled "Alvin" here), 1970, woodblock, 12 × 9 inches (30.5 × 23 cm), San Francisco. Collection of Alcatraz Indian Occupation Records, San Francisco History Center, San Francisco Public Library.

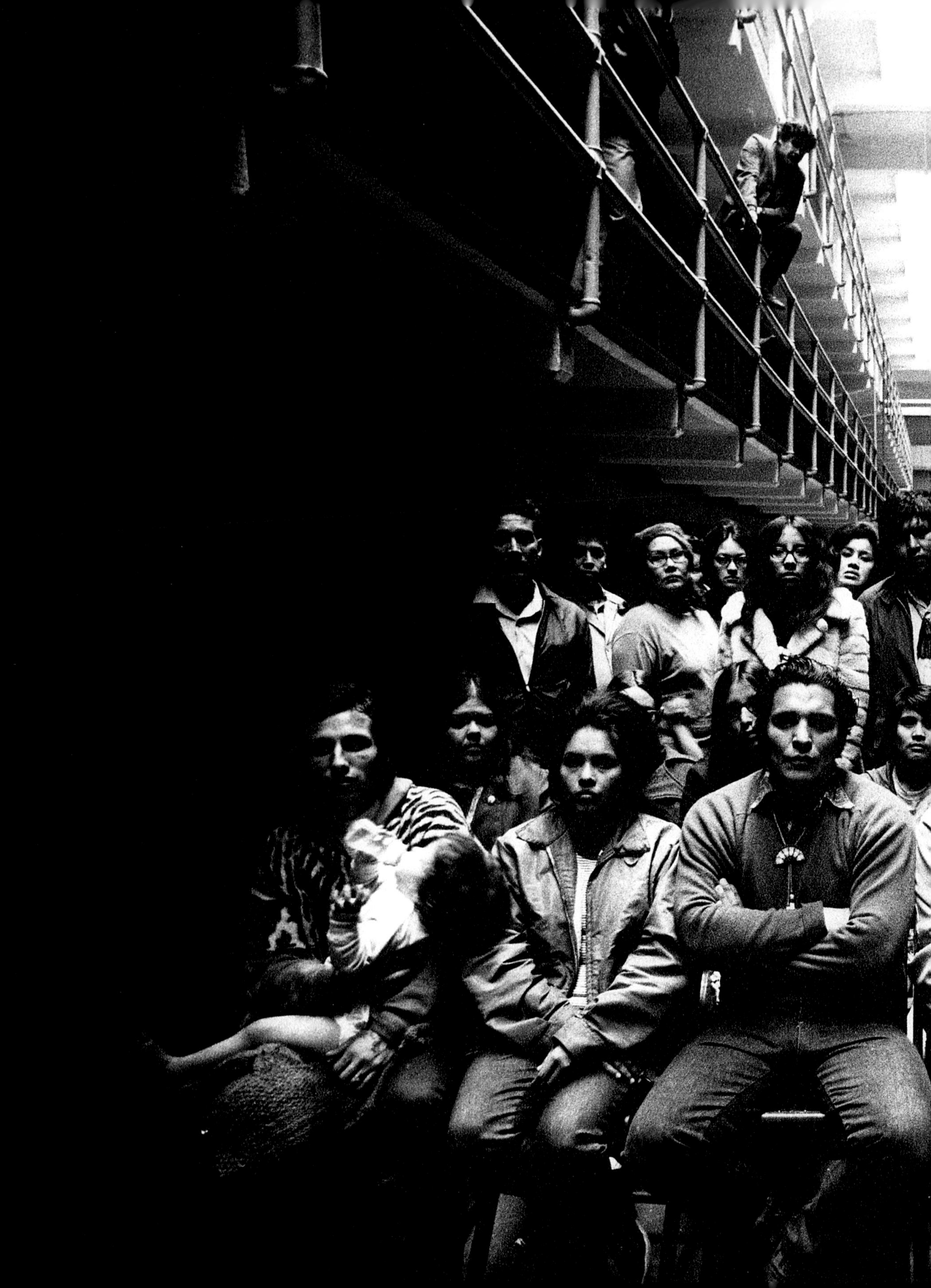

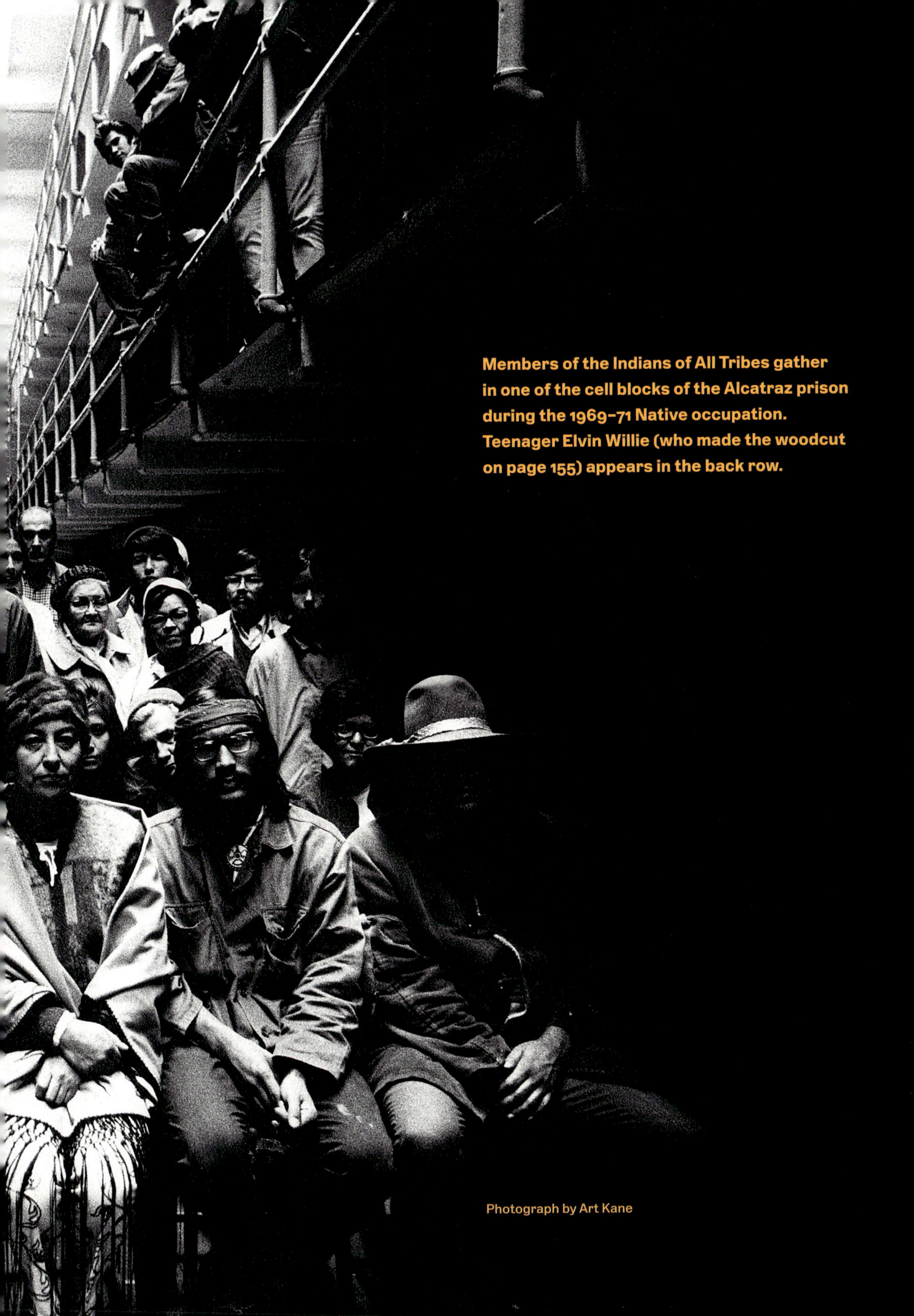

Members of the Indians of All Tribes gather in one of the cell blocks of the Alcatraz prison during the 1969–71 Native occupation. Teenager Elvin Willie (who made the woodcut on page 155) appears in the back row.

Photograph by Art Kane

"The colors of our skins, the languages of our cultural and native origins, the lack of formal education, the exclusion from the democratic process, the numbers of our slain in recent wars—all these burdens generation after generation have sought to demoralize us, to break our human spirit. But God knows that we are not beasts of burden, we are not agricultural implements or rented slaves, we are men."

—Cesar Chavez, letter from Delano, California, 1969

From 1965 to 1970, the Delano Grape Strike brought the working conditions and pay of farm laborers to the forefront of the American consciousness. This poster by famed designer Milton Glaser is direct but surprising, and the image—a bunch of grapes, radioactive in color and shaped like a skull—transmits its message through lethal connotation.

After the 1962 publication of Rachel Carson's conservationist warning *Silent Spring*, the harmful effects of pesticides became a critical issue for both environmental and labor movements. The Delano strike was a joint effort by the Agricultural Workers Organizing Committee (AWOC), a Filipino labor organization led by Larry Itliong, and the predominantly Mexican National Farm Workers Association (NFWA), led by Cesar Chavez and Dolores Huerta. The two organizations soon merged to form the United Farm Workers (UFW). Rare at the time for its coalition across ethnicities, which had often been pitted against each other, the movement harnessed grassroots methods of door-to-door education, civic meetings, marches, nonviolent resistance, and boycotts. In solidarity, union dockworkers refused to load nonunion grapes, while consumers refused to buy them.

Playing off the layout style of magazine ads of the time, Glaser's poster functions as a sort of anti-advertisement. With a headline in Helvetica Black, the text below the skull excerpts a letter—set in News Gothic—from Chavez decrying the discrimination against the workers.

Five years after the strike began, under the duress of the boycott, the grape companies of Delano, California, caved to union demands. Ten thousand farm workers were guaranteed a wage increase from $1.65 to $1.80, employer contributions to healthcare, and safety protections from pesticides. The UFW is still active today.

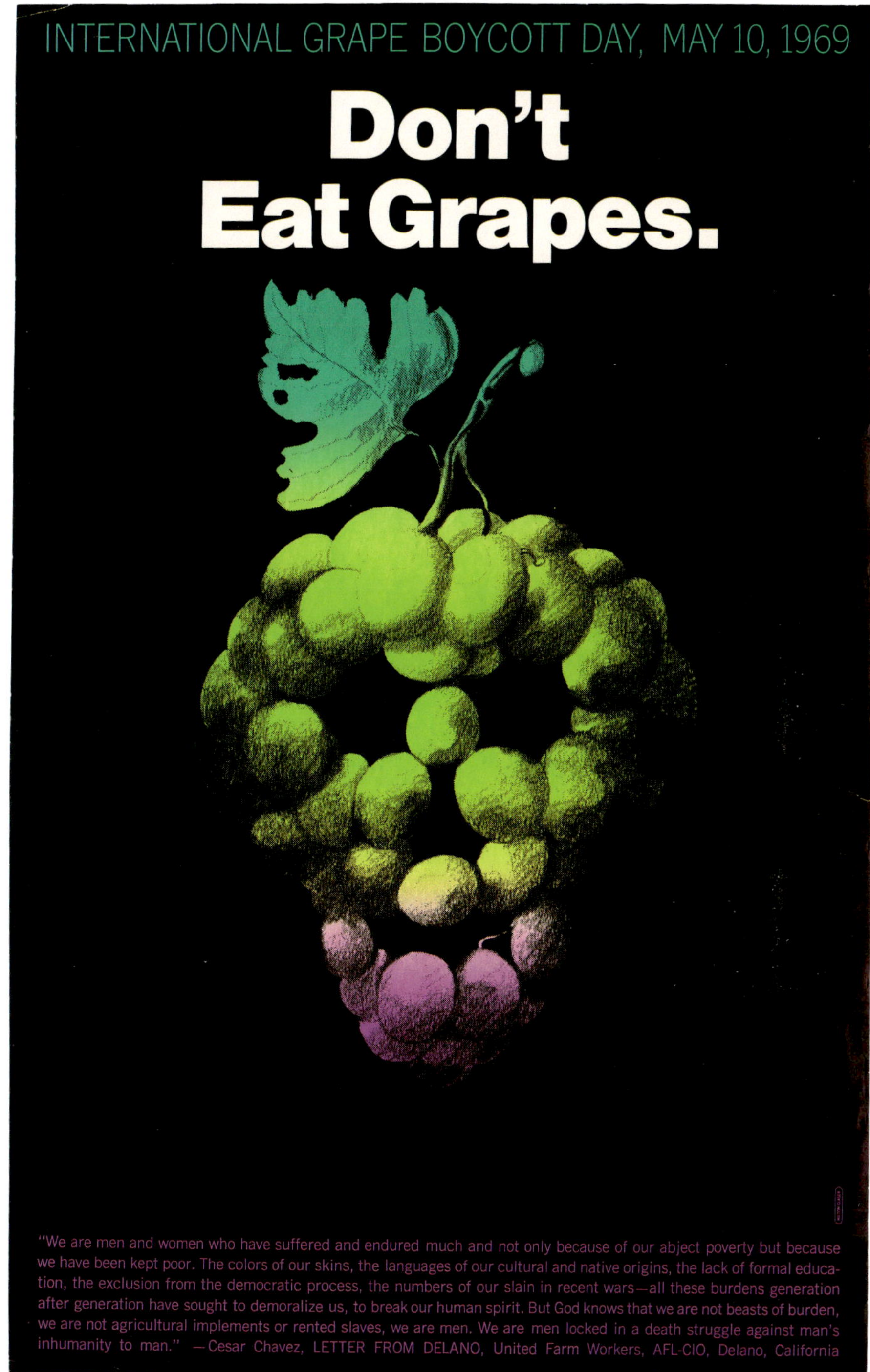

Milton Glaser, *Don't Eat Grapes*, 1969, offset, 36½ × 23½ inches (92.5 × 59.5 cm), New York.

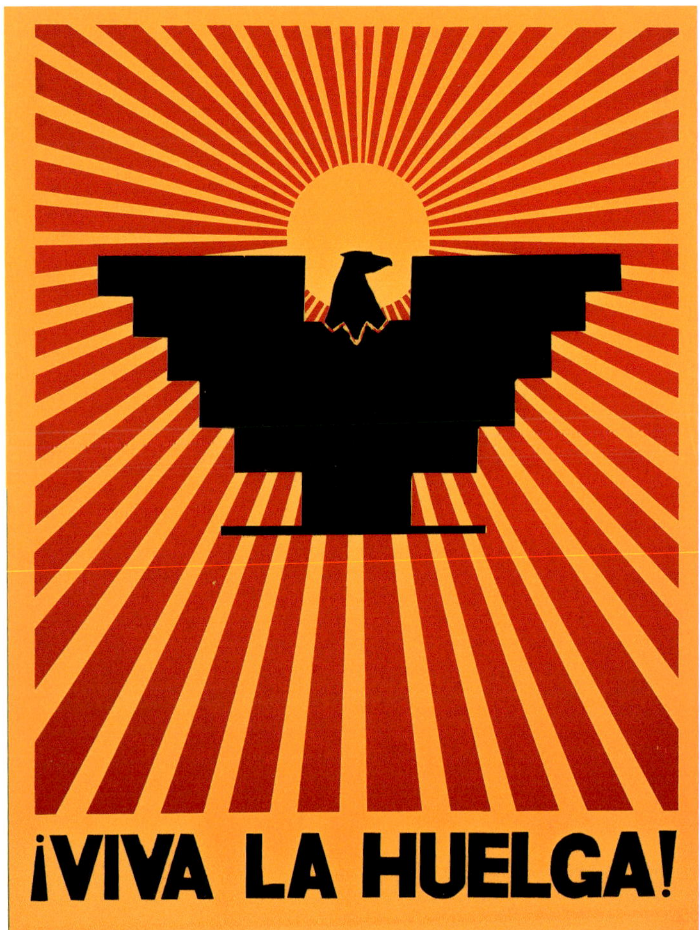

Unknown designer for the United Farm Workers, *Long Live the Strike!* (*¡Viva La Huelga!*), circa 1965, screen print, 26 × 20 inches (61 × 51 cm), Delano, California. Collection of the Oakland Museum of California. This union poster for the Delano Grape Strike features the Aztec eagle, a symbol of Mexican pride. The bird itself (now known as the UFW Eagle®) was designed in 1962 by Cesar Chavez's brother, Richard.

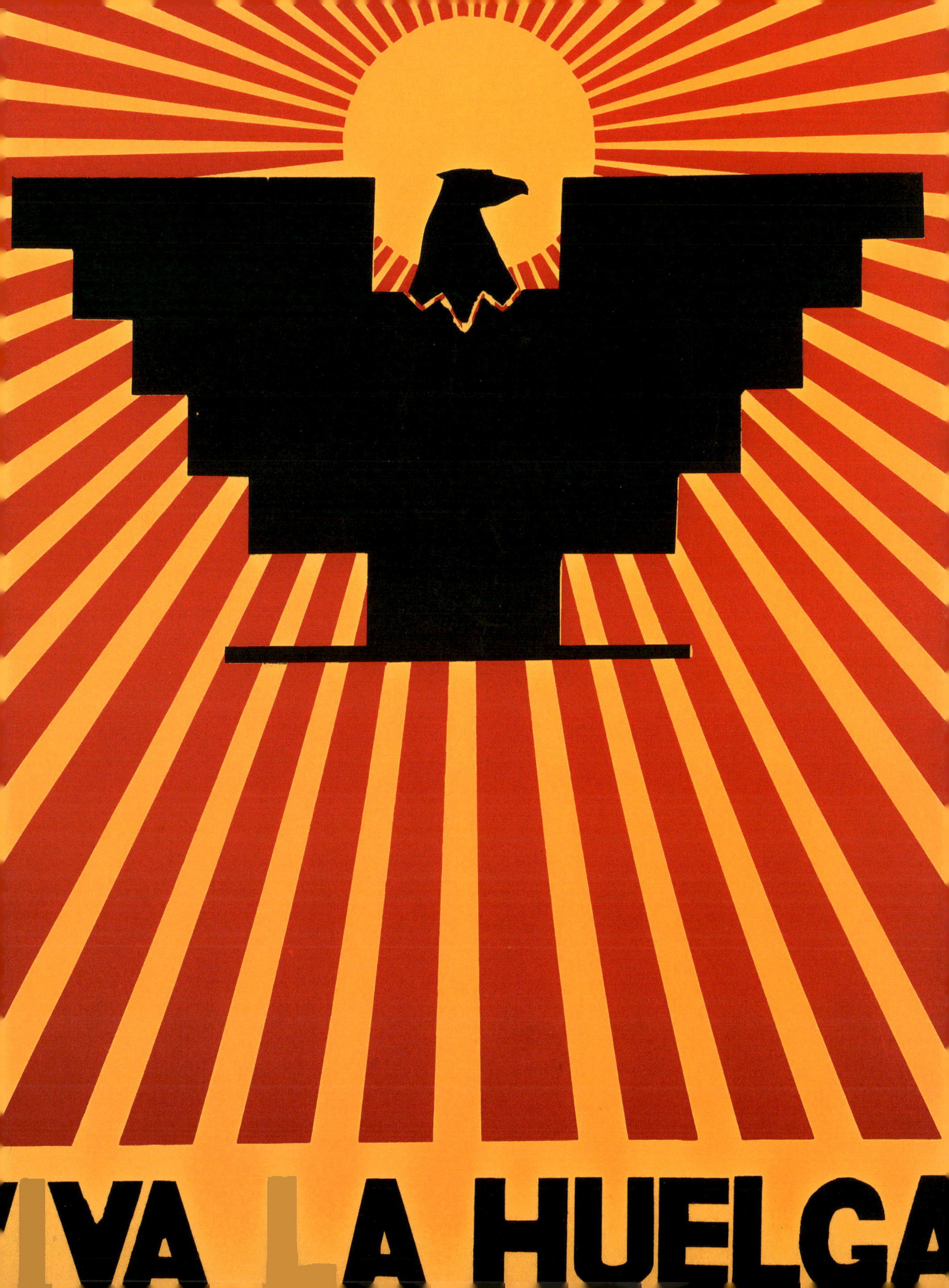
VIVA LA HUELGA

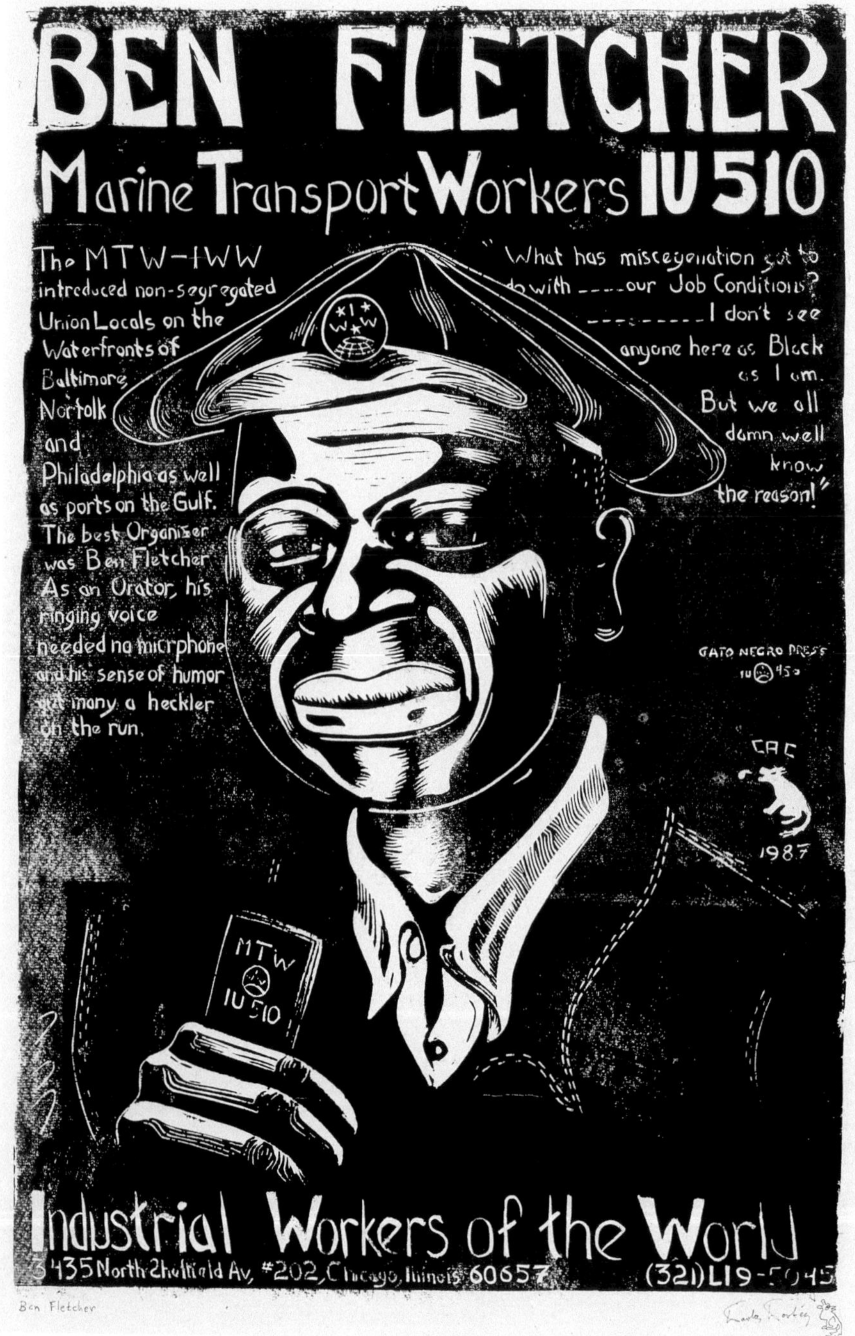
BEN FLETCHER
Marine Transport Workers IU 510
The MTW-IWW introduced non-segregated Union Locals on the Waterfronts of Baltimore, Norfolk and Philadelphia as well as ports on the Gulf. The best Organizer was Ben Fletcher. As an Orator, his ringing voice needed no micrphone and his sense of humor
many a heckler on the run.
"What has miscegenation got to do with ---- our Job Conditions? ---------- I don't see anyone here as Black as I am. But we all damn well know the reason!"
MTW IU 510
GATO NEGRO PRESS
CAC
1987
Industrial Workers of the World
3435 North Sheffield Av, #202, Chicago, Illinois 60657
Ben Fletcher

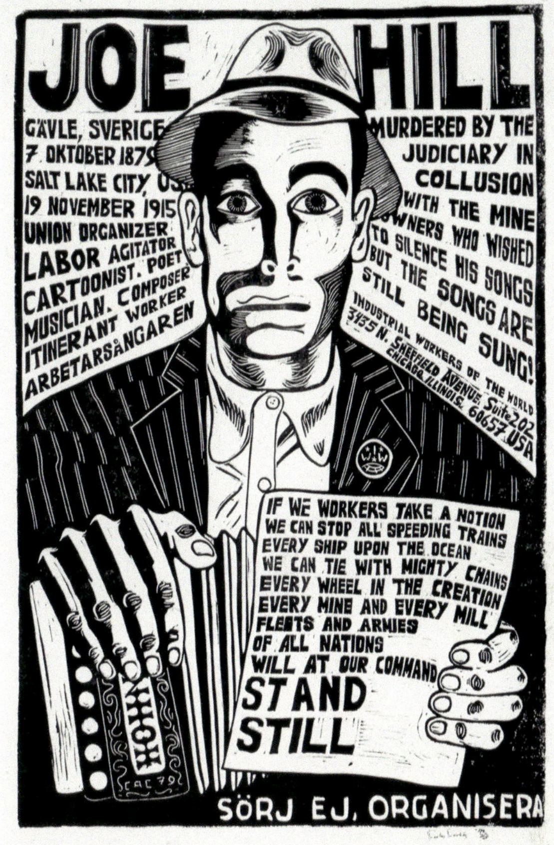

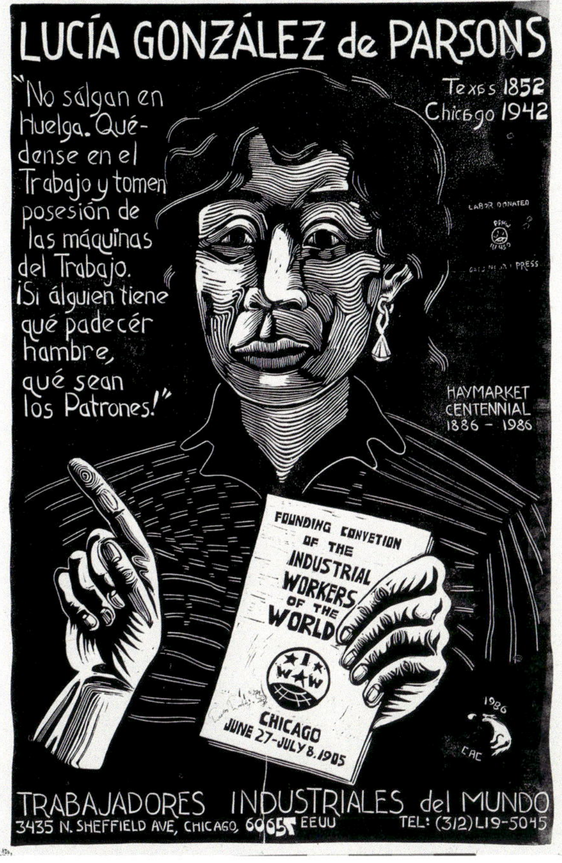

Carlos Cortez, linocut, 30 × 20 inches (76 × 51 cm), Chicago. From left to right: *Ben Fletcher*, 1987; *Lucía González de Parsons*, 1986; *Joe Hill*, 1979. Collection of the National Museum of Mexican Art.

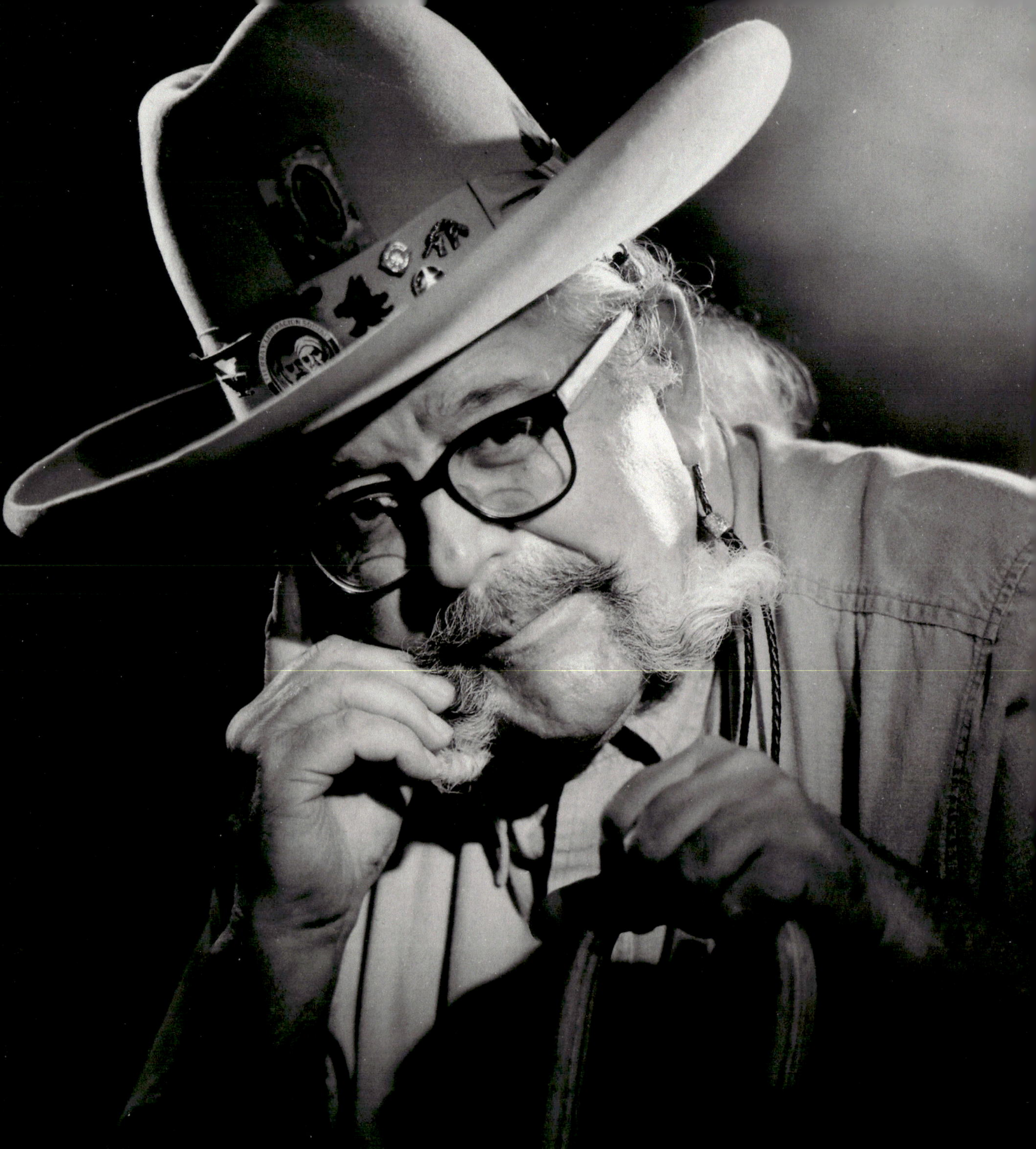

Designer as Protester

Carlos Cortez

“There is no such thing as nonpolitical art.”

—Carlos Cortez

Carlos Cortez was a self-described “harvest hand, construction worker, loafer, jailbird, vagabond, factory stiff,” and, of course, poet and print maker. Born in Milwaukee, Wisconsin, in 1923, he received an early education in working-class politics thanks to his Mexican-Indigenous father, who was an organizer with the Industrial Workers of the World (IWW), and his German mother, a socialist and pacifist. When called up to fight in World War II, his principled refusal landed him in federal prison. After his release, he enrolled in evening art classes, joined the IWW, and began submitting articles, drawings, and later linocuts and woodcuts to its publication, the *Industrial Worker*, which he would eventually edit.

As a Wobbly (a popular name for IWW card-carriers), Cortez advocated for workers' direct control over production in their struggles against capitalist exploitation. From its founding in 1905, the IWW organized toward this end, building solidarity in parts of the working class previously excluded from trade unions, including women, Black, and immigrant workers. In a series of linocut posters from the 1970s and 1980s, Cortez shares the stories of its early rank-and-file leaders with a new generation. One poster features Black longshoreman and soapbox orator Ben Fletcher (see page 162), who helped unite workers on Philadelphia's waterfront in one of the most diverse and effective locals of the 1910s and 1920s. On another, Lucy Parsons, an anarcho-communist organizer born into slavery, points to a paraphrase of her speech at the IWW founding convention: “Don't go out on strike. Stay on the job and take possession of its machines. If someone has to starve, let it be the bosses!” (see page 163). Printing her words in Spanish, Cortez nods to the Mexican-Indigenous heritage Parsons claimed and addresses his Chicano community in Chicago, where he lived after 1965.

In Cortez's portraits, historical facts and slogans take the foreground in a style resembling chalk on a blackboard, as in his Fletcher and Parsons posters. In his portrait of legendary Wobbly organizer and songwriter Joe Hill, the lettering beams forth in strong black capitals (see page 163). The economy of form in Cortez's work originated, in part, from a desire to create impact at minimal cost. In the 1950s, when the *Industrial Worker* could not afford to electrotype line drawings for print, Cortez began carving his submissions in cheap linoleum flooring. When linoleum prices rose, he made woodcuts on repurposed panels from discarded cedar furniture. Even after he gained recognition in the 1980s, he insisted on printing unlimited editions on inexpensive papers.

This populist ideal hearkens back to Mexican print maker José Guadalupe Posada, whose thousands of similarly coarse relief prints satirized authority and chronicled the Mexican Revolution. It also carries on the Wobbly tradition of working-class art, symbolized in Cortez's poster of Joe Hill with a squeezebox in one hand, song lyrics in the other. Depicting Hill as a martyr whose death in 1915 by firing squad occurred amid widespread efforts to suppress revolutionary unionism, Cortez celebrates the resilient culture of the anticapitalist left. “The mine owners [. . .] wished to silence his songs,” he writes on his poster. “But the songs are still being sung!”

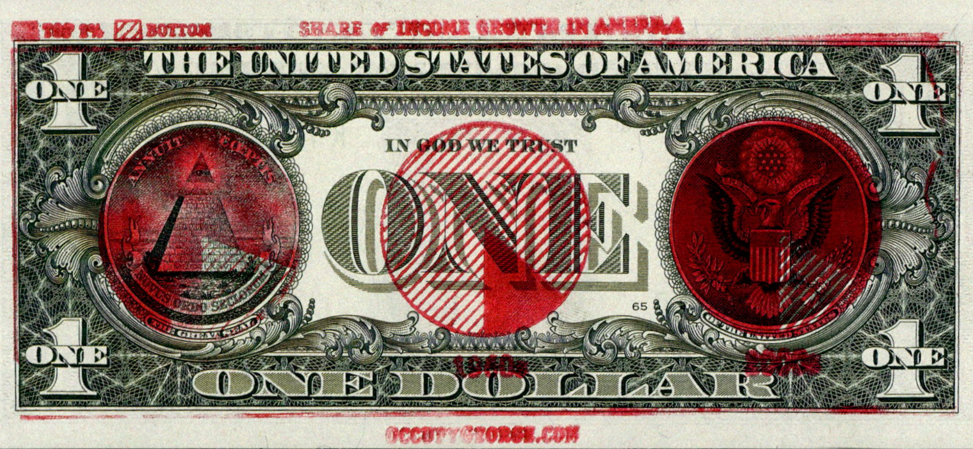

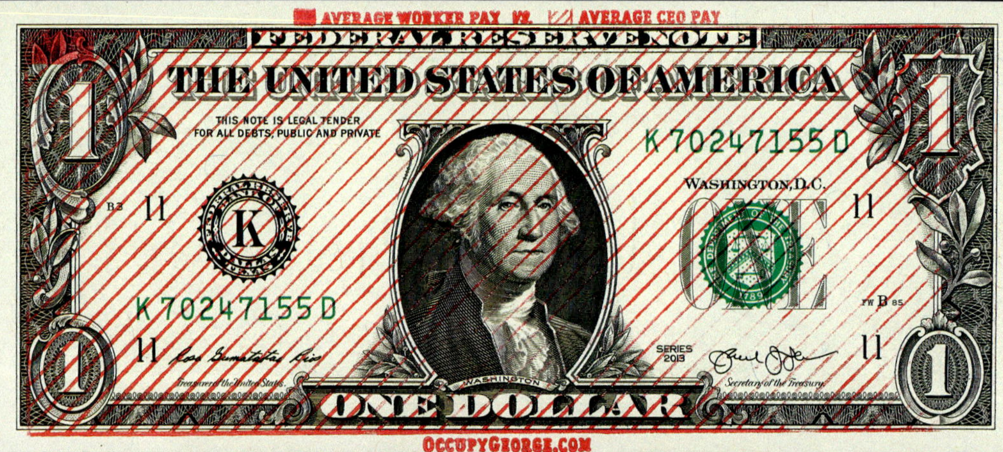

Ivan Cash and Andy Dao, *Occupy George Dollar 2: Share of Income Growth in America* and *Occupy George Dollar 3: Average Worker Pay vs. Average CEO Pay*, 2011, rubber stamped, 2¾ × 6¼ inches (7 × 16 cm), San Francisco.

BlackDog (Mark Fox), *Patriotism ≠ Consumption*, 2002, screen print, 2¾ × 6¼ inches (7 × 16 cm), San Rafael, California.

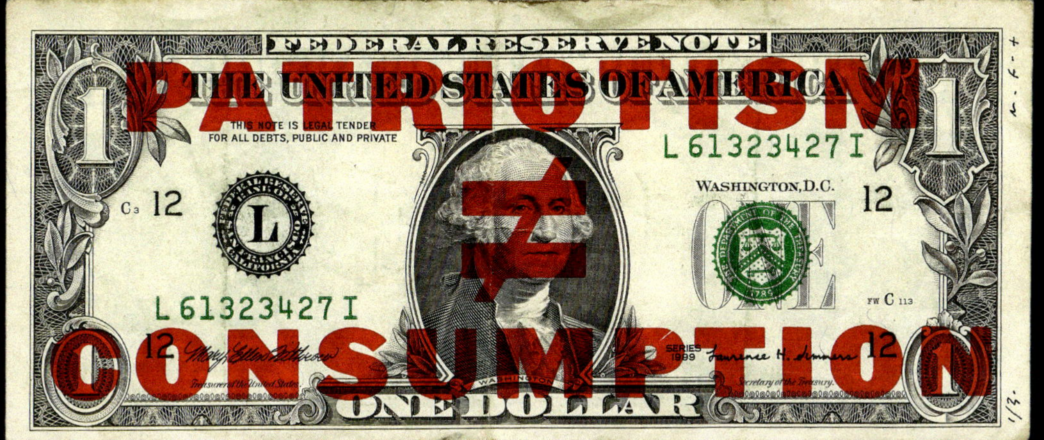

Call and Response

Emblazoned with official seals and portraits of leaders, a nation's currency is often one of its most recognizable statements of design. And in the United States, a single bill can circulate for years, guaranteeing that each gets thousands of views. This ubiquity, coupled with the transgressive force of currency defamation, makes it an enticing substrate for designers looking to interrogate institutional power.

In 2002, San Francisco designer Mark Fox created an edition of thirty $1 bills stamped with "Patriotism ≠ Consumption" in response to President George W. Bush, who had urged Americans to shop to show their love of country and prevent an economic crash after 9/11.

Almost a decade later, designers Ivan Cash and Andy Dao also modified the dollar bill for political purposes—this time, in support of the burgeoning Occupy movement. On September 17, 2011, spurred by a call to arms printed in the anti-consumerist magazine *Adbusters*, protesters set up an encampment in Lower Manhattan's Zuccotti Park. By October 9, similar camps had sprung up in nearly one thousand cities around the world. Under the rallying cry "We are the 99 percent," their grievances were many: the 2008 mortgage crisis and the U.S. government's bailout of the banks that had defrauded the American people, the ever-widening income disparity, and predatory student loans and mortgages. Critics in the media cast this diversity of ideas as a lack of clear principle. In response, Cash and Dao devised *Occupy George*, a series of dollar bills stamped with economic infographics—such as charts showing how much the average worker earns compared to the average CEO, and the difference in income growth between the top 1 percent and the bottom 99 percent.

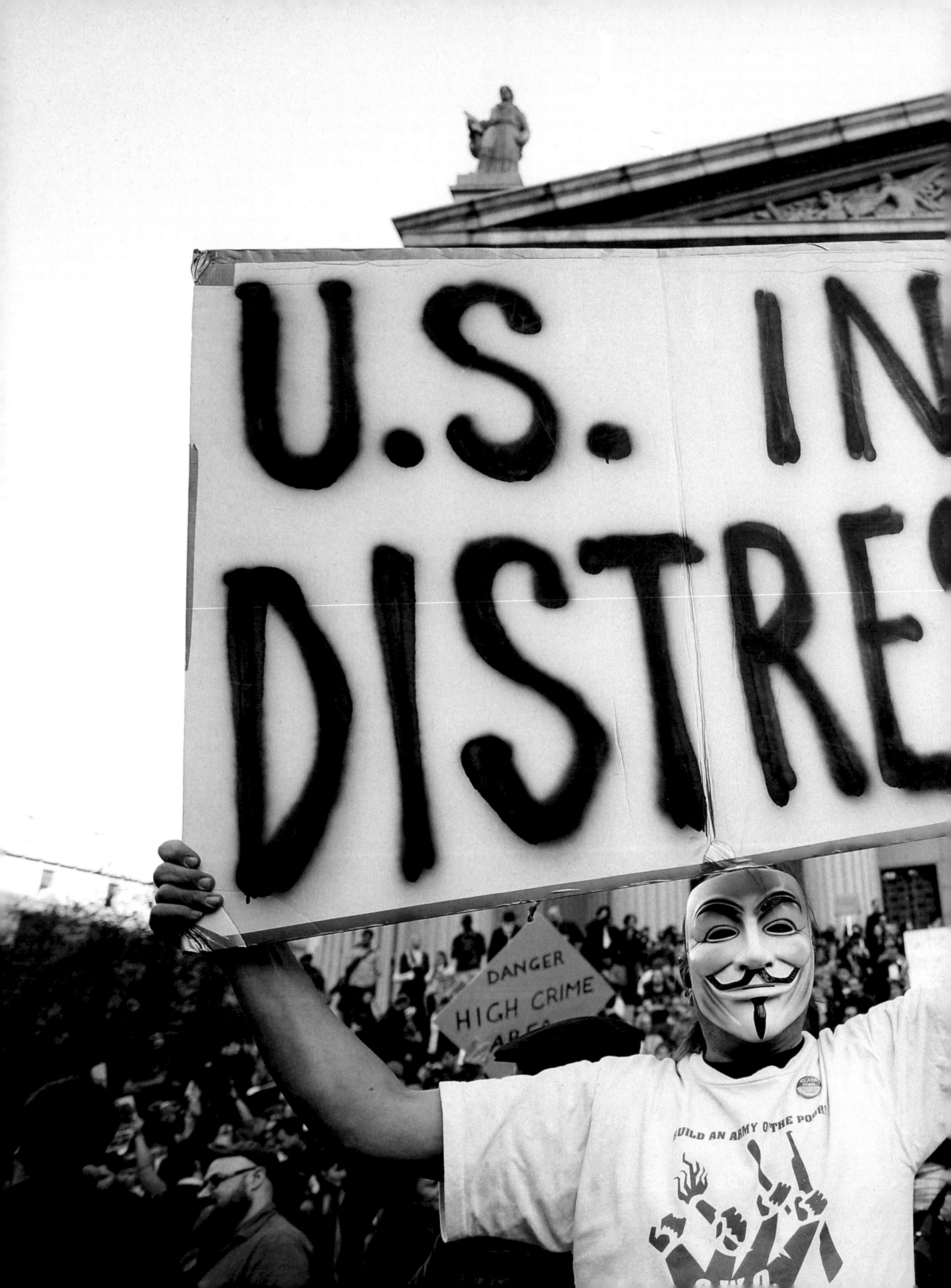

U.S.
DANGER
HIGH CRIME

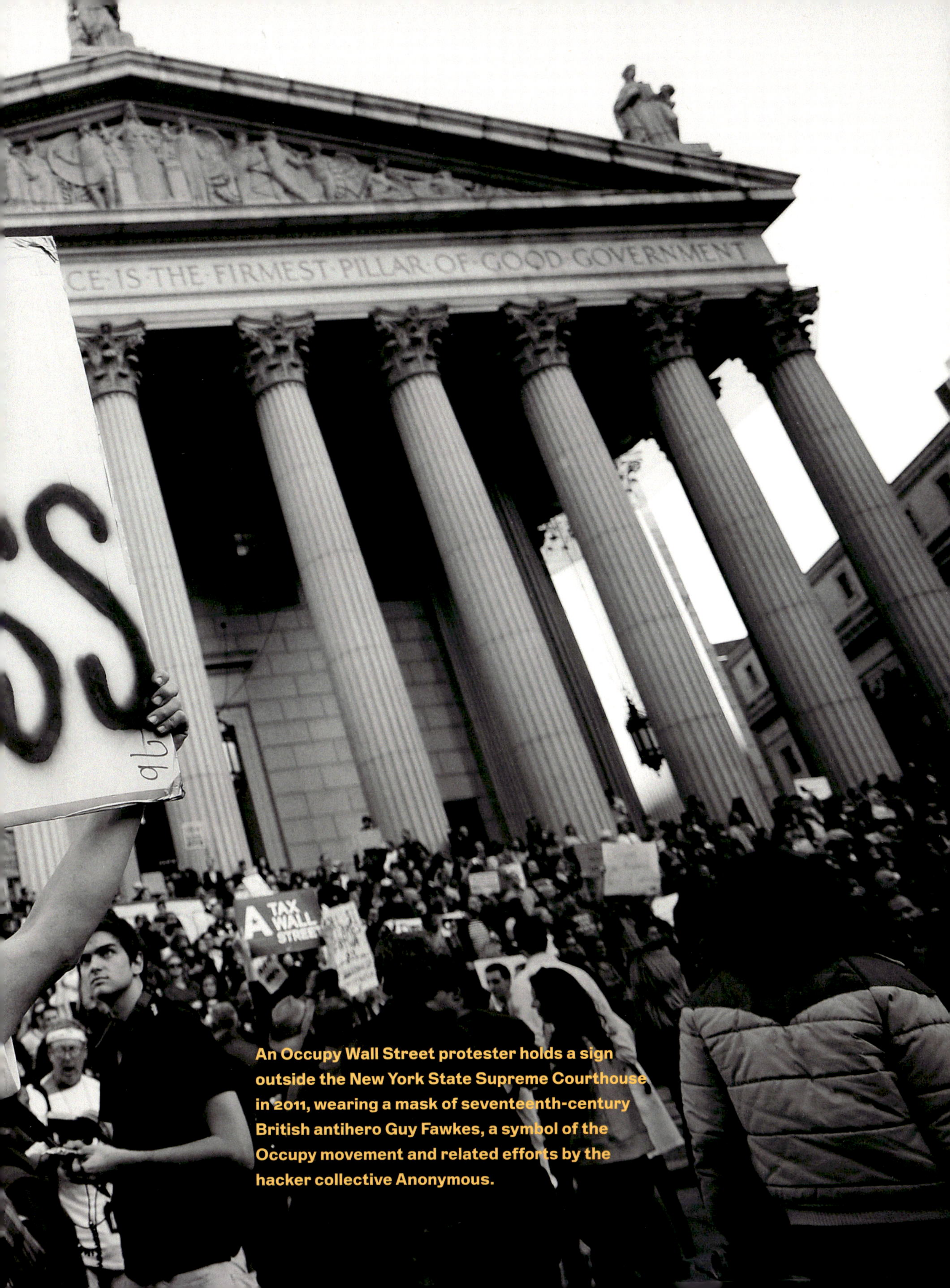

An Occupy Wall Street protester holds a sign outside the New York State Supreme Courthouse in 2011, wearing a mask of seventeenth-century British antihero Guy Fawkes, a symbol of the Occupy movement and related efforts by the hacker collective Anonymous.

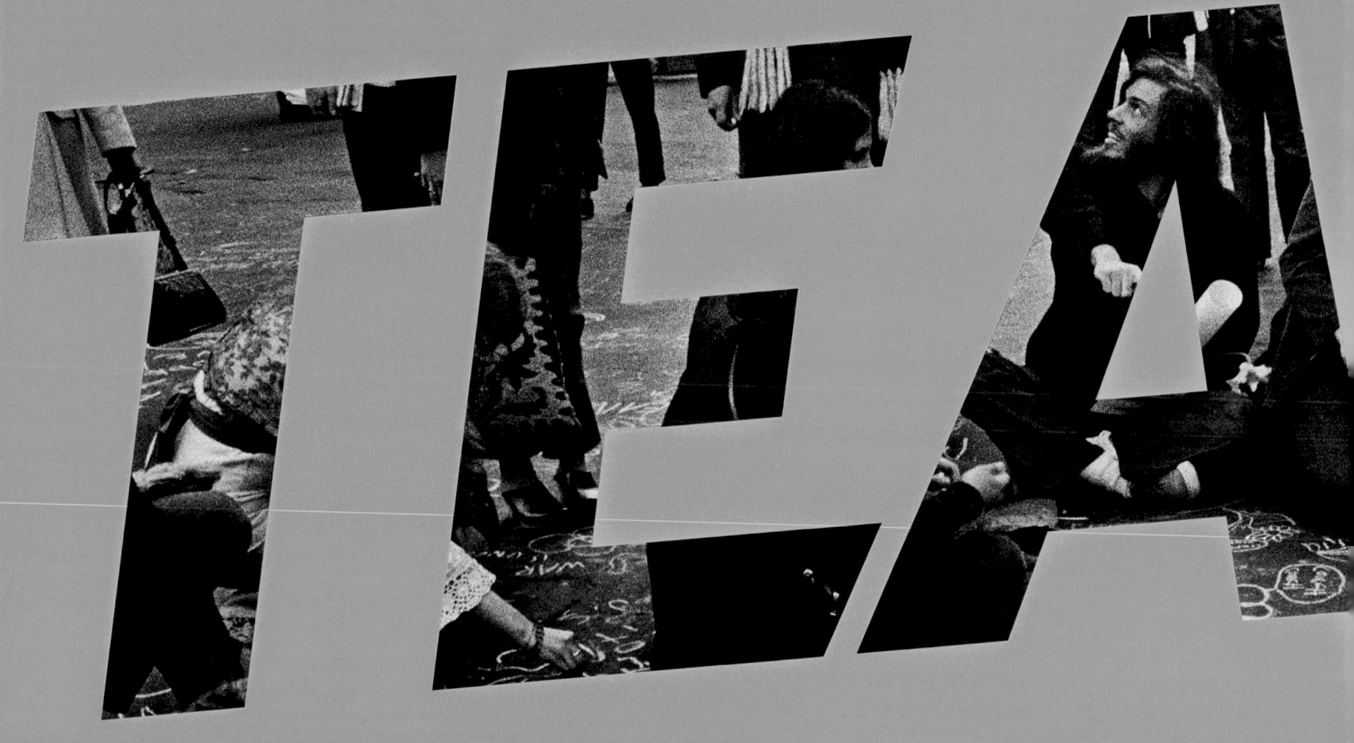
TEA

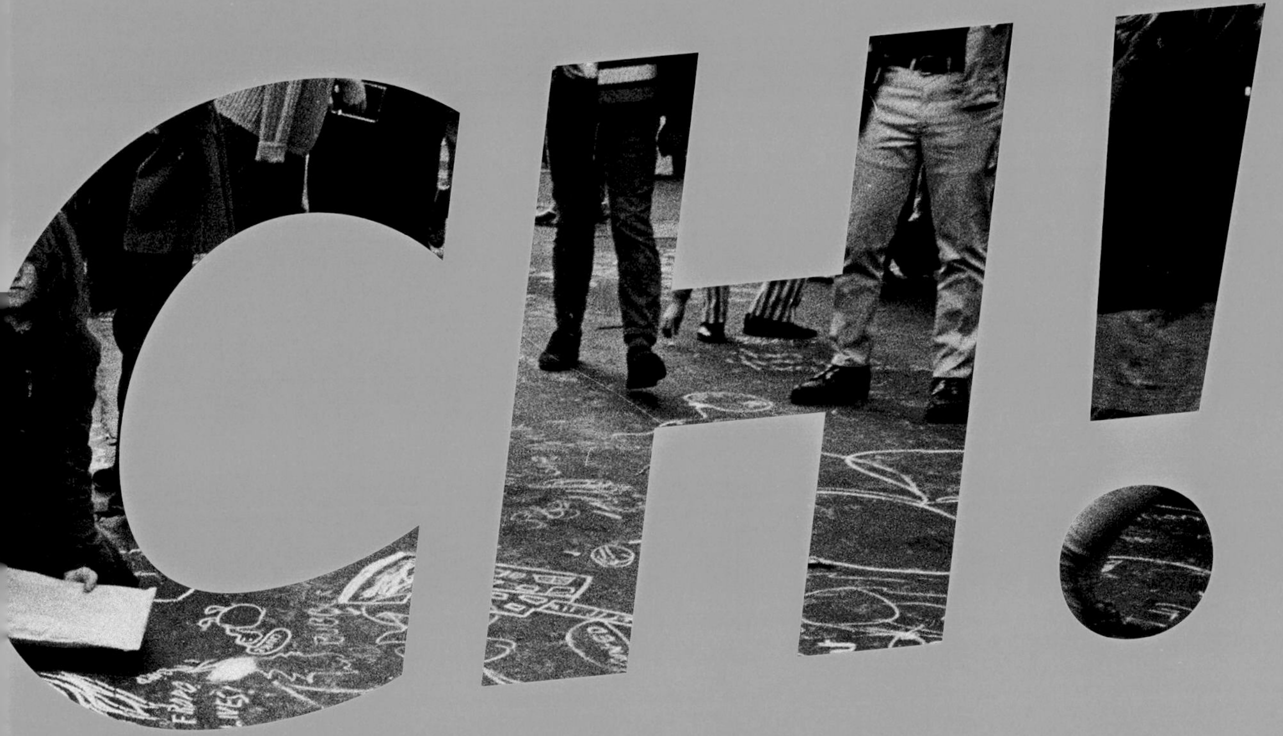
CH!

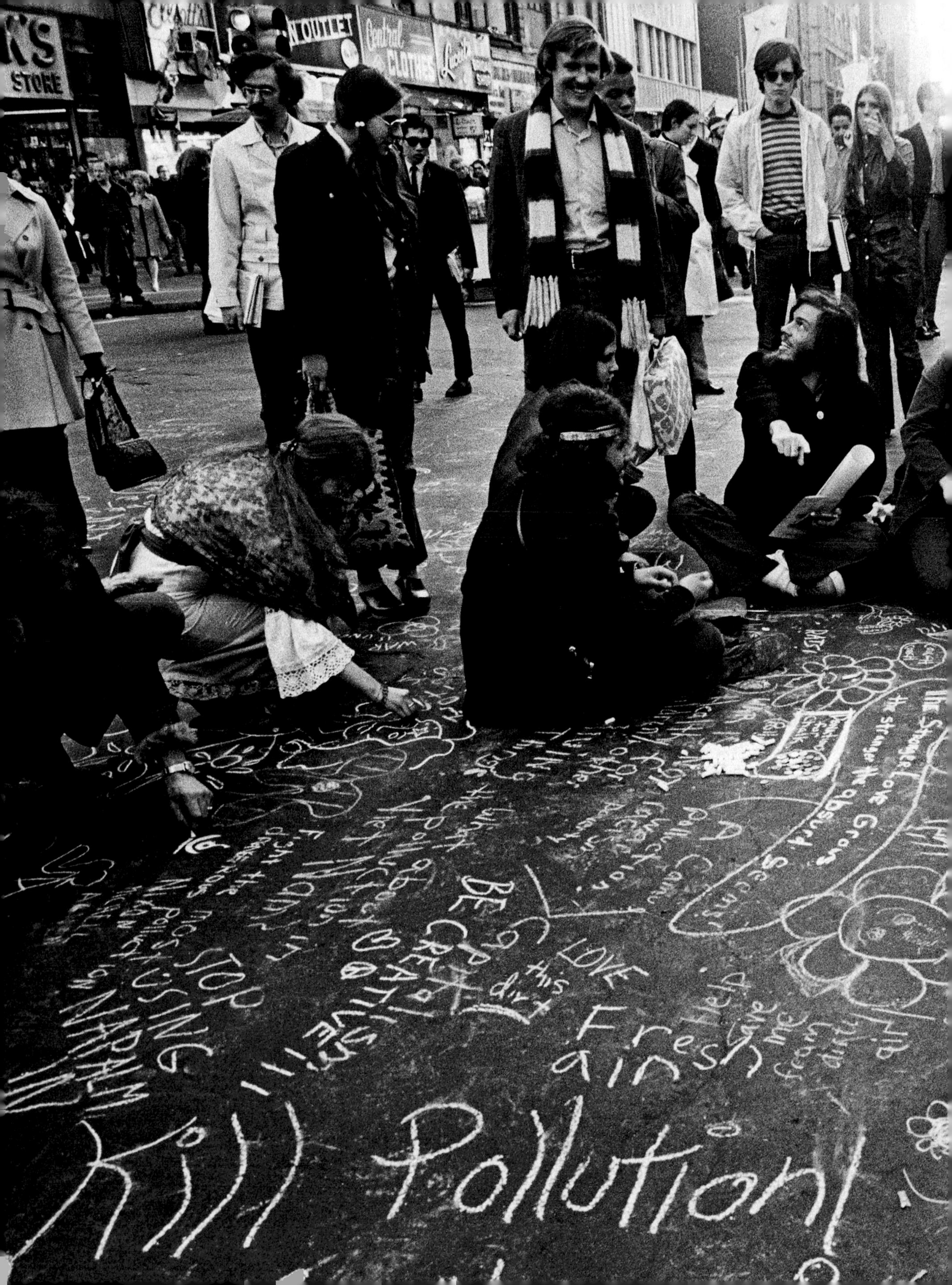
STORE
N OUTLET
Central
CLOTHES
STOP USING NAPALM
BE CREATIVE!!
LOVE this dirt
Fresh air
Kill Pollution!

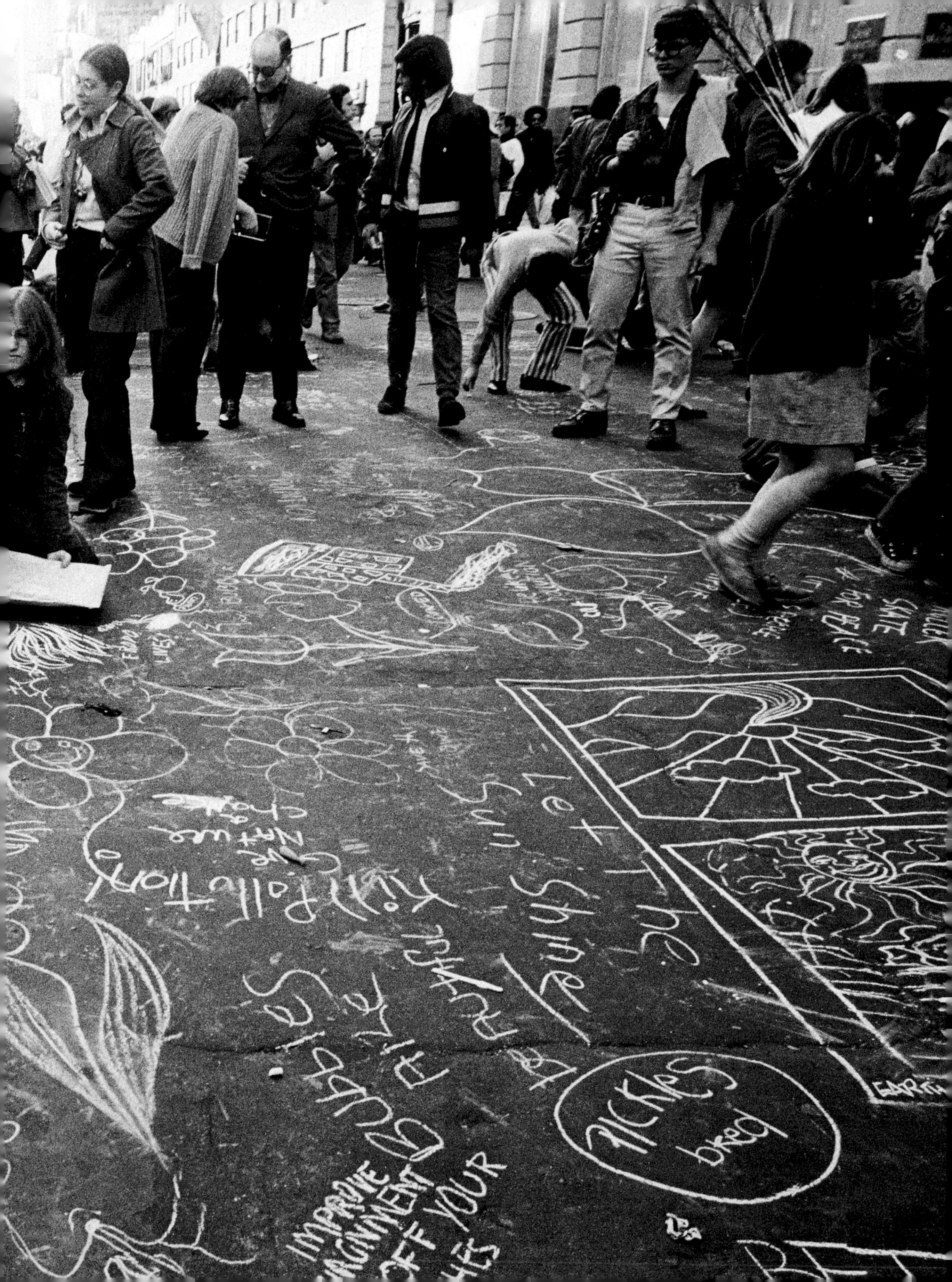

Kill Pollution
Let the sun shine
PICKLES
bred
SKATE FOR PEACE

"The classroom, with all its limitations, remains a location of possibility. In that field of possibility we have the opportunity to labor for freedom, to demand of ourselves and our comrades, an openness of mind and heart that allows us to face reality even as we collectively imagine ways to move beyond boundaries, to transgress. This is education as the practice of freedom."

—bell hooks, *Teaching to Transgress*, 1994

TEACH!

Protest itself is a form of pedagogy. Through uniting in solidarity, we learn from each other the tools by which we can improve the conditions of our lives. And the ephemera of protest movements—their pamphlets and flyers, posters and publications, all designed to inform, persuade, and motivate the masses—make up a powerful reading list in the course of social justice.

We begin with the infographics of W. E. B. Du Bois and his Black students at Atlanta University (now Clark Atlanta University), who pounded the streets in 1899 to gather statistical data on the lives of African Americans in Georgia. Displayed the next year in an exhibition at the 1900 world's fair in Paris, the resulting large-format charts awakened millions of fairgoers to the ongoing struggles of Black people in the United States. Graphic and vivid in color, they also exhibit a protomodernism that predates the Bauhaus, de Stijl, and other aesthetic movements linked with social change in Europe.

Additional examples of countercanonical teaching materials include *Proletarian Education and Social Justice in Mexico*. Made in the 1930s, following Mexico's decade-long peasant-led revolution, these booklets display the typographic influence of Russian constructivism, which emerged as a key style of socialist propaganda after the 1917 Bolshevik revolution.

The simple demand for education—for access to quality information about one's history and culture—can be an act of defiance against exclusionary narratives. A circa-1970 poster by Emory Douglas features what appears to be a young Black person of indeterminate gender dressed in a tunic that can be read as both African and Greco-Roman. The student holds an automatic rifle and a single hardbound book with "BLACK STUDIES" across the cover in bold typography. This lesser-known piece from Douglas's prolific oeuvre for the Black Panther Party renders the protester as an emissary of education. While the

Party's visual record is most often told through its newspapers' iconic front and back covers (which, when isolated, read as broadsheets or posters), the publications were also dense with teachings, including counterarguments against white supremacy and plans for holistic Black education. Deeper cuts in the Party's publishing—pamphlets like "On the Ideology of the Black Panther Party," which appears in this chapter—circulated the tenets of their platform in a concise format.

If protest is a teacher, then students are active participants in shaping the curriculum to align with their values. Designed in 1970 by David L. Burke, *Right On!* uses a hybrid of cinematic photography and lettering abstracted from DIY signs to present data and research on protest activity on college campuses. Issued in a run of 100,000 by Bantam Books, *Right On!* leverages the efficiencies of traditional book publishing to take its progressive message to the masses.

The twentieth century's mass-media explosion allowed new Black publications to reframe narratives about Black life, too. Among them was *Ebony*, one of the magazines created by media trailblazer John H. Johnson. A 1969 special issue uses an elegant, highly modernist approach to elevate Black issues on the nation's newsstands. Bookshelves were similarly changing, with titles such as *The Black Book*, edited by Toni Morrison, proving that there was an appetite for Black history. With rich typographic styling and images that both expose the devastation and celebrate the more jubilant aspects of Black history, it became a *New York Times* best seller.

Twenty years later, editor and designer Tibor Kalman took a similarly no-holds-barred approach to visuals in *Colors: A Magazine About the Rest of the World*. Its pages harnessed eye-catching design to heighten awareness of issues like global warming, racism, and AIDS. Feminist art collective Guerrilla Girls also borrow the idiom of the public service announcement, appropriating the advertorial voice of consumerism to skewer the art world's worst tendencies.

While these print materials inform and influence the public, two projects provide a stark reminder of what happens when freedom of information is denied: Mirtha Dermisache's *Diario* and Jeremy Mickel and Forest Young's typeface Redaction, which both use illegible text to indict state-sanctioned abuses of power.

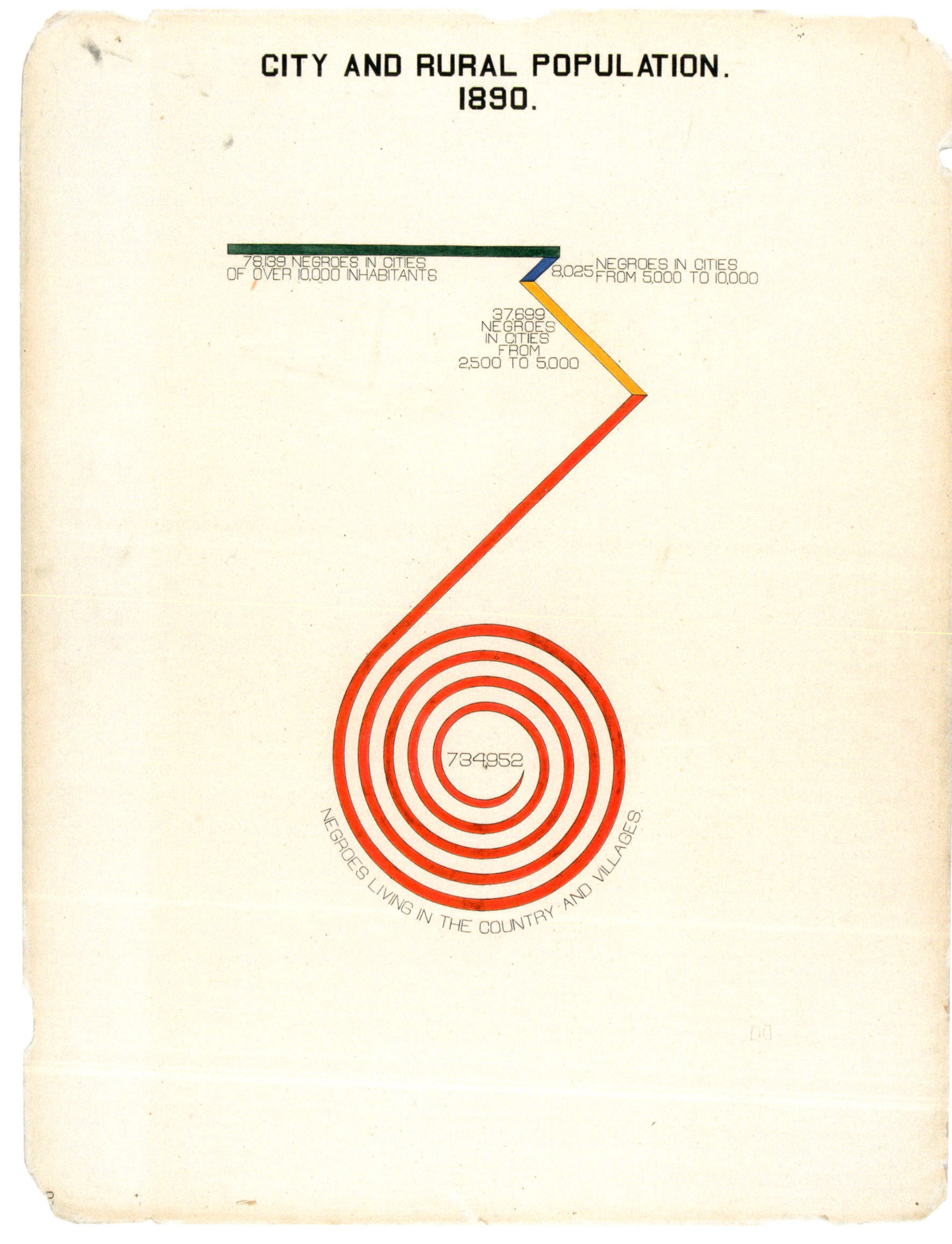
CITY AND RURAL POPULATION.
1890.
78,139 NEGROES IN CITIES
OF OVER 10,000 INHABITANTS
8,025 NEGROES IN CITIES
FROM 5,000 TO 10,000
37,699
NEGROES
IN CITIES
FROM
2,500 TO 5,000
734,952
NEGROES LIVING IN THE COUNTRY AND VILLAGES.

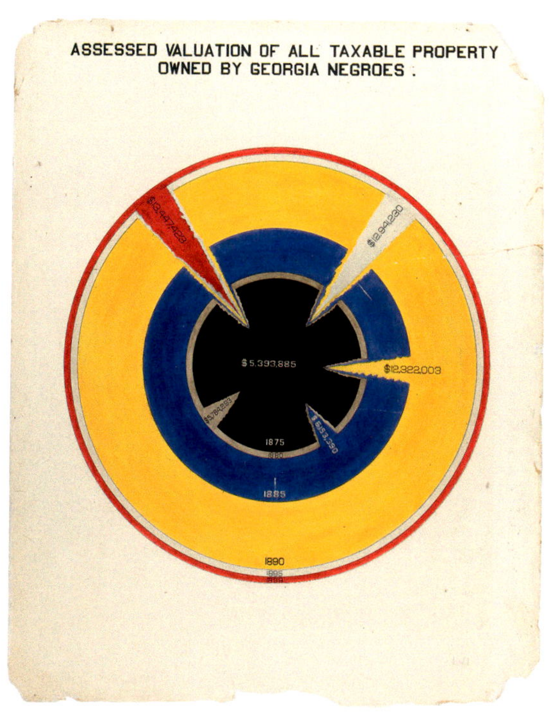

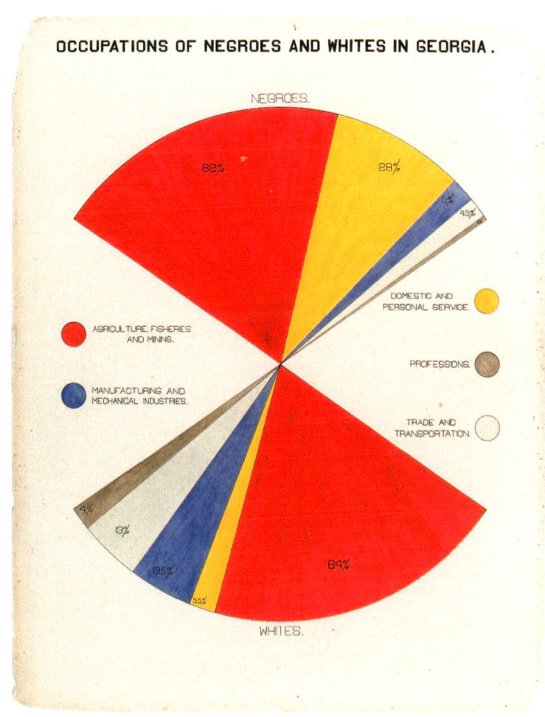

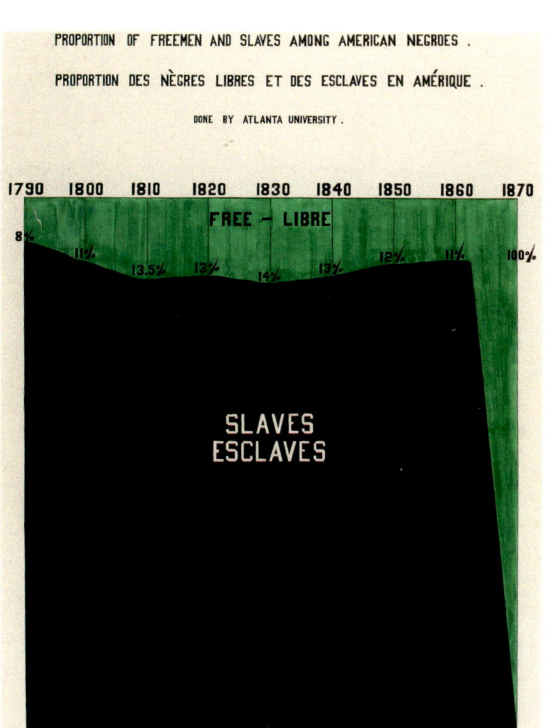

W. E. B. Du Bois and unknown Atlanta University students (researchers and designers), diagrams from *The Georgia Negro: A Social Study*, 1900, ink and watercolor on newsprint, 28 × 22 inches (71 × 56 cm), Atlanta. Left: *City and Rural Population, 1890*; clockwise from top left: *Assessed Valuation of All Taxable Property Owned by Georgia Negroes*; *Occupations of Negroes and Whites in Georgia*; *Proportion of Freemen and Slaves Among American Negroes*.

Designer as Protester

W. E. B. Du Bois

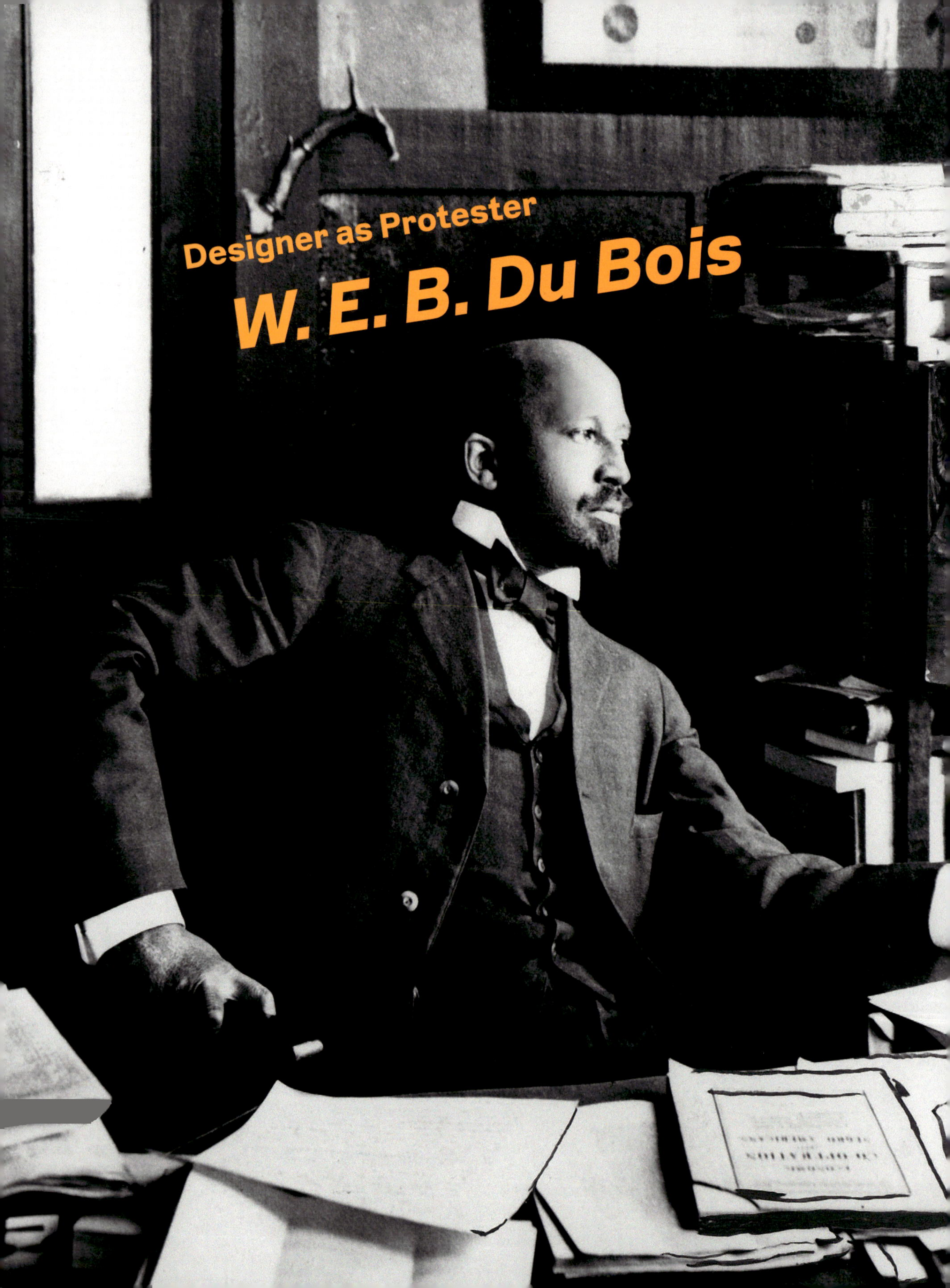

"Education and work are the levers to uplift a people. Work alone will not do it unless inspired by the right ideals and guided by intelligence. Education must not simply teach work—it must teach Life."

—W. E. B. Du Bois

One of the twentieth century's foremost intellectuals, W. E. B. Du Bois shaped our ideas about Black life in America and helped create the field of modern sociology through books such as *The Souls of Black Folk* and *Black Reconstruction in America*. A founder of the National Association for the Advancement of Colored People (NAACP), he also helped lead an international charge against injustice. Although less well known, his early forays into information design present another facet in Du Bois's legacy of teaching in the service of social advancement.

Invited to participate in the American Negro exhibit at the 1900 Paris Exposition, a world's fair that drew more than 50 million visitors, Du Bois devised two series of poster-sized graphs, maps, and tables in which he would "attempt to give, in as systematic and compact a form as possible, the history and present condition of a large group of human beings." On a short deadline and a shoestring budget, he collaborated with Black students and alumni of Atlanta University to condense volumes of empirical data into around sixty impactful displays.

With their bright primary colors, modular shapes, and compact, dynamic arrangements, Du Bois's infographics seem to anticipate a century's worth of graphic innovation, including the modernism of Russian constructivism and the Bauhaus. One striking tree-ring diagram from the series *The Georgia Negro: A Social Study* (see page 177, top left) marks the growing value of property held by Black Georgians since the end of Reconstruction. Styled as a target, its labels fit within triangular fissures that point viewers' attention inward. Another circular chart compares employment distributions among Black and white Georgian workers, balancing two reflected wedges in an immediately clear image of stratified labor (see page 177, top right).

Handpainted in opaque watercolor, these modern forms enticed fairgoers to flip through the complete series, which was displayed in movable wing frames mounted at eye level. Lettered using templates for technical blueprints, with a tube-tipped stylographic pen that yields narrow strokes, each plate's facts and figures appear in a rational style of sans-serif block capitals built entirely of straight lines.

In total, Du Bois's infographics challenge the scientific racism of his day with detailed research and precise visuals that demonstrate the collective achievements of Black Americans. A chart from his series on the conditions of formerly enslaved people and their descendants shows, in a mass of black (see page 177, bottom), both the long shadow of slavery across U.S. history and the dramatic success of what Du Bois later deemed Black workers' "general strike" for emancipation. Another diagram, titled *City and Rural Population, 1890* (see page 176), employs a spiral to depict the concentration of Black people in the rural South—a legacy of slavery that, as other graphs make clear, raised questions about the precarious conditions faced by tenant farmers. Suggesting the shape of a question mark across the page, the diagram is a reminder of Du Bois's belief that a lifelong pursuit of knowledge can be a powerful factor of liberation.

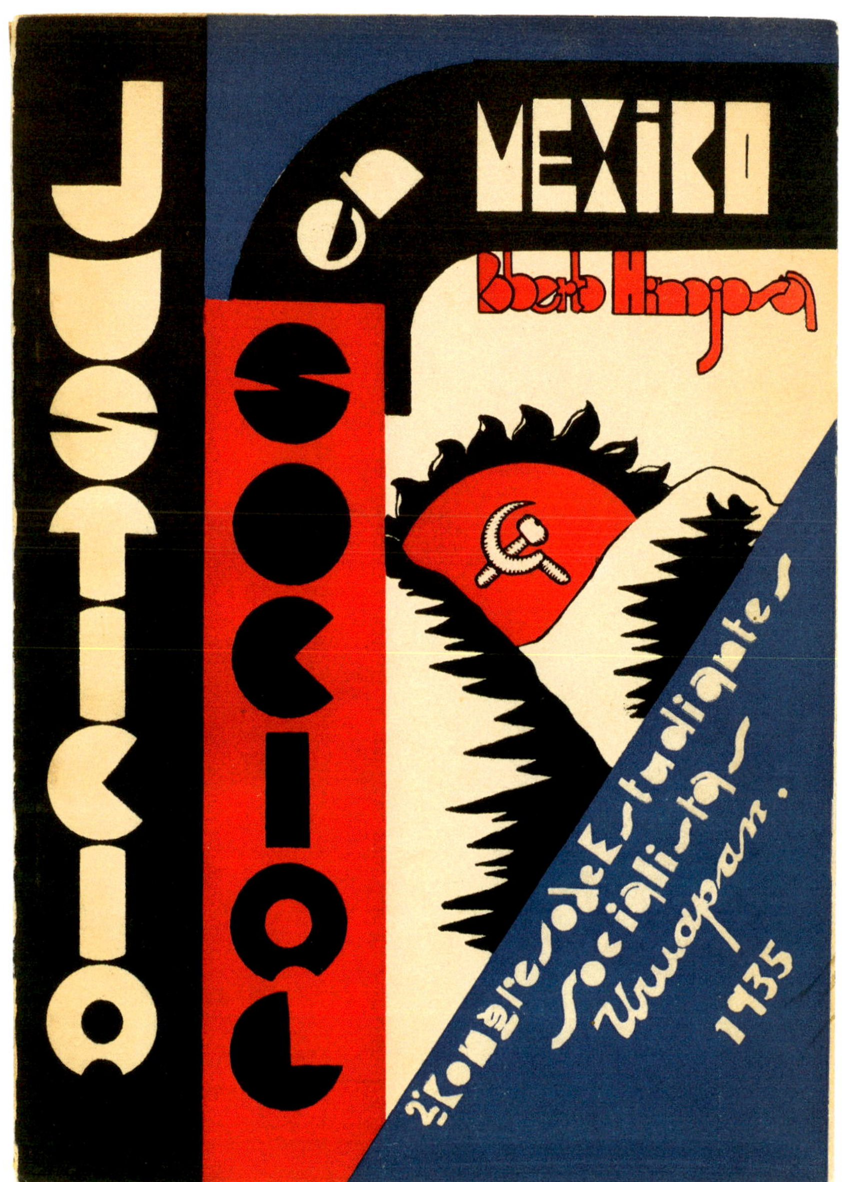

Unknown designer, Roberto Hinojosa (author), *Social Justice in Mexico* (*Justicia Social en México*), 1935, letterpress, 9 × 6½ inches (23 × 16.5 cm), Uruapan, Mexico. This report on the second Socialist Students of Mexico Conference addresses university reform and education in a socialist state. On its cover, a small hammer and sickle—representing the unification of factory and agriculture workers—visually reinforces the Soviet influence.

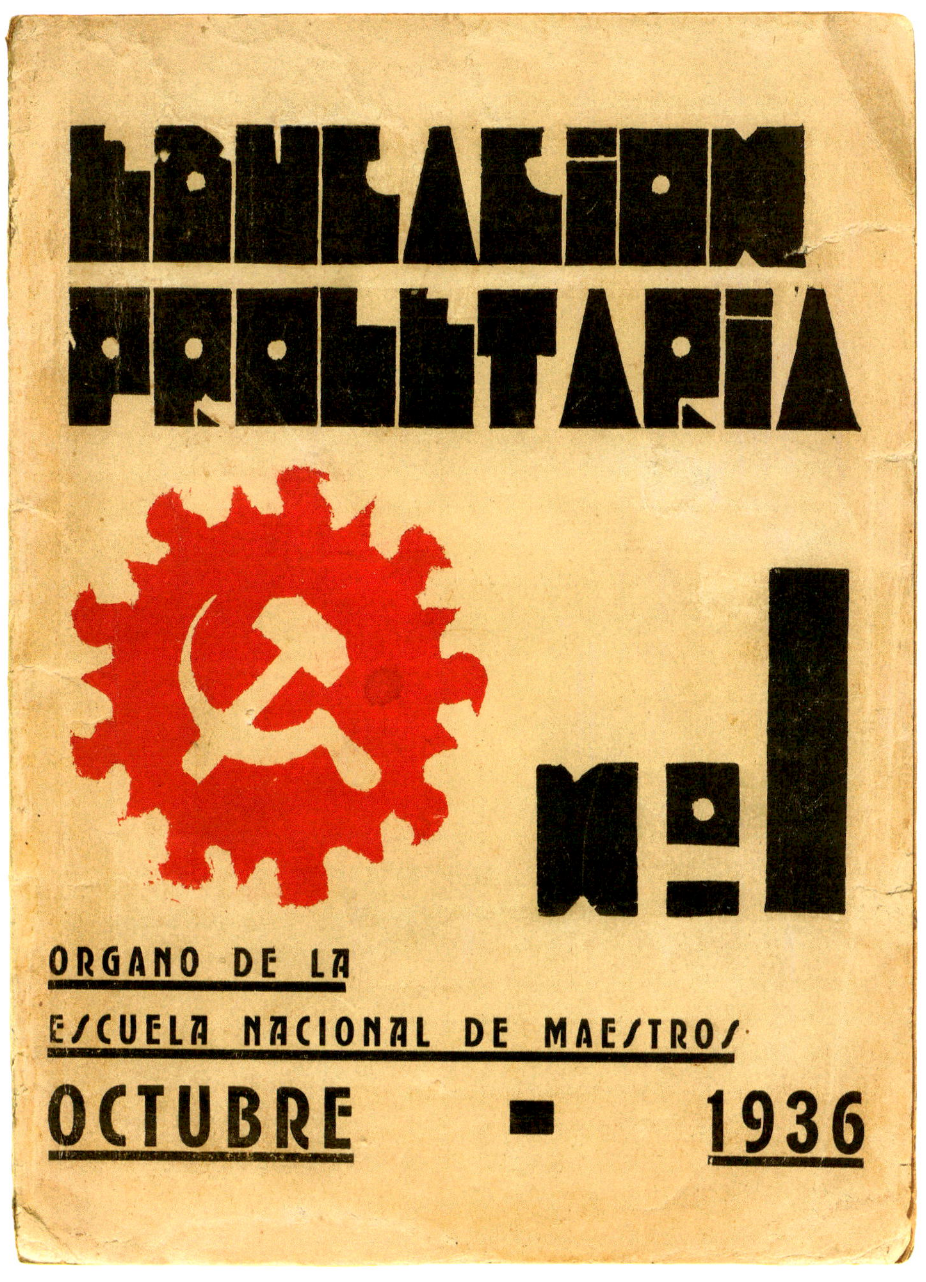

E. A. Ugarte, Ricardo Cabrera Lamadrid, and Raúl Mejía (designers), *Proletarian Education* (*Educación Proletaria*), vol. 1, no. 1, 1936, letterpress, 9¼ × 6⅞ inches (23.5 × 17.5 cm), Mexico City. This pamphlet's chunky, constructed letterforms are as revolutionary as any from the Russian avant-garde but could also be informed by a simplified style of art deco that was popular in the Americas at the time.

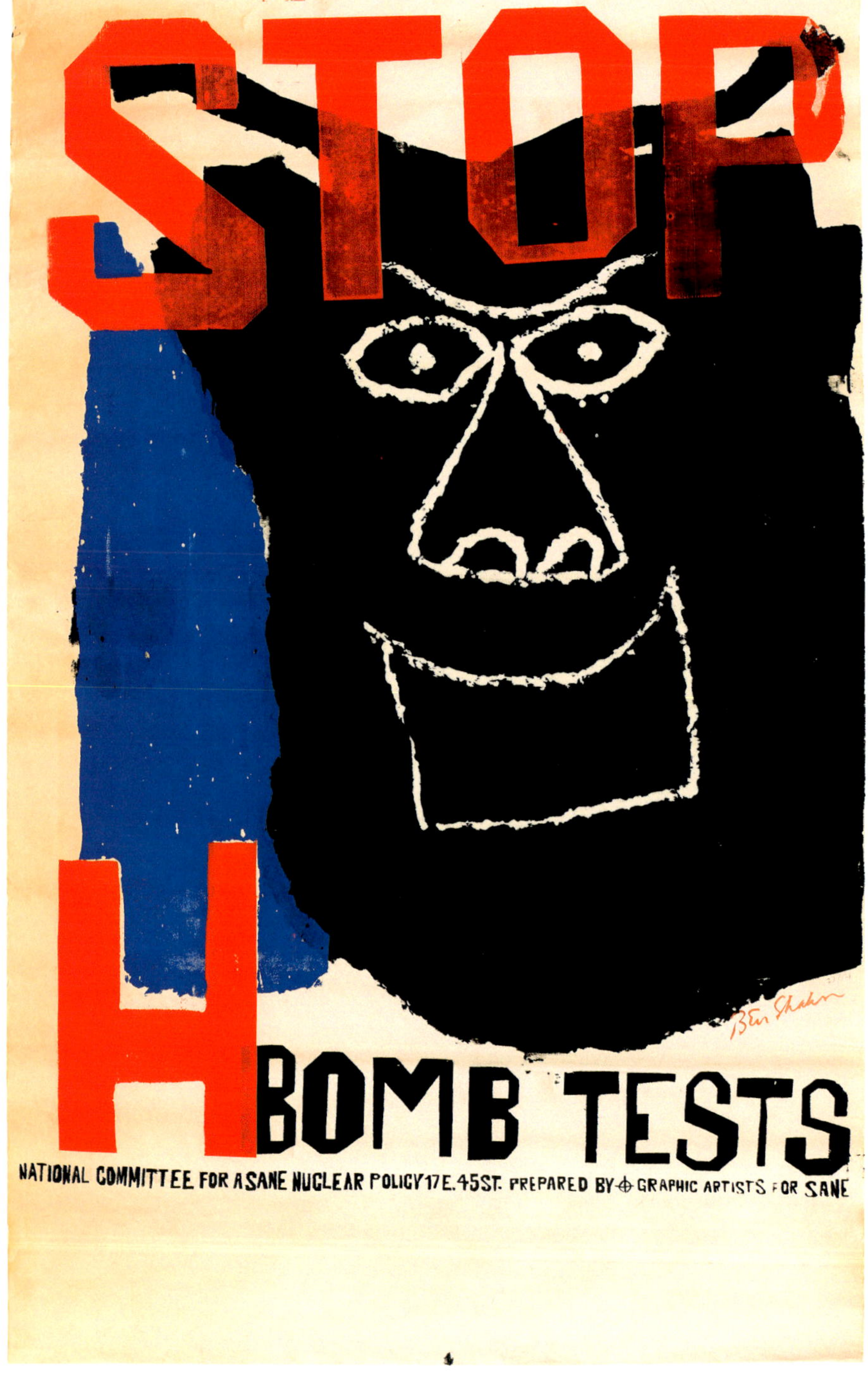

Ben Shahn, *Stop H Bomb Tests*, 1960, screen print, 46⅜ × 29¾ inches (117.5 × 75.5 cm), New York. In this poster for the Committee for a SANE Nuclear Policy, Shahn's letterforms demonstrate a characteristic mix of wild and straight strokes and unpredictable weight placement, mirroring his cut-paper illustration style.

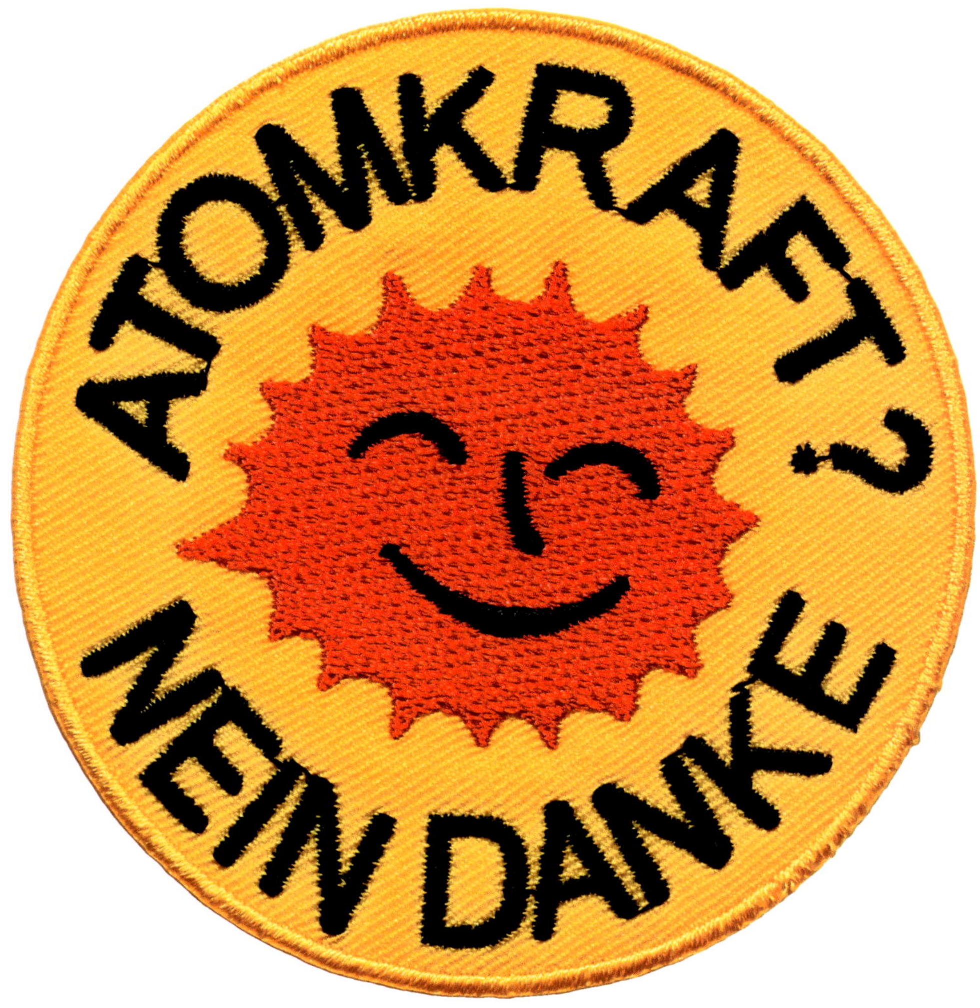

Anne Lund, *Nuclear Power? No Thanks* (*Atomkraft? Nein Danke*), a.k.a. the Smiling Sun, 2020, machine embroidery, 3 × 3 inches (7.5 × 7.5 cm), Aarhus, Denmark. This patch features the German-language version of Lund's internationally popular 1975 design protesting nuclear power, which has been made in sixty languages. Lund was an activist, not a trained designer, who created the logo to appeal to women demonstrators. The soft terminals of the typeface on this version, Helvetica Rounded, further the design's amiability.

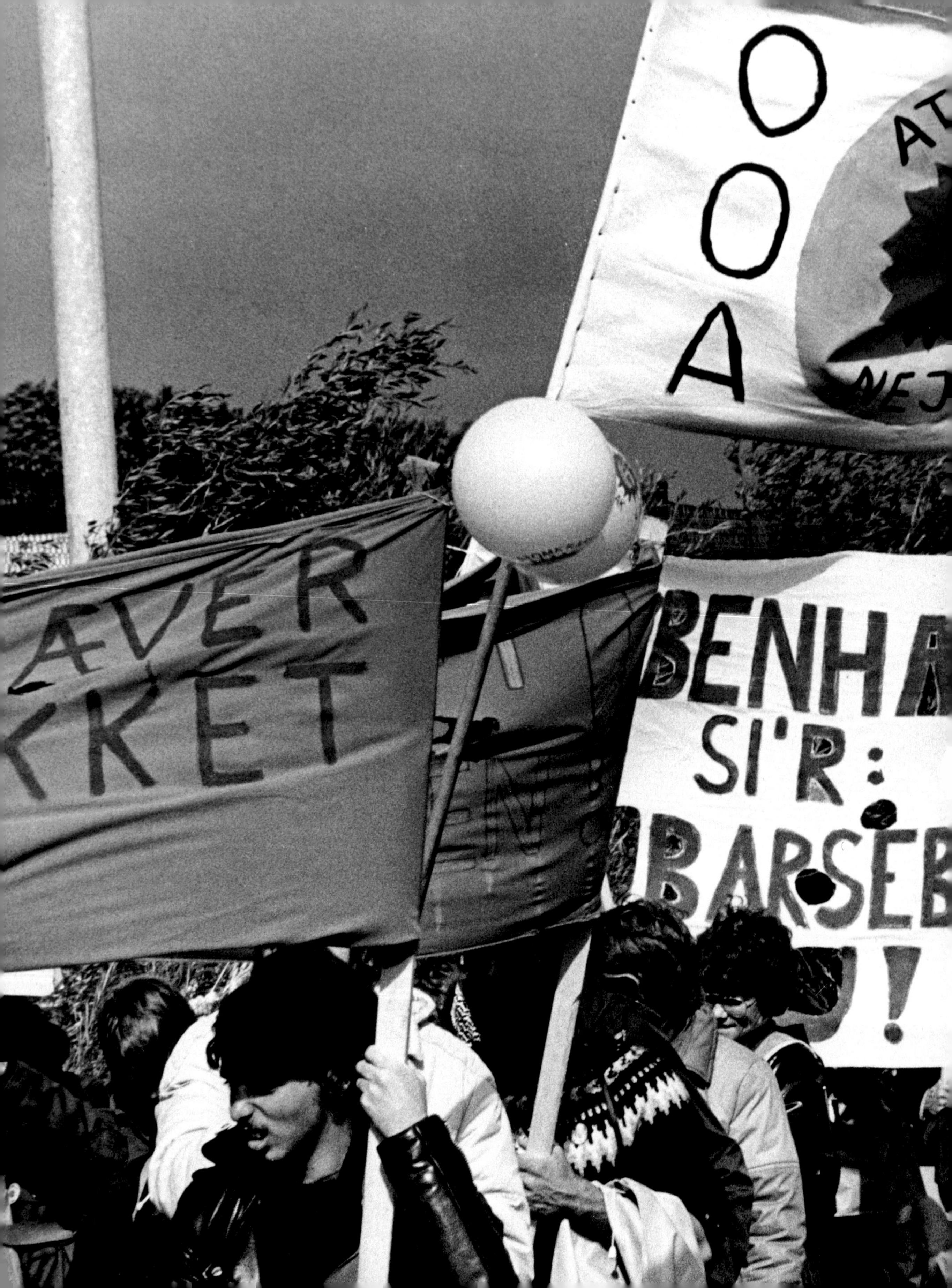
OOA
NEJ
ÆVER
KKET
BENHA
SI'R:
BARSEB

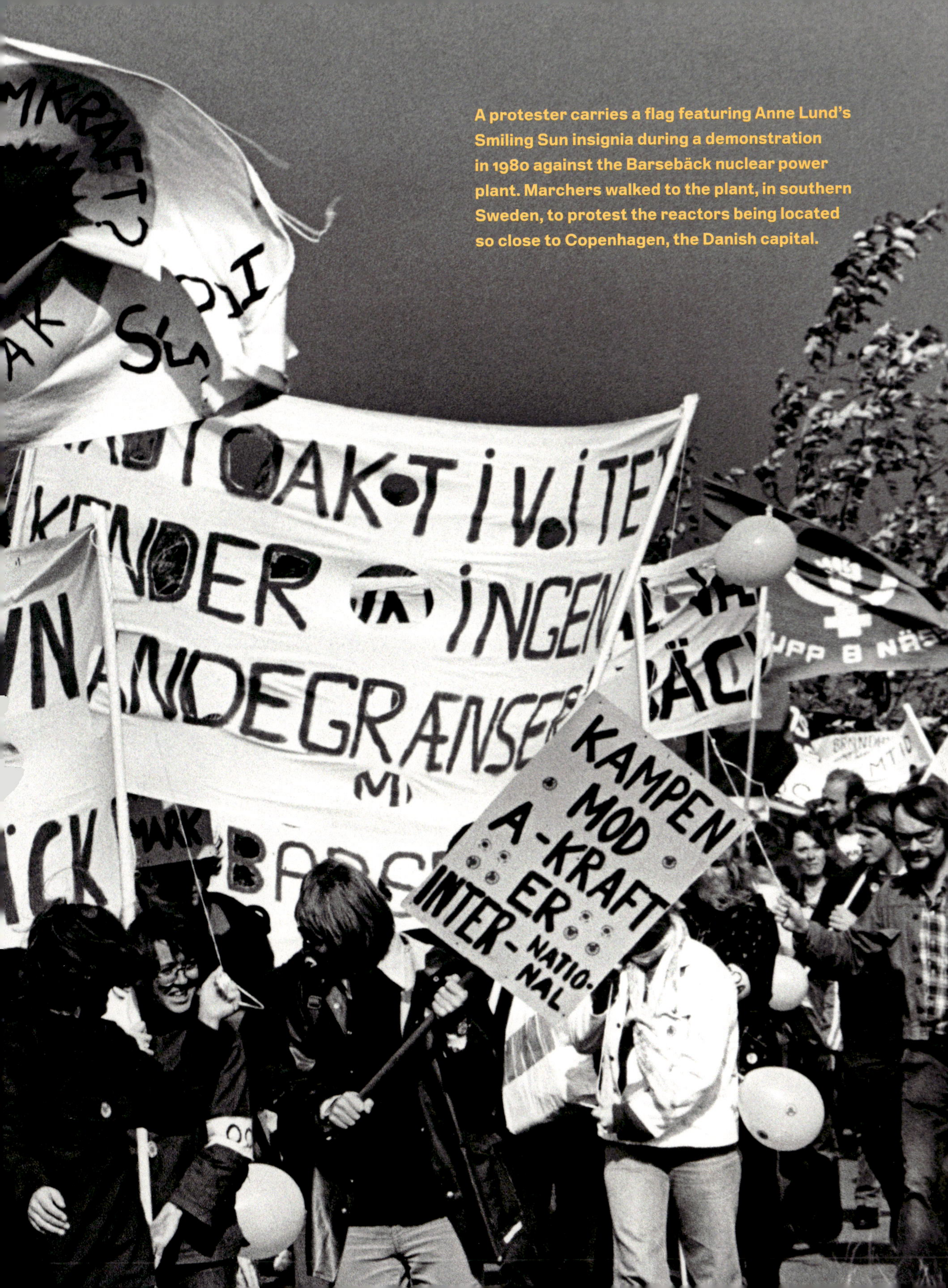

A protester carries a flag featuring Anne Lund's Smiling Sun insignia during a demonstration in 1980 against the Barsebäck nuclear power plant. Marchers walked to the plant, in southern Sweden, to protest the reactors being located so close to Copenhagen, the Danish capital.

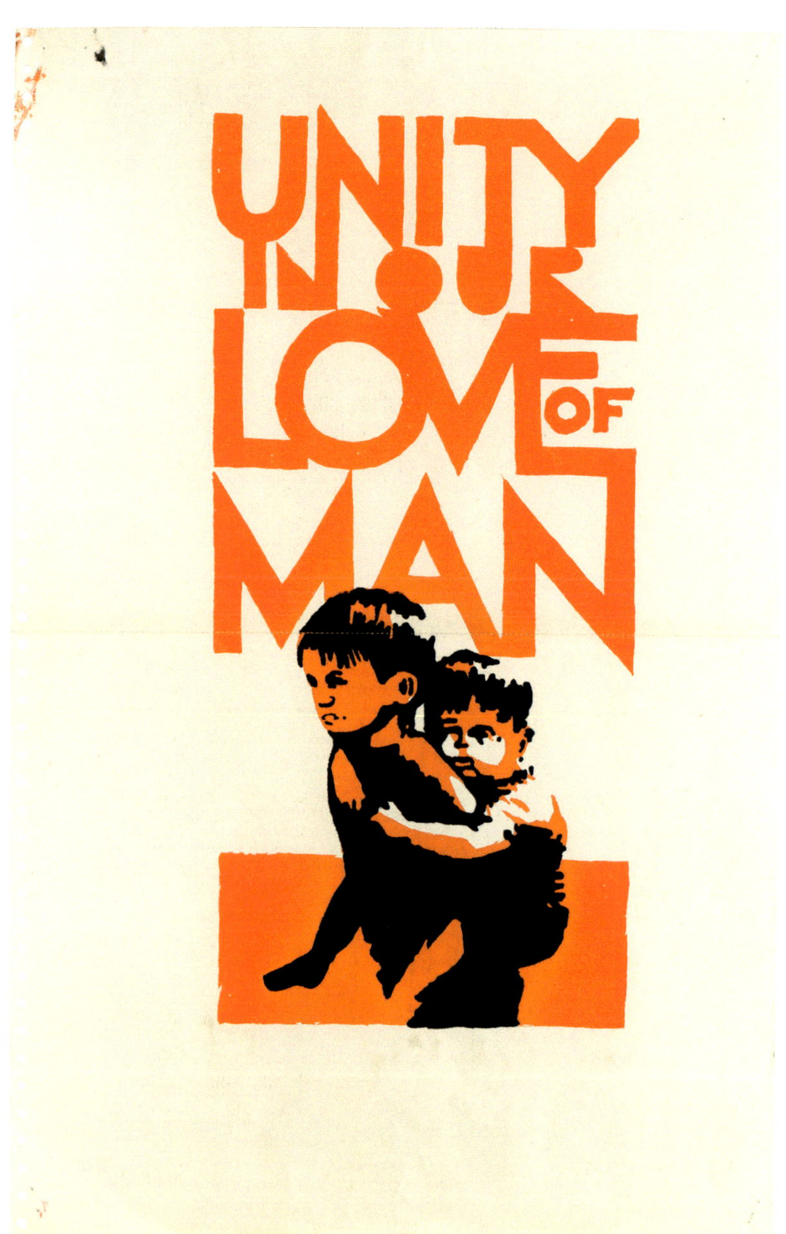

Unknown designers for the Berkeley Political Poster Workshop, *Unity in Our Love of Man*, 22 × 14⅜ inches (56 × 36.5 cm), and *Hunger Is Violence*, 33 × 14⅞ inches (84 × 38 cm), 1970, screen print on reused dot-matrix printer paper, Berkeley, California. The poster at right uses rudimentary letters—all harshly cut and devoid of curved lines—to connect the brutality of hunger to violence, while stacked, interlocking all-caps communicate the above poster's theme of unity. Both were made in student workshops at the University of Berkeley, California, in the wake of the student massacres at Kent State in Ohio and Jackson State in Mississippi.

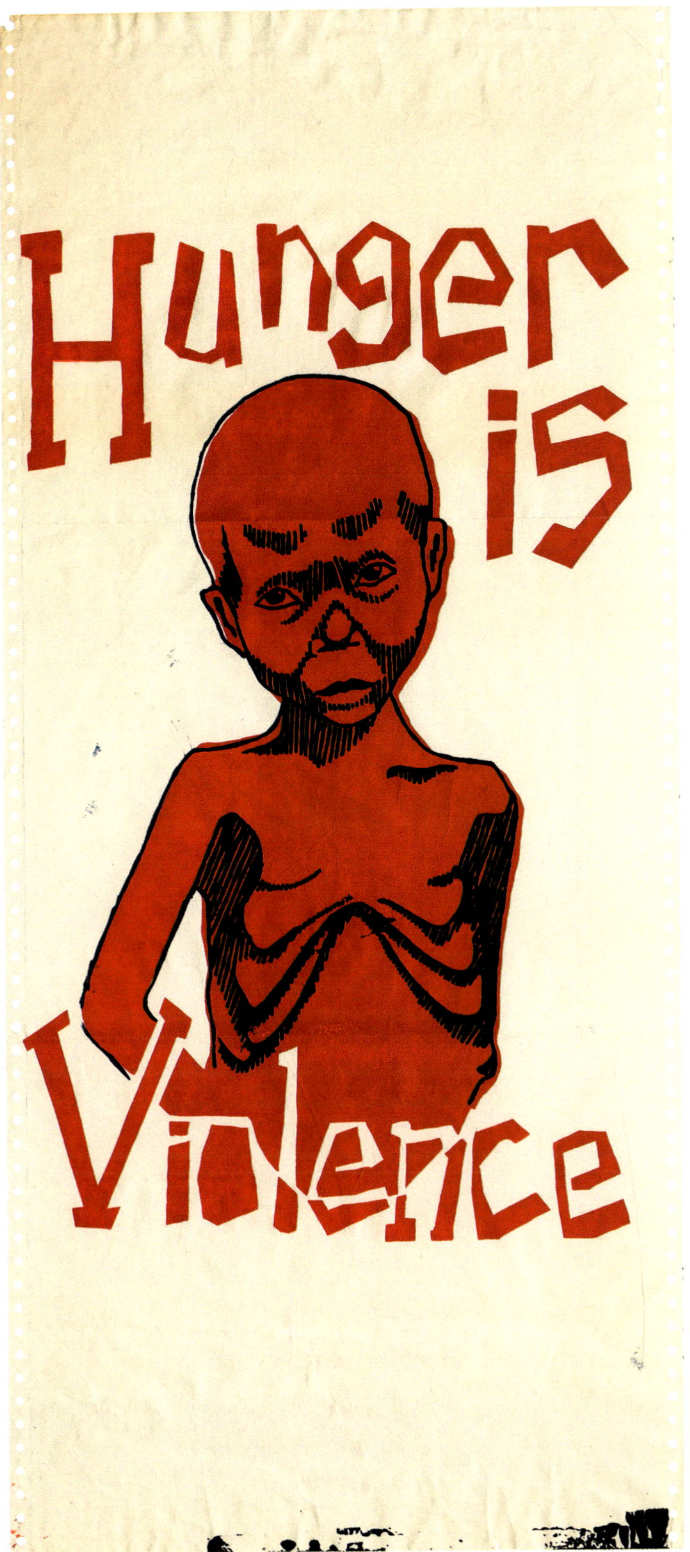
Hunger
is
Violence

"We attempted, on a severely limited budget, to capture the spirit of the conflict between the establishment and the students in a book form that can compete with other media."

—David L. Burke

In 1970, the Urban Research Corporation conducted a study of 292 campus protests held over the previous two years. It found that, along with antiwar themes, students demanded more representation in school government, greater faculty diversity, and the creation of Black studies programs. *Right On!* publishes data from the report alongside news coverage and quotes from students. It reads like a documentary film in paperback form: Straightforward charts and survey results in sterile Helvetica serve as the only narration, which is interspersed with dynamic, full-bleed layouts featuring cinematic street photography and reproductions of expressive DIY protest graphics that seem wheatpasted onto the page. *Right On!* appears to have been influenced by Marshall McLuhan's *The Medium Is the Massage*, a 1967 title from the same publisher, Bantam Books. Assembled by designer Quentin Fiore in a compilation that defied typographic norms and mimicked multimedia (with an intentional typo in "message" in the title), the earlier book is a seminal example of "designer as author." In *Right On!*, Burke similarly animates the text, situating the students' activism within a fittingly active page.

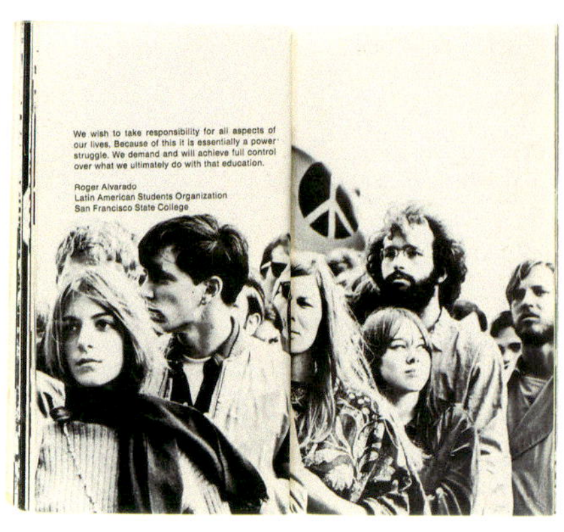

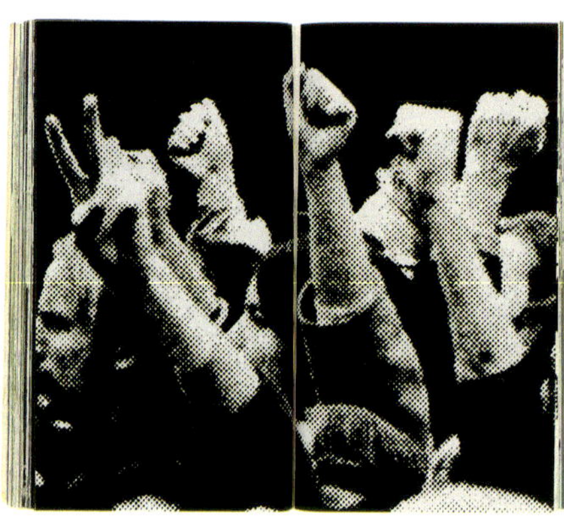

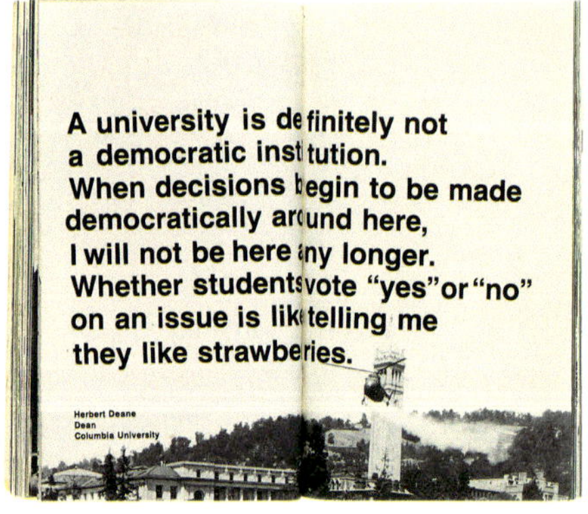

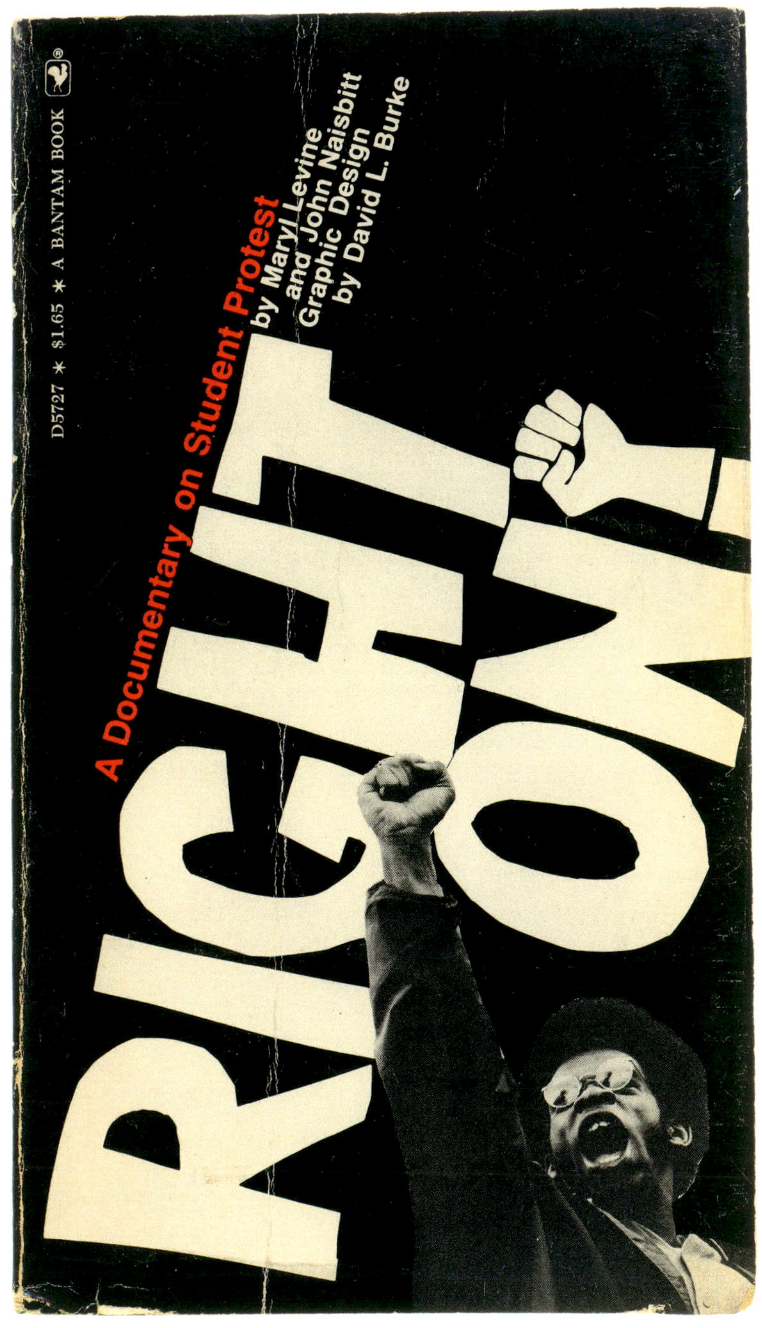

David L. Burke (designer), Maryl Levine and John Naisbitt (authors), *Right On!: A Documentary of Student Protest*, 1970, offset, 7⅛ × 4¼ inches (18 × 11 cm), New York.

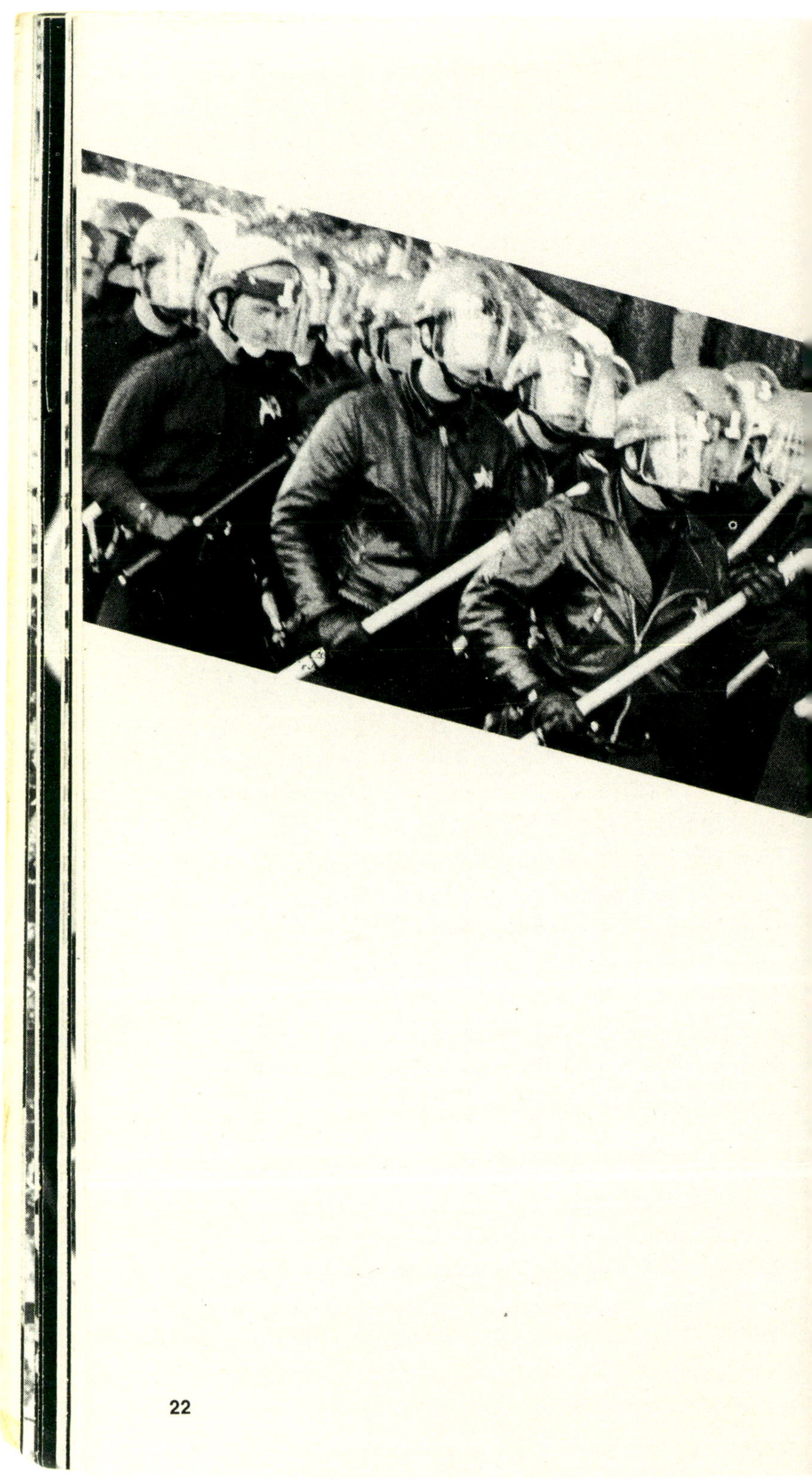

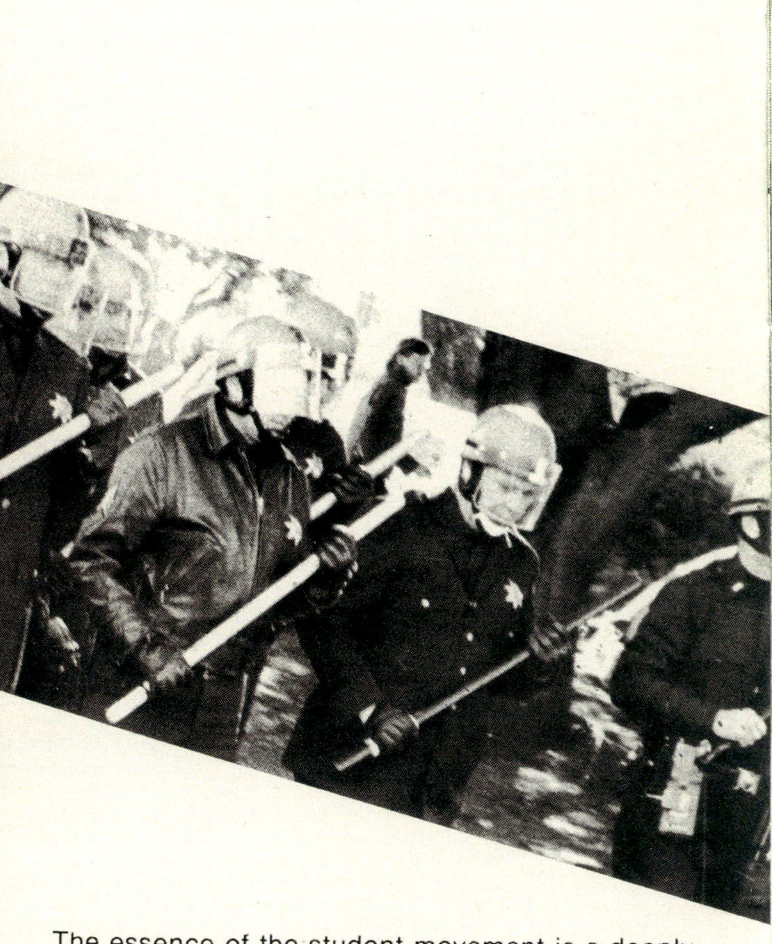

The essence of the student movement is a deeply moral protest against a society that glosses over injustices.

Harold Taussig
Professor
Kentucky Southern College

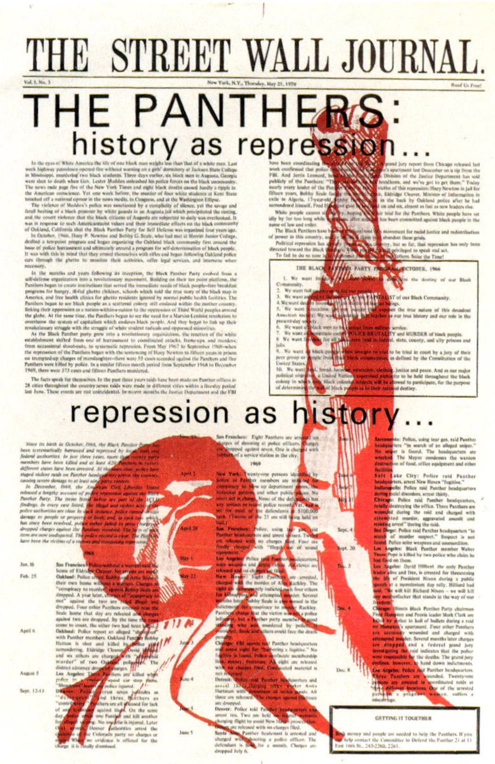

THE STREET WALL JOURNAL.

THE PANTHERS:
history as repression...

repression as history...

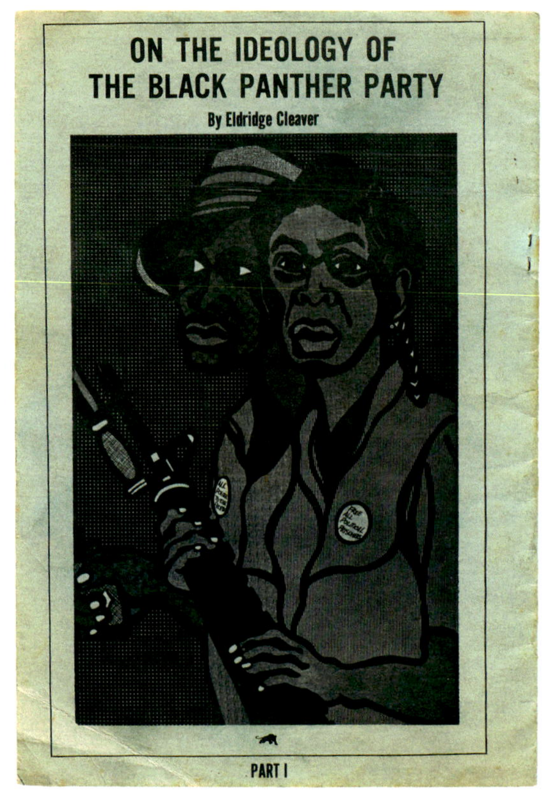

Unknown designer, *The Street Wall Journal*, vol. 1, no. 3, 1970, letterpress, 22 × 15½ inches (56 × 39.5 cm), New York. Here, a mock newspaper front page riffs on the conservative *Wall Street Journal* to educate the public about twenty-one Black Panthers who were charged with (and later acquitted of) conspiracy to carry out rifle attacks.

Emory Douglas (designer), Eldridge Cleaver (author), "On the Ideology of the Black Panther Party," 1967, offset, 10 × 7 inches (25.5 × 17.5 cm), Oakland, California. This educational pamphlet details the Black Panther Party's Marxist-socialist roots. It includes the Ten-Point Program, which demands restitution for slavery, access to safe housing, exemption from military service, full employment, and an end to police brutality.

Emory Douglas, *Black Studies*, circa 1970, offset, 22¾ × 8⅛ inches (58 × 20.5 cm), Oakland, California. In Douglas's portrait, the revolutionary student is doubly armed—with a weapon against police brutality and an account of Black history.

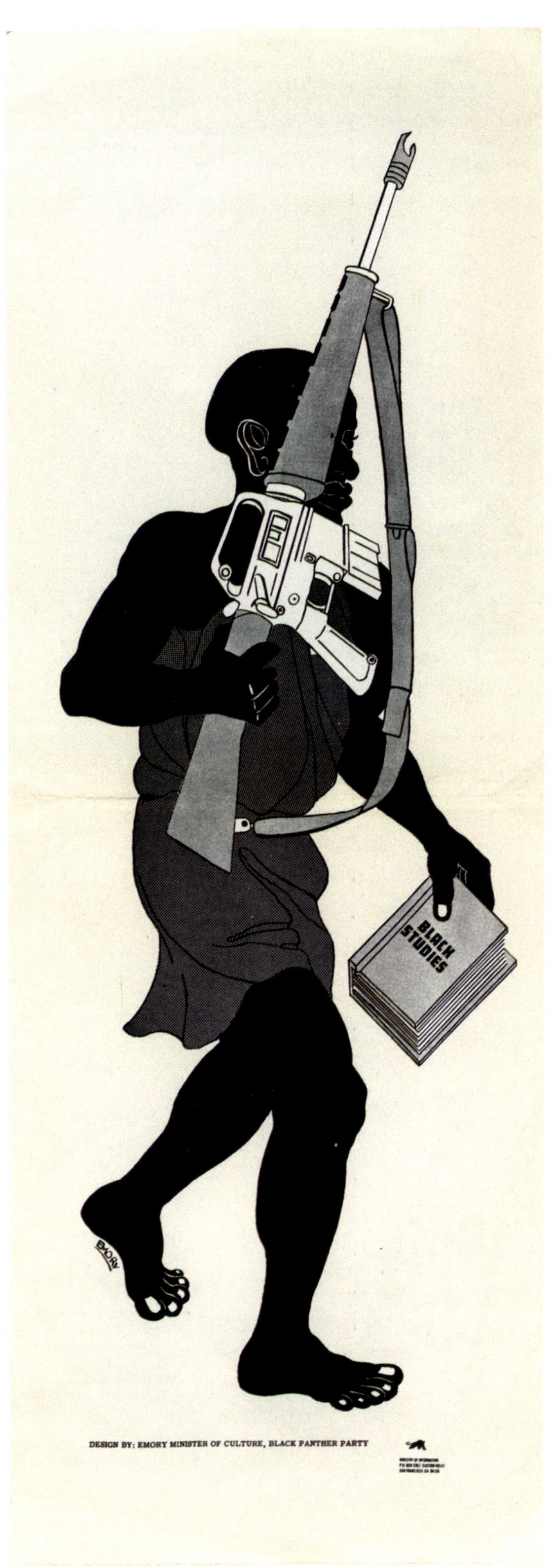

"We want education for our people that exposes the true nature of this decadent American society. We want education that teaches us our true history and our role in the present-day society."

—Eldridge Cleaver, "On the Ideology of the Black Panther Party," 1967

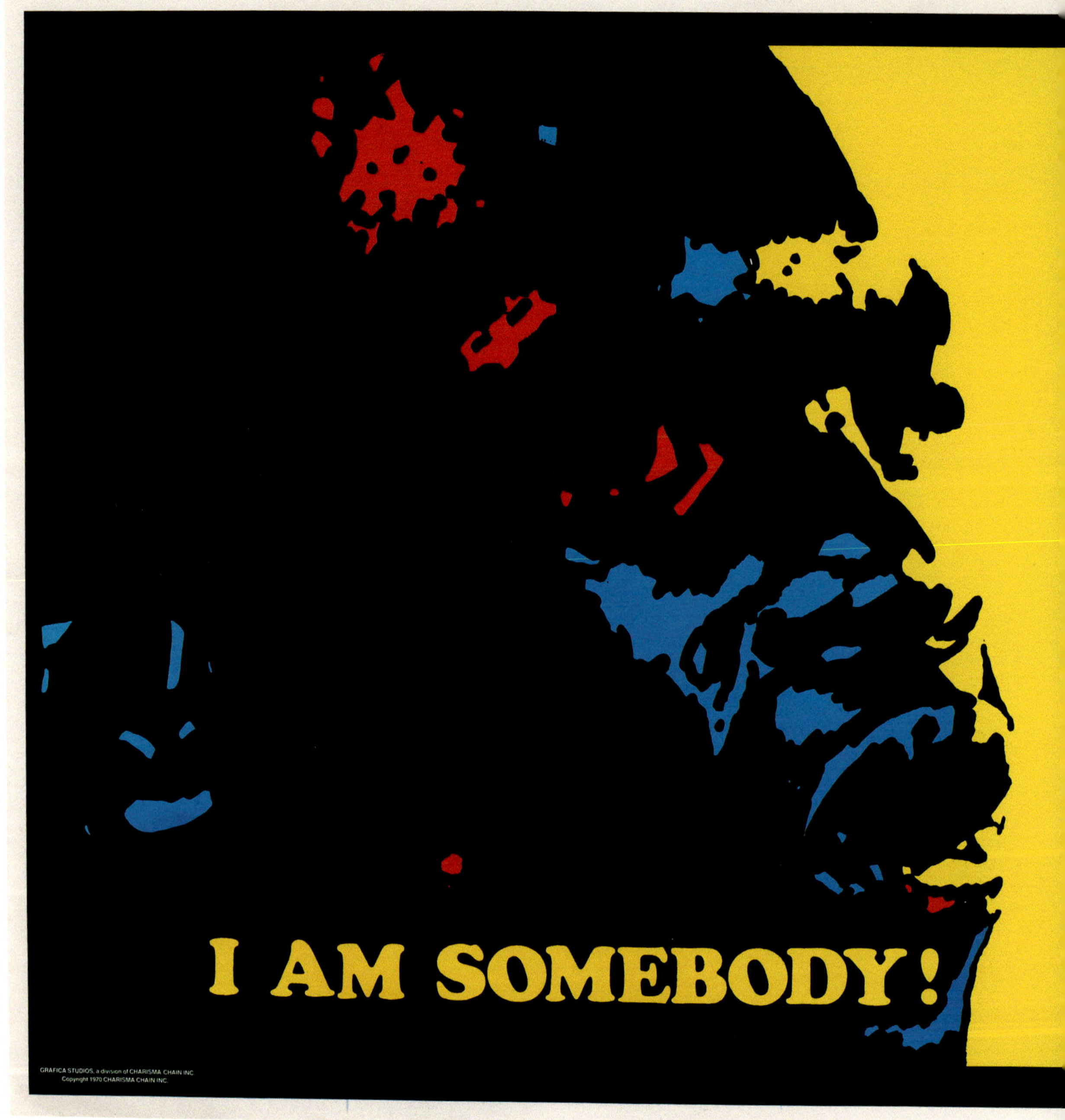

Herb Bruce for Gráfica Studios/Charisma Chain Inc., *I Am Somebody!*, 1970, offset, 24 × 36 inches (61 × 91.5 cm), Chicago. This black-light poster features the lyrics to a song written in the 1950s by civil rights activist Reverend William Holmes Borders, Sr. It was popularized by Reverend Jesse Jackson, who performed it on the children's television show *Sesame Street* as part of an education PSA for children of color. The type is set in Cooper Black, a strong typeface with roots in handlettering.

I AM SOMEBODY
I may be poor,
I may be on welfare,
I may be in jail,
but...
I AM SOMEBODY
I am BLACK
I am BEAUTIFUL
I must be RESPECTED
I must be PROTECTED
I am... SOMEBODY!!

I AM SOMEBODY
I may be poor,
I may be on welfare,
I may be in jail,
but...
I AM SOMEBODY
I am BLACK
I am BEAUTIFUL
I must be RESPECTED
I must be PROTECTED
I am... SOMEBODY!!

I AM SOMEBODY
I may be poor,
I may be on welfare,
I may be in jail,
but...
I AM SOMEBODY
I am BLACK
I am BEAUTIFUL
I must be RESPECTED
I must be PROTECTED
I am... SOMEBODY!!

I AM SOMEBODY
I may be poor,
I may be on welfare,
I may be in jail,
but...
I AM SOMEBODY
I am BLACK

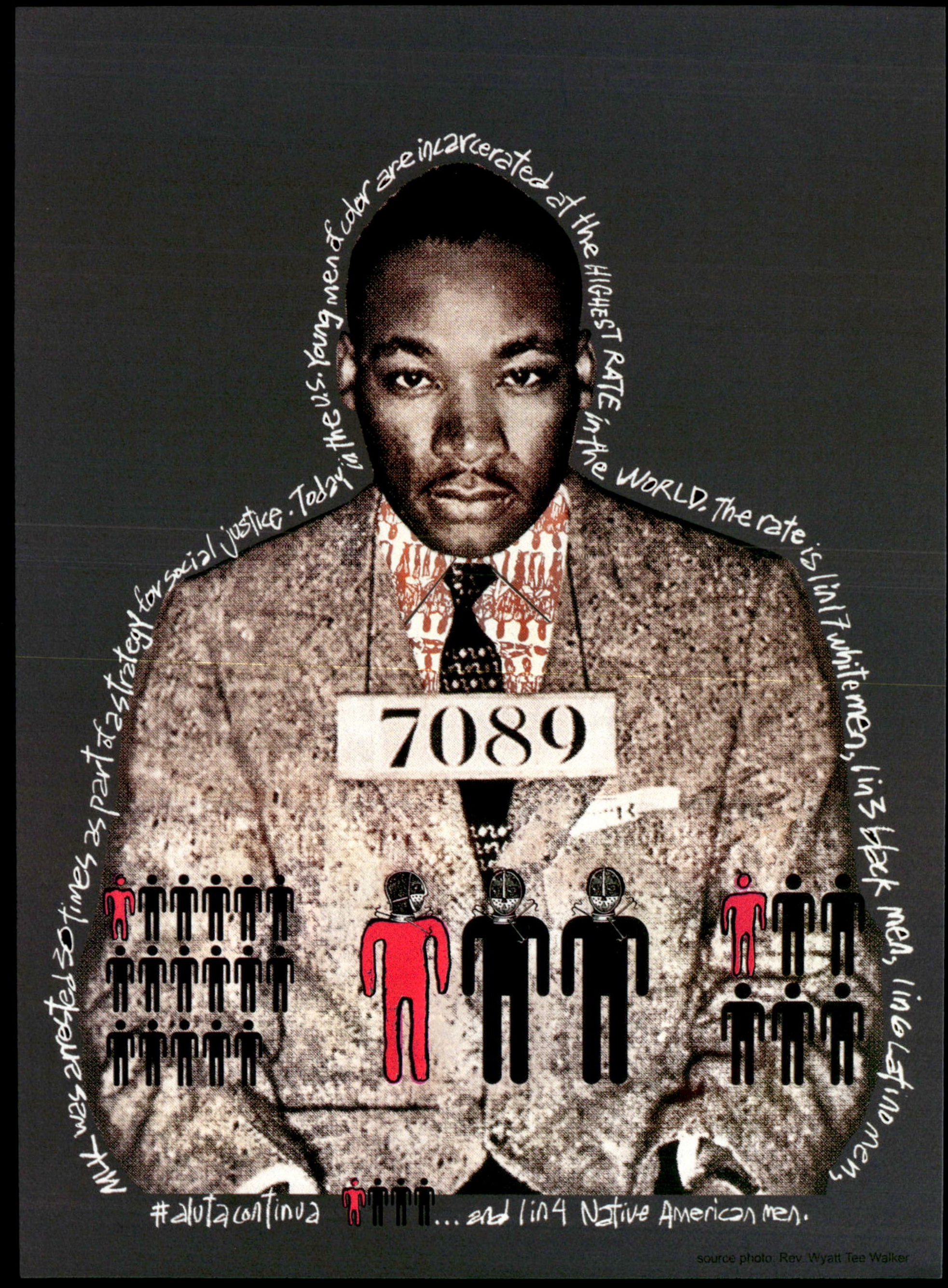

Chip Thomas, *Criminal Justice Reform Now*, 2016, screen print, 24 × 18 inches (61 × 46 cm), Chicago.

Unknown designer, *The Black Scholar: The Journal of Black Studies and Research*, vol. 2, no. 2, 1970, offset, 10¼ × 7¼ inches (26 × 18.5 cm), San Francisco.

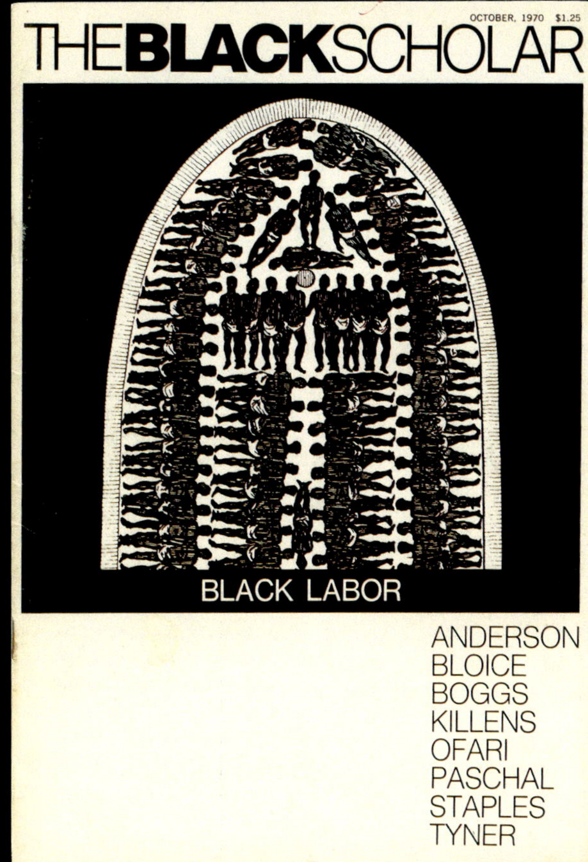

Call and Response

In 1791, British abolitionist Thomas Clarkson commissioned a diagram of the slave ship *Brookes* to detail how nearly five hundred humans were packed into the hull and made to lie on shallow shelves for the monthslong transatlantic journey. A powerful teaching tool, Clarkson's diagram demonstrated the stark and cruel reality of the slave trade, which his efforts helped outlaw in Britain in 1807.

This symbol has since been reclaimed on artwork ranging from protest posters (see *News of the Week* by Corita Kent on page 52) to album covers (like Bob Marley's 1979 *Survival*). In 1970, *The Black Scholar*, a journal of culture and politics based in the San Francisco Bay Area, reprised the graphic for the cover of an issue on Black labor.

In 2016, Chip Thomas, a photographer, public artist, activist, and physician for the Navajo Nation, repurposed the image to illustrate what is often referred to as slavery's modern-day incarnation: the U.S. prison-industrial complex. Thomas patternizes the artwork onto the shirt worn by Dr. Martin Luther King, Jr., in a mugshot taken after his arrest for leading the 1956 bus protest in Montgomery, Alabama. Thomas contrasts the utilitarian stencil of King's booking number with handwritten facts about the contemporary incarceration rates of white, Black, and Native American men. Layered over the photo, infographic representations of these statistics echo Clarkson's original diagram, creating a multigenerational meme that charts institutionalized racism and brutality.

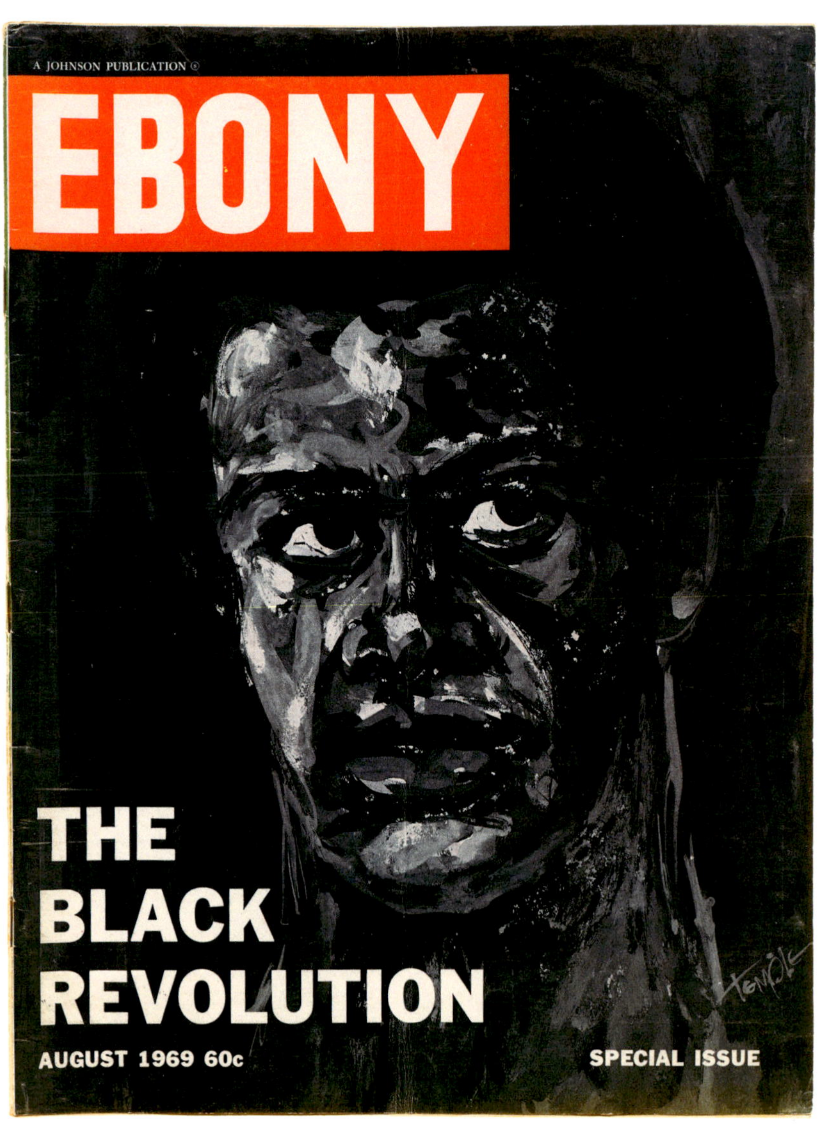

Herbert Temple (designer and cover artist), John H. Johnson (editor), *Ebony*, *The Black Revolution* special issue, vol. 24, no. 10, 1969, offset, 13¼ × 10⅛ inches (33.5 × 25.5 cm), Chicago. Temple set the nameplate in a basic sans within a red rectangle to create deliberate product confusion with *Life*—and to get Black issues in front of a mass white audience. His use of Franklin Gothic in the title conveys straightforward journalism—part of *Ebony*'s bid to be seen as part of the established press.

EBONY

THE BLACK REVOLUTION

UGUST 1969 60c

SPECIAL ISSUE

Curated by collector and historian Middleton A. Harris and compiled by Toni Morrison as a countertext to whitewashed schoolbooks, *The Black Book* tells the four-hundred-year history of Black people in America. Its coverage begins in Africa, with the first-person tale of two young brothers kidnapped into the slave trade. It then follows Black life through slavery, the Civil War, Reconstruction, and the Jim Crow era. Intercut with public records of slave auctions, graphic newspaper clippings of lynchings, lyrics to lullabies and hymnals, announcements of Black talent in sports, music, and entertainment, and recipes for hoe cake and voodoo talismans alike, *The Black Book* is a scrapbook of injustice and hatred as well as beauty and achievement. Its design is a pastiche of primary sources and wide-ranging print technologies: Woodcut scenes, reproductions of government notices in various resolutions, and blurred long-exposure portraiture sit alongside glitzy, highly produced movie stills, technical diagrams of innovations, and bigoted ads that were shamelessly printed in full color.

For the text, designer Jack Ribik chose a three-column grid set in Cheltenham (long a mainstay for headlines in the *New York Times*) in order to re-create the sense of an artfully crammed nineteenth-century newspaper. For the cover, he stacked the title in Parsons, a distinctive typeface based on the lettering of a popular Chicago sign-painter by the same name, over a patchwork of images of Black life.

Without a table of contents, distinct chapters, sidebars, an index, or other navigation elements, *The Black Book* maintains the sense of a loose collection: a violent, sorrowful, joyous, and triumphant history to be continuously reassembled—and reckoned with—by today's reader.

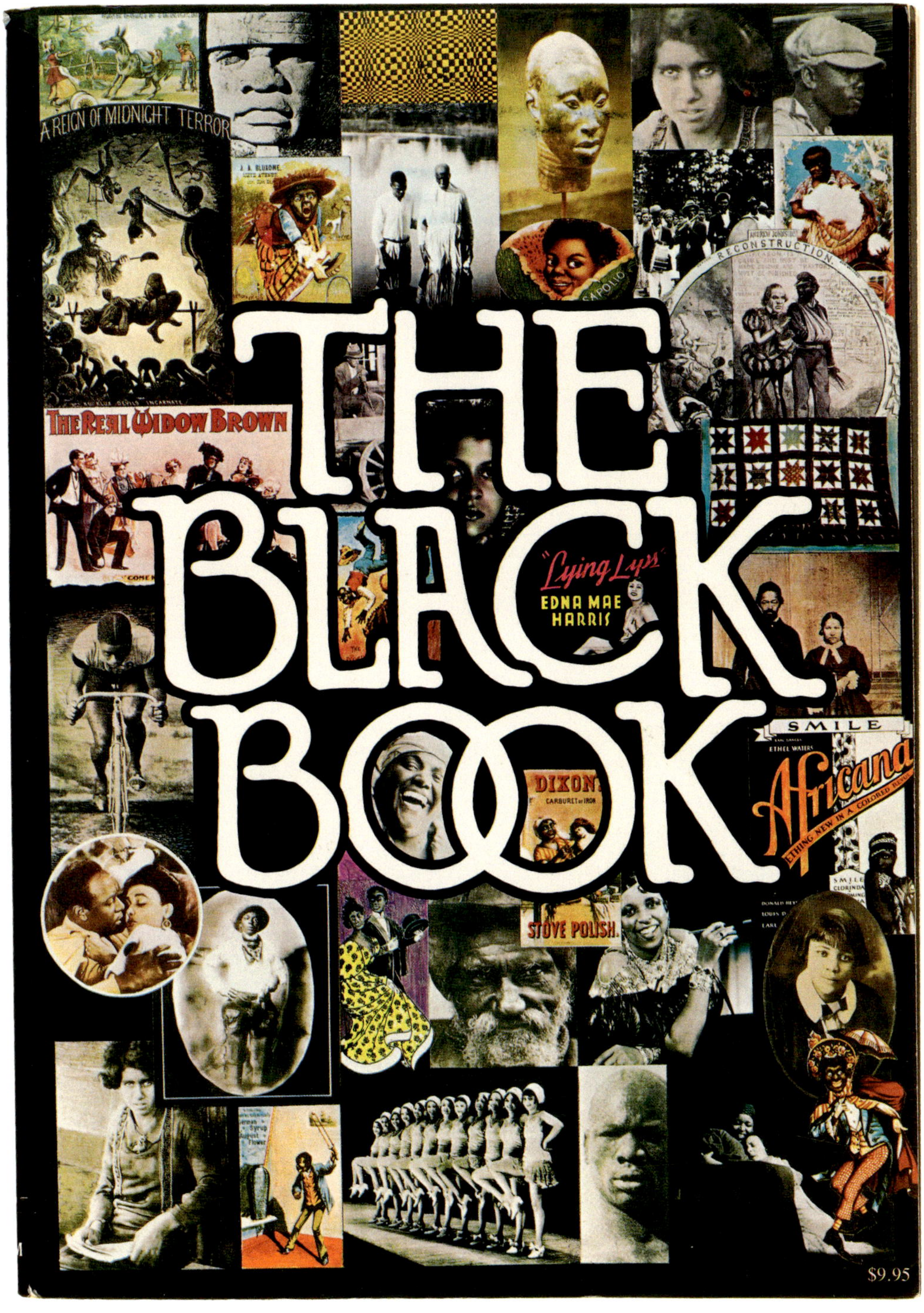

Jack Ribik (designer), Middleton A. Harris with Morris Levitt, Roger Furman, and Ernest Smith (contributing editors), Toni Morrison (editor), *The Black Book*, 1974, offset, 11⅜ × 8¼ inches (29 × 21 cm), New York.

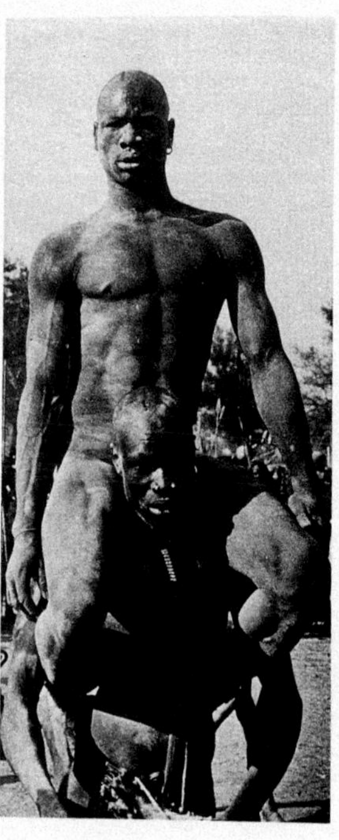

as he himself was too young to lift or carry such weight like me, so by that he was unable to lift me to a distance of about ten feet before he would fall down four times or more.

When he tried all his power for several times and failed and again at that moment the smell of the gun-powder of the enemies' guns which were shooting repeatedly was rushing to our noses by the breeze and this made us fear more, so my brother lifted me again a very short distance, but when I saw that he was falling several times, then I told him to leave me on the road and run away for his life perhaps he might be safe so that he would be taking care of our mother as she had no other sons more than both of us and I told him that if God saves my life too then we should meet again, but if God does not save my life we should meet in heaven.

But as I was telling him these sorrowful words both his eyes were shedding tears repeatedly, of course I did not shed tears at all on my eyes as I put hope that no doubt I would be easily captured or killed. And it was that day I believed that if fear is overmuch, a person would not fear for anything again. But as the smoke of the enemies' guns was rushing to our view, then my brother left me on that road with sorrow, and then he stopped and put his hand into his pocket and brought out the fruits which fell down from the tree under which we were about to hide ourselves before; he gave me both fruits instead of one. After that he started to run as fast as he could along this road towards the enemies unnoticed and he was still looking at me as he was running away.

So after I saw him no more on the road I put both fruits into my pocket and then got back to that fruit tree under which we picked them and I stood there only to shelter myself from the sun. But when the enemies were at a distance of about an eighth of a mile to that place where I stood I was unable to hear again because of the noises of the enemies' guns and as I was too young to hear such fearful noises and wait, so I entered into the bush under this fruit tree. This fruit tree was a "SIGN" for me and it was on that day I called it—THE "FUTURE SIGN."

Now it remained me alone in the bush, because no brother, mother, father or other defender could save me or direct me if and whenever any danger is imminent. But as these enemies had approached us closely before my brother left because of me he was captured within fifteen minutes that he left me, but he was only captured as a slave and not killed, because I heard his voice when he shouted louder for help.

African Word	*Afro American Word*	*Meaning*
Yaw Kay	OK	All right
Hipi	Hip	Aware
Cat	Cat	Person
Goy	Guy	A young man of no standing
Dega	Dig	Understand
Kuta	Cooter	Tortoise
Podzo	Poor Joe	Blue Heron
Taki	Tackies	Small wild horses
Tota	Tote	Carry
Dzogal (to rise)	Joggle board	Seesaw
Saut (to run around the Kaaba)	Shout	Religious ecstasy
Banzar	Banjo	Musical instrument with neck of wood fitted with four strings

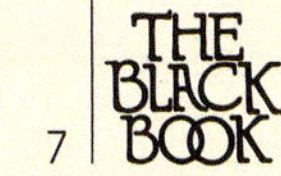

And they sold us like beasts, and they counted our teeth . . . and they felt our testicles and they tested the lustre or dullness of our skin . . .

—Cesaire

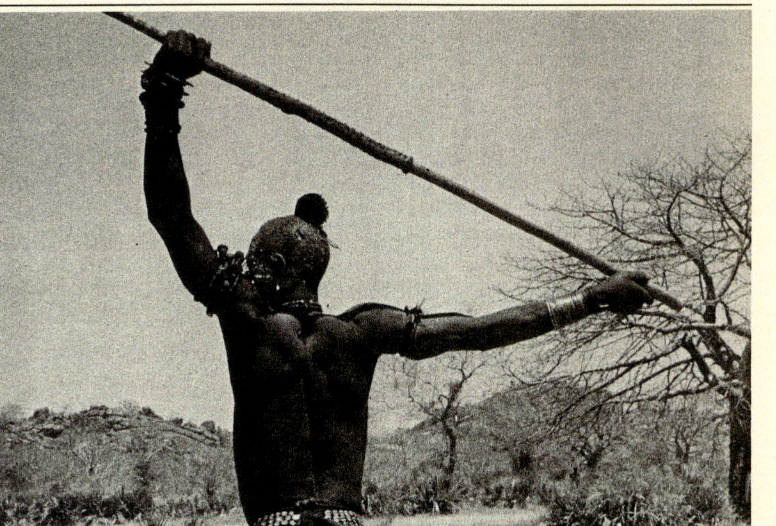

EX SIGNÉ

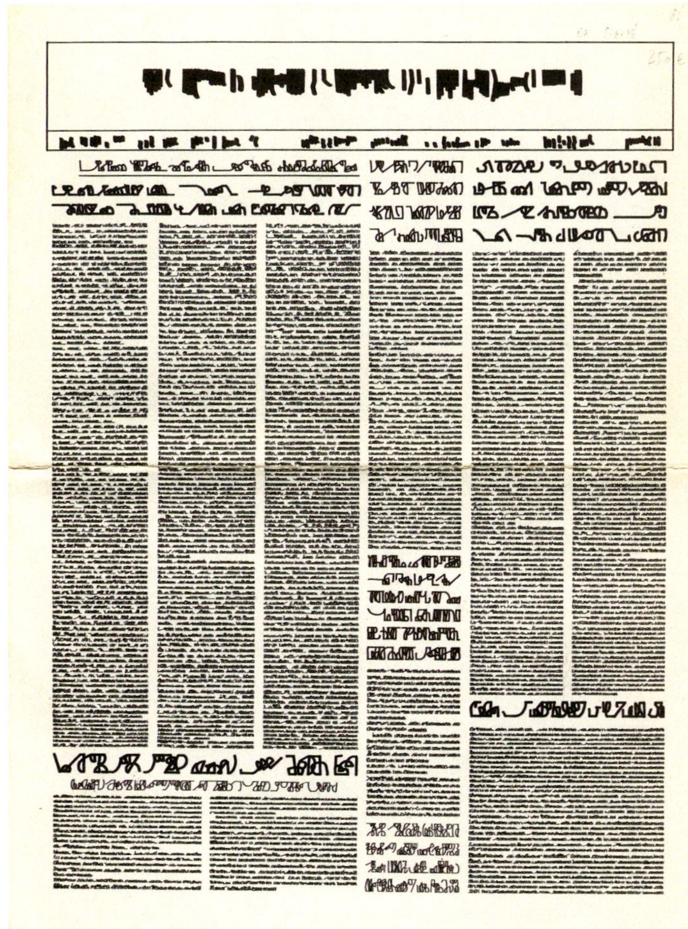

Mirtha Dermisache (designer), *Newspaper* (*Diario*), vol. 1, no. 1, 1975 (third edition of the 1972 original), offset, 18⅝ × 14¼ inches (47.5 × 36 cm), Buenos Aires. In this piece, created at least in part as a commentary on the Trelew massacre, the Argentine military's 1972 murder of sixteen political prisoners, Dermisache translated a newspaper into *asemic* (nonsensical) writing, calligraphically obscuring some text in resistance of the government's misrepresentation of the massacre in the media. She left folded copies on public benches as part of an exhibition, which the police destroyed in an effort to censor criticism.

DESTROY SUPERABUNDANCE. STARVE THE FLESH, SHAVE THE HAIR, EXPOSE THE BONE, CLARIFY THE MIND, DEFINE THE WILL, RESTRAIN THE SENSES, LEAVE THE FAMILY, FLEE THE CHURCH, KILL THE VERMIN, VOMIT THE HEART, FORGET THE DEAD. LIMIT TIME, FORGO AMUSEMENT, DENY NATURE, REJECT ACQUAINTANCES, DISCARD OBJECTS, FORGET TRUTHS, DISSECT MYTH, STOP MOTION, BLOCK IMPULSE, CHOKE SOBS, SWALLOW CHATTER. SCORN JOY, SCORN TOUCH, SCORN TRAGEDY, SCORN LIBERTY, SCORN CONSTANCY, SCORN HOPE, SCORN EXALTATION, SCORN REPRODUCTION, SCORN VARIETY, SCORN EMBELLISHMENT, SCORN RELEASE, SCORN REST, SCORN SWEETNESS, SCORN LIGHT. IT'S A QUESTION OF FORM AS MUCH AS FUNCTION. IT IS A MATTER OF REVULSION.

"Symbols are more important than things themselves .... There's a fine line between information and propaganda .... Your actions are pointless if no one notices them."

—Jenny Holzer, *Truisms*, 1979

In the 1970s, artist Jenny Holzer worked as a typesetter for *Laundry News*, a trade publication for the coin-operated-laundry industry. The skills she learned there (namely, precision and legibility) form the foundation of her artwork, in which text becomes image, and image becomes a site for public discourse.

Produced around this time, one of Holzer's first projects was *Inflammatory Essays*, a collection of ten prints on colored paper. Their text is inscrutable—bewildering instructions mix with snippets of contradictory fascist rants, inspired by a reading list that includes figures such as anarchist writer Emma Goldman and Chinese communist revolutionary Mao Zedong.

Holzer anonymously wheatpasted these essays around New York City, pairing their messaging with the characters of the various boroughs. (She was arrested one night, though released when police couldn't figure what to make of her activities.) Encountered on message boards, urban walls, and signposts, her essays can be read as public service announcements, ranging in tone from absurdist to dark humor or satire. It is in this public realm that her text—a poetic doxology, printed line after line with repetitive constructions like those found in prayerbooks or sacred texts—asks the reader to question the written word's vague but absolute claim to power. In order to present these short dictums as fact, she set them simply in Times New Roman (a default typeface known for its ubiquity in institutional documents), while using italics and capitalization to undermine their neutrality and give them a sense of enigmatic screed. In the example at left, Holzer allows for stacks (repeated words at the start or end of a line, considered poor for legibility), which create further discomfort in the reader.

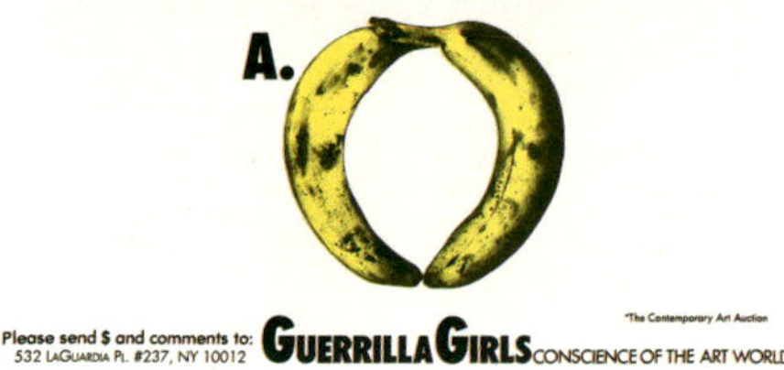

"Dearest art collector," begins a note in curlicue script across a hot pink handkerchief. "It has come to our attention that your collection, like most, does not contain enough art by women." Such an official complaint, ironically packaged in the hallmarks of stereotypical femininity, is the handiwork of Guerrilla Girls, a feminist collective that has been calling out the art world for its inequitable gender representation since 1985. The anonymous members of the troupe—who avoid identification by wearing gorilla masks and using the names of major women artists as pseudonyms—got their start counting rare nude male figures in paintings at museums and galleries in New York City. They then distributed handbills or tacked up posters decrying the results. Styled as cheeky advertisements or public service announcements, their designs pose rhetorical questions, such as, "Q: How many works by women artists were in the Andy Warhol and Tremaine auctions at Sotheby's?" which is answered with a zero formed by two bananas—a nod to the double meaning in the *guerrilla* of their nom de protest (as well as to Warhol's famous artwork for the Velvet Underground and Nico's 1967 album). This humor is key to their messaging, which seeks to undo stereotypes of feminism as overly serious. Guerrilla Girls has also addressed racism, as in *How Long Did It Take to Loot South Central L.A.?*, which questions the media's framing of community unrest after the Los Angeles police who were caught on camera beating Rodney King, a Black man, were acquitted in 1992.

GUERRILLA GIRLS SOCIAL STUDIES QUIZ

HOW LONG DID IT TAKE TO LOOT SOUTH CENTRAL L.A.?

A. 81 seconds *Length of videotaped beating of Rodney King*
B. 72 hours *Length of L.A. riots*
C. 12 years *Length of Reagan-Bush administrations*

A PUBLIC SERVICE MESSAGE FROM GUERRILLA GIRLS 532 LAGUARDIA PL. #237, NY 10012

"POP'S" QUIZ

HOW MANY WHITE MALE GENIUSES EMPLOY UNDOCUMENTED CHILDCARE WORKERS?

A. None of your goddamn business.
B. Same as the number of U.S. senators.
C. Those who have wives to take the blame.

A PUBLIC SERVICE MESSAGE FROM GUERRILLA GIRLS 532 LAGUARDIA PL. #237, NY 10012

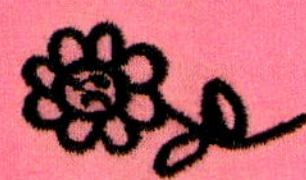

Guerrilla Girls, at left, from the *Guerrilla Girls Most Wanted* series, offset, 17 × 22 inches (43 × 56 cm), New York. From top to bottom: *How Many Works by Women Artists Were in the Andy Warhol and Tremaine Auctions at Sotheby's?*, 1989; *How Long Did It Take to Loot South Central L.A.?*, 1992; *"Pop's" Quiz*, 1999. Above: *Dearest Art Collector*, 2015 adaptation of a 1986 poster, digital print and embroidery on a cotton handkerchief, 11⅜ × 8¼ inches, New York.

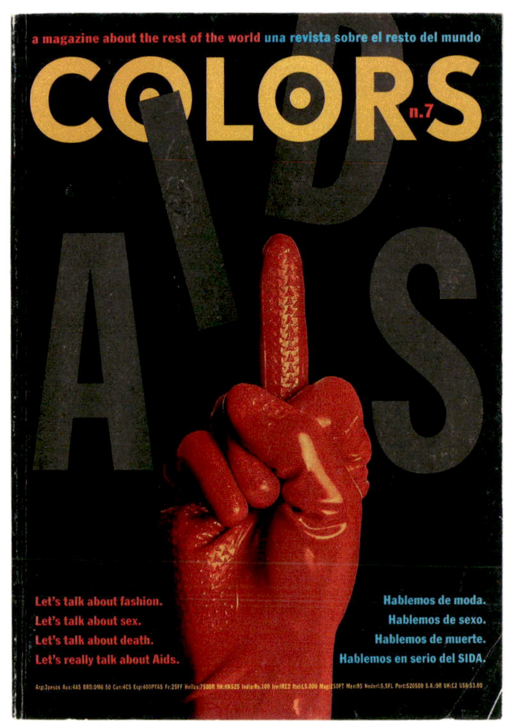
a magazine about the rest of the world una revista sobre el resto del mundo
COLORS
n.7
AIDS
Let's talk about fashion.
Let's talk about sex.
Let's talk about death.
Let's really talk about Aids.
Hablemos de moda.
Hablemos de sexo.
Hablemos de muerte.
Hablemos en serio del SIDA.

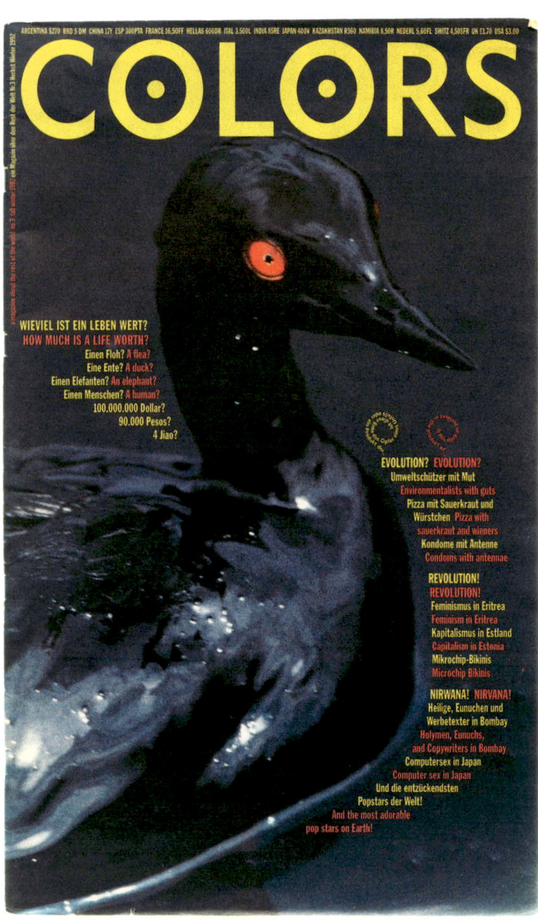
COLORS
WIEVIEL IST EIN LEBEN WERT?
HOW MUCH IS A LIFE WORTH?
Einen Floh? A flea?
Eine Ente? A duck?
Einen Elefanten? An elephant?
Einen Menschen? A human?
100.000.000 Dollar?
90.000 Pesos?
4 Jiao?
EVOLUTION? EVOLUTION?
Umweltschützer mit Mut
Environmentalists with guts
Pizza mit Sauerkraut und Würstchen
Pizza with sauerkraut and wieners
Kondome mit Antenne
Condoms with antennae
REVOLUTION! REVOLUTION!
Feminismus in Eritrea
Feminism in Eritrea
Kapitalismus in Estland
Capitalism in Estonia
Mikrochip-Bikinis
Microchip Bikinis
NIRWANA! NIRVANA!
Heilige, Eunuchen und Werbetexter in Bombay
Holymen, Eunuchs, and Copywriters in Bombay
Computersex in Japan
Computer sex in Japan
Und die entzückendsten Popstars der Welt!
And the most adorable pop stars on Earth!

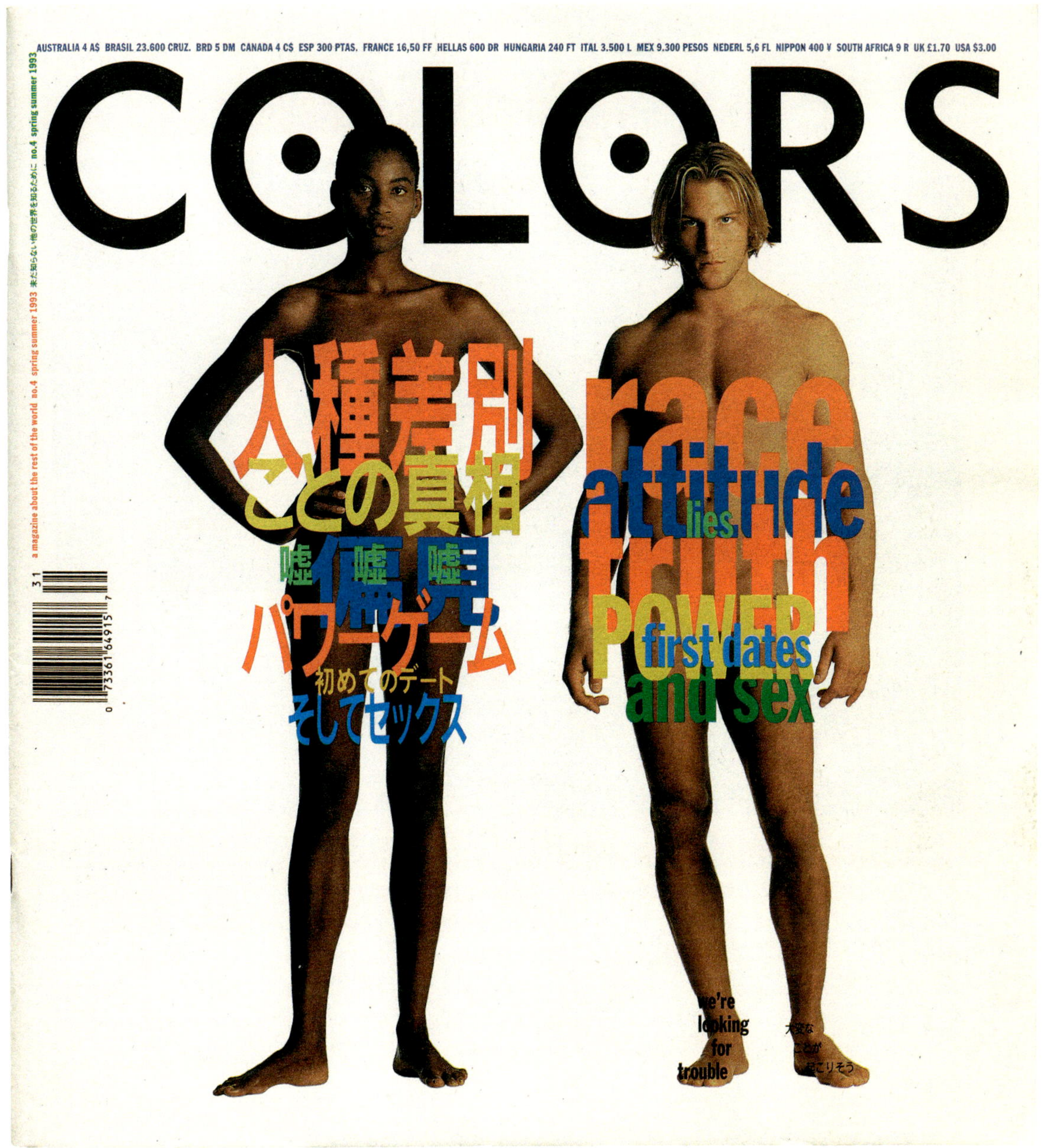

Various designers, Tibor Kalman (editor), *Colors: A Magazine About the Rest of the World*, offset. From left to right: **Paul Ritter (designer),** no. 3, 1992, 18½ × 11½ inches (47 × 29 cm), New York; **Scott Stowell (designer),** no. 7, 1994, 10⅝ × 7½ inches (27 × 19 cm), Rome; **Paul Ritter (designer)**, no. 4, 1993, 12⅛ × 11½ inches (31 × 29 cm), Rome. Page 212: **Scott Stowell (designer),** no. 7, 1994, 10⅝ × 7½ inches (27 × 19 cm), Rome. Page 213: **Paul Ritter (designer),** no. 14, 1996, 13¼ × 9⅞ inches (33.5 × 25 cm), Paris.

Where did AIDS come from?

experts say...

AIDS was caused by radiation from French nuclear testing in the Sahara Desert![2]

AIDS CAME FROM GREEN MONKEYS

Humans caught the virus — by eating raw monkey brains!

HIV was created by Soviet scientists...

...while testing new biological weapons![3]

AIDS IS A C.I.A. PLOT

U.S. soldiers were the first to get HIV... ...from sex with monkeys in Vietnam![5]

AIDS STARTED IN AFRICA

... brought in by white TOURISTS!

[1] Cited as a myth by *The Guardian*, November 1993. [2] Attributed to American scientist Ernest Stirnglass in De Thé, *Sur la piste du cancer*, Flammarion, Paris, 1984. [3] Cited as a myth by *The Guardian*, November 1993. [4] Cited as a myth alleged by Soviet newspapers by Langone in *AIDS: The Facts*, Little, Brown & Company, 1991. Also cited as a myth in *New Internationalist*, December 1993. [5] Alleged by *Islam*, a Turkish magazine, August 1987. This rumor soon became widespread in the Middle East. Cited as a myth by Renée Sabatier in *Blaming Others*, Panos Institute, 1988. [6] Rumor from the streets of Kampala, Uganda. Cited by local COLORS reporter. [7] Cited as a myth by Langone in *AIDS: The Facts*, Little, Brown & Company, 1991.

GAY SEX DRUG CAUSED AIDS!

It doesn't matter.

¿De dónde viene el SIDA?

los expertos dicen que...

¡El SIDA fue causado por la radiación emitida por las pruebas nucleares realizadas por los francéses en el desierto del Sahara!

EL SIDA VIENE DE UNOS MONOS VERDES

El hombre contrajo el virus: ¡comiendo el cerebro crudo de los monos![2]

El VIH fue creado por los científicos soviéticos... ...¡mientras hacían pruebas con las nuevas armas biológicas![3]

EL SIDA ES UN COMPLOT DE LA C.I.A.[4]

Los soldados de EE.UU.fueron los primeros en contagiarse el VIH...

...¡teniendo relaciones con monos en Vietnam![5]

EL SIDA APARECIO EN AFRICA

[1] Atribuido al científico americano Ernest Stringlass en De Thé, *Sur la piste du cancer*, Flammarion, París, 1984. [2] Citado como mito por *The Guardian*, Noviembre 1993. [3] Citado como mito por *The Guardian*, noviembre 1993. [4] Citado por los periodicos soviéticos como mito citado por Langone en *SIDA: Los hechos*, Little, Brown & Company, 1991. También citado como mito en *New Internationalist*, diciembre 1993. [5] Afirmado por *Islam*, una revista turca, Agosto 1987. Este rumor se difundió pronto en oriente medio. Citado como mito por Renée Sabatier en *Blaming Others*, Panos Institute, 1988. [6] Rumor de las calles de Kampala, Uganda. Citado por un corresponsal local de COLORS. [7] Citado como mito por Langone en *SIDA: Los hechos*, Little, Brown & Company, 1991.

...¡llevado por los turistas blancos![6]

¡La droga sexual de los homosexuales causó el SIDA![7]

No tiene importancia.

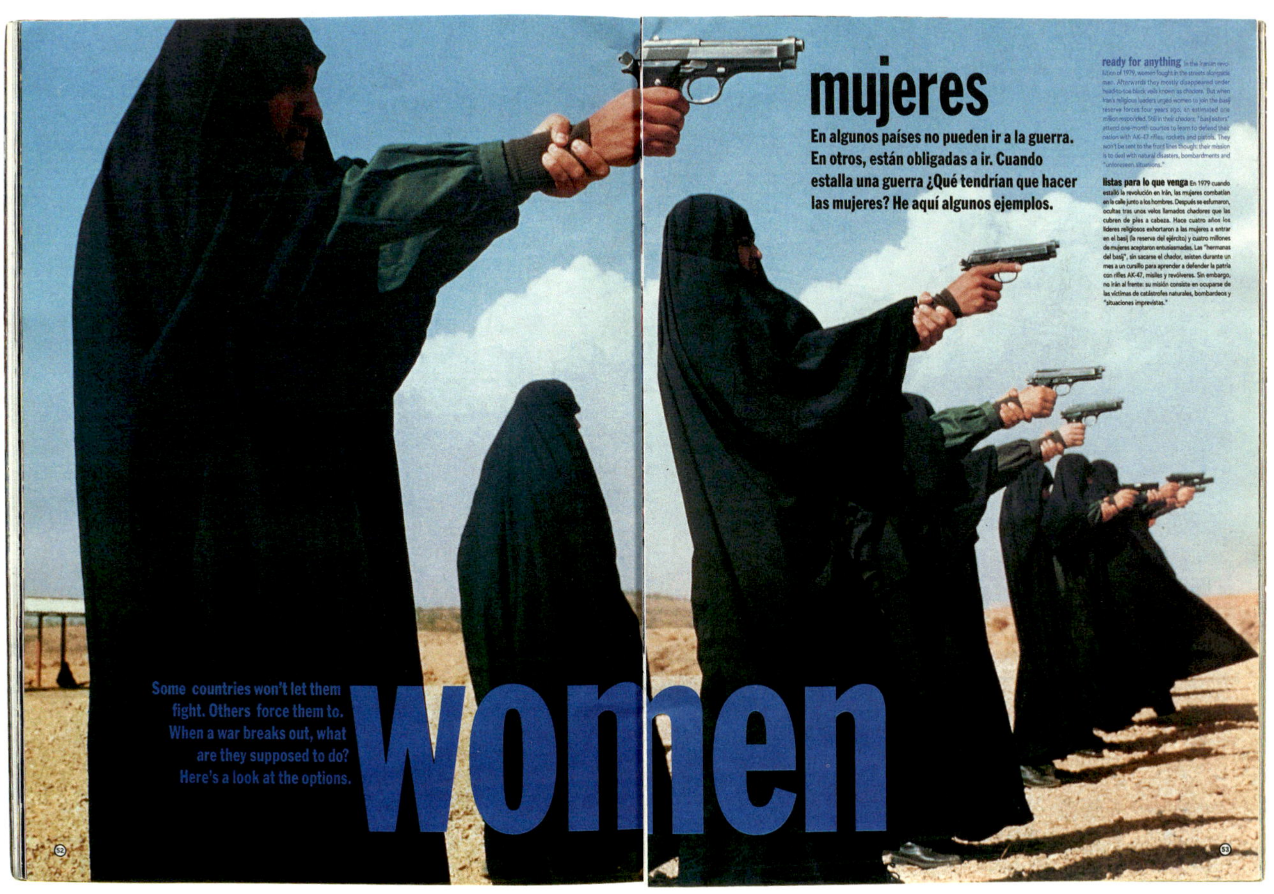
mujeres
En algunos países no pueden ir a la guerra. En otros, están obligadas a ir. Cuando estalla una guerra ¿Qué tendrían que hacer las mujeres? He aquí algunos ejemplos.
ready for anything In the Iranian revolution of 1979, women fought in the streets alongside men. Afterwards they mostly disappeared under head-to-toe black veils known as chadors. But when Iran's religious leaders urged women to join the basij reserve forces four years ago, an estimated one million responded. Still in their chadors, "basij sisters" attend one-month courses to learn to defend their nation with AK-47 rifles, rockets and pistols. They won't be sent to the front lines though: their mission is to deal with natural disasters, bombardments and "unforeseen situations."
listas para lo que venga En 1979 cuando estalló la revolución en Irán, las mujeres combatían en la calle junto a los hombres. Después se esfumaron, ocultas tras unos velos llamados chadores que las cubren de pies a cabeza. Hace cuatro años los líderes religiosos exhortaron a las mujeres a entrar en el basij (la reserva del ejército) y cuatro millones de mujeres aceptaron entusiasmadas. Las "hermanas del basij", sin sacarse el chador, asisten durante un mes a un cursillo para aprender a defender la patria con rifles AK-47, misiles y revólveres. Sin embargo, no irán al frente: su misión consiste en ocuparse de las víctimas de catástrofes naturales, bombardeos y "situaciones imprevistas."
Some countries won't let them fight. Others force them to. When a war breaks out, what are they supposed to do? Here's a look at the options.
women
52
53

Designer as Protester

Tibor Kalman

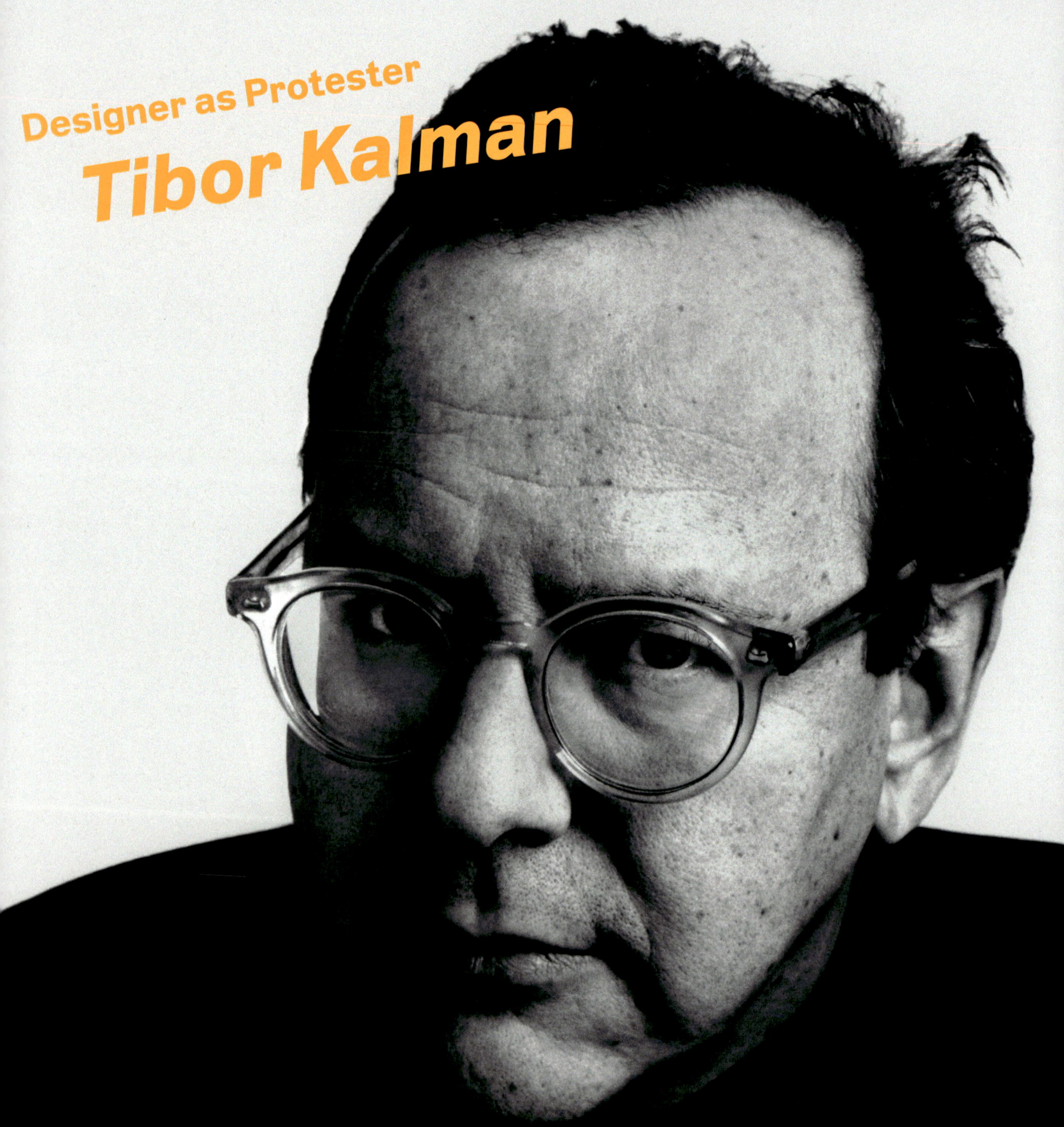

"If we approach clients with our own agenda, we may be able to make them better, or smarter, or more socially responsible."

—Tibor Kalman

Born in Budapest in 1949, Tibor Kalman immigrated with his family to the United States in 1957 after the failed Hungarian uprising against the Soviet Union. This early exposure to revolution, plus his childhood experiences as an outsider, laid the foundation for a life in graphic rebellion.

Kalman's own independent forays into advocacy began in 1968 when, as a student at New York University, he partook in the massive demonstrations against the Vietnam War organized by Students for a Democratic Society (SDS). He covered the protests for the group's newspaper and witnessed firsthand the NYPD's billy club attacks against students at Columbia University. Kalman followed his radical instincts to Cuba in 1970, working in solidarity with farmers to challenge the U.S. government's embargo.

After a brief stint organizing factory workers while living in a New Jersey commune, Kalman made it back to New York City. In 1971, he stumbled into a job as a display designer for a small bookstore that would one day grow into the corporate giant Barnes & Noble. With no training in graphic design, Kalman made it up as he went.

This unskilled start in the field was a start nonetheless. In 1979, Kalman formed M&Co, a design agency that ultimately catered to clients ranging from the Limited clothing retailer to the band the Talking Heads. With this commercial success came an acute awareness of how design propped up business, and Kalman began using his position to argue for social responsibility. For instance, at a 1989 AIGA conference, he presented "Dangerous Ideas," one of the first industry-wide calls to action to challenge design professionals to investigate their role in environmental and economic crises.

As the editor-in-chief of *Colors: A Magazine About the Rest of the World*, Kalman forged a unique opportunity to take what he'd learned in corporate design and wield it for more than commercial gain; in short, to weaponize the language of consumerism against the monoculture that it spawned. With striking often controversial images, pithy and provocative copywriting, and cutting-edge infographics, each issue of *Colors* educated its sophisticated readership on a single topic, such as war, immigration, art, protest, and happiness. Ironically, its anticommercial stance and lavish art direction were funded by the Italian clothing company Benetton, which had already sparked debate with its own advertising campaigns.

Embracing global diversity, *Colors* was published in seven languages, with Italian, Chinese, French, Korean, Spanish, or Portuguese translations mirroring the original English text across the gutter. Examples of this typographic strategy appear on the cover of the race issue (see page 211) and inside the AIDS issue (page 212). On the covers on pages 210–11, Kalman and his design team use the same typeface, Franklin Gothic Extra Condensed—a standby American headliner since the early 1900s—but apply it differently on every issue, from all caps on an irregular baseline ("AIDS"), to overlapping lowercase ("race"), to sentence style capitalization wrapped around an oil-soaked bird for the Evolution issue.

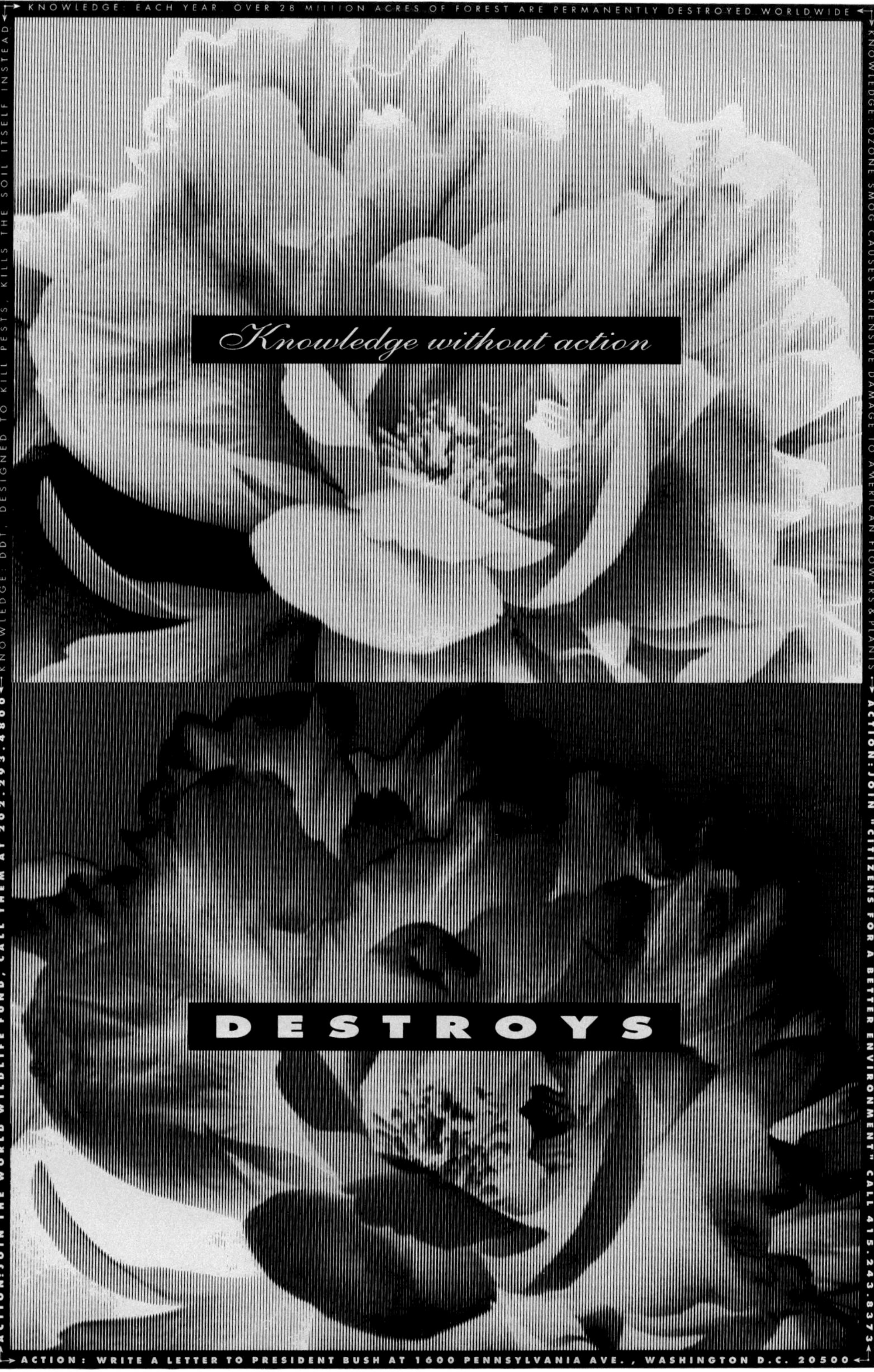
KNOWLEDGE: EACH YEAR, OVER 28 MILLION ACRES OF FOREST ARE PERMANENTLY DESTROYED WORLDWIDE
KNOWLEDGE: OZONE SMOG CAUSES EXTENSIVE DAMAGE TO AMERICAN FLOWERS & PLANTS
KNOWLEDGE: DDT, DESIGNED TO KILL PESTS, KILLS THE SOIL ITSELF INSTEAD
Knowledge without action
DESTROYS
ACTION: JOIN "CITIZENS FOR A BETTER ENVIRONMENT" CALL 415.243.8373
ACTION: JOIN THE WORLD WILDLIFE FUND, CALL THEM AT 202.293.4800
ACTION: WRITE A LETTER TO PRESIDENT BUSH AT 1600 PENNSYLVANIA AVE., WASHINGTON D.C. 20500

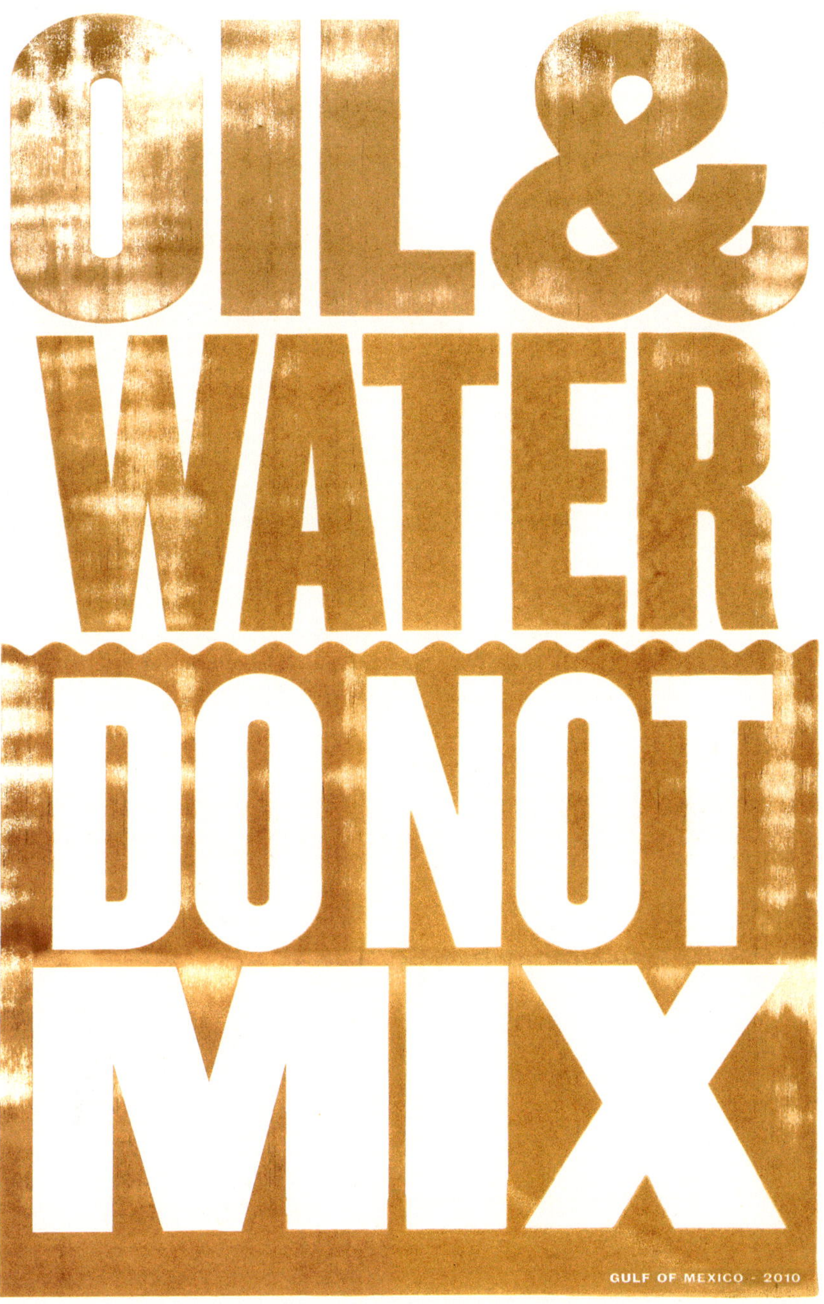

Jennifer Morla, *Knowledge without Action Destroys*, 1991, offset, 36 × 24 inches (91.5 × 61 cm), San Francisco. This poster urges citizens to write to George H. W. Bush's White House about environmental legislation, the administration's alignment with chemical industries, and the loosening of EPA guidelines.

Anthony Burrill for Happiness Brussels, *Oil & Water*, 2010, screen print with oil-soaked sand, 30 × 20 inches (76 × 51 cm), New Orleans. Featuring an emphatic environmental warning in all-caps Champion Gothic, Burrill's poster was made with oil from the 2010 Deepwater Horizon oil spill off the Gulf of Mexico.

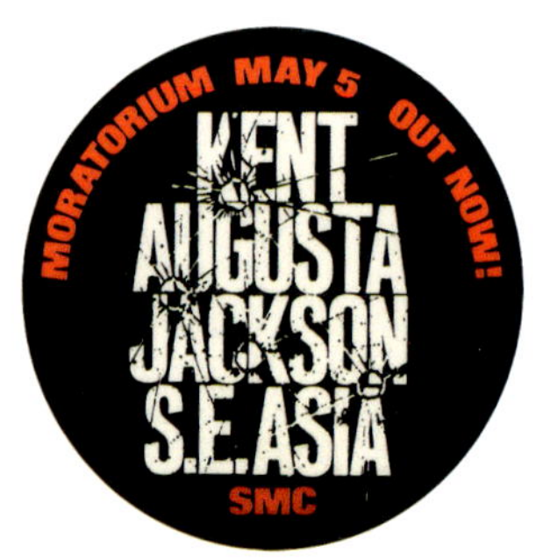
MORATORIUM MAY 5 OUT NOW!
KENT
AUGUSTA
JACKSON
S.E.ASIA
SMC

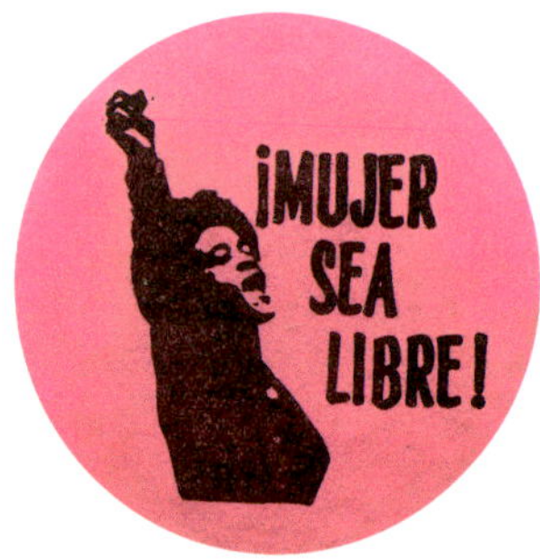
¡MUJER
SEA
LIBRE!

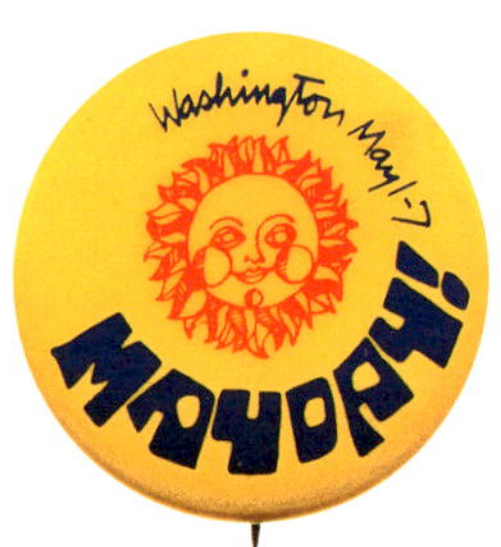
Washington May 1-7
MAYDAY!

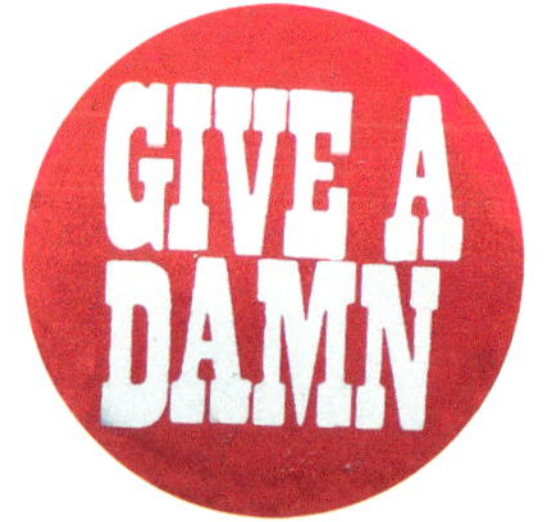
GIVE A
DAMN

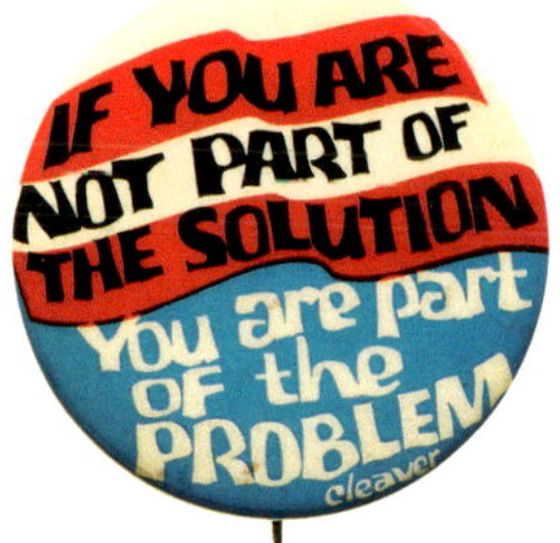
IF YOU ARE
NOT PART OF
THE SOLUTION
You are part
of the
PROBLEM
cleaver

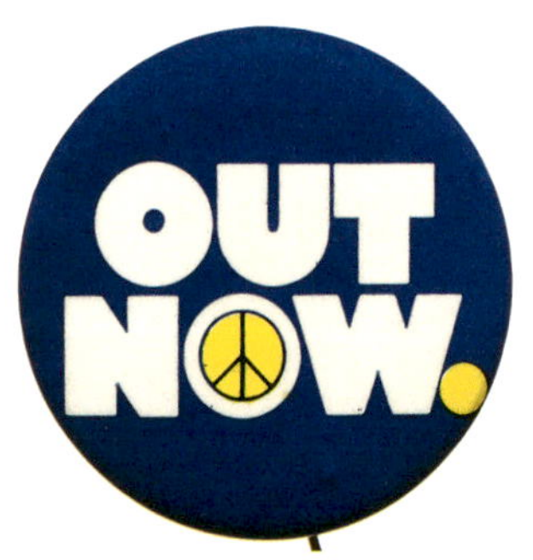
OUT
NOW.

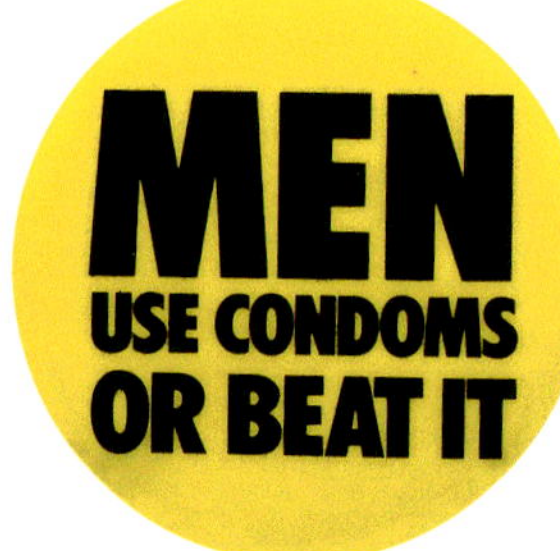
MEN
USE CONDOMS
OR BEAT IT

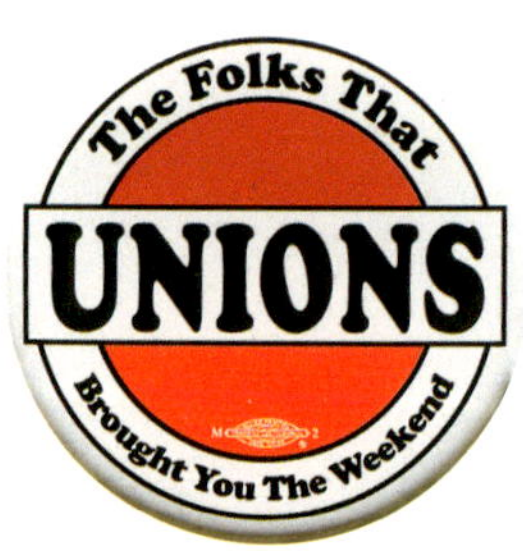
The Folks That
UNIONS
Brought You The Weekend

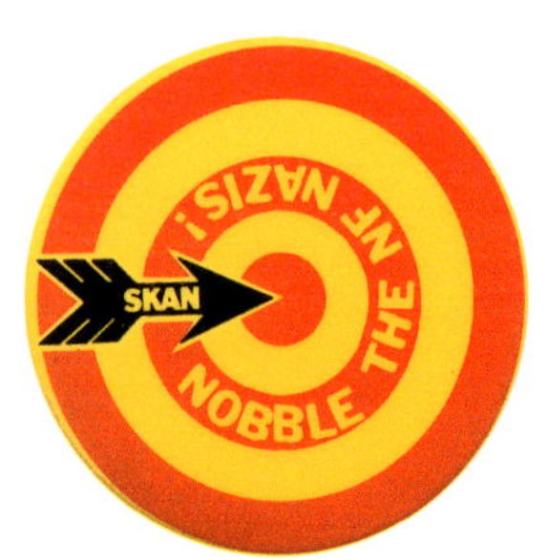
SKAN
NOBBLE THE
NF NAZIS!

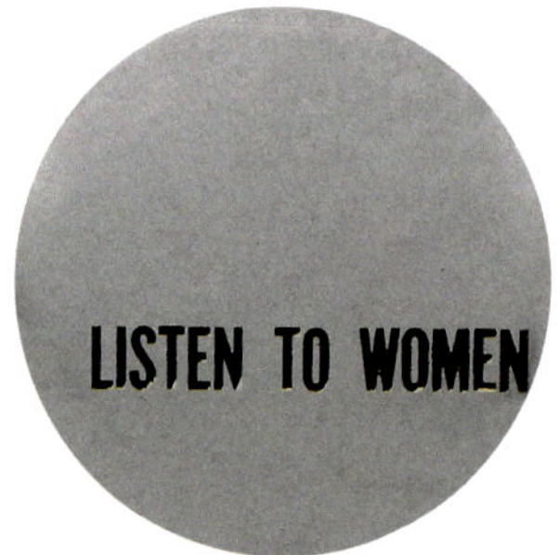
LISTEN TO WOMEN

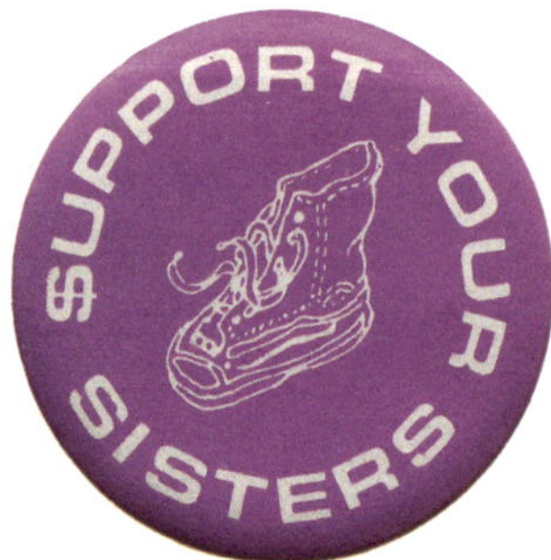
SUPPORT YOUR
SISTERS

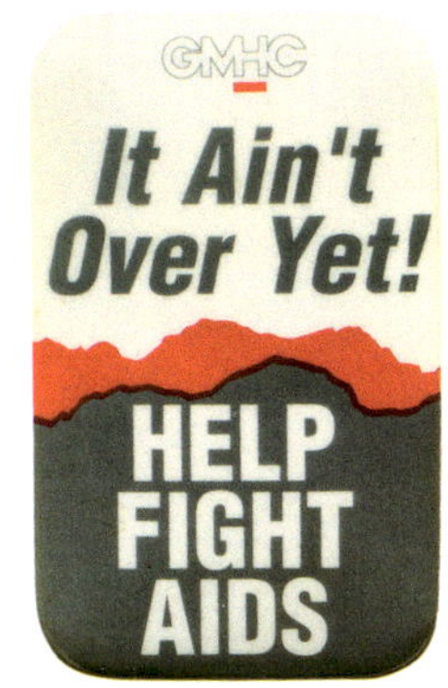

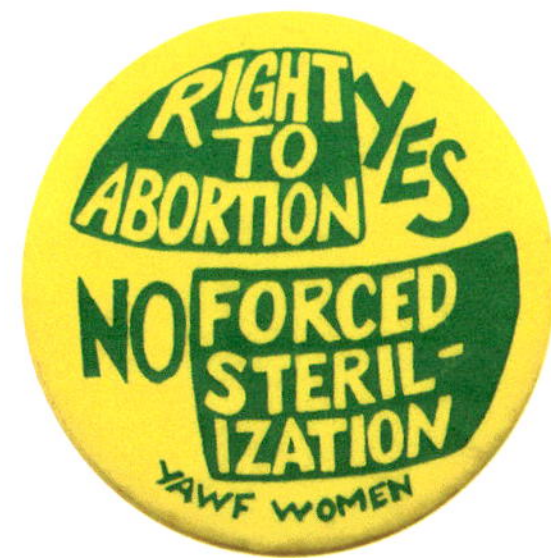

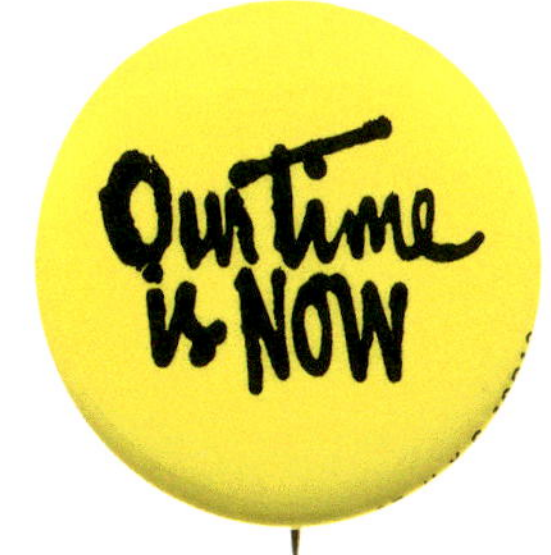

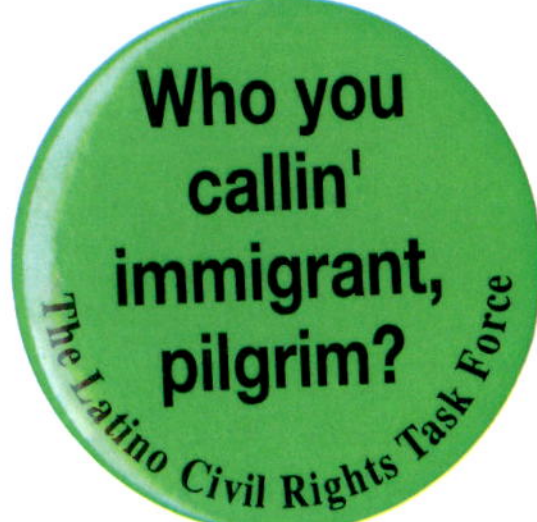

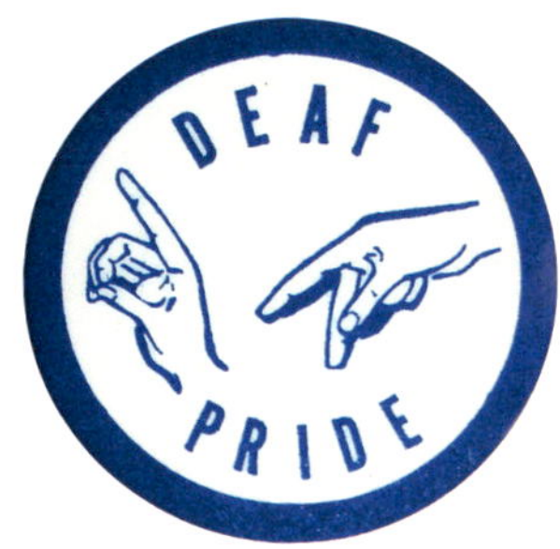

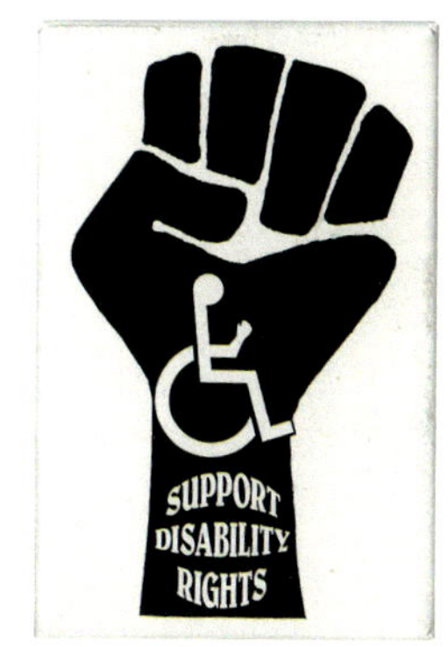

Since 1896, when New Jersey inventor Benjamin S. Whitehead patented a badge with a metal pin on its back, the political button as we know it has been used to proclaim just about everything. Its lineage, however, extends back one hundred years earlier, when British ceramicist Josiah Wedgwood produced a medallion depicting an enslaved Black man and labeled "Am I not a man and a brother?" for abolitionists to wear when campaigning for the antislavery cause.

Today, pins serve as conversation starters for a host of issues, thanks in part to cheap, readily available tabletop button-makers. Their limited size and traditionally circular shape make ideal conditions for freshly commissioned lettering, which can work around original artwork, as seen here in *Mayday*, or dynamically fill the frame, as in *Right to Abortion*. Visual shorthand helps, too: *Our Time Is Now* grabs attention for its anti-Vietnam message by playing on the lettering of the popular *Apocalypse Now* movie poster, while *Out Now* relies on the geometry of the typeface Gill Kayo to unite the circle of the button with that of the peace sign and an emphatic period. Simplicity also reigns with the generous field of *Listen to Women*, which seems ready to hold space for whatever exchange might ensue, should its message be heeded.

With hands making the American Sign Language gestures for *D* and *P*, *Deaf Pride* can be read not only as a signal of advocacy but also as a notice that the wearer might be hard of hearing. The *Support Disability Rights* button fuses the fist—a perennial emblem of power—with the universal symbol for disability: a wheelchair in profile, first designed in 1968 and later modified to include a simplified icon for a human head. Here, an arm has been added as well, tellingly raising a fist.

See page 277 for caption information.

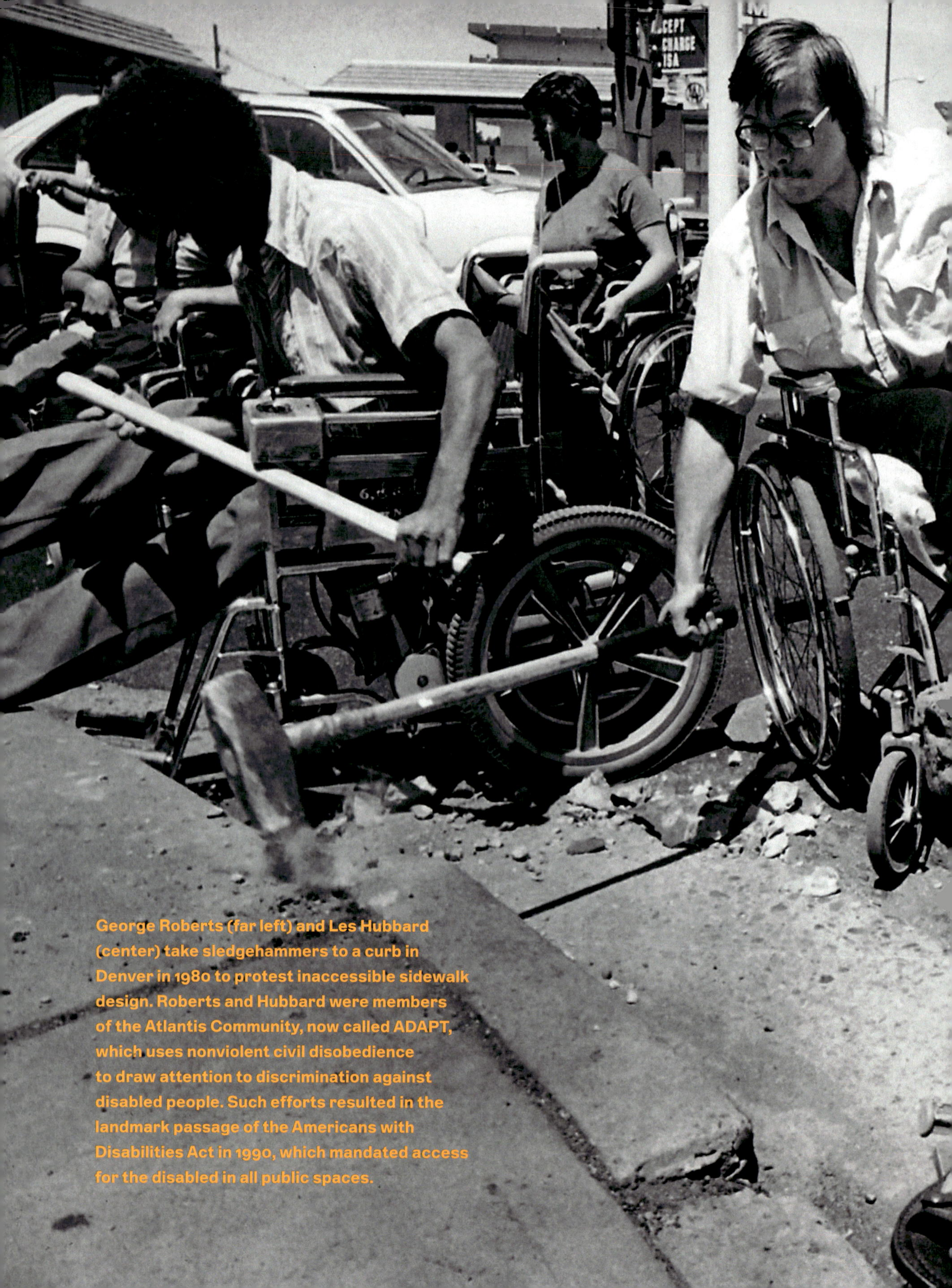

George Roberts (far left) and Les Hubbard (center) take sledgehammers to a curb in Denver in 1980 to protest inaccessible sidewalk design. Roberts and Hubbard were members of the Atlantis Community, now called ADAPT, which uses nonviolent civil disobedience to draw attention to discrimination against disabled people. Such efforts resulted in the landmark passage of the Americans with Disabilities Act in 1990, which mandated access for the disabled in all public spaces.

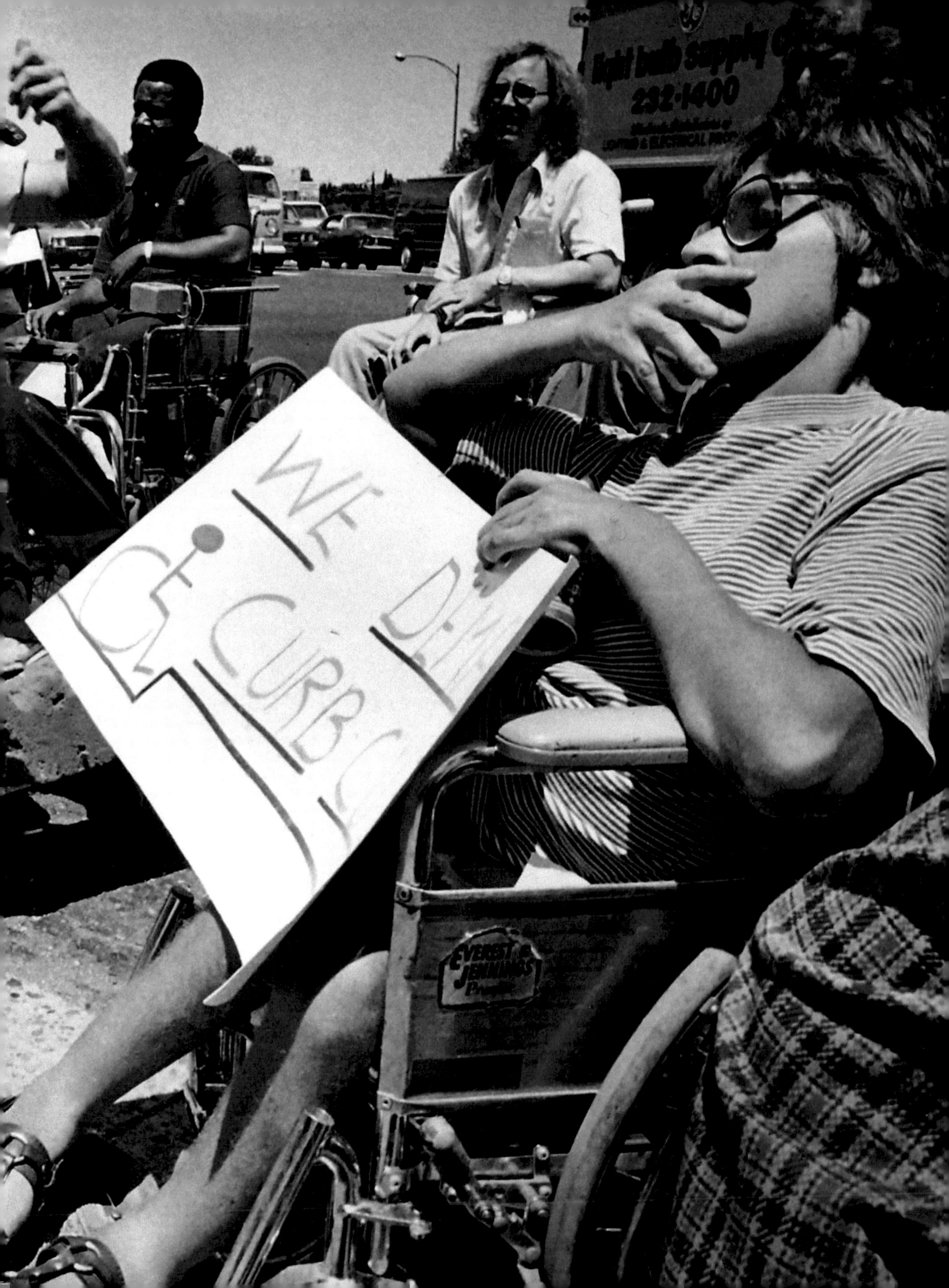
light bulb supply
232-1400
WE
JENNINGS

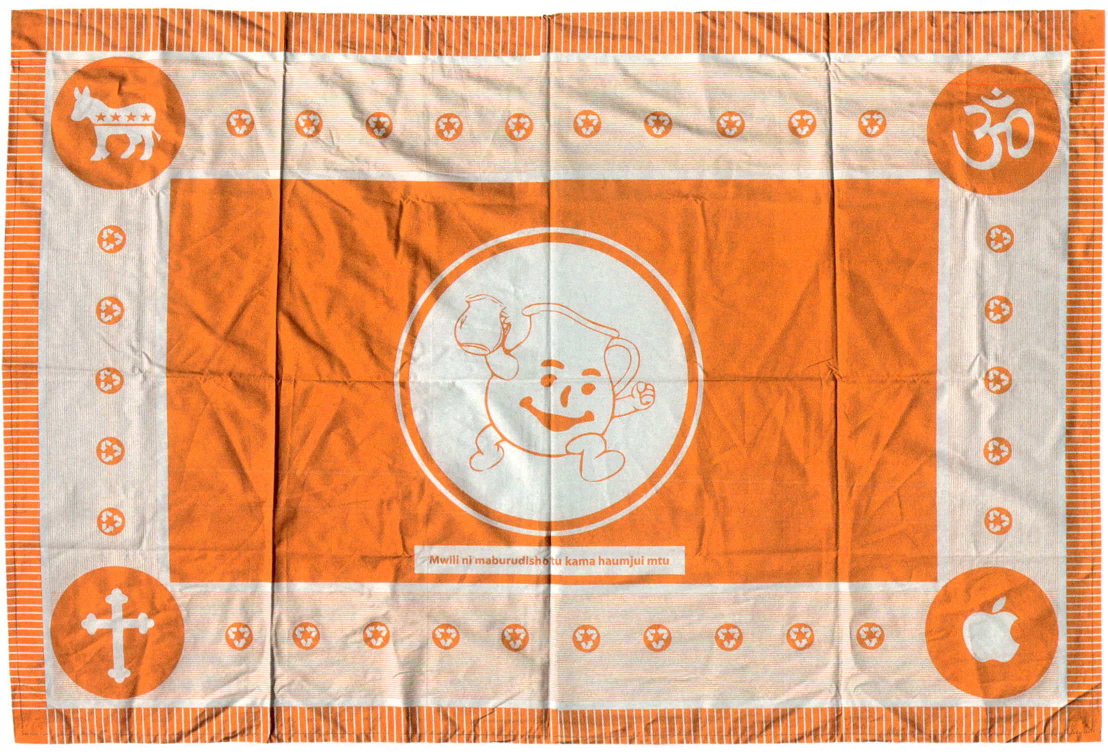

This cloth by Tanzanian-born designer Ziddi Msangi offers a contemporary take on *kanga*, a one-hundred-year-old textile tradition that plays a role in visual communication in East Africa. Originally worn in Tanzania, Uganda, and Kenya, kanga are a true product of their geopolitics, which were shaped by trade connecting East Africa to the rest of the world. Historically, different cloths were used to make the multipurpose garment. A cheap cotton option, *merkani*, was first imported from the United States to the island of Zanzibar (now part of Tanzania) in the 1800s; it was worn by enslaved peoples in both America and East Africa.

At the end of the nineteenth century, when slavery was abolished in East Africa, newly liberated people began decorating their kanga with symbols and borders. They also began adding a proverb in Swahili to the cloth's center. Over time, the patterns came to correspond to the text, so even when the proverb was not visible, viewers would still get the message. Women especially found them a powerful way to share their values as part of daily life. And, for a country speaking back to colonial British rule at midcentury, the garments allowed Tanzanians to signal their support of independence. When it was achieved in 1963, kanga evolved from a symbol of enslavement to one of liberation.

Today, kanga are seen from Japan to Dubai. Msangi's own designs explore his personal narrative using the East African idiom. In *The Body Is Just a Distraction If One Doesn't Know the Person*, shown here, he creates a pattern out of cultural icons—the Apple logo, a cross, the U.S. Democratic Party's mule, the *om* symbol, the recycle symbol, and the Kool-Aid Man—to critique his own ideological makeup.

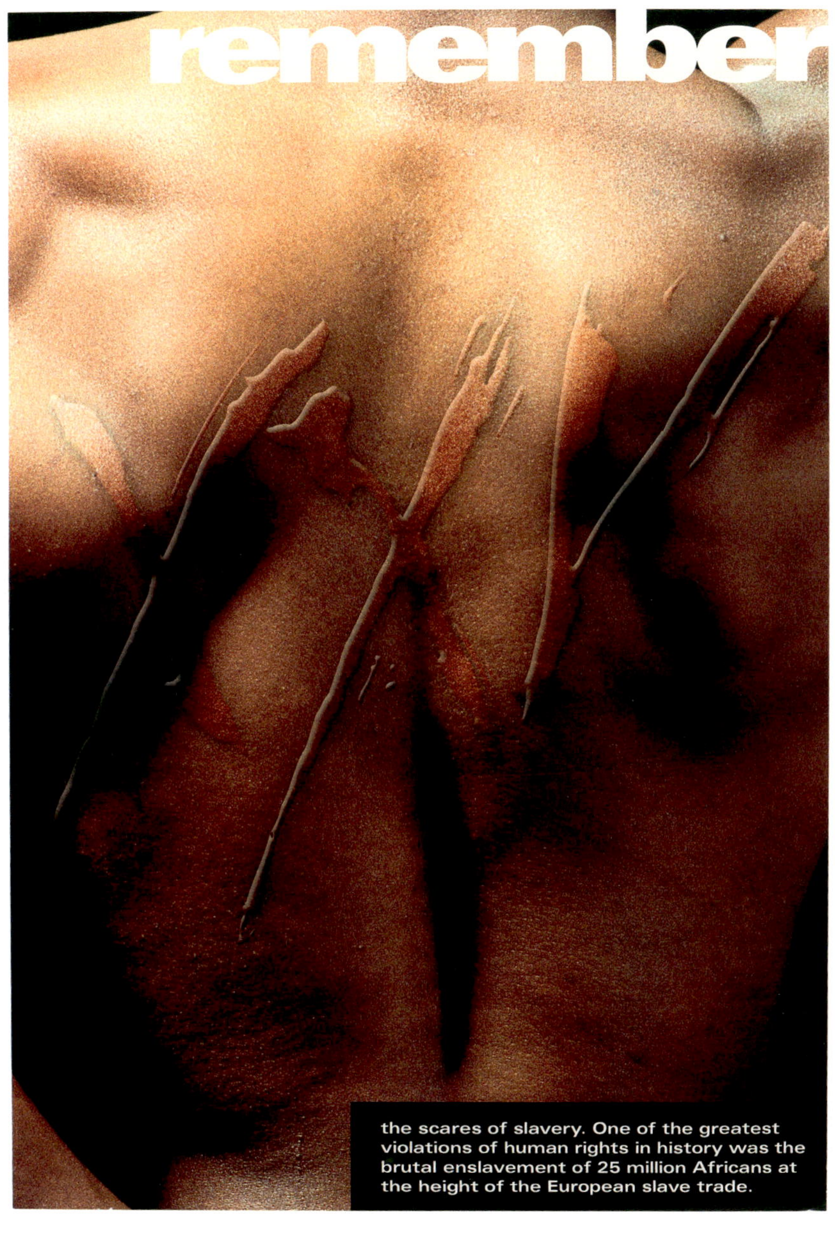

Ziddi Msangi, *The Body Is Just a Distraction If One Doesn't Know the Person* (*Mwili ni maburudisho tu kama mtu hajui mtu*), 2011, digital printing on fabric, 38⅝ × 58 inches (98 × 148 cm), Seekonk, Massachusetts.

Chaz Maviyane-Davies, *Remember XXV*, 2011, offset, 23⅜ × 16⅜ inches (59.5 × 41.5 cm), Harare, Zimbabwe. In his poster series, Zimbabwe-born designer Maviyane-Davies uses "remember" to set up his description of a human rights violation. Here, he digitally cast the roman numeral 25 as a scar to signify the 25 million people enslaved at the worst point of the slave trade.

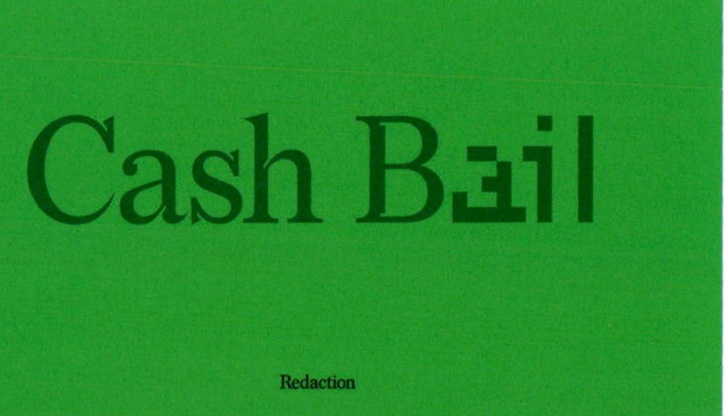

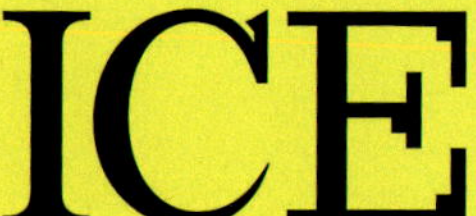

Redaction

re —
dac a multiplicity of
ti typographic,
on legal, and human
histories

Forest Young and Jeremy Mickel, samples of the typeface Redaction, 2019, digital font, Los Angeles. Mickel and Young created this typeface in critique of cash bail and court fees, which disproportionately result in longer prison sentences for people of color. Its compromised, eroded letterforms mimic those seen on repeatedly photocopied court documents, effectively linking the endless bureaucracy of the U.S. criminal justice system to the erasure of the lives trapped within it.

Heather Snyder Quinn and Adam DelMarcelle (designers), Flor Salatino (developer), the augmented-reality mobile application Mariah, 2019–22.

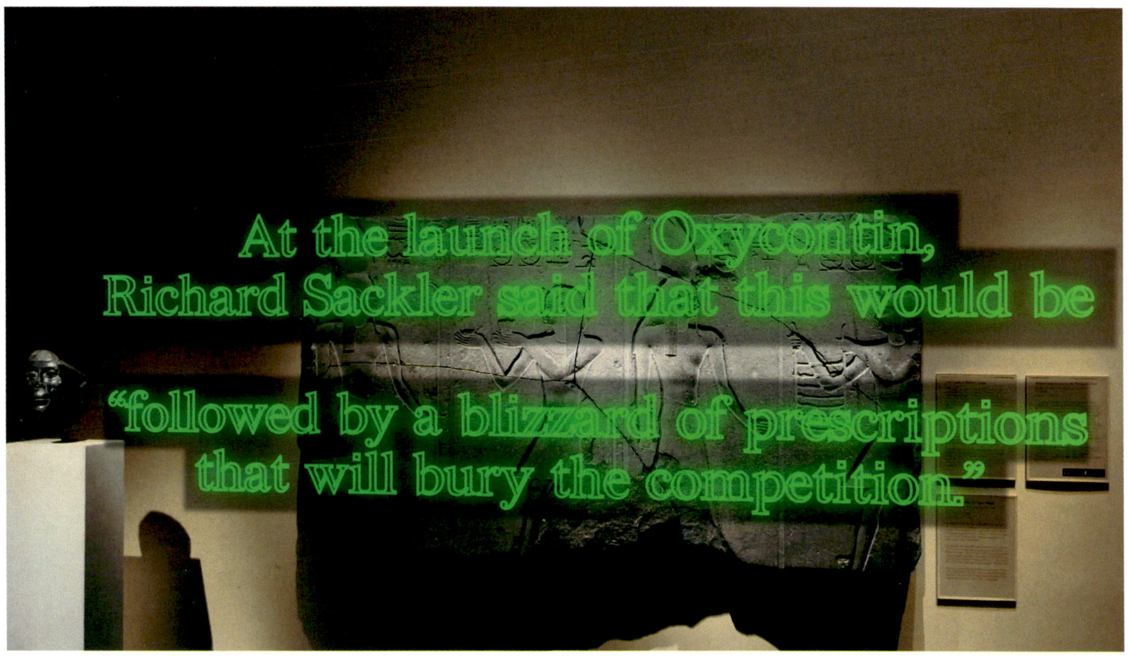

Developed by Heather Snyder Quinn, Adam DelMarcelle, and Flor Salatino in 2019, the mobile app Mariah uses augmented reality to call out the tainted financial support provided to cultural institutions by the Sackler family. Their company, Purdue Pharma, makes the painkiller OxyContin, a key contributor to the opioid epidemic that has claimed more than half a million lives in the United States. Named after Mariah Lotti, a Massachusetts teenager who died by overdose in 2011, the app allows users to point their phones at art and artifacts donated by the Sacklers and see superimposed data and information about the crisis. Set in Redaction (see left), the text details Purdue Pharma's predatory marketing efforts, with the type's digital bitmapping suggesting moral degradation. The app also launches audio and video of victims and their families, giving a face to the statistics.

Quinn, DelMarcelle, and Salatino first used the app to transform the Metropolitan Museum of Art's Sackler Wing, home to the popular Egyptian galleries and the Temple of Dendur, into a virtual memorial for Lotti and others who have lost their lives to opiate addiction, including DelMarcelle's brother, Joe, who died in 2014. In 2021, Mariah expanded to the Louvre, which is also Sackler-funded. App users there can interact with a virtual sculpture of a number that updates to represent overdose fatalities in real time.

While Mariah no doubt serves to raise awareness of the opioid epidemic, it also asks larger questions about the moral cover that philanthropy provides, probing who ultimately pays for such donations (in this case, the overdose victims and their loved ones). Mariah also presents a new form of protest, in which citizens digitally overtake a cultural space in order to reframe the narratives of its artifacts.

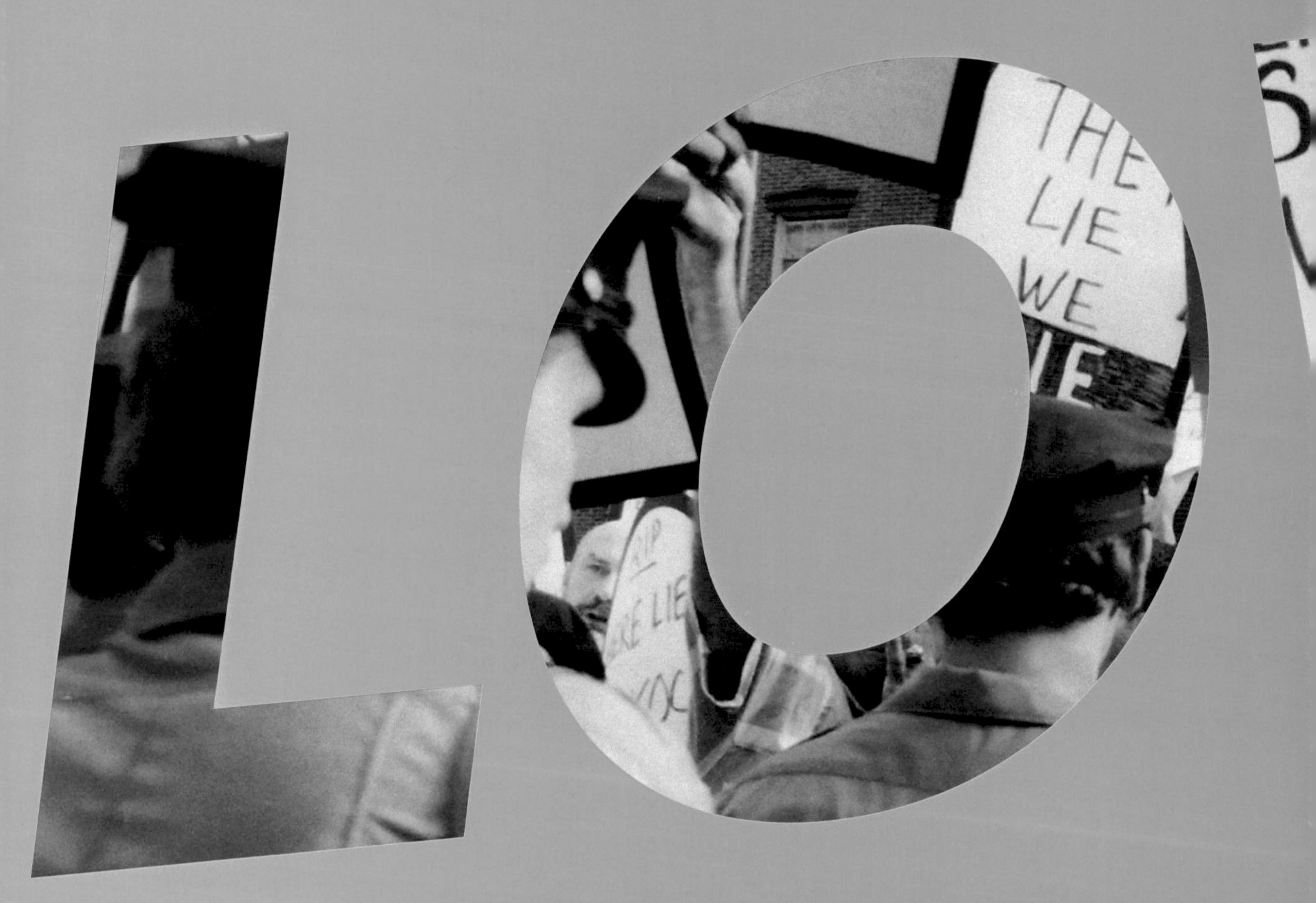
THE
LIE
WE

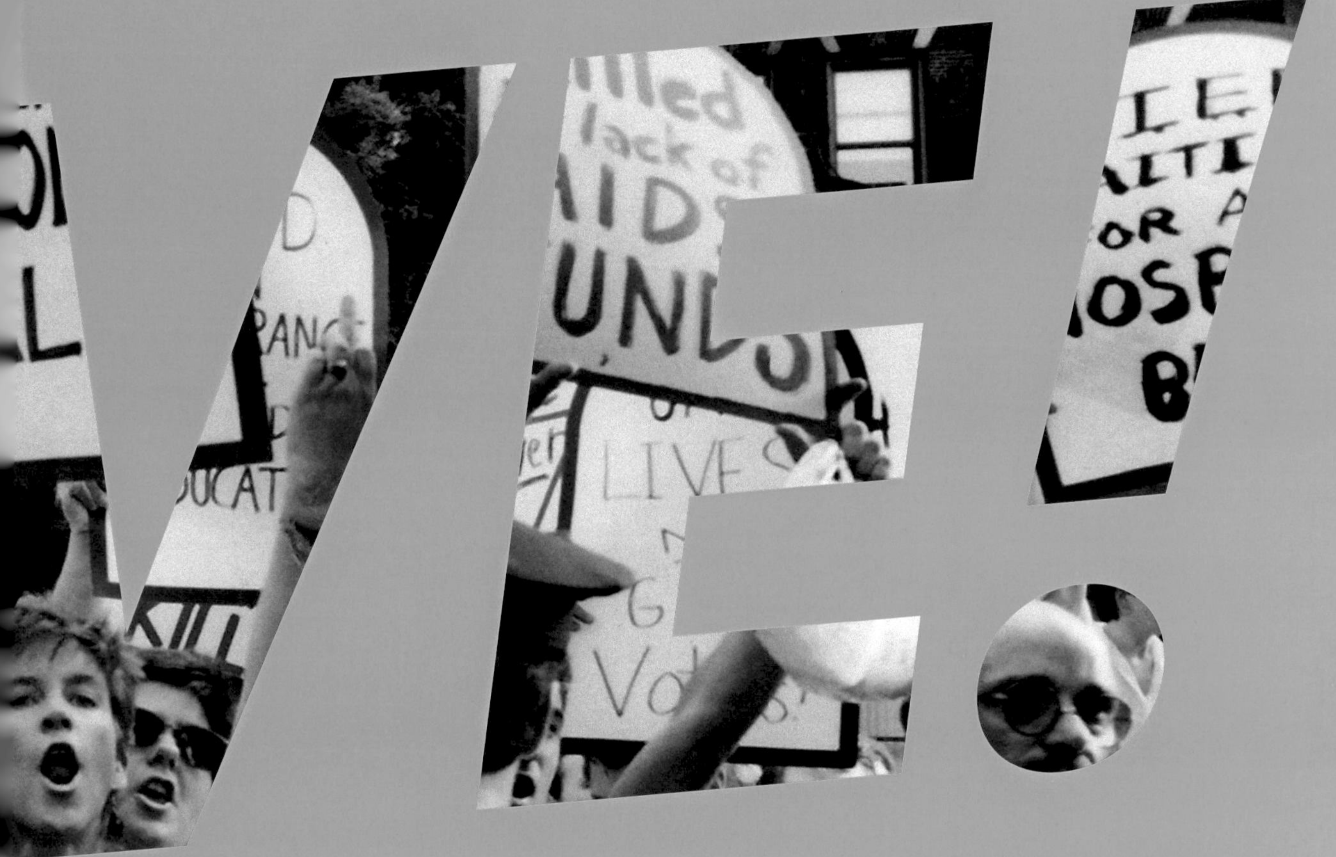
VE!
lack of
LIVES

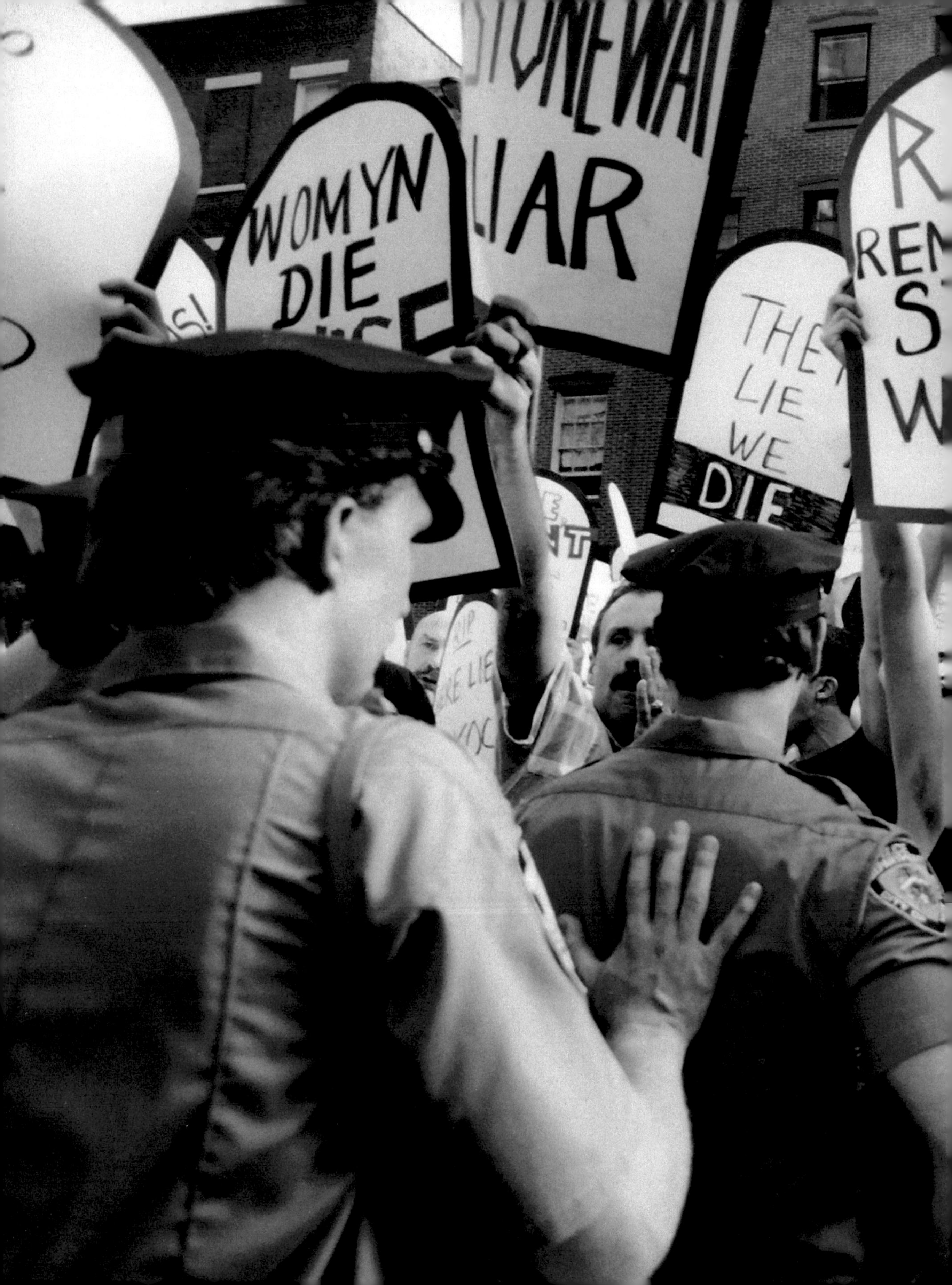
WOMYN
DIE
LIAR
LIE
WE
DIE

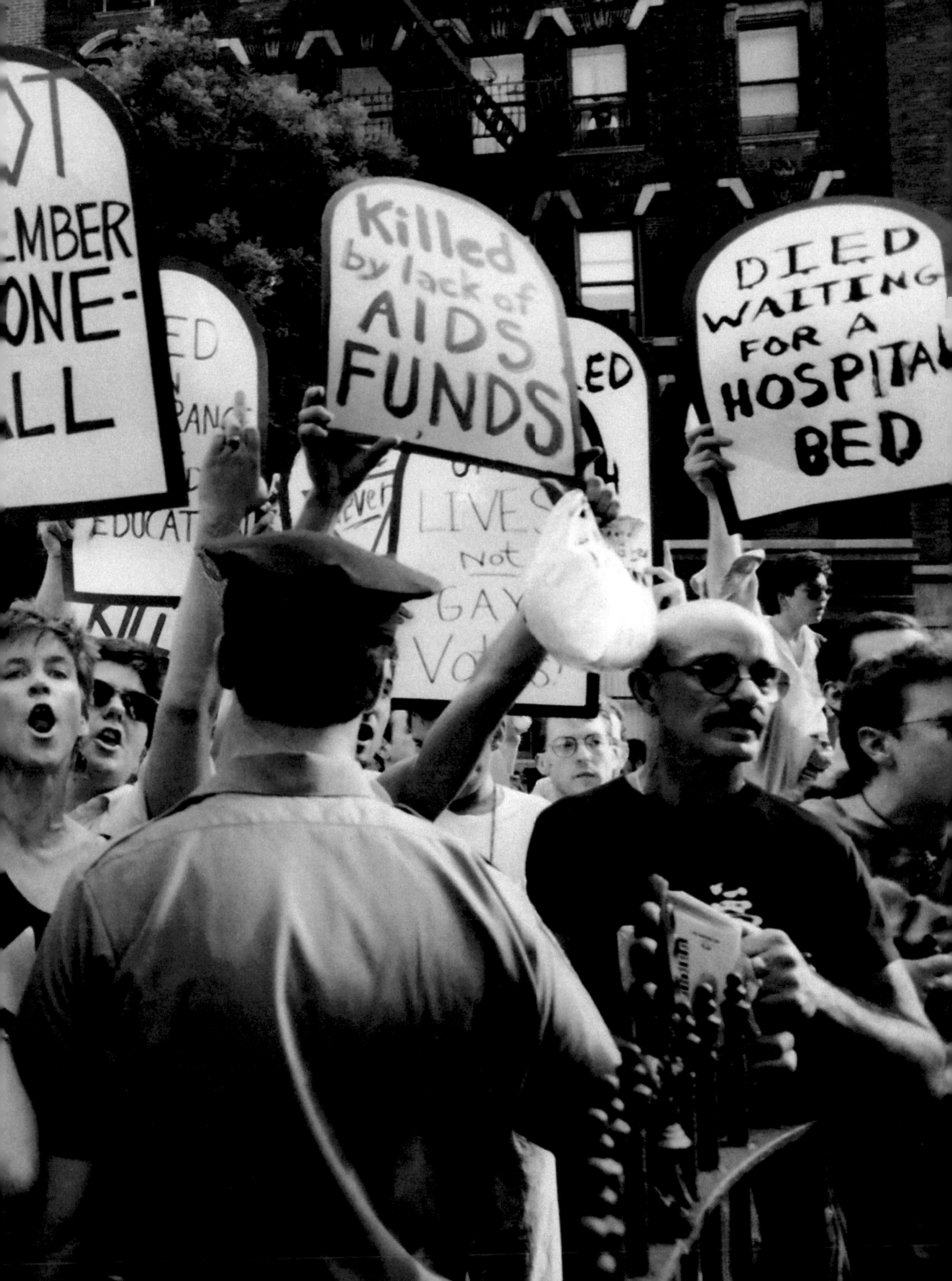

Killed by lack of AIDS FUNDS
DIED WAITING FOR A HOSPITAL BED
LIVES Not GAY Votes

"We're going to keep on struggling for brighter days. We're going to keep on struggling until we win your love."

—*The Black Panther*, vol. 7, no. 5, 1971

LOVE!

For an emotion said to be universal, love has never been static. And while erotic attraction in all gender configurations has been around since sex itself, the last one hundred years have seen a dramatic shift in how desire in its many expressions impacts identity. Along the way, visibility and acceptance for these notions of self, including lesbian, gay, bi, queer, trans, and more, have dramatically expanded, and today include identities that transcend the gender binary.

These identities, however, have also been silenced, forbidden, outlawed, or, as in the case of the gay men and trans folks who were abandoned by the U.S. government's neglect during the AIDS crisis, left for dead. This discrimination and abuse has taken many forms, from the refusal to recognize marriages and civil unions between people of the same sex to open violence against queer people, fantastically viewed as a threat to heteronormative existence. In the midst of this oppression, a vibrant array of communities has arisen to create safe and playful spaces for the expression of love and the possibility of a thriving existence. This chapter presents a small sampling of the graphic output created by these communities.

A product of the 1920s Harlem Renaissance, *Fire!!* is the first known publication to present openly gay Black people through a mix of literature, visual art, and graphic design. Featuring a dozen Black contributors, many of them queer, its editorial approach is an early example of a principle of inclusion that we now call "For us, by us" or "Nothing about us without us." With this publication, the collective of self-described Niggerati, which included Wallace Thurman, Langston Hughes, Zora Neale Hurston, and Richard Bruce Nugent, sought to burn down old ideas that insisted Black people live by a particular moral code (heterosexual, with no interracial partnerships) in order to gain respect and, with it, freedom.

Almost fifty years later, on June 28, 1969, the push for equality that we now know as the gay liberation movement erupted into the streets of Manhattan when patrons of the Stonewall Inn, a gay bar in the West Village, rebelled against a raid conducted by the NYPD. Protests over the raid extended for days, with queer and trans patrons, including Marsha P. Johnson, rising up to defend their right to have a drink without being harassed or surveilled. A year later, the community held the first gay pride marches to commemorate their resilience. In this chapter, pieces like the 1971 poster *Gay Is Angry*, by Argentine immigrant designers Juan Carlos Vidal and Néstor Latrónico, communicate the ebullient rage of this era with colorful butterflies—a symbol of transformation—flittering about a typographic time bomb.

The late 1960s were a period in which many sought to claim their right to erotic expression, with sexual liberation reaching not just to members of the LGBTQIA+ movements but to cis women as well. Inclusions like Mari Tepper's psychedelic poster *Hallelujah the Pill!!* provide crucial context to the era of free love, in which love could not be free until women stopped paying the price with their futures.

In 1966, *Fact* magazine, published by Ralph Ginzburg and art-directed by Herb Lubalin, used a heart filled with a black-and-white gradient to illustrate an article on interracial marriage—a controversial topic at the time. Ginzburg and Lubalin formed this radical publication after the former served jail time for publishing *Eros*, their intellectual yet racy book-as-magazine.

By the end of the 1980s, HIV/AIDS brought the era of free love to an abrupt and tragic end. Art collectives General Idea, Gran Fury, and fierce pussy worked to call out the U.S. government's blatant disregard of the crisis, an attitude that largely stemmed from the fact that many of the first victims were queer people of color or intravenous drug users. fierce pussy's *For the Record* typographically details the incalculable human loss that has accumulated over the intervening half-century, in which more than 36 million people have died of the disease.

We close on Nat Pyper's twenty-first-century type design project, *A Queer Year of Love Letters*, a series of fonts that function as typable tributes to queer revolutionaries.

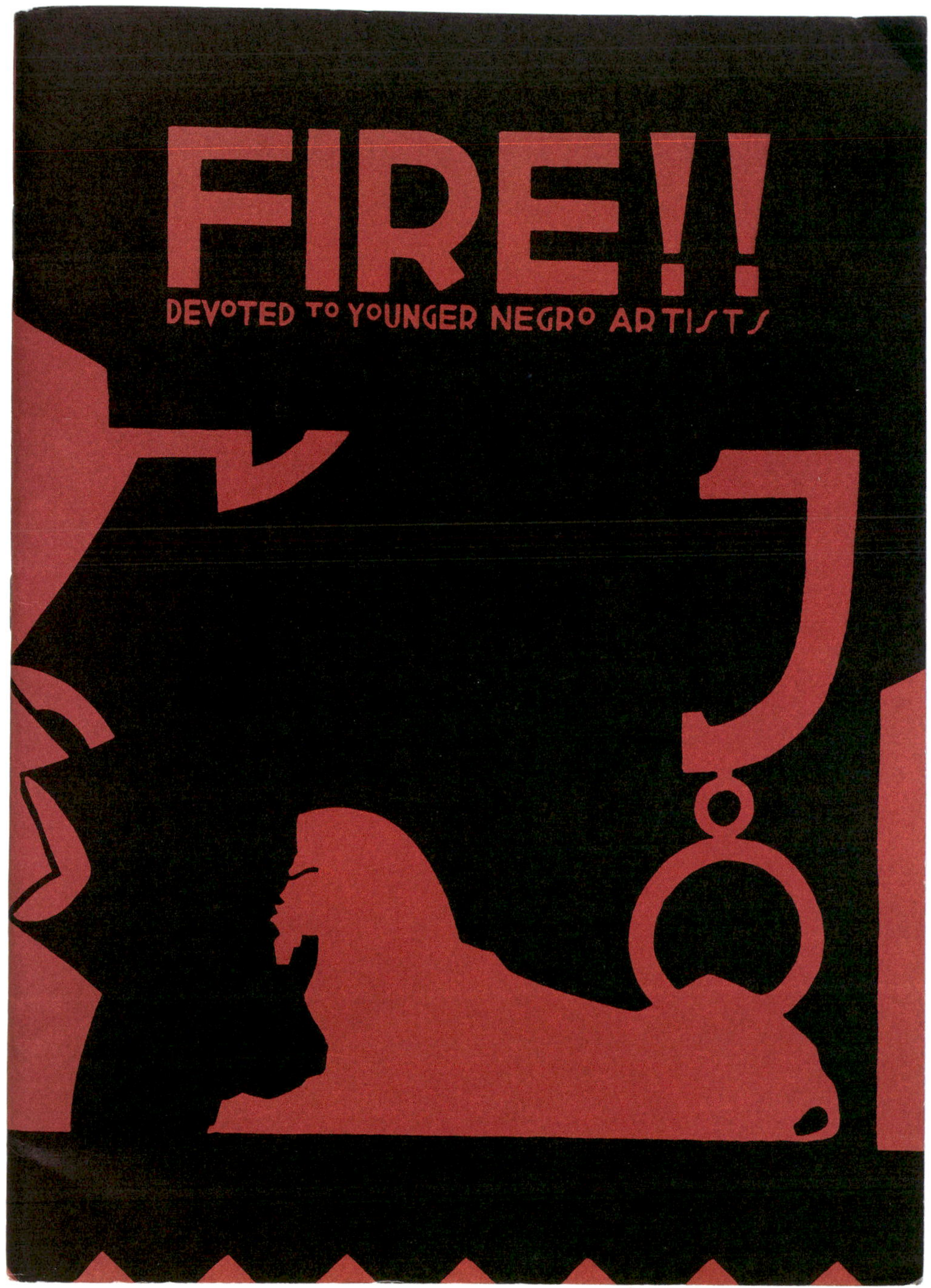

Aaron Douglas (cover designer), Wallace Thurman (editor), Richard Bruce Nugent (interior illustrator), facsimile reissue of the 1926 journal *Fire!!: Devoted to Younger Negro Artists*, issue 1, 1985, offset, 10⅞ × 8½ inches (27.5 × 21.5 cm), New York.

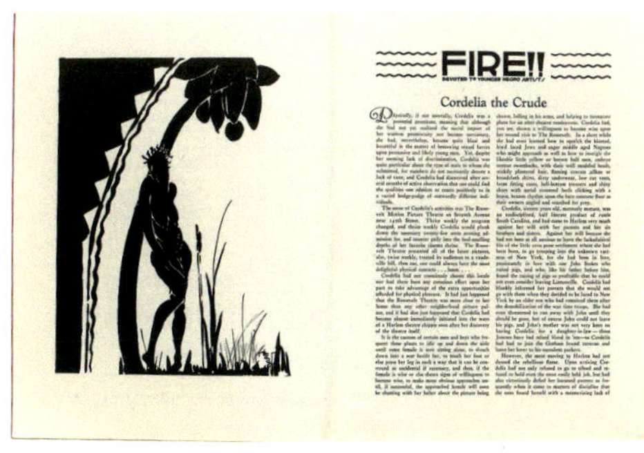
FIRE!!

Cordelia the Crude

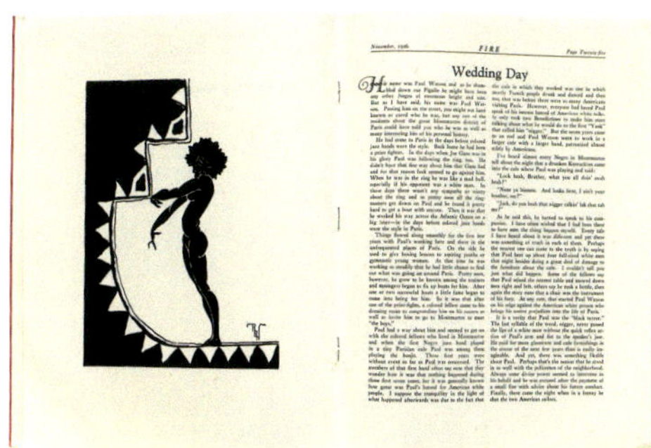
Wedding Day

Published in 1926, at the height of the Harlem Renaissance, *Fire!!* was one of the earliest magazines in the United States to explore Black queer life in print. Editor Wallace Thurman organized its pages, which included literary and artistic contributions from Langston Hughes, Zora Neale Hurston, Aaron Douglas, Richard Bruce Nugent, Gwendolyn Bennett, and others. Its text covered a host of taboo topics of the era, such as Bennett's story about interracial love, Nugent's on Black homosexual desire (accompanied by his own sapphic illustrations), Hurston's play about colorism, and Thurman's short story on teenage prostitution. *Fire!!* sought to make a bold statement against ideas espoused by figures such as W. E. B. Du Bois, who at the time viewed Black art as a vehicle for convincing the white middle class that Black people were their equals, with straight sexuality an apparent prerequisite. (Both Hughes and Nugent were queer; it is widely speculated that Thurman was, too.)

To forge a distinctly modern African American art, *Fire!!* cover artist Aaron Douglas blended formal aspects of the sculptures and masks of West Africa with the angular modernism of cubism. His cover illustration presents an abstract close-up of an androgynous Black profile, regally made up and wearing a bold earring. The flickering relationship between foreground and background, in which a sphinx (an Egyptian symbol of protection) is the first thing viewers see, presents a coded depiction of queer Blackness—if you don't know the signs, you might miss them. Douglas's lettering for the title also reflects the art deco style of the time: square caps, a big-bowled *R* with an angled leg, a leaning *S*, and raised and reduced *O*s.

Banned in Boston and decried in the conservative Black press, *Fire!!* is an example of the moral policing of queer creators of color. (This censure carries on today in the restrictive community guidelines of social media platforms, in which QTPOC artists are often warned or banned at a disproportionate rate.) While the magazine never saw a second issue due to debt and, ironically, a fire that destroyed its office and stock, it is today seen as a watershed moment in early Black and queer publishing.

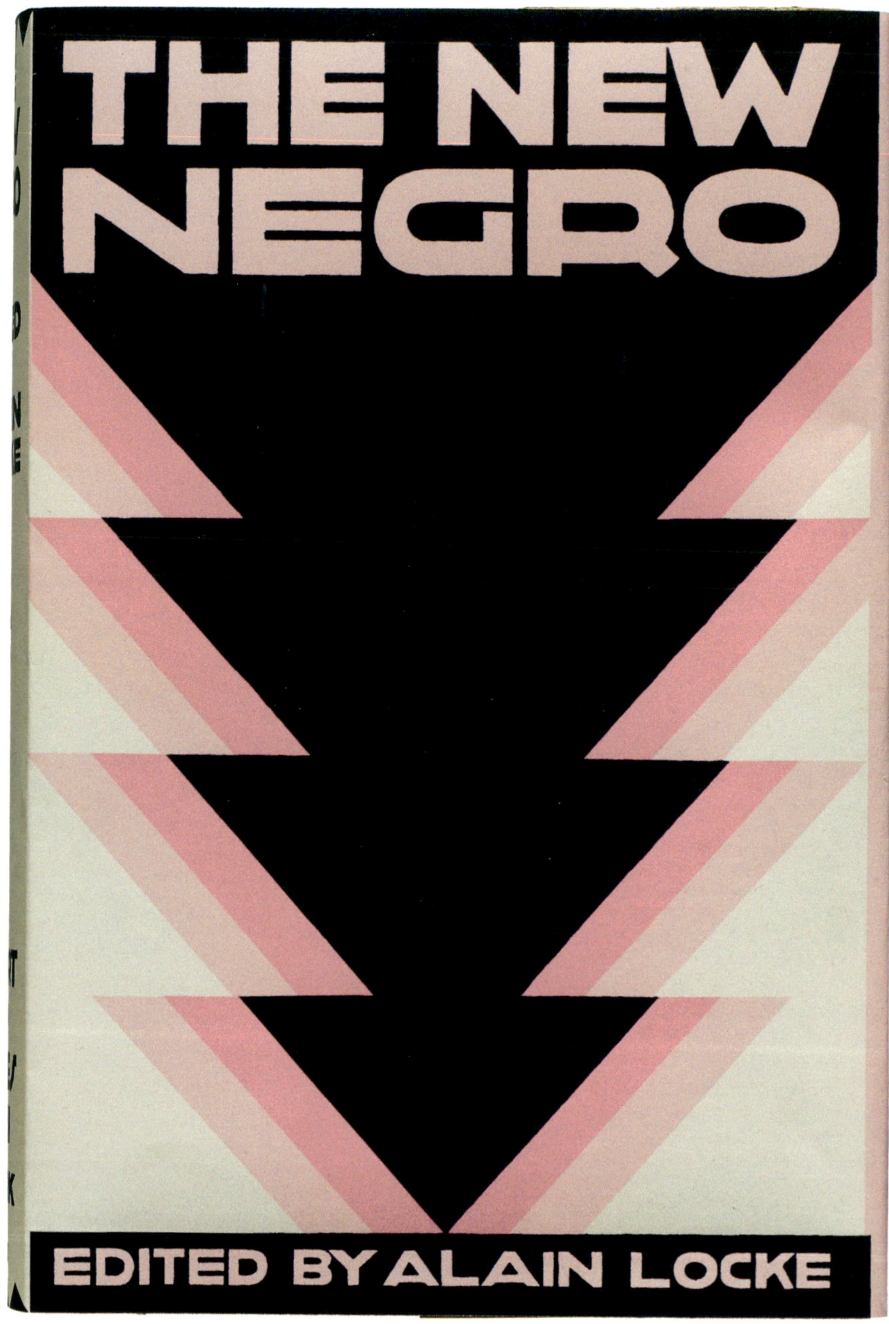

Winold Reiss (designer), Alain Locke (editor), Aaron Douglas and Michael Covarrubias (graphic apprentices), *The New Negro: An Interpretation*, with facsimile dust jacket, 1925, letterpress, 8⅞ × 6⅛ inches (22.5 × 15.5 cm), New York.

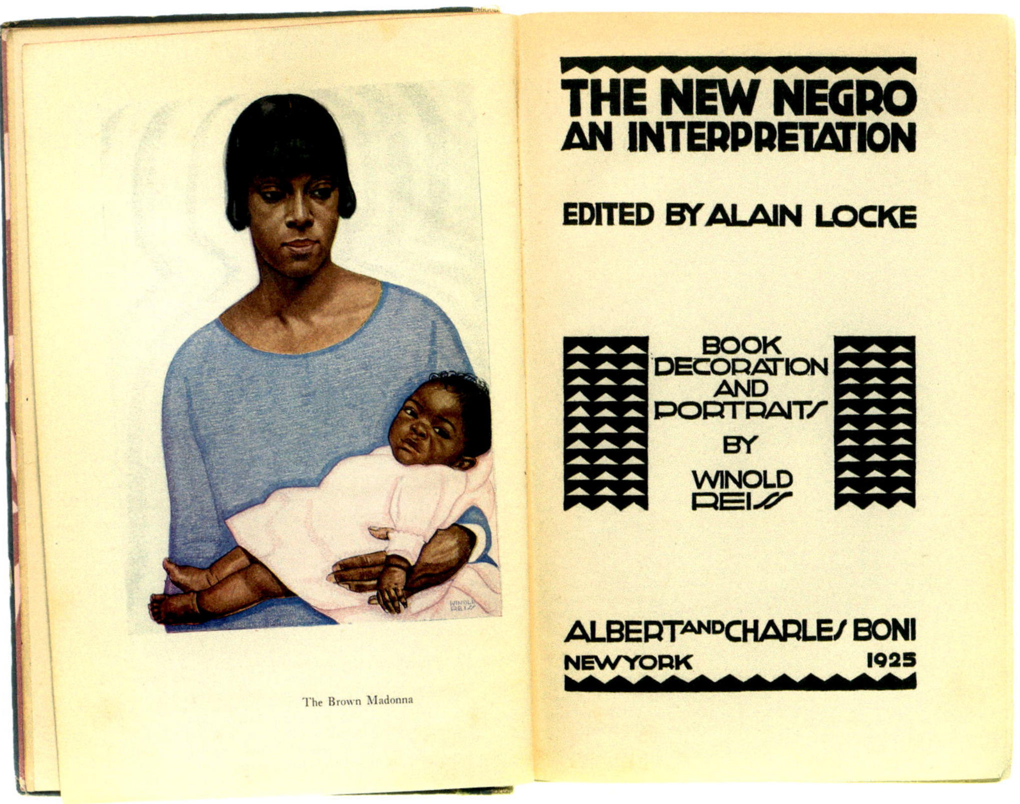

Edited by Black scholar Alain Locke, *The New Negro* collects the literary voices of the Harlem Renaissance, including writers Langston Hughes, Zora Neale Hurston, James Weldon Johnson, Jean Toomer, Countee Cullen, and Claude McKay. In its compilation, Locke sought to urge African Americans to demand their civil rights and overturn simplified stereotypes. Locke, a Black man who privately had gay relationships, came up with the name "New Negro" in Italy, shortly after Langston Hughes refused his romantic advances.

The lettering on the jacket and throughout is by Winold Reiss, a white German artist who lent his graphic style to early-twentieth-century publications, including the sociopolitical journal *Survey Graphic*. (Locke's main essay in *The New Negro* first appeared as a cover feature in *Survey Graphic*'s "Harlem: Mecca of the New Negro" issue.) Reiss also created the portraits that appear in the first edition, including *The Brown Madonna*, a modern depiction of a Black mother and child, opposite the book's title page. Both the jacket and interior lettering are in his signature art deco style, with bold, blocky capital letters and geometric ornaments used to fill gaps and frame headlines. These graphic shapes echo in the small artworks provided by Aaron Douglas and Miguel Covarrubias, Reiss's students and apprentices on the project.

The endpapers (see pages 236–37) feature two androgynous figures reclining in a stylized jungle. While this illustration only subtly nods to Black queerness, it is telling that Locke chooses to both begin and conclude his book with it.

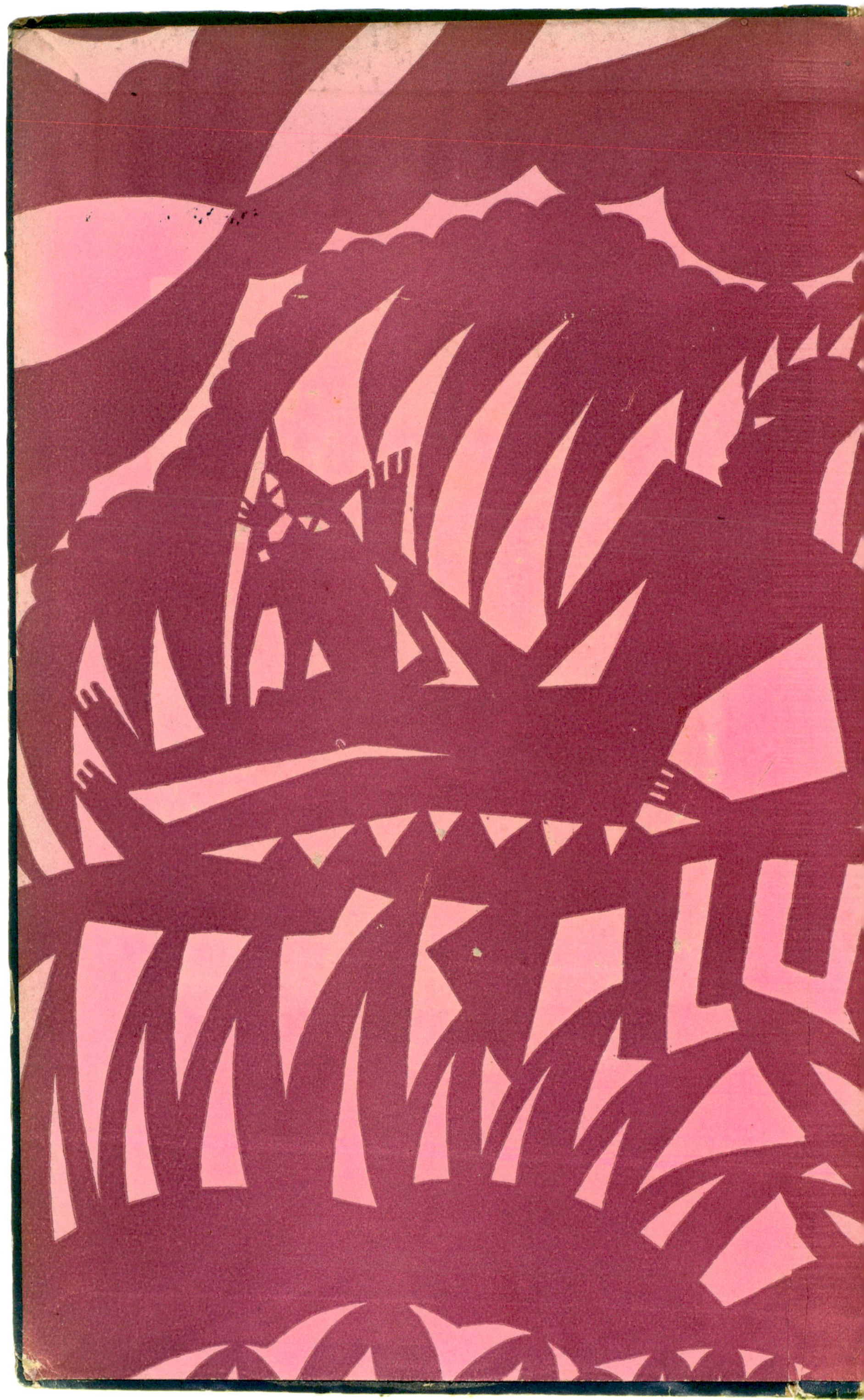

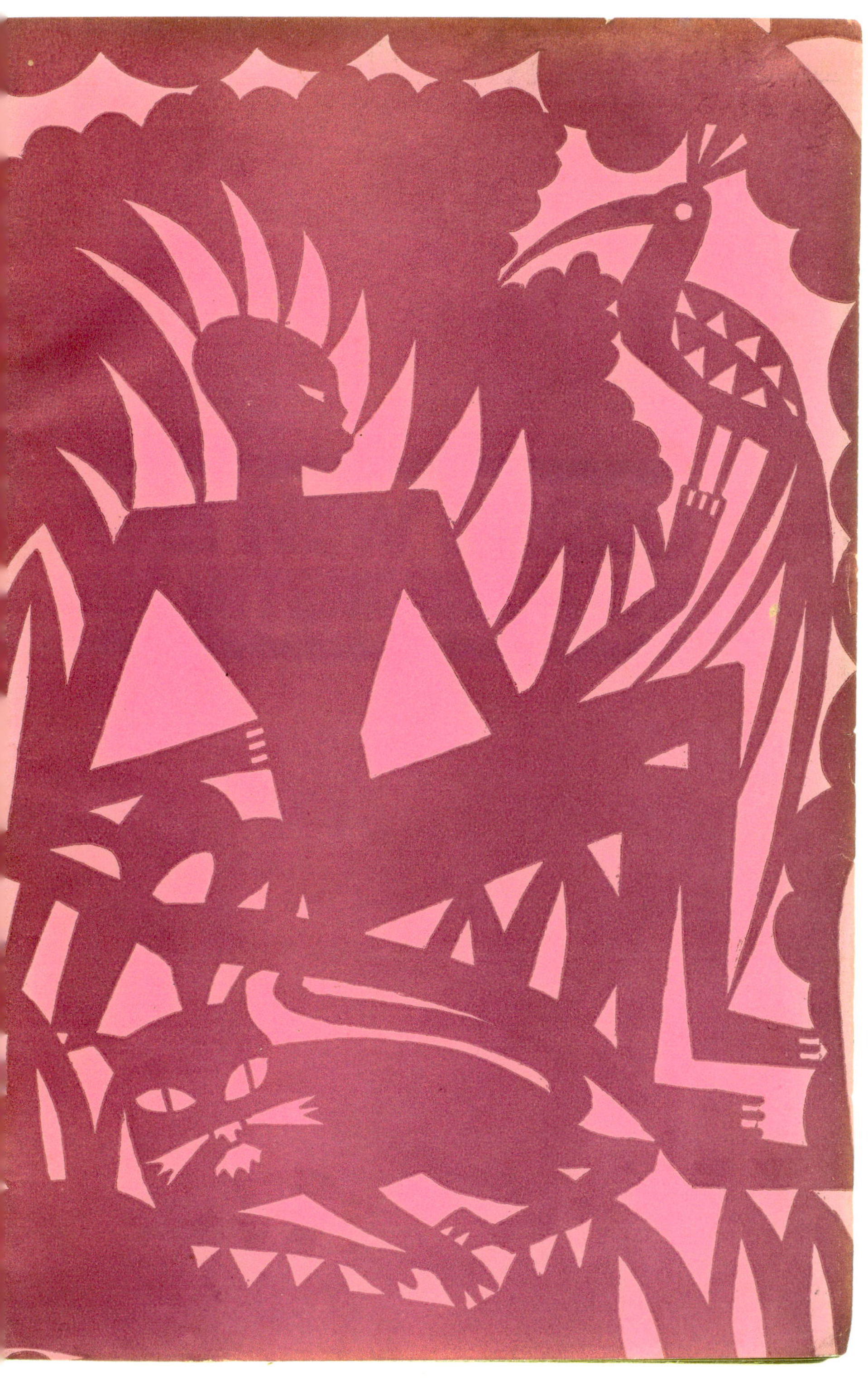

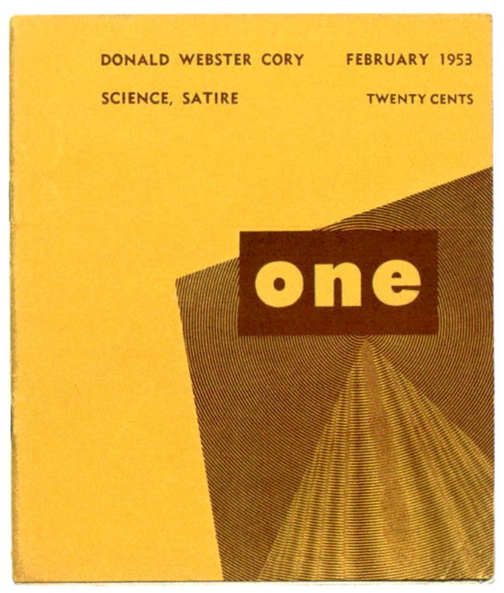
DONALD WEBSTER CORY
FEBRUARY 1953
SCIENCE, SATIRE
TWENTY CENTS
one

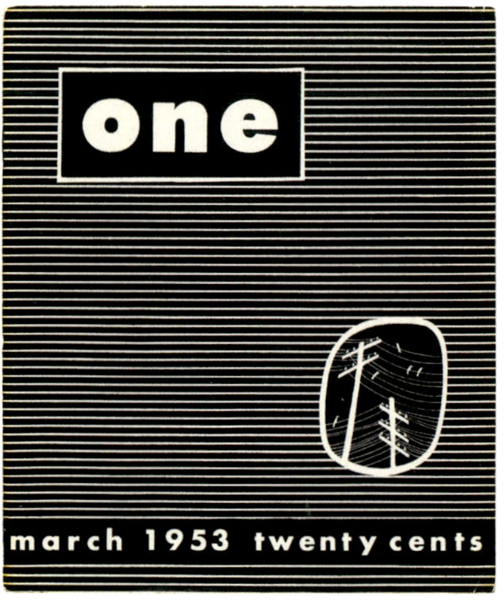
one
march 1953 twenty cents

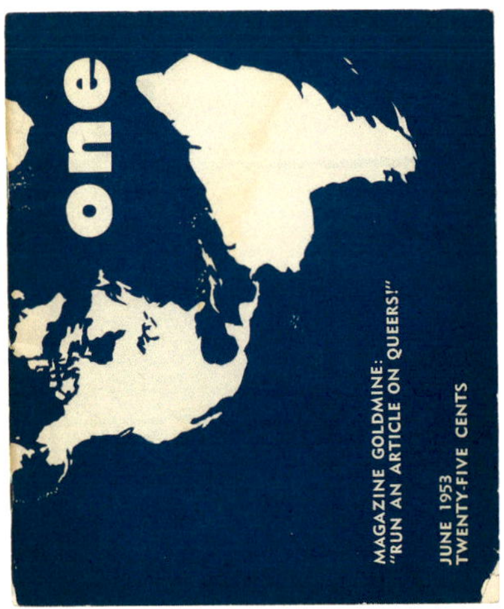
one
MAGAZINE GOLDMINE:
"RUN AN ARTICLE ON QUEERS!"
JUNE 1953
TWENTY-FIVE CENTS

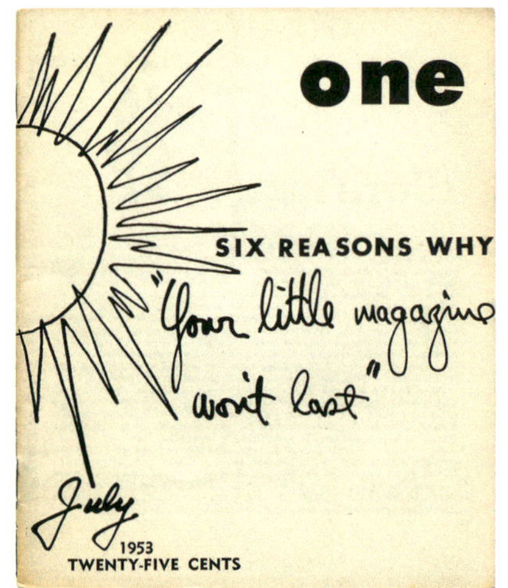
one
SIX REASONS WHY
"Your little magazine
won't last"
July
1953
TWENTY-FIVE CENTS

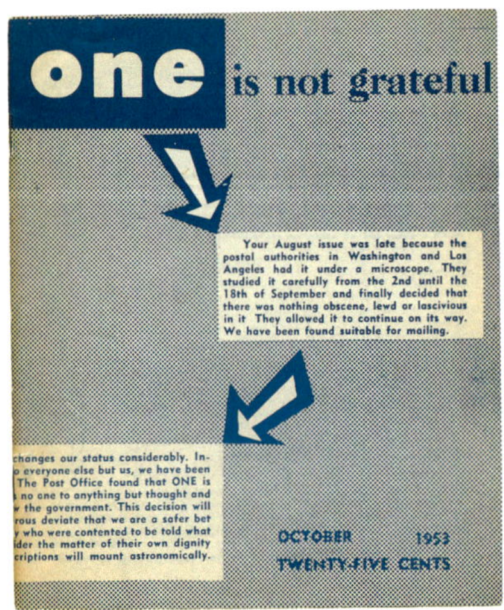
one
is not grateful
Your August issue was late because the postal authorities in Washington and Los Angeles had it under a microscope. They studied it carefully from the 2nd until the 18th of September and finally decided that there was nothing obscene, lewd or lascivious in it They allowed it to continue on its way. We have been found suitable for mailing.
changes our status considerably. In-
everyone else but us, we have been
The Post Office found that ONE is
no one to anything but thought and
the government. This decision will
rous deviate that we are a safer bet
who were contented to be told what
ider the matter of their own dignity
criptions will mount astronomically.
OCTOBER 1953
TWENTY-FIVE CENTS

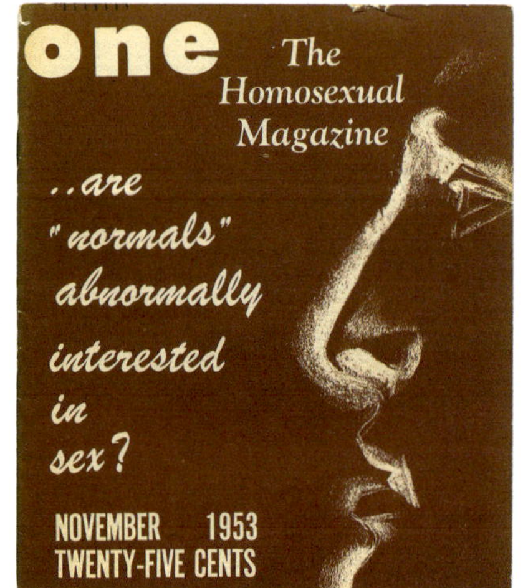
one
The
Homosexual
Magazine
..are
"normals"
abnormally
interested
in
sex?
NOVEMBER 1953
TWENTY-FIVE CENTS

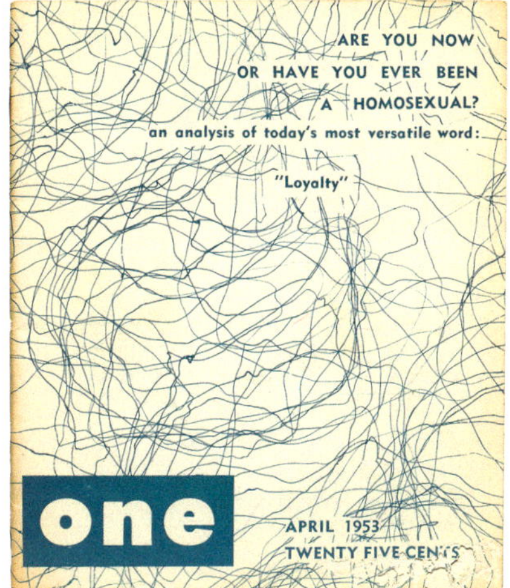

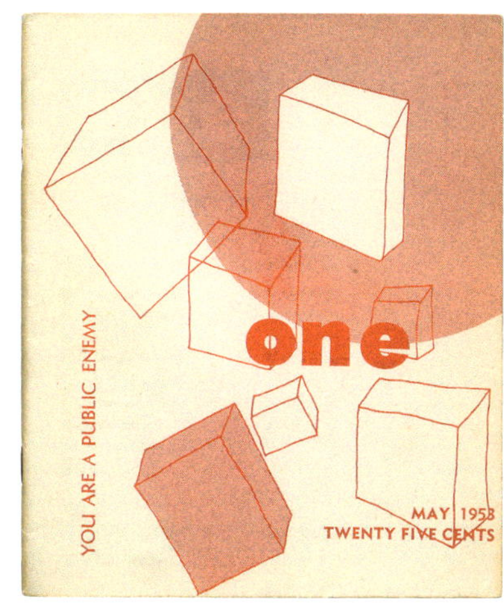

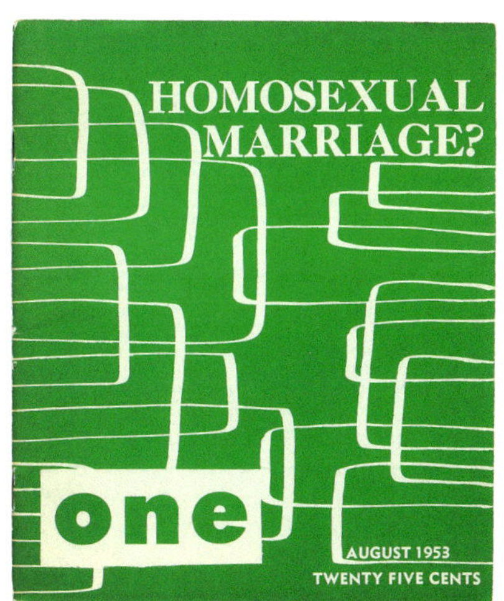

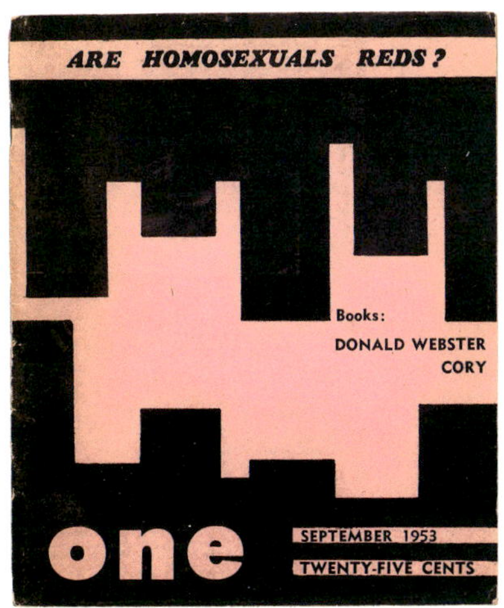

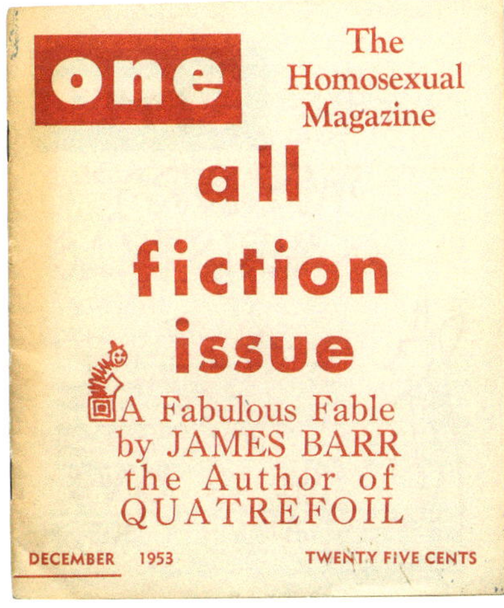

Eve Elloree, a.k.a. Joan Corbin (designer), *ONE*, vol. 1, nos. 2–12, 1953, offset, 7 × 6 inches (17.5 × 15 cm), Los Angeles. Funded by early gay and lesbian rights groups the Mattachine Society and the Daughters of Bilitis, *ONE* was the nation's first queer magazine. It was designed by Joan Corbin, a lesbian who also served on its editorial board. With a logo in Twentieth Century Ultrabold (an American version of Futura), her covers showcase a midcentury-modern approach to illustration that cleverly (and necessarily) abstracted the contents. Nonetheless, *ONE* was briefly banned by the U.S. Postal Service under obscenity laws.

Mari Tepper's *Hallelujah the Pill!!* celebrates one of the key contributors to the sexual revolution: the U.S. Food and Drug Administration's approval of the first oral contraceptive in 1960 (and the Supreme Court's ruling that people could use it in 1965). Tepper grew up in San Francisco's Haight-Ashbury District in the 1960s, where, as a teenager, she made psychedelic concert posters for Bill Graham's Fillmore Auditorium. Her 1967 poster shown here situates the iconic pack of birth control pills at the center of a mandala, a circular array used in prayer in various religions. From this central ring, with the seven days of the week clearly labeled, radiates a kaleidoscopic pattern of colorful lovers in various sexual positions. A geometric border pattern contains these festivities, trumpeting its own prayer, "Hallelujah the Pill!!" in an emphatic, all-caps hand.

Created in the historic Summer of Love, in which 100,000 young people pilgrimaged to the Haight, Tepper's handpainted homage, though ecstatic, is hardly naive. Snakes twist between the couples, recalling Eve's original sin in Genesis, as well as hinting at potential side effects of the era's new embrace of drug use and casual sex. Most of Tepper's figures, however, are standing, suggesting that the pill—which allowed women to decouple sex from childbearing—might permit a measure of equal footing between the sexes.

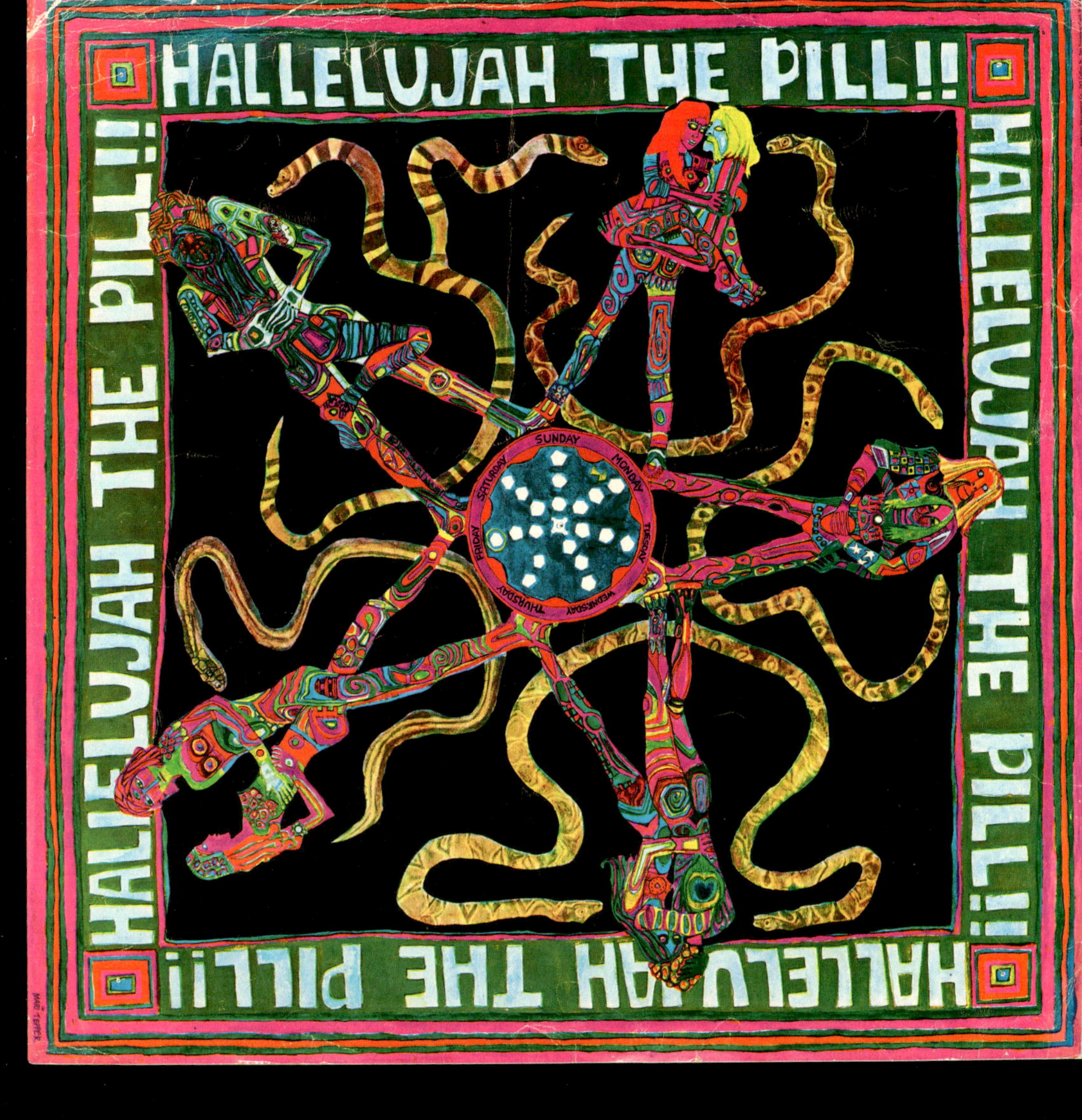
HALLELUJAH THE PILL!!
HALLELUJAH THE PILL!!
HALLELUJAH THE PILL!!
HALLELUJAH THE PILL!!
SUNDAY
MONDAY
TUESDAY
WEDNESDAY
THURSDAY
FRIDAY
SATURDAY

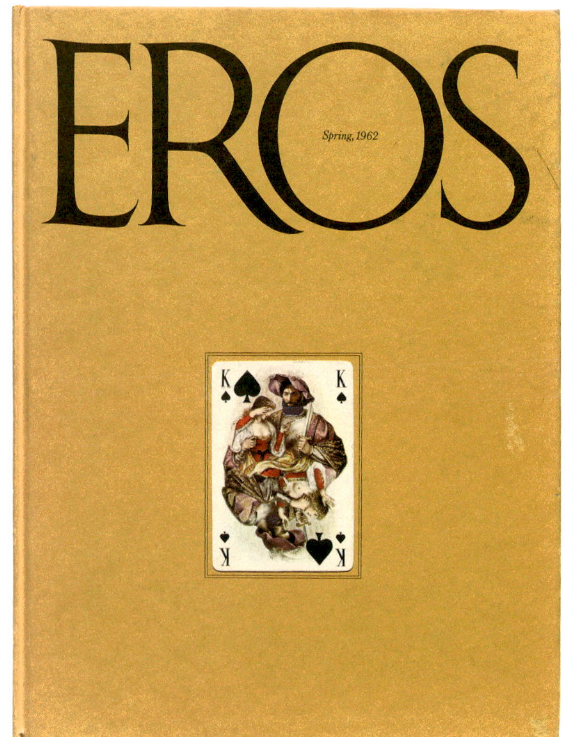
EROS
Spring, 1962

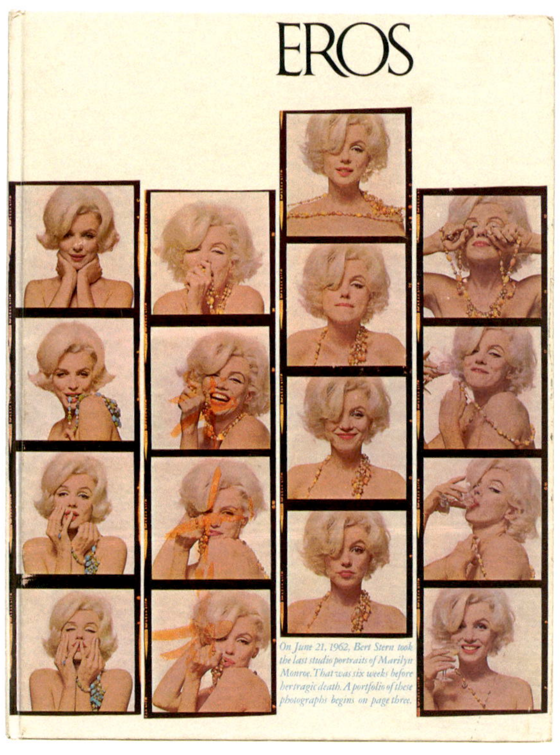
EROS
On June 21, 1962, Bert Stern took the last studio portraits of Marilyn Monroe. That was six weeks before her tragic death. A portfolio of these photographs begins on page three.

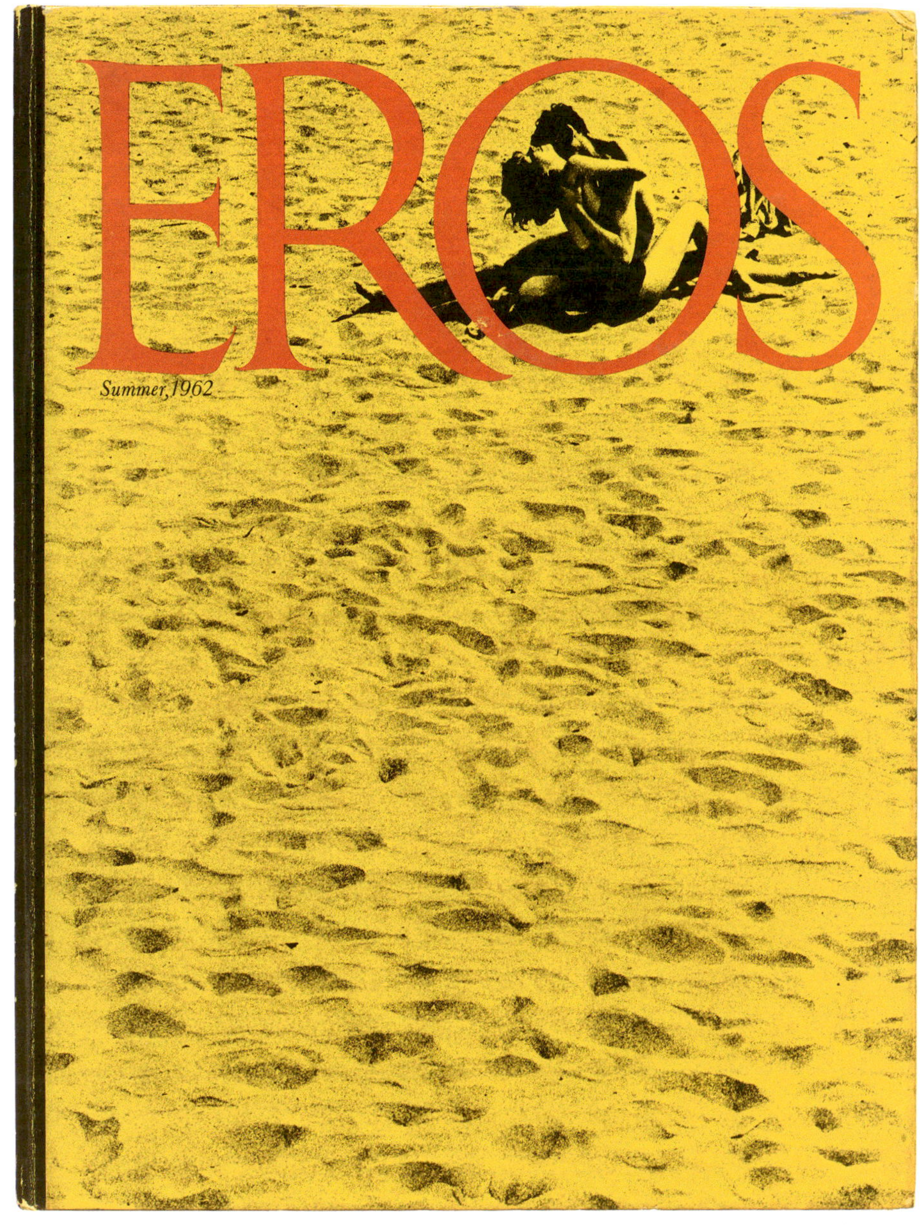

Herb Lubalin (designer), Ralph Ginzburg (editor), *Eros*, 1962, offset, 13 × 10⅛ inches (33 × 25.5 cm), New York. From left to right: vol. 1, nos. 1, 3, and 2. More book than magazine, this hardback quarterly was among the first to cater to audiences intrigued by the sexual revolution. Lubalin's strategically elegant nameplate for the cover draws on the classic Roman capitals of the Trajan inscription, with the wide-open bowl of the *O* providing an opportunity for interesting framing, as in the spyglass effect above.

"Lubalin and I worked together like Siamese twins. It was a rare and remarkable relationship. I had no experience or training as a graphic designer. Herb brought a graphic impact. I never tried to overrule him and almost never disagreed with him."

—Ralph Ginzburg

Herb Lubalin is one of the most referenced designers of advertising's Mad men era. Much of his work treated type as image by forming masses of bold and/or decorative letters that intertwined or interlocked, often for use in ads and logos—a novel approach that he called typographics. But it was his collaborations with controversial editor Ralph Ginzburg that earned him a reputation as a rule breaker.

The second magazine Lubalin and Ginzburg produced together, *Fact*, certainly broke both typographic and social conventions. While not officially part of the magazine's name, a colon appears after the logo on every cover. Lubalin invented this brilliantly simple device as a way to proclaim the focus of each issue with a controversial statement in plain, black-and-white text. The logo is based on a straightforward but eye-grabbing editorial serif, Caslon 540, and was modified by Lubalin's righthand lettering man, Tom Carnase, who tweaked the *f* so it echoes the *t*. For the first issue of its third volume, with a feature on interracial marriage, *Fact*'s cover took a subtle turn, with a graphic—not text—used to complete the sentence. Here, love itself, regardless of skin color, is presented as fact. Published the year before the U.S. Supreme Court's landmark ruling in *Loving v. Virginia*, which deemed antimiscegenation laws unconstitutional, this issue elicited a wide range of opinions on interracial marriage, a taboo subject in the press at the time.

Before *Fact*, Ginzburg and Lubalin had partnered on *Eros*, "a quarterly magazine entirely devoted to Love and Sex" (see pages 242–43). As a magazine, it stood out: *Eros* was ad free, mail-order only, large format, and hardcover. Under Lubalin's art direction, its pages were also unlike other periodicals of its time, mixing art historical overviews of eroticism (including that seen in Romantic painting and the pagodas of ancient India) with more suggestive photo essays and headlines, including "A Plea for Polygamy" and "My Quest for a French Tickler in Japan." This freedom was made possible by Ginzburg's innovative idea to make the magazine available only by subscription, thus freeing it from the constraints of the newsstand. But *Eros* ceased publication after just one year, with Ginzburg convicted of obscenity charges. The final straw was evidently a photo essay in the fourth issue featuring an interracial couple.

After the trial reached the Supreme Court, Ginzburg ended up serving eight months of a five-year sentence in prison. Lubalin is reported to have said, "I should have gone to jail, too."

fact:

VOLUME THREE, ISSUE ONE $1.25

Interracial marriage: in this issue Mort Sahl, the KKK's Robert Shelton, Godfrey Cambridge, Nat Hentoff, Judy Collins, Arthur Krock, Rudy Vallee, Ralph Ellison, Murray Kempton, Lillian Smith, Rona Jaffe, Paul Goodman, Harper Lee, Dave Garroway, Dore Schary, Harry Golden, Dr. Kenneth Clark, Gov. Ross Barnett of Mississippi and others give their personal views.

Herb Lubalin (designer), Ralph Ginzburg (publisher), Warren Boroson (editor), *Fact*, vol. 3, no. 1, 1966, offset, 11 × 8⅜ inches (28 × 21 cm), New York.

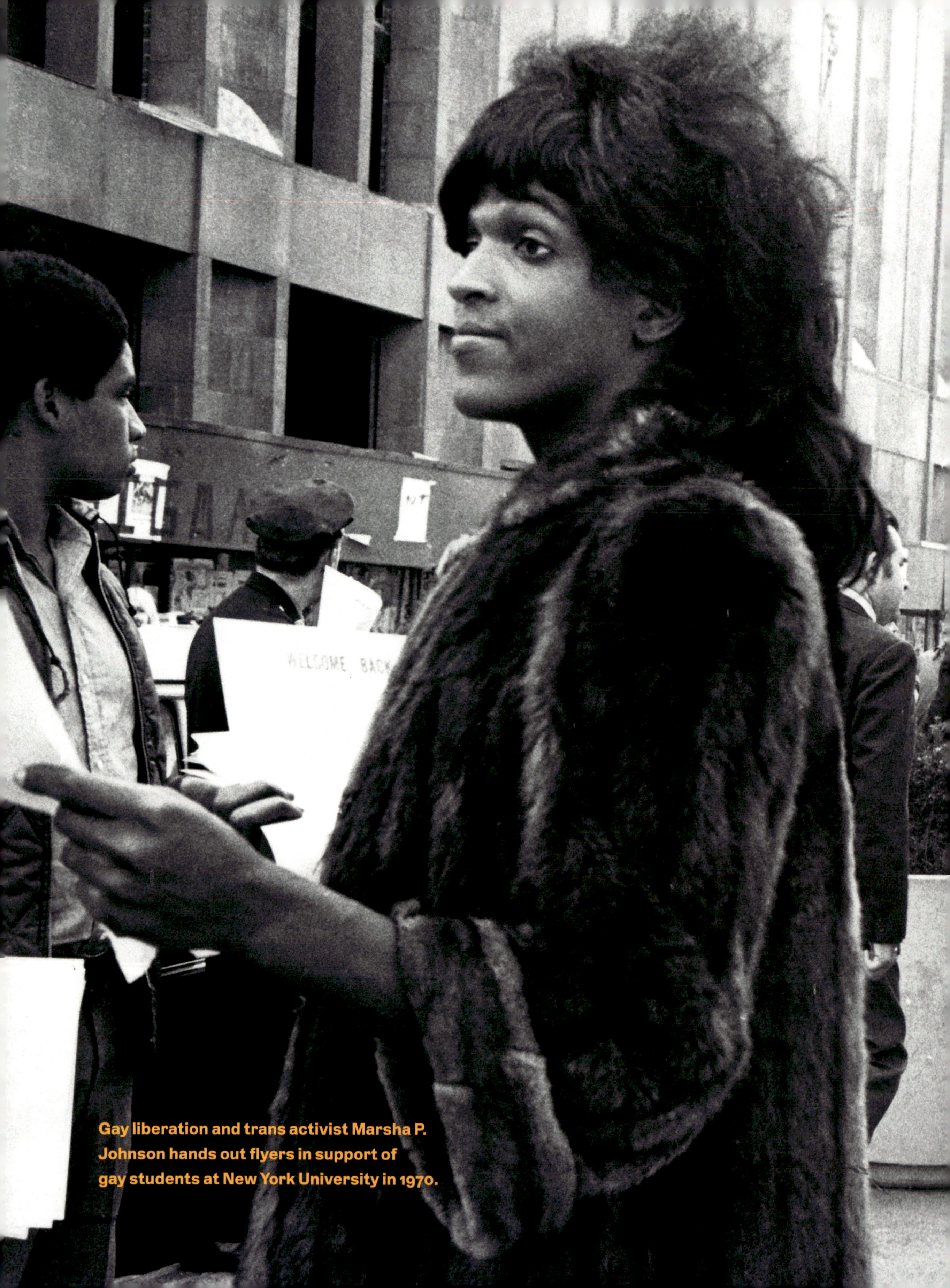

Gay liberation and trans activist Marsha P. Johnson hands out flyers in support of gay students at New York University in 1970.

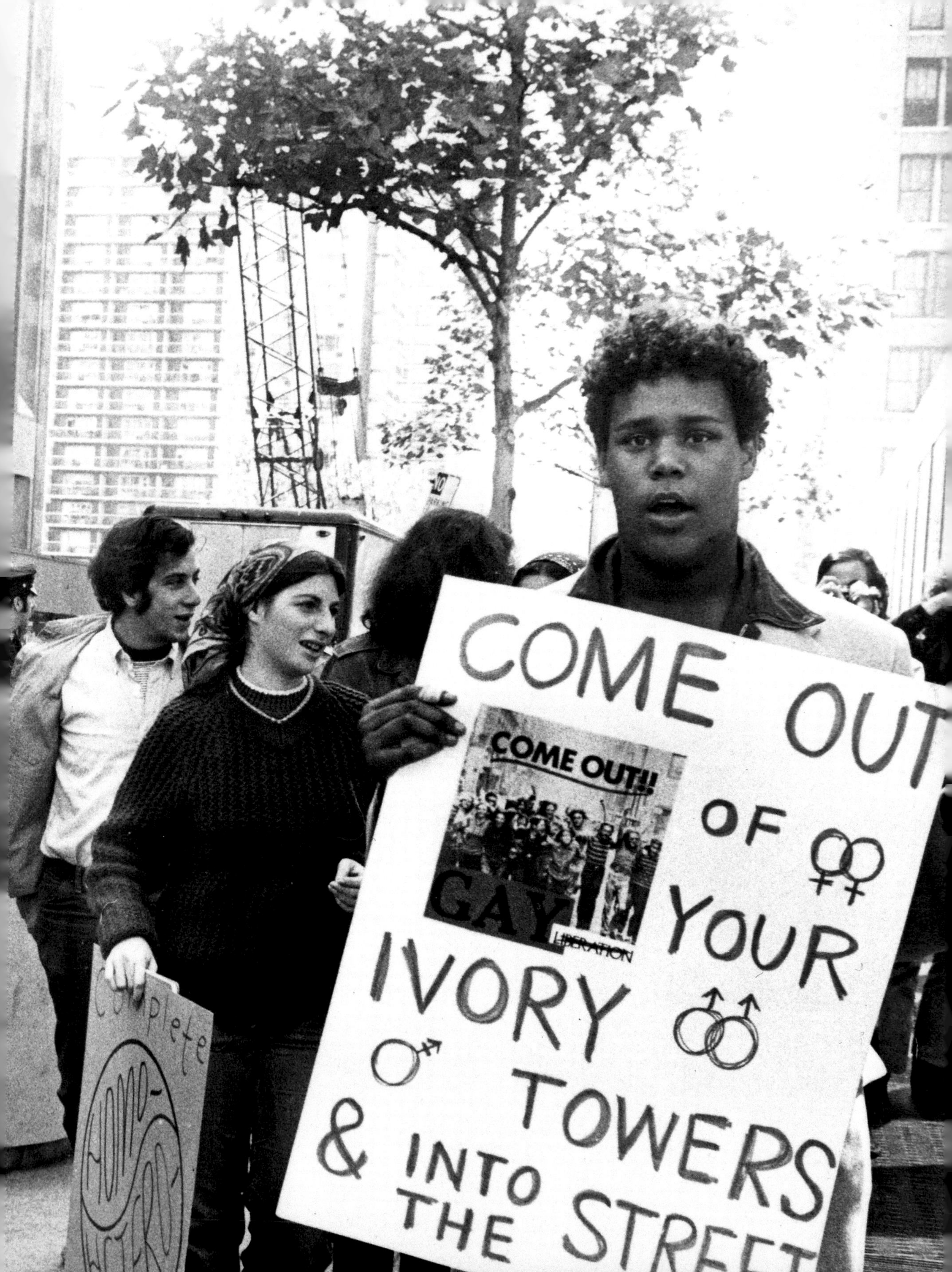
COME OUT
OF
YOUR
IVORY
TOWERS
& INTO
THE STREE
COME OUT!!
GAY
LIBERATION
Complete

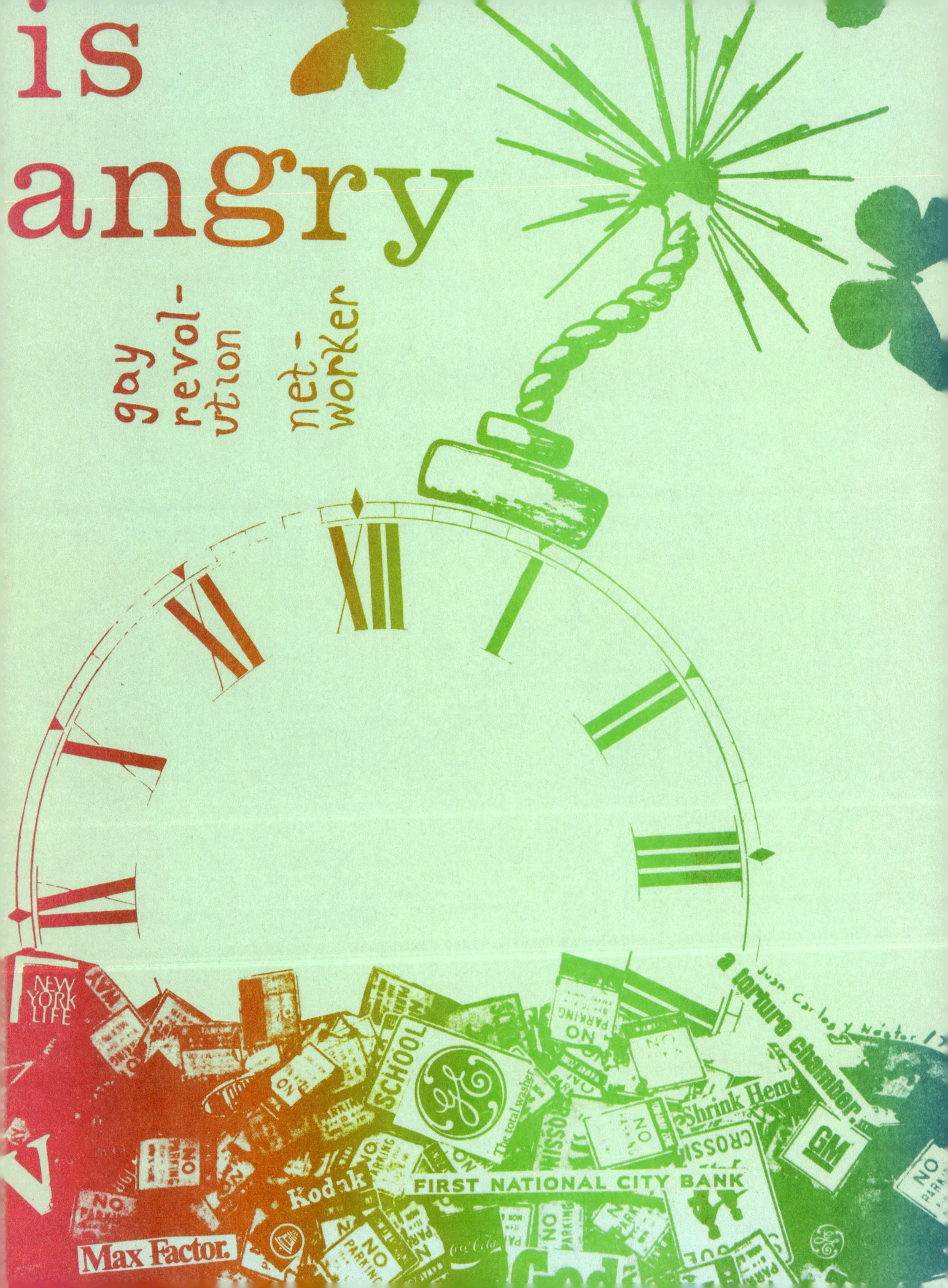
is
angry
gay
revol-
ution
net-
worker
a torture chamber
NEW YORK LIFE
SCHOOL
NO PARKING
The total washer
Kodak
Max Factor.
FIRST NATIONAL CITY BANK
GM

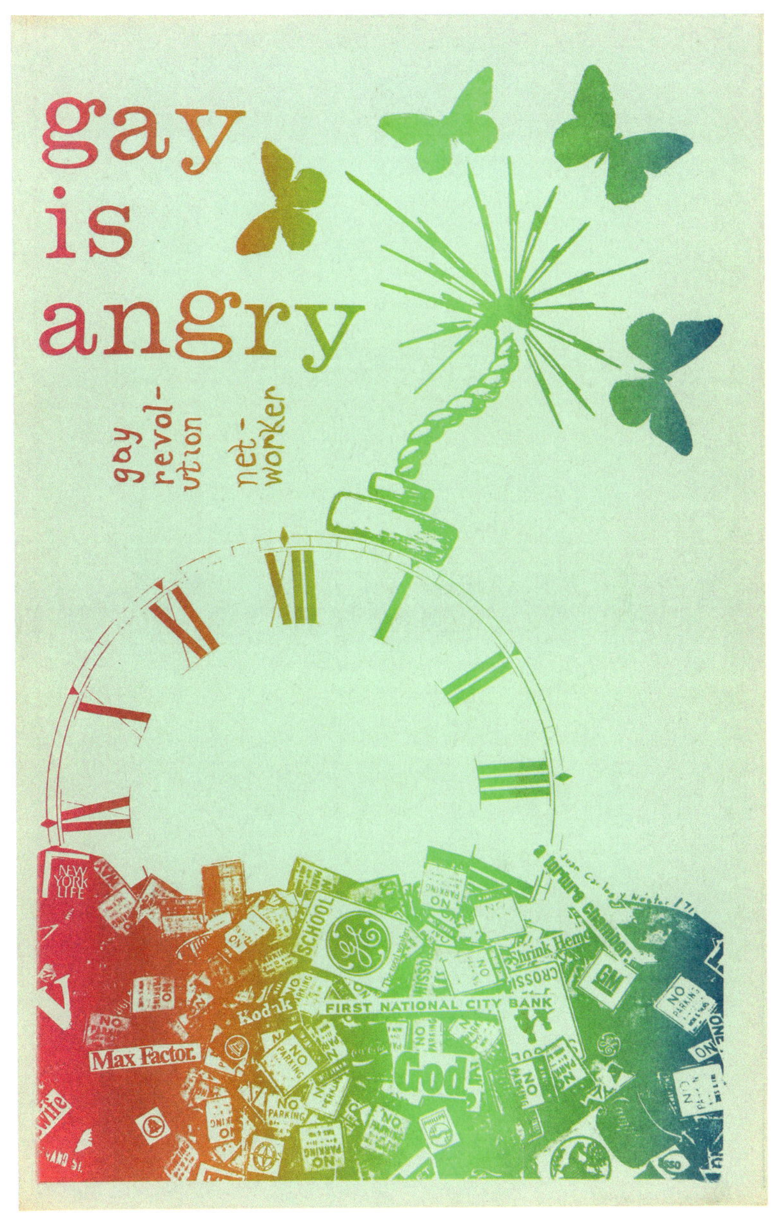

Juan Carlos Vidal and Néstor Latrónico, *Gay Is Angry*, 1971, screen print, 17 × 11 inches (43.5 × 28 cm), New York. Collection of ONE Archives. Here, the sense of collective agency that followed the Stonewall uprising takes the form of a ticking time bomb on a heap of text fragments that include corporate logos and headlines, as well as a procession of signs, all likely clipped from newspapers or magazines and then distorted on a photocopier. The title is set in an all-lowercase slab serif with a playfully wavy baseline. The poster's creators were members of the Third World Gay Revolution (TWGR), a group of Black and Latinx queers in the New York gay liberation movement.

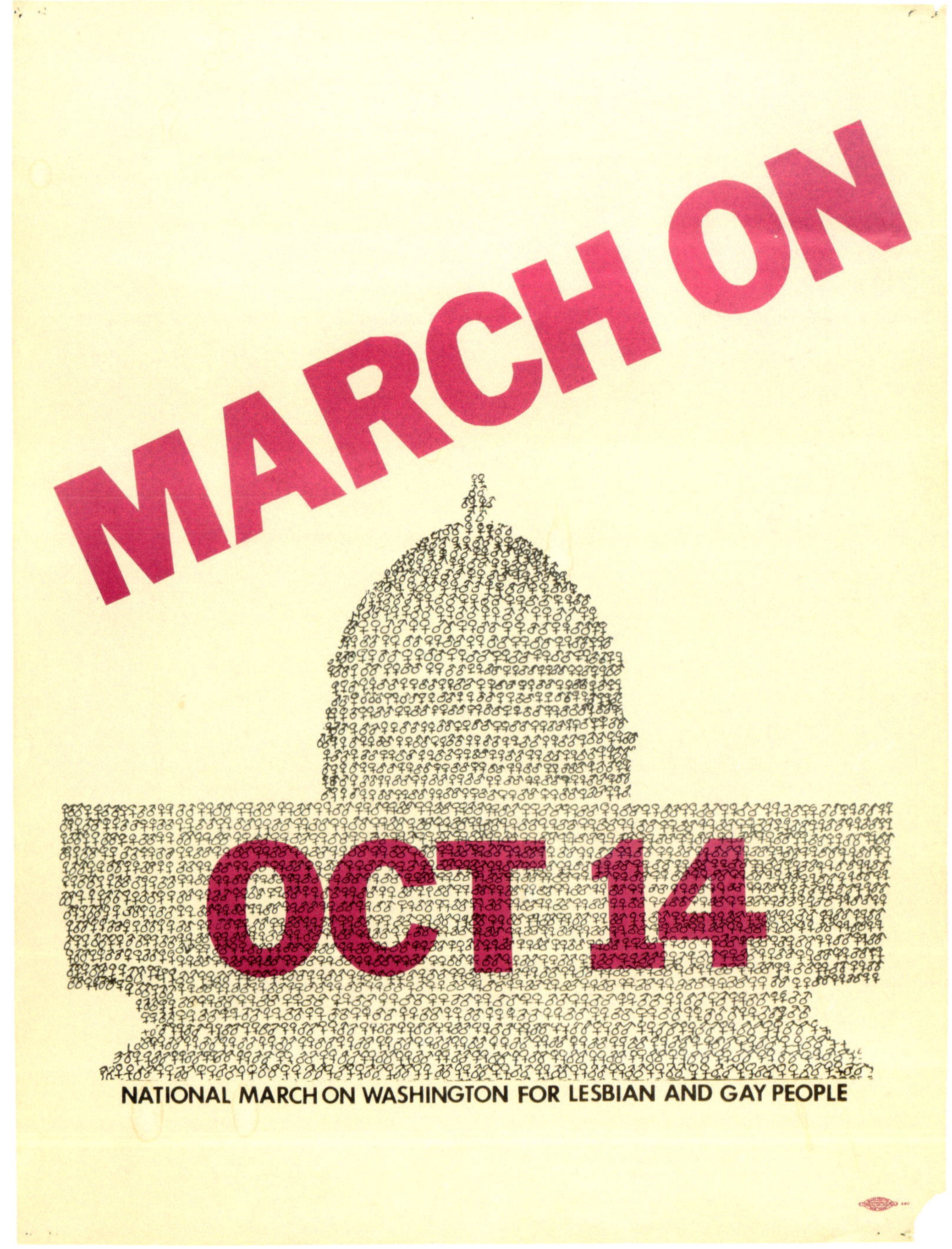

Unknown designer, *March on Oct 14*, 1979, offset, 22 × 17¼ inches (56 × 44 cm), Washington, D.C. Collection of ONE Archives. This poster advertises the first large-scale gay rights rally at the U.S. Capitol, the shape of which is here composed of same-sex pairs of the symbols for man and woman. More than 100,000 people attended the rally.

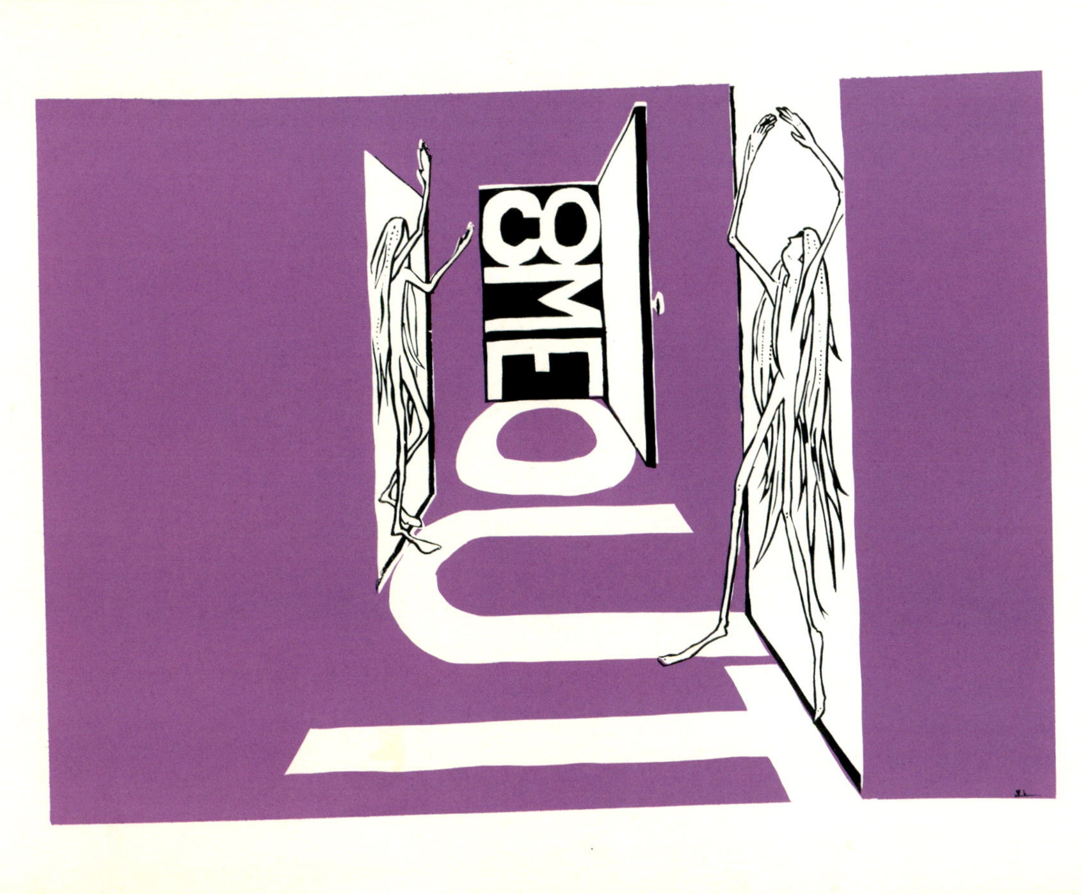

Unknown designer, *Come Out*, date unknown, screen print, 17¾ × 22⅞ inches (45 × 58 cm), location unknown. Collection of ONE Archives. Here, original lettering leads the viewer down a hallway and out of the proverbial closet, as androgynous, fantastical figures emerge dancing out of their own.

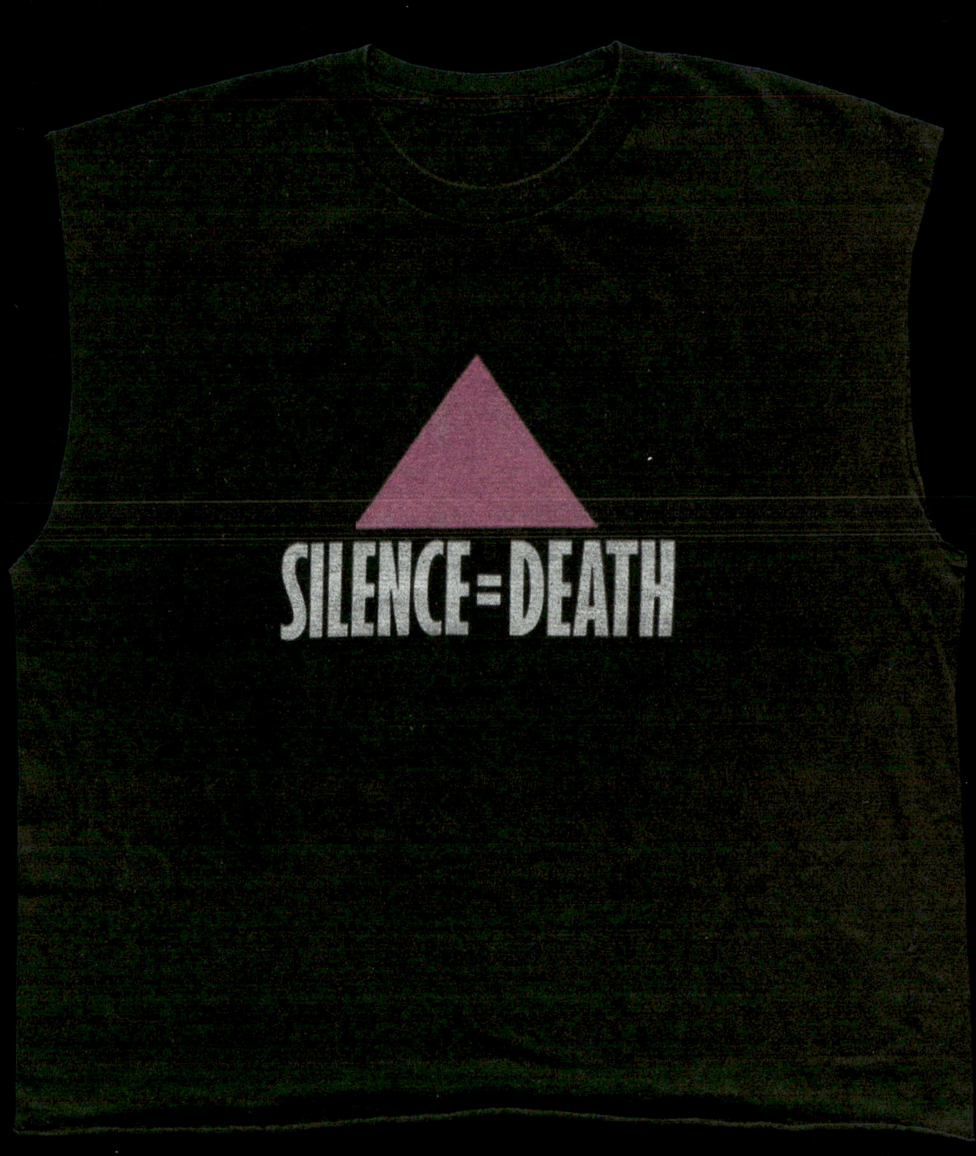

The Silence=Death Project, *Silence=Death* T-shirt, circa 1987, screen print, 25½ × 23 inches (64 × 58.5 cm), New York.

Unknown designer, English translation of a chart of prisoner badges used in the Nazi concentration camp Dachau, Germany, circa 1938–1942. Collection of the United States Holocaust Memorial Museum.

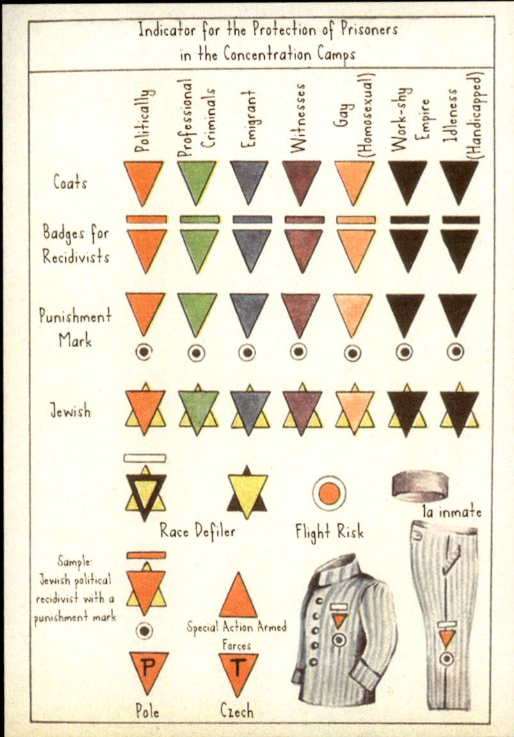

Call and Response

In 1981, the first cases of what would come to be called AIDS were reported in the United States. In the beginning, as it ravaged communities of gay people and people of color, predominantly in New York City and Los Angeles, the U.S. government and the public at large turned a blind eye. This immoral vacuum created an urgent need for public education to prevent the spread of the disease, as well as to create awareness about the conditions of those suffering and to channel helpless rage into purposeful activism.

Avram Finkelstein, Brian Howard, Oliver Johnston, Charles Kreloff, Chris Lione, and Jorge Socarrás came together in 1986 to help address this need. Their design, *Silence=Death*, appropriated the pink triangle, a symbol originally used by the Nazis to persecute gay people, who were forced to wear it as a badge in concentration camps beginning in the 1930s. In addition to the estimated 6 million Jewish people murdered in the Holocaust, the Nazis killed between 5,000 and 15,000 gay men, as well as an unknown number of others regarded as sexual deviants.

Silence=Death inverted the orientation of the pink triangle and boosted its pastel hue to a hot pink in an act of reclamation and rejection of its original purpose. The group's font selection, Gill Sans Bold Extra Condensed, was inspired by the work of the Guerrilla Girls (see pages 208–9), who also used a plain sans serif borrowed from advertising. First issued as a poster, the *Silence=Death* design became emblematic of the gay community's response to the crisis, and it soon appeared in many forms of media, including this T-shirt. Its creators were among the activists who formed ACT UP (the AIDS Coalition to Unleash Power) to advocate for medical research and antidiscrimination legislation. In 1988, Finkelstein became a founding member of Gran Fury, the arts group affiliated with ACT UP.

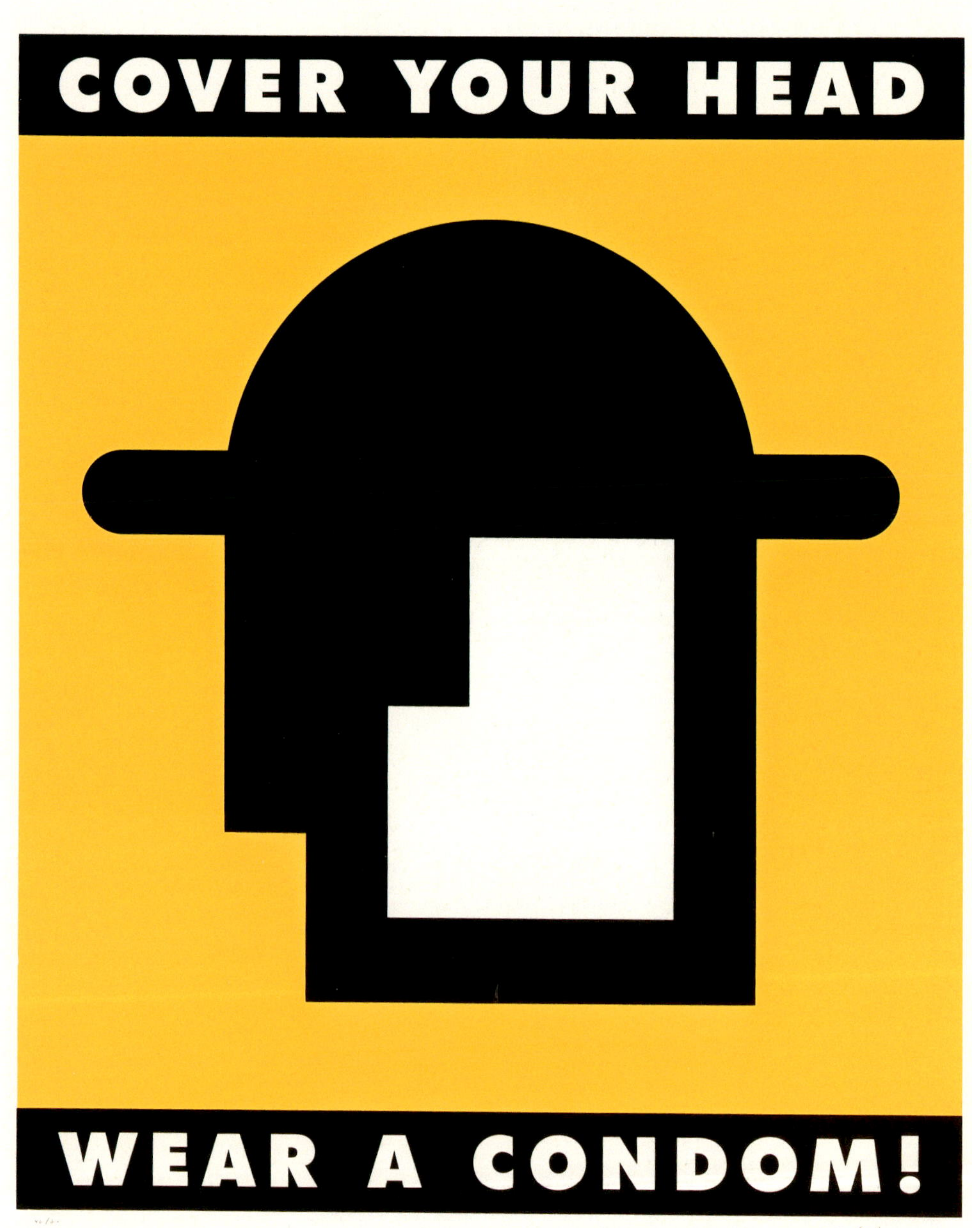

BlackDog (Mark Fox), *Cover Your Head: Wear a Condom!*, 1992, screen print, 30⅞ × 26 inches (78.5 × 66 cm), San Rafael, California. Fox submitted this safe-sex poster—with its anatomical pun—for ACT UP.

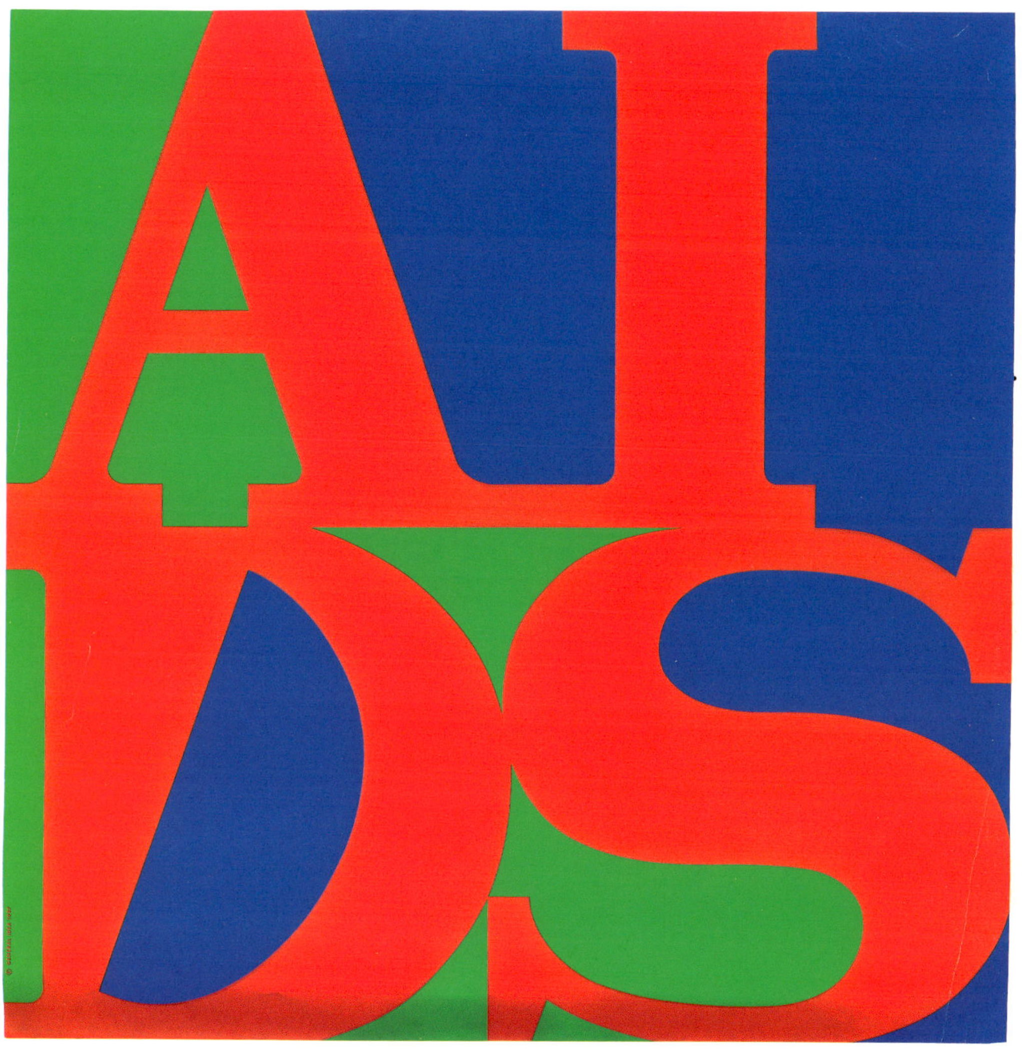

General Idea, *AIDS*, 1987, screen print, 26⅞ × 26⅞ inches (68 × 68 cm), New York. Here, AA Bronson, Felix Partz, and Jorge Zontal call out the public's apathy regarding the AIDS crisis by mimicking Robert Indiana's famed 1966 *LOVE* sculpture. They set *AIDS* in the same colorway and bracketed slab serif (based on Clarendon Bold), angling the interior of the *D* to recall Indiana's slanted *O*. In 1994, both Partz and Zontal died of AIDS.

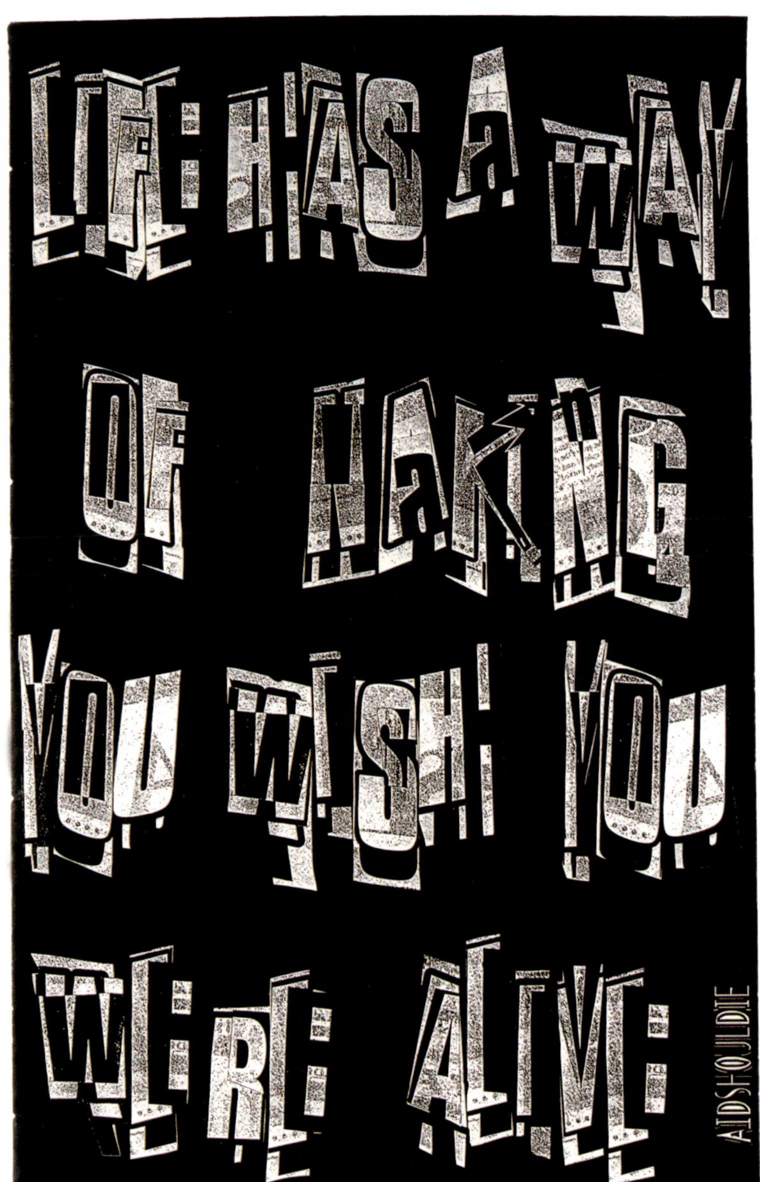

Rick Valicenti, *AIDS Should Die* and *God Has AIDS*, circa 1992, digital prints, 36 × 24 inches (91.5 × 61 cm), Chicago. Above: Collection of Cooper Hewitt, Smithsonian Design Museum. The pair of posters exudes the postmodern expressionism of the 1990s, when trends like digital manipulation and grunge emerged. These nearly dimensional collages feature upper- and lowercase letters in Compacta Bold (with both shadow and outline effects) clipped from car ads. The static background texture in *God Has AIDS* resulted from multiple passes through a Xerox machine.

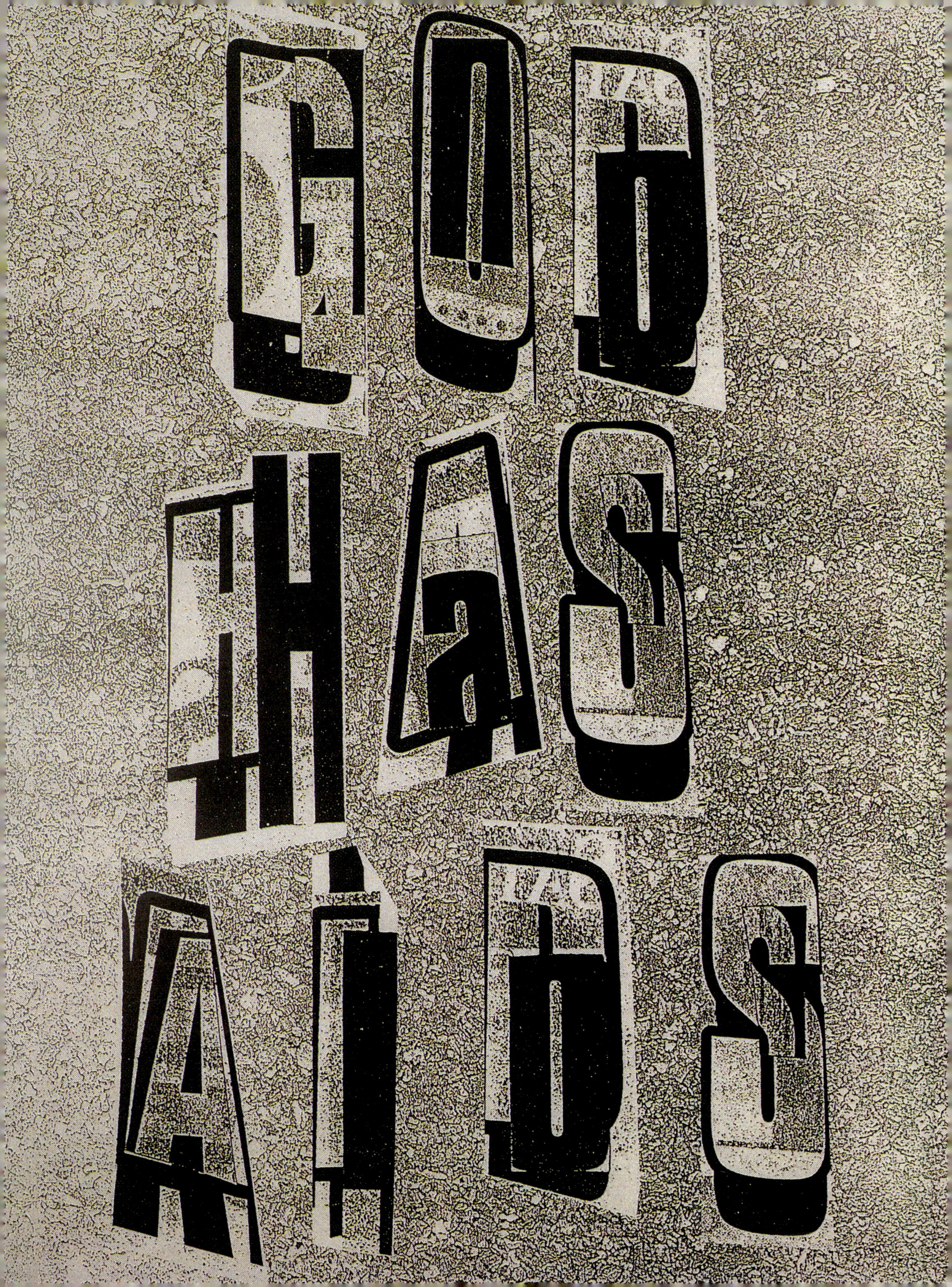

GOD
HAS
AIDS

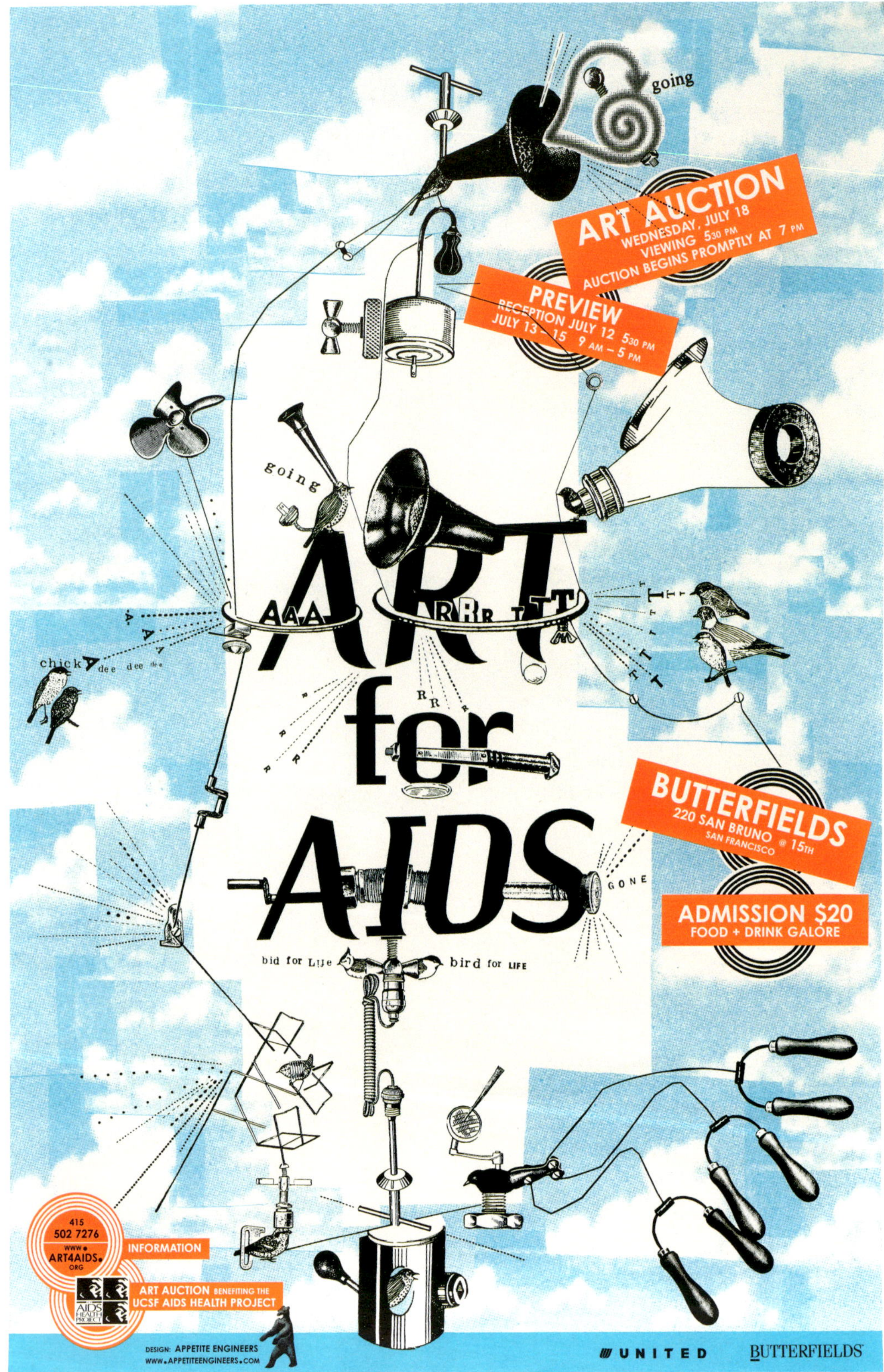
going
ART AUCTION
WEDNESDAY, JULY 18
VIEWING 5:30 PM
AUCTION BEGINS PROMPTLY AT 7 PM
PREVIEW
RECEPTION JULY 12 5:30 PM
JULY 13 – 15 9 AM – 5 PM
going
ART
for
AIDS
chick A dee dee dee
GONE
bid for Life
bird for LIFE
BUTTERFIELDS
220 SAN BRUNO @ 15TH
SAN FRANCISCO
ADMISSION $20
FOOD + DRINK GALORE
415
502 7276
WWW.ART4AIDS.ORG
INFORMATION
ART AUCTION BENEFITING THE UCSF AIDS HEALTH PROJECT
DESIGN: APPETITE ENGINEERS
WWW.APPETITEENGINEERS.COM
UNITED
BUTTERFIELDS

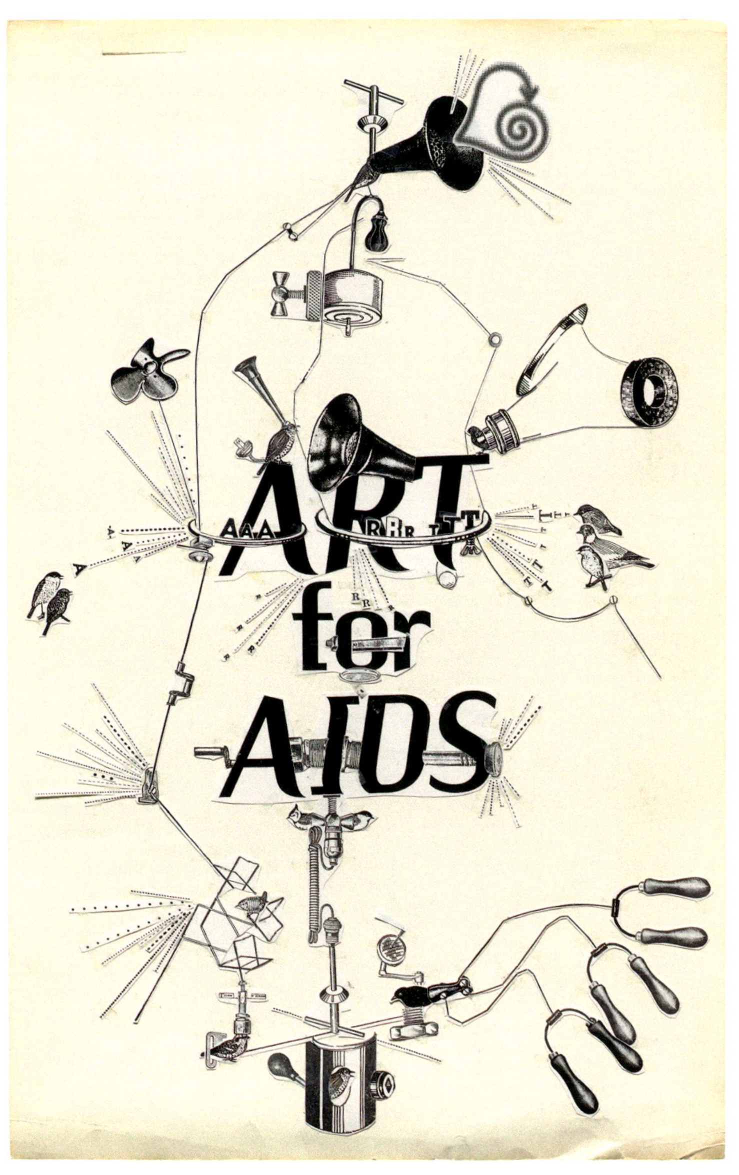

Martin Venezky for Appetite Engineers, poster and process work for *Art for AIDS*, 2001, San Francisco. Offset, 22 × 14⅜ inches (56 × 36.5 cm), and collage, 17 × 11 inches (43 × 28 cm). This poster reflects the public's changing attitude toward AIDS, a shift that led to support for research into prevention and treatment. Venezky's meticulous cut-paper collage, which was assembled with tweezers before being digitally colorized, presents an AIDS fundraiser auction as a mechanical whirligig urging viewers to "bid for life."

if he were
alive today
he'd still
be living
with AIDS

For the Record, 2nd edition, 2nd printing for Visual AIDS www.visualaids.org fierce pussy 2015 www.fiercepussy.org

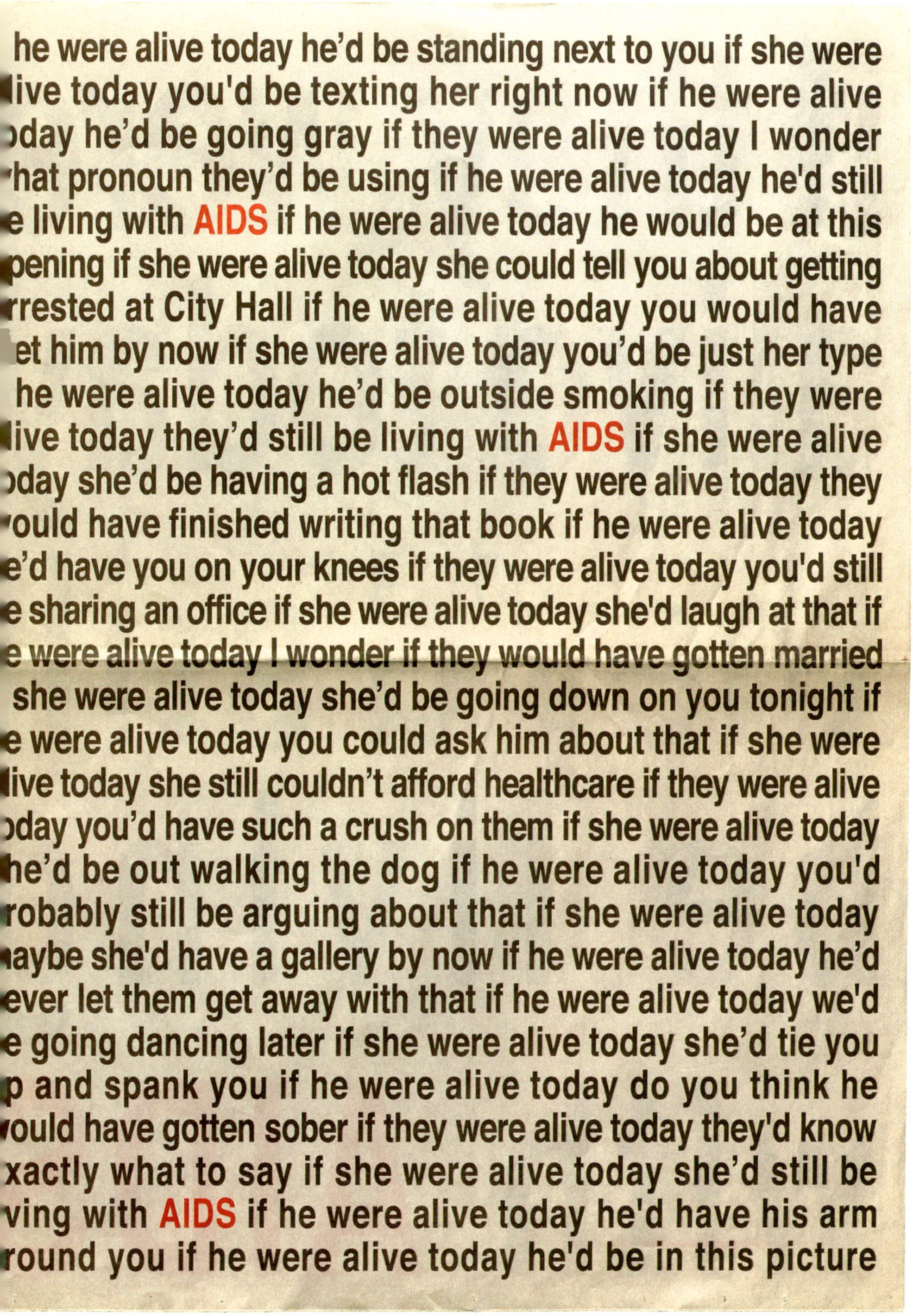

he were alive today he'd be standing next to you if she were
ive today you'd be texting her right now if he were alive
day he'd be going gray if they were alive today I wonder
hat pronoun they'd be using if he were alive today he'd still
e living with AIDS if he were alive today he would be at this
pening if she were alive today she could tell you about getting
rrested at City Hall if he were alive today you would have
et him by now if she were alive today you'd be just her type
he were alive today he'd be outside smoking if they were
ive today they'd still be living with AIDS if she were alive
day she'd be having a hot flash if they were alive today they
ould have finished writing that book if he were alive today
e'd have you on your knees if they were alive today you'd still
e sharing an office if she were alive today she'd laugh at that if
e were alive today I wonder if they would have gotten married
she were alive today she'd be going down on you tonight if
e were alive today you could ask him about that if she were
ive today she still couldn't afford healthcare if they were alive
day you'd have such a crush on them if she were alive today
he'd be out walking the dog if he were alive today you'd
robably still be arguing about that if she were alive today
aybe she'd have a gallery by now if he were alive today he'd
ever let them get away with that if he were alive today we'd
e going dancing later if she were alive today she'd tie you
p and spank you if he were alive today do you think he
ould have gotten sober if they were alive today they'd know
xactly what to say if she were alive today she'd still be
ving with AIDS if he were alive today he'd have his arm
round you if he were alive today he'd be in this picture

fierce pussy, *For the Record*, 2013, offset, 22¾ × 34 inches (57.5 × 86.5 cm), New York. This double-sided print was included in the Visual AIDS series, which contained newsprint posters, stickers, postcards, and digital broadsides created by the lesbian feminist collective called fierce pussy.

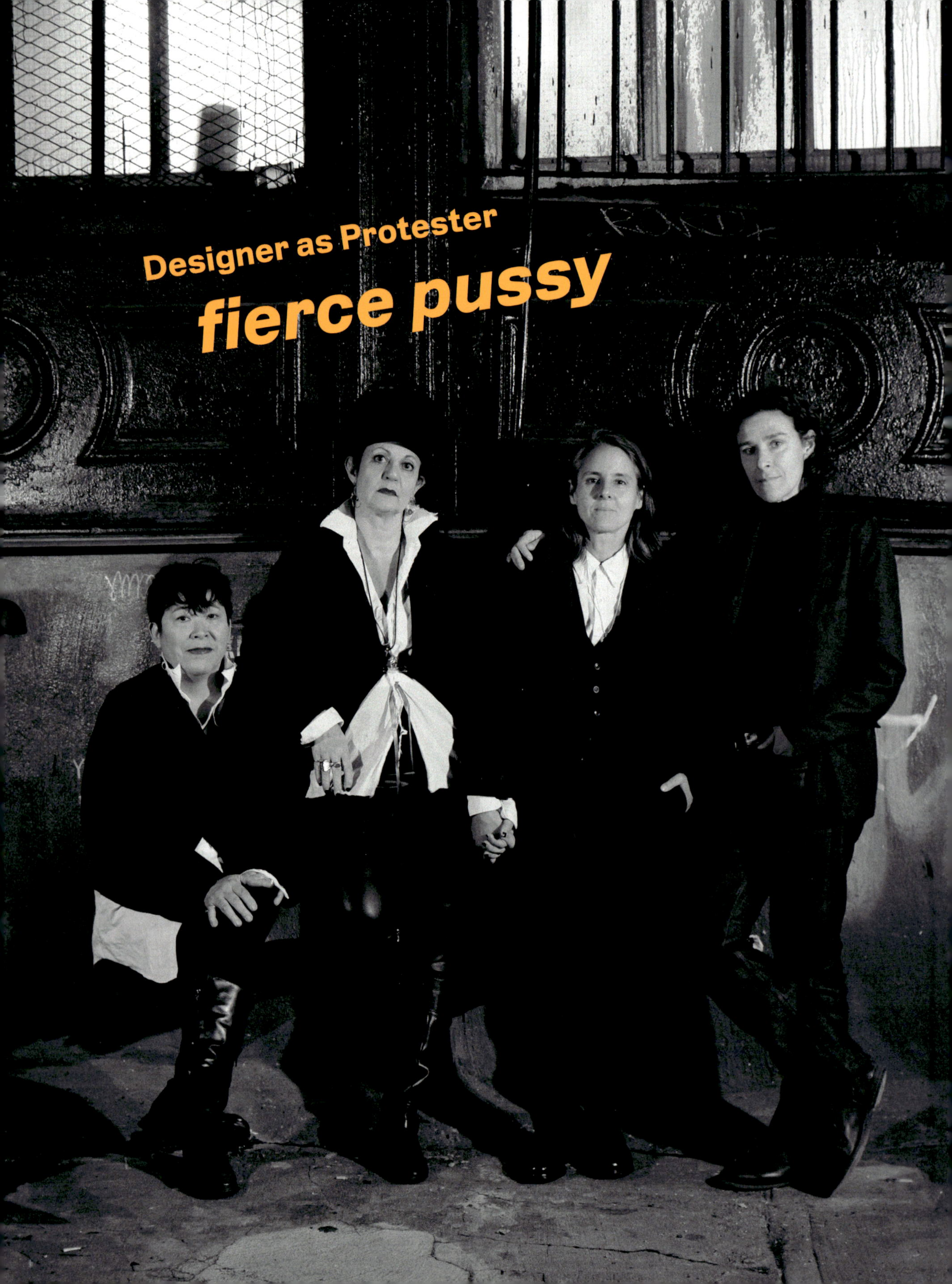

Designer as Protester

fierce pussy

"I am a stone butch / androgyne / femme / tomboy / girlfriend / sapphic / deviant / AND PROUD."

—fierce pussy

In 1991, at an ACT UP meeting in New York's East Village, a group of advocates announced the formation of a new group—one that, at a moment of intense focus on the experiences of gay men during the AIDS crisis, would give voice to the lesbian feminist perspective. At their first meetup, founding members Joy Episalla, Carrie Yamaoka, Nancy Brooks Brody, and Zoe Leonard made a work of art on the spot: a list of derogatory terms for queer women (*lezzie*, *dyke*, *bulldagger*), bookended with the words "I AM A" and "AND PROUD" to indicate their fiery reclamation of language. Made with readily available paper, an old typewriter, and a pair of scissors, then photocopied and wheatpasted out in the streets, fierce pussy's inaugural project brazenly declared a communal "I" for queer women during an era of conservative government and increasing homophobia, just a few years before the enforcement of "Don't ask, don't tell."

From the start, typography figured in the collective's identity. The choice to set their name in lowercase was in part to signal their embrace of nonhierarchical structure. The words on their early posters—set in the single typeface available on their typewriter, then enlarged and subjected to repeated photocopying—lost crispness over time but gained power through being multiplied for the masses. Ultimately, the type's graininess is a visual testament to its reach. (Ironically, the group's subversive output was unofficially subsidized by a major media corporation: Condé Nast, where Episalla and Yamaoka worked in magazine design departments and used the copy machines to crank out posters and flyers.)

Among the group's other work is the 1991 series *Family Pictures and Found Photos*, which juxtaposes childhood images of the collective's members with labels like "Tomgirl" and taunts like "Find the dyke in this picture." These graphic pairings force viewers to interrogate society's imposition of gender norms at birth. In 1993, after Colorado passed homophobic legislation, fierce pussy responded with a 1906 photo of an arrested suffragette overprinted with text equating the persecution of women seeking the vote with the discrimination still experienced by lesbians nearly a century later.

After going dark in 1995, the collective's original four members came back together in 2008, producing new work as well as remixing their earlier posters with updated text that addresses the shifting sociopolitical position of lesbians within contemporary capitalism. One of their newer pieces, created in 2013, *For the Record*, details what those lost to AIDS would be doing had they lived, including the domestic ("walking the dog"), the erotic ("going down on you tonight"), the political ("still not being able to afford healthcare"), and the wistful ("going gray"). Justified between narrow margins in Helvetica, the evenly spaced text offers the eye no reprieve, with the narrative shifting between the pronouns *he*, *she*, and *they* to communicate the health crisis's brutal inclusivity. In this way, it also expands fierce pussy's original concern—lesbian visibility in the era of AIDS—to encompass those who are trans and nonbinary.

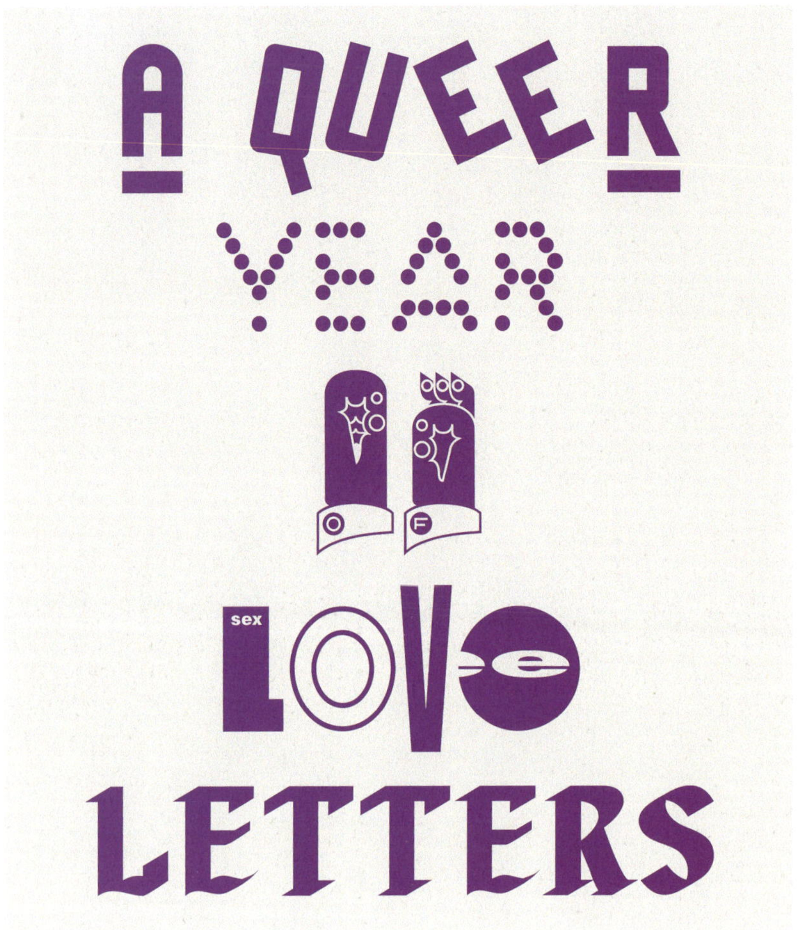

For *A Queer Year of Love Letters*, nonbinary alphabet artist Nat Pyper researched overlooked figures in queer liberation history as a way of paying homage to their ancestors. The resulting digital fonts draw on the letterforms produced by activists including Ernestine Eckstein, a Black lesbian organizer who was the only person of color to picket the White House at a 1965 gay rights demonstration. In photos of the historic pre-Stonewall event, Eckstein carries a sign reading "Denial of Equality of Opportunity Is Immoral"—the words Pyper displays in the specimen for the typeface that bears her name. For a font honoring Robert Ford, the Chicago-based maker of the early 1990s Black queer zine *Thing*, Pyper adapted various type featured in the publication and used them to form *Thing*'s tagline, "She Knows Who She Is." The typeface named after Martin Wong, a gay Chinese American painter who died of AIDS, references his landscapes of 1980s New York City that included rows of hands gesturing in American Sign Language. Another font pays tribute to the lettering of *Moonstorm*, a zine produced by the Women's Car Repair Collective, a lesbian-operated garage that offered repairs by and for women in St. Louis, Missouri, during the 1970s. With the series as a whole, Pyper aims to "make the act of remembering these overlooked and illegitimate histories . . . as easy as typing."

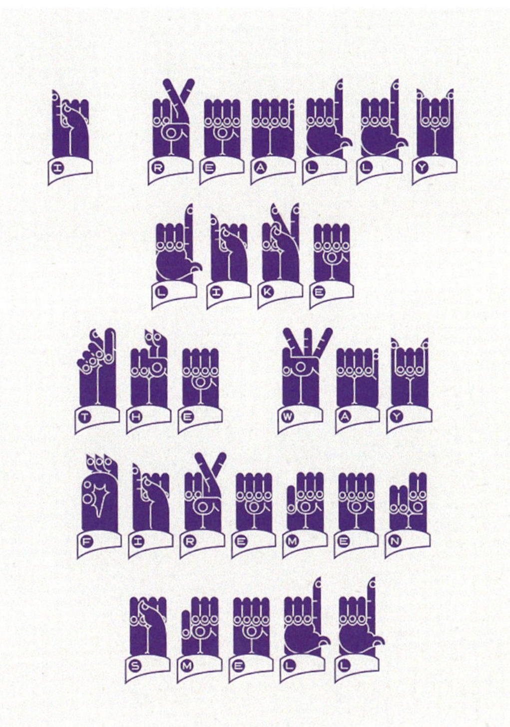

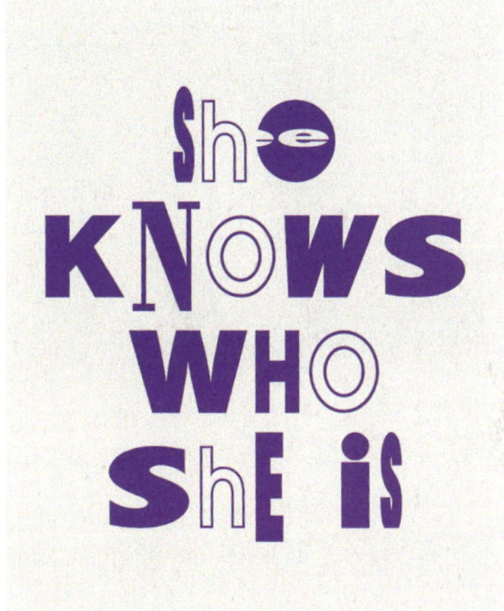

A DENIAL OF EQUALITY OF OPPORTUNITY IS IMMORAL

"WE MUST CREATE OUR OWN LESBIAN-IDENTIFIED STRUCTURES."

Nat Pyper, samples from the typeface series *A Queer Year of Love Letters*, 2018, digital fonts, Chicago and New Haven, Connecticut. From top to bottom: Martin Wong, Robert Ford, Ernestine Eckstein, and Women's Car Repair Collective.

STRIKET

IROUGH!

Notes

Curatorial Statement

Silas Munro

1 Bryan C. Keene, "Medieval Copyediting," published on *The Iris*, the blog of the J. Paul Getty Trust, April 8, 2014, https://blogs.getty.edu/iris/medieval-copyediting/.

2 Helen Williams, *Laurence Sterne and the Eighteenth-Century Book* (Cambridge: Cambridge University Press, 2021).

3 Insup Taylor and Maurice Martin Taylor, *Writing and Literacy in Chinese, Korean, and Japanese* (Amsterdam: John Benjamins Publishing Company, 1995).

4 Noam Cohen, "Crossing Out, for Emphasis," *New York Times*, July 23, 2007.

5 Robert Bringhurst, *The Elements of Typographic Style* (Vancouver: Hartley & Marks Publishers, 1992).

6 Nat Pyper website, https://www.natpyper.com/.

7 Nat Pyper, "Queer Year of Love Letters," Library Stack, https://www.librarystack.org/queer-year-of-love-letters/.

8 Harold Courlander, *A Treasury of Afro-American Folklore: The Oral Literature, Traditions, Recollections, Legends, Tales, Songs, Religious Beliefs, Customs, Sayings, and Humor of Peoples of African Descent in the Americas* (New York: Marlowe & Company, 1976).

NOW! Demanding Black Liberation with Typography

Colette Gaiter

1 Lincoln Cushing, "Red in Black and White: The New Left Printing Renaissance of the 1960s—and Beyond," *Peace Press Graphics 1967–1987: Art in the Pursuit of Social Change*, ed. Ilee Kaplan and Carol A. Wells, exh. cat. (Long Beach: University Art Museum, California State University, Long Beach, 2011). Reprinted on *Docs Populi* (website), August 15, 2021, https://www.docspopuli.org/articles/New_Left_Printing.html.

2 Hal Elliott Wert, *George McGovern and the Democratic Insurgents: The Best Campaign and Political Posters of the Last Fifty Years* (Lincoln: University of Nebraska Press, 2015), 4.

3 For example, the United States' Counterintelligence Program, or COINTELPRO, "zealously directed its energy toward destroying what it deemed 'militant black nationalist groups,' particularly the Black Panther Party . . . . Until its accidental discovery in 1971 by an activist group digging through files in an FBI field office in Media, Pennsylvania, COINTELPRO had contributed to the deaths of at least four Panthers, including Fred Hampton and Mark Clark on December 4, 1969, and the imprisonment of dozens of Panthers." Santi Elijah Holley, "The Black Panther Party Has Never Been More Popular. But Actual Black Panthers Have Been Forgotten," *New Republic*, April 22, 2021, https://newrepublic.com/article/162144/black-panther-party-never-popular-actual-black-panthers-forgotten.

4 Tamar Sarai Davis, "Released after Decades in Prison, a Former Black Panther Still Faces Threats to His Freedom," *Prism*, January 27, 2021, https://prismreports.org/2021/01/27/for-black-radicals-released-after-decades-in-prison-the-carceral-system-is-still-a-threat/.

5 Neal, Larry. "The Black Arts Movement," *Drama Review: TDR* 12, no. 4 (Summer 1968): 28–39, https://doi.org/10.2307/1144377/.

6 According to scholar Leah Donnella, describing the colors of the Pan-African flag of unity, "Red stood for blood—both the blood shed by Africans who died in their fight for liberation, and the shared blood of the African people. Black represented, well, black people. And green was a symbol of growth and the natural fertility of Africa." Leah Donnella, "On Flag Day, Remembering the Red, Black and Green," NPR, June 14, 2017, https://www.npr.org/sections/codeswitch/2017/06/14/532667081/on-flag-day-remembering-the-red-black-and-green.

7 Michele Wallace, "Faith Ringgold's Political Posters: Power to the People," *The 1960s* (website), May 26, 2010, https://ringgold-inthe1960s.blogspot.com/2010/05/blog-post.html.

8 Huey Copeland, "Conditions Reporting," lecture presented at *Fearless Endeavors: Daring Art History Methodologies and Art Practices*, the 2022 James A. Porter Colloquium on African American Art and Art of the African Diaspora, April 8, 2022.

9 Andrea Estrada, "Collective Intelligence," *The Current* (news website for UC Santa Barbara), January 13, 2017, https://www.news.ucsb.edu/2017/017564/collective-intelligence.

Suggested Reading

Campbell, Andy. 2019. *Queer X Design: 50 Years of Signs, Symbols, Banners, Logos, and Graphic Art of LGBTQ*. New York: Black Dog & Leventhal.

Cushing, Lincoln. 2003. *Revolución! Cuban Poster Art*. San Francisco: Chronicle Books.

Cushing, Lincoln, and Timothy W. Drescher. 2009. *Agitate! Educate! Organize! American Labor Posters*. Ithaca, NY: Cornell University Press.

Susan Dackerman, ed. 2015. *Corita Kent and the Language of Pop*. Boston: Harvard Art Museums.

Douglas, Emory. 2007. *Black Panther: The Revolutionary Art of Emory Douglas*. Edited by Sam Durant. New York: Rizzoli.

Glaser, Milton, and Mirko Ilić. 2017. *The Design of Dissent, Expanded Edition: Greed, Nationalism, Alternative Facts, and the Resistance*. Beverly, MA: Rockport.

Godfrey, Mark, and Zoé Whitley, eds. 2017. *Soul of a Nation: Art in the Age of Black Power*. London: D.A.P./Tate.

Kugelberg, Johan, and Philippe Vermès, eds. 2011. *Beauty Is in the Street: A Visual Record of the May '68 Paris Uprising*. London: Four Corners Books.

Lampert, Nicholas. 2013. *A People's Art History of the United States: 250 Years of Activist Art and Artists Working in Social Justice Movements*. New York: New Press.

Lupton, Ellen, et al. 2021. *Extra Bold: A Feminist, Inclusive, Anti-Racist, Nonbinary Field Guide for Graphic Designers*. New York: Princeton Architectural Press.

MacPhee, Josh, and Alec Dunn, eds. *Signal: A Journal of International Political Graphics & Culture*. Oakland, CA: PM Press, 2010–2021.

McQuiston, Liz. 2019. *Protest!: A History of Social and Political Protest Graphics*. Princeton, NJ: Princeton Architectural Press.

McQuiston, Liz. 1997. *Suffragettes to She-Devils: Women's Liberation and Beyond*. London: Phaidon.

Ramos, E. Carmen, ed. 2020. *¡Printing the Revolution! The Rise and Impact of Chicano Graphics, 1965 to Now*. Princeton, NJ: Smithsonian American Art Museum with Princeton University Press.

Rickett, Helen, ed. 2018. *The Art of Feminism: Images that Shaped the Fight for Equality, 1857–2017*. San Francisco: Chronicle Books.

Riemer, Matthew, and Leighton Brown. 2019. *We Are Everywhere: Protest, Power, and Pride in the History of Queer Liberation*. Emeryville, CA: Ten Speed Press.

Rogger, Basil, Jonas Voegeli, Ruedi Widmer, Zurich University of the Arts, and the Museum für Gestaltung Zürich, eds. 2018. *Protest: The Aesthetics of Resistance*. Zürich: Lars Müller.

Young, Ralph, ed. 2016. *Make Art Not War: Political Protest Posters from the Twentieth Century*. New York: Washington Mews Books.

Index

Credits

Image & Artwork Credits

All images © Letterform Archive unless listed below. All artwork collection of Letterform Archive unless noted in the caption where the artwork appears.

All artwork still under copyright is registered with the artists, artists' estates, heirs, or appointed licensing agencies. The publisher has made every attempt to locate the proper heirs and agencies for artwork still under copyright. Please contact Letterform Archive Books with any questions or corrections pertaining to credits or rights.

Unless otherwise noted below, all artwork still under copyright is registered with the creators listed in the captions where the artwork appears. Further acknowledgments to image licensors and lending institutions also appear below.

Front cover Unknown photographer **Back cover, clockwise from top left** © Ganzeer; permission courtesy of *People's World*; image courtesy of and © See Red Women's Workshop; © 2022 Emory Douglas/Licensed by AFNYLAW.com; collection of the Oakland Museum of California H73.347.5/the UFW Eagle® is a registered trademark of the United Farm Workers union and is used with permission.

Front endpapers *I Am a Man* protesters photo © Dr. Ernest C. Withers, Sr., courtesy of the Withers Family Trust; Black women voters photo courtesy of the Smithsonian National Museum of African American History and Culture/Cox Studio **pages 4–5** Getty Images/David Fenton **page 7** Image courtesy of the Smithsonian National Museum of African American History and Culture **page 10** © 2022 Emory Douglas/Artists Rights Society (ARS), New York **page 11** © *IGTimes* **page 12** Image courtesy of Ganzeer **page 13** Image courtesy of Nat Pyper **page 14** © 2022 Emory Douglas/Artists Rights Society (ARS), New York **page 17** © Danny Lyon/Magnum Photos TEST 01-Stock (Photogs) **page 18** Photo courtesy of Hank Willis Thomas and Jack Shainman Gallery, New York/Artwork © Hank Willis Thomas **page 19** © 2022 Emory Douglas/Artists Rights Society (ARS), New York **page 20** © Estate of Barbara Jones-Hogu; image courtesy of Lusenhop Fine Art **page 21** © 2022 Faith Ringgold/Artists Rights Society (ARS), New York; image courtesy of ACA Galleries, New York **page 24** © Penguin Random House **page 26** © 2022 Emory Douglas/Licensed by AFNYLAW.com **pages 28–31** Getty Images/Graeme Robertson **page 34** Image courtesy of the Smithsonian National Museum of African American History and Culture **page 36** Image courtesy of the Library of Congress **page 37** Image courtesy of the Boston Public Library **pages 39–41** Images courtesy of the Library of Congress **pages 42–43** Images courtesy of the Smithsonian National Museum of African American History and Culture **page 45** © 2022 Estate of George Maciunas/Artists Rights Society (ARS), New York **pages 52–54** © 2022 Estate of Corita Kent/Immaculate Heart Community/Licensed by Artists Rights Society (ARS), New York; images courtesy of Corita Art Center **pages 57–61** © 2022 Emory Douglas/Artists Rights Society (ARS), New York **page 62** Photo courtesy of and © 2022, Stephen Shames/Steven Kasher Gallery **page 65 (right)** Permission courtesy of *People's World* **pages 66–67** Getty Images/Robert Altman **pages 74–77** Images courtesy of and © See Red Women's Workshop **pages 79–81** © *IGTimes* **pages 88–89** Images courtesy of and © Nadine Chahine **page 91** © 2022 Estate of Ben Shahn/Licensed by VAGA at Artists Rights Society (ARS), New York **page 92** Image courtesy of the Smithsonian National Museum of African American History and Culture **pages 96–99** © Nephi Sicajan/photos by Ramona Mia (page 96, bottom; page 97, top), Anthony Cruz (pages 98–99), and Michael Sandoval/filmdotorg (page 97, bottom) **pages 102–5** Photo courtesy of the Smithsonian National Museum of African American History and Culture/Cox Studio **page 109** Image courtesy of the Smithsonian National Museum of African American History and Culture **page 110** © 2022 The Heartfield Community of Heirs/Artists Rights Society (ARS), New York **pages 112–13** © 2022 Estate of Ben Shahn/Licensed by VAGA at Artists Rights Society (ARS), New York **page 114** Gjon Mili/The LIFE Picture Collection/Shutterstock **pages 116–17** Permission courtesy of the Herb Lubalin Study Center and the Estate of Ralph Ginzburg **pages 122–23** Getty Images/Bettman **page 128** Photo courtesy of and © Garrett MacLean **pages 134–35** Photo © Kyle Depew; courtesy of Brick x Brick **pages 136 & 138** © 2022 Favianna.com **page 140** Image courtesy of and © 2022 Favianna.com **pages 142–45** © Dr. Ernest C. Withers, Sr.; image courtesy of the Withers Family Trust **page 148** Photo by and courtesy of Igor Alves, DreamPlay Media **page 149** Image courtesy and collection of the Smithsonian National Museum of African American History and Culture, gift of Arthur J. "Bud" Schmidt **page 152** Photo by Marc Riboud/Fonds Marc Riboud au MNAAG/Magnum Photos TEST 02-Stock (Estate) **page 155** Image courtesy of Alcatraz Indian Occupation Records, San Francisco History Center, San Francisco Public Library **pages 156–57** Photo courtesy of and © Art Kane **page 159** Permission of the Estate of Milton Glaser and © Milton Glaser **pages 160–61** Collection of the Oakland Museum of California H73.347.5; the UFW Eagle® is a registered trademark of the United Farm Workers union and is used with permission. **pages 162–63** Images by Kathleen Culbert-Aguilar; images courtesy and collection of the National Museum of Mexican Art Permanent Collection: *Ben Fletcher*: 1992.118, gift from Carlos Cortez; *Lucía González de Parsons*: 1992.118, gift from the Carlos Cortez Estate; *Joe Hill*: 1990.27, gift from Carlos Cortez **page 164** Photo courtesy of the National Museum of Mexican Art Permanent Collection, 2005.287, gift from the Carlos Cortez Estate/© Don Ontiveros Fotografia **pages 168–69** Getty Images/Emmanuel Dunand **pages 170–73** Getty Images/Santi Visalli **pages 176–77** Images courtesy of the Library of Congress **page 178** Photo courtesy of the W. E. B. Du Bois Papers, Robert S. Cox Special Collections and University Archives Research Center, UMass Amherst Libraries **page 182** © 2022 Estate of Ben Shahn/Licensed by VAGA at Artists Rights Society (ARS), New York **pages 184–85** Photo © Søren Rud **pages 188–191** © Penguin Random House **page 192 (right)**

& 193 © 2022 Emory Douglas/Artists Rights Society (ARS), New York **pages 198–99** © *Ebony* **pages 201–3** Excerpts from *The Black Book* © 1974 by Middleton A. Harris, Morris Levitt, Roger Furman, and Ernest Smith; used by permission of Random House, an imprint and division of Penguin Random House LLC, all rights reserved **pages 204–5** © Courtesy Legado Mirtha Dermisache, Buenos Aires, 2022 **page 206** © 2022 Jenny Holzer, member Artists Rights Society (ARS), New York **pages 208–9** Permission courtesy guerrillagirls.com **pages 210–13** © *Colors*; photos by Steve McCurry (page 210, left), Oliviero Toscani (page 210, right, and page 211), Jean Gaumy/Magnum/Contrasto (page 213) **page 214** Photo by and © Chalkie Davies **page 217** Image courtesy of and © Anthony Burrill **page 218** (second row, center; yellow equals sign on blue background) © 2022 Human Rights Campaign, Inc. All Rights Reserved. Reproduced with permission. Any further use without the express written consent of Human Rights Campaign is prohibited. **page 219 (bottom row)** Images courtesy of the Division of Political and Military History, National Museum of American History, Smithsonian Institution **pages 220–21** Getty/John Sunderland **page 224** Images courtesy and © Forest Young and Jeremy Mickel **page 225** Photo courtesy of Heather Snyder Quinn and Adam DelMarcelle **pages 226–29** Getty/Newsday LLC/Erica Berger **page 232** © 2022 Heirs of Aaron Douglas/Licensed by VAGA at Artists Rights Society (ARS), New York **pages 238–39** Permission courtesy of ONE Archives at the USC Libraries **pages 242–45** Permission courtesy of the Herb Lubalin Study Center and the Estate of Ralph Ginzburg **pages 246–47** Photo by Diana Davies, Manuscripts and Archives Division, The New York Public Library 1582220, © NYPL **pages 248–51** Images courtesy of ONE Archives at the USC Libraries **page 253** Matteo Omied/Alamy Stock Photo **page 256** Cooper Hewitt, Smithsonian Design Museum, gift of Rick Valicenti, 1995-73-5; photo © Smithsonian Institution **page 262** Photo by Alice O'Malley; courtesy of fierce pussy **pages 264–65** Images courtesy of and © Nat Pyper **Back endpapers** Photo of Marsha P. Johnson by Diana Davies, Manuscripts and Archives Division, The New York Public Library 1582202, © NYPL; AIDS activists photo Getty Images/Newsday LLC/Erica Berger

Additional Caption Information

pages 4–5 Black Panther Party members outside the New York County Criminal Court in April 1969, rallying in support of the acquittal of the Panther 21 **pages 28–31** Antiwar demonstrators in London rally against the war in Iraq in March 2003 **pages 102–5** Women from the San Francisco chapter of the National Council of Negro Women hold signs encouraging Bay Area residents to vote as part of the Citizenship Education Project in 1956 **page 118** unknown designer, unknown symbol on black patch, 5¼ × 5⅛ inches (13.5 × 13.5 cm); unknown designer, *Tegen Sexisme*, 5½ × 6 inches (14 × 15 cm); unknown designer, *Shell to Hell, Kill a Multi*, 5⅝ × 4¼ inches (14.5 × 11 cm); Clifford Harper, *Keep Warm, Burn Out the Rich*, 5⅝ × 6 inches (14.5 × 15 cm) **page 119** Seth Tobocman, *You Don't Have to Fuck People Over to Survive*, 1984, 6 × 4¼ inches (15 × 11 cm); unknown designer, *Until All Are Free, We Are All Imprisoned*, 5⅛ × 6¾ inches (13 × 17 cm) **pages 142–45** Memphis sanitation workers gathered in front of Clayborn Temple during the 1968 solidarity march protesting the lack of compensation given to families of Black workers who had been killed on the job **pages 170–73** A chalk art demonstration on the first Earth Day in 1970 in New York City **page 218 (from left to right)** Student Mobilization Committee, *Kent, Augusta, Jackson, S. E. Asia, Moratorium May 5, Out Now!*, 1971, 2½ × 2½ inches (6.5 × 6.5 cm); Revolutionary Socialist League, *Woman Be Free! (¡Mujer Sea Libre!)*, 1981, 2¼ × 2¼ inches (5.5 × 5.5 cm); unknown designer, *Mayday: Washington May 1–7*, circa 1970s, 1¼ × 1¼ inches (3 × 3 cm); Corita Kent, *Give a Damn*, circa 2010s, 1¼ × 1¼ inches (3 × 3 cm); Human Rights Campaign, =, 2016, 1¾ × 1¾ inches (4.5 × 4.5 cm); Black Panthers, *If You Are Not Part of the Solution*, circa 1960, 2¼ × 2¼ inches (5.5 × 5.5 cm); unknown designer, *Out Now*, circa 1960s, 2¼ × 2¼ inches (5.5 × 5.5 cm); Gay Men's Health Crisis and Gran Fury, *Men, Use Condoms or Beat It*, circa 1980s, 1½ × 1½ inches (3.5 × 3.5 cm); Ricardo Levins Morales/RLM Art Studio, *Unions: The Folks that Brought You the Weekend*, 2011, 2¼ × 2¼ inches (5.5 × 5.5 cm); School Kids Against the Nazis (SKAN), *Nobble the NF Nazis!*, circa 1970s, 1¾ × 1¾ (4.5 × 4.5 cm); Mia Christopher and Open Windows Cooperative, *Listen to Women*, 2016, 2⅛ × 2⅛ inches (5.5 × 5.5 cm); unknown designer, *$upport Your Sisters*, circa 1980s, 2¼ × 2¼ inches (5.5 × 5.5 cm) **page 219 (from left to right)** Gay Men's Health Crisis, *It Ain't Over Yet! Help Fight AIDS*, 1989, 2¾ × 1¾ inches (7 × 4.5 cm); YAWF Women, *Right to Abortion Yes, No Forced Sterilization*, circa 1970s; 1¾ × 1¾ (4.5 × 4.5 cm); designer unknown, *Our Time Is Now*, 1979, 1¼ × 1¼ inches (3 × 3 cm); all bottom row collection of the Division of Political and Military History, National Museum of American History, Smithsonian Institution, unknown designers: *Who You Callin' Immigrant, Pilgrim?*, 1996, 2¼ × 2¼ inches (6 × 6 cm); *Deaf Pride*, 1¼ × 1¼ inches (3 × 3 cm), gift of Janine Kemp Bertram; *Support Disability Rights*, 3 × 2 inches (7.5 × 5 cm) **pages 226–29 & back endpapers** Activists protesting the ongoing AIDS epidemic at the dedication ceremony for the Stonewall monument at Stonewall Place in New York City in 1989 **Back endpaper** Marsha P. Johnson pickets Bellevue Hospital to protest the treatment of unhoused people and gay people.

Epigraph Credits

page 106 From *Our Time Is Now: Power, Purpose, and the Fight for a Fair America* © 2020 Stacey Abrams, Henry Holt and Co. **page 146** Reprinted by arrangement with the Heirs to the Estate of Martin Luther King, Jr., c/o Writers House as agent for the proprietor, New York, NY. © 1964 by Dr. Martin Luther King, Jr. Renewed © 1992 by Coretta Scott King. **page 174** From *Teaching to Transgress: Education as the Practice of Freedom* © 1994 bell hooks, Routledge. Reproduced with permission of Taylor & Francis Group through PLSclear.

Acknowledgments

Author Acknowledgments

It's been said that writing is a solitary act. *Strikethrough* has proven quite the opposite. While writing, curating, and designing a show about the graphics of protest and collective action, the solidarity, collaboration, and teamwork I experienced within the interconnected teams of Letterform Archive and my design studio, Polymode, is beyond measure. The call and response between us all has changed the way I practice.

Thank you to Brian Johnson of Polymode, who grounded our work. Cheers go to Michelle Lamb for her typographic dexterity and tenacity, as well as to Randa Hadi, Audrey Davies, and Edgar Casarin, for demonstrating what studio as family truly means. Stephen Coles, your wisdom, craft, and ability to find the most obscure typographic artifacts are vital to the scholarship in this book. You kept me company and in awe. Molly O'Neil Stewart, your grace in stewarding so many materials ensured rich connections near and far. And I—as someone raised by editors—owe my enduring gratitude to Lucie Parker for helping us find a voice that is equal parts visionary and inclusive.

Thank you to Rob Saunders for creating a space where nerdy and curious typographers can learn, reflect, and be inspired by the many stories found in letterforms worldwide.

Lastly, thank you to my husband, Bill Hildebrand; you fortified my heart as I worked with such powerful and challenging material.

Research Acknowledgments

Research doesn't happen in a vacuum. We want to thank the numerous activists, designers, scholars, typographers, and type designers who introduced us to objects and stories in this exhibition and book, including Ahmed Ansari, Tasheka Arceneaux-Sutton, Audrey Bennett, Pierre Bowins, Andy Campbell, Christopher Dingwall, Jason Forrest, Colette Gaiter, Jon Key, Ellen Lupton, Saki Mafundikwa, Cheryl D. Miller, Ziddi Msangi, Tanvi Sharma, Omari Souza, Ramon Tejada, Kelly Walters, and Lauren Williams. And thanks go to my design history teachers who ignited the spark that led me to study in this field: Brockett Horne, Louise Sandhaus, Doug Scott, and Lorraine Wild.

We also want to thank Tré Seals for his research into the type and lettering on protest signs, which yielded Equals, the display type specially created for this book by his foundry, Vocal Type.

Publisher Acknowledgments

Thank you to Kate Long Stellar, Henry Cole Smith, sair goetz, and Paola Zanol for collections assistance; 42-line, April Harper, and Ellis Martin for digitization; and Lisa K. Marietta, Mark Nichol, and Ken DellaPenta for editorial aid. We are also grateful to Colette Gaiter for her introduction and to Lincoln Cushing for his content review.

With special thanks to the Boston Public Library, Anthony Burrill, the Corita Art Center, *Ebony* magazine, the Library of Congress, the New York Public Library, the Oakland Museum of California, ONE Archives, the San Francisco Public Library, the Smithsonian National Museum of African American History and Culture, and the National Museum of American History, Smithsonian Institution. Also many thanks to Kathy Spillar, Eleanor Smeal, and Kathy Bonk of the Feminist Majority Foundation.

In addition to the exhibition's curators, the following people contributed text to this catalog: Brian Johnson, Kate Long Stellar, Lucie Parker, Molly O'Neil Stewart, and Chris Westcott.

About the Contributors

About Silas Munro

Silas Munro is a partner of Polymode, a studio that leads the edge of contemporary graphic design for clients in the cultural sphere. Collaborations include works with the City of Los Angeles Mayor's Office; the Cooper Hewitt, Smithsonian Design Museum; the Getty Museum; the David Kordansky Gallery; Mark Bradford at the Venice Biennale; MoMA; and MOCA. Munro's writing appears in *W. E. B. Du Bois's Data Portraits: Visualizing Black America*, published by Princeton Architectural Press and featured in *Smithsonian Magazine*, the *New Yorker*, and *Black Perspectives*. Munro expanded this research as a coauthor of the first BIPOC-centered design history course, Black Design in America: African Americans and the African Diaspora in Graphic Design, which will be published in book form in 2023. Munro holds an MFA from CalArts and a BFA from RISD. He is founding faculty and cochair of the MFA in Graphic Design program at Vermont College of Fine Arts.

About Stephen Coles

Born in Salt Lake City, Stephen Coles moved to San Francisco in 2004 to serve as FontShop's creative director. He later worked as an independent consultant, connecting font makers with font users, and wrote the bestselling book *The Anatomy of Type*. With his background in design and journalism, combined with an obsession for type history, Stephen is responsible for the online face and voice of Letterform Archive, where he is editorial director and associate curator. He also publishes the influential websites Typographica and Fonts In Use.

About Colette Gaiter

Colette Gaiter is a professor in the departments of Africana studies and art & design at the University of Delaware. After working as a graphic designer in New York City, she became an educator, an artist, and a writer. Her visual work, exhibited internationally, ranges from digital prints and artist books to websites and interactive installations. Since 2005, she has written about former Black Panther artist Emory Douglas's work, including his current international human rights artist activism. Her essays on his work appear in *Black Panther: The Revolutionary Art of Emory Douglas* (for which she wrote a new introduction to the 2014 edition); *West of Center: Art and the Counterculture Experiment in America, 1965–1977*; *Art, Global Maoism, and the Chinese Cultural Revolution*; and other publications. The 2022 book *The Black Experience in Design: Identity, Expression & Reflection* includes her essay on evolving visual literacy. After many trips to Cuba, she has also written about Afro-Cuban art, design, and culture—especially as they relate to issues of race. Her visual work and writing investigate creative activism, while her teaching focuses on the ways that popular culture influences social change.

About Letterform Archive

Founded in 2015 in San Francisco, Letterform Archive is a nonprofit center for design inspiration. Letterform Archive Books produces titles based on its collection of more than 75,000 artifacts spanning the history of graphic design, type design, and lettering.

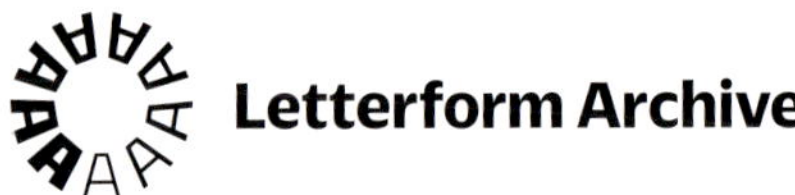

2339 Third Street, Floor 4R
San Francisco, CA 94107
letterformarchive.org

Publisher
Rob Saunders

Associate Publisher
Lucie Parker

Associate Managing Editor
Molly O'Neil Stewart

Associate Acquisitions Editor & Marketing Coordinator
Chris Westcott

Design
Silas Munro, Brian Johnson, and Michelle Lamb of Polymode

Print Production
Thomas Bollier

Available through ARTBOOK | D.A.P.
75 Broad Street, Suite 630
New York, NY 10004
www.artbook.com

ISBN: 978-1-7368633-0-5

Library of Congress Control Number: 2022936589
10 9 8 7 6 5 4 3 2 1
2022 2023 2024 2025 2026

Printed in China by 1010 Printing

Strikethrough: Typographic Messages of Protest is the official catalog for the 2022–2023 Letterform Archive exhibition of the same name, cocurated by Silas Munro and Stephen Coles.

The text of *Strikethrough* is set in Polymode Sans, designed by Ben Kiel and Jesse Ragan of XYZ Type. Redrawn from historical resources, including Lining Gothic, which was designed by Charles Henry Beeler and released by MacKellar, Smiths & Jordan in 1885, Polymode Sans is a variable font that shifts to reference a range of idiosyncrasies linked to qualities of "extra-ness" connected to queer and BIPOC lineages.
The display type of *Strikethrough* is Equals, a typeface designed by Tré Seals of Vocal Type and derived from italic brush lettering found in protest signs, including women's suffrage, civil rights, anti–Vietnam war, women's rights, Chicano rights, and anti-apartheid movements.

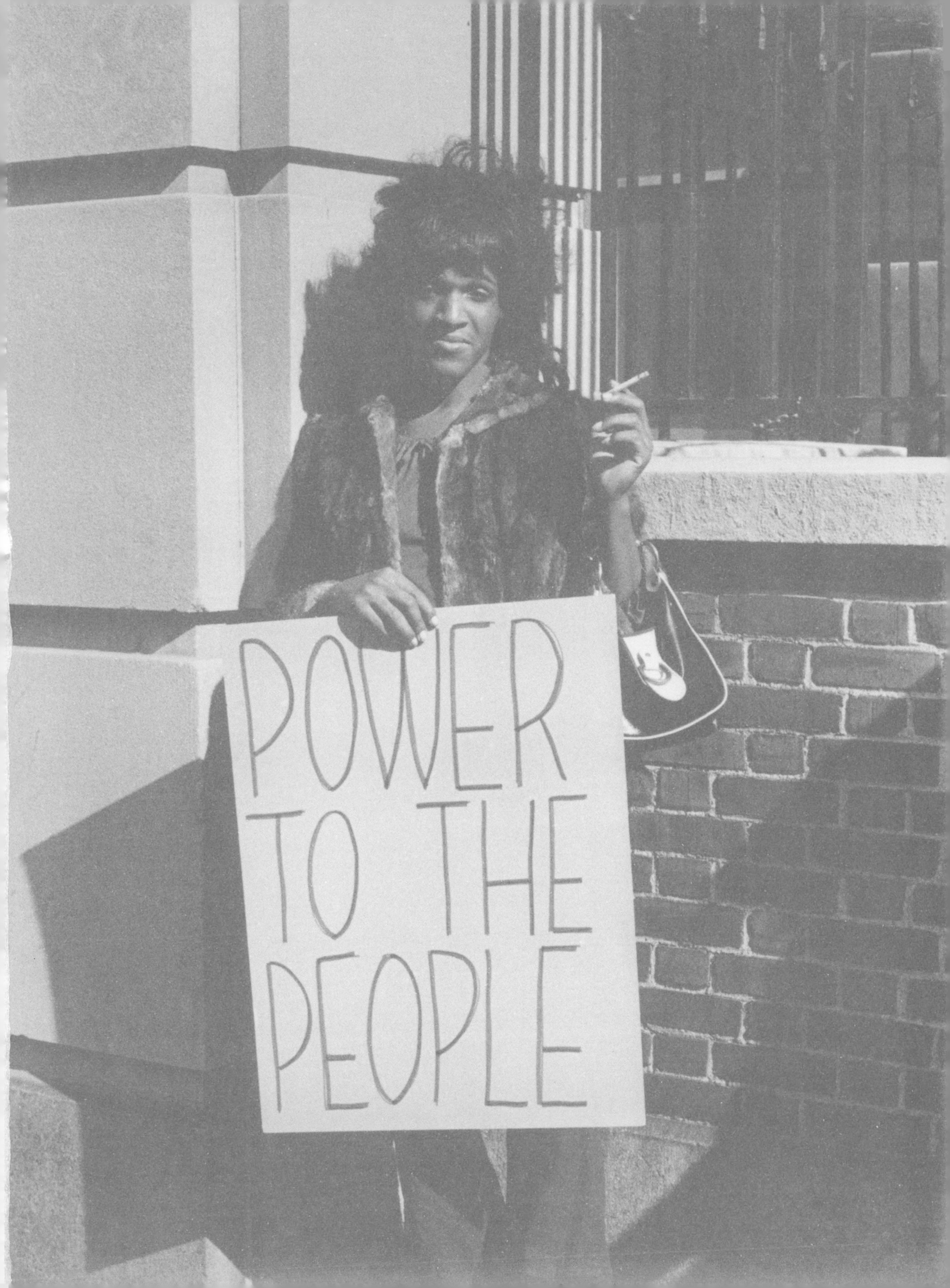

POWER
TO THE
PEOPLE

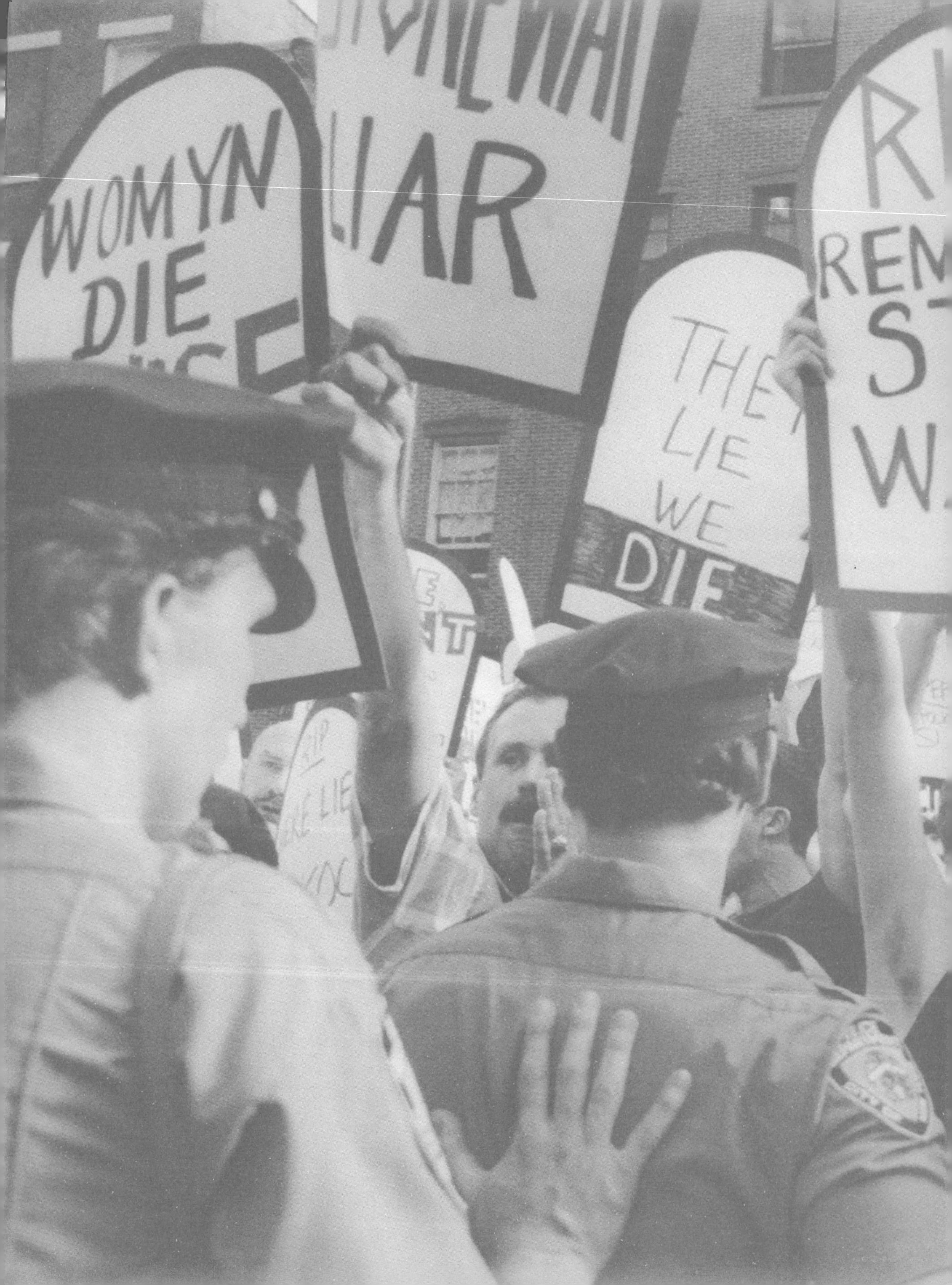
WOMYN DIE
LIAR
THEY LIE WE DIE
RIP